Managing and Maintaining a Microsoft® Windows Server™ 2003 Environment (70-290)

Textbook

Craig Zacker

PUBLISHED BY
Microsoft Press
A Division of Microsoft Corporation
One Microsoft Way
Redmond, Washington 98052-6399

Library of Congress Cataloging-in-Publication Data
Zacker, Craig.
    Managing and Maintaining a Microsoft Windows Server 2003 Environment / Craig Zacker, Mark Fugatt.
      p. cm.
    Includes index.
    ISBN 0-7356-2031-8
    (Microsoft Press)
    ISBN 0-07-294487-0
    (McGraw-Hill)
    1. Microsoft Windows Server.   2. Operating systems (Computers).   I. Title.

  QA76.76.O63Z345   2004
  005.4'47682--dc22   2003064855

Printed and bound in the United States of America.

  2 3 4 5 6 7 8 9   QWT   8 7 6 5 4 3

Distributed in Canada by H.B. Fenn and Company Ltd.

A CIP catalogue record for this book is available from the British Library.

Microsoft Press books are available through booksellers and distributors worldwide. For further information about international editions, contact your local Microsoft Corporation office or contact Microsoft Press International directly at fax (425)
936-7329. Visit our Web site at www.microsoft.com/learning. Send comments to *moac@microsoft.com*.

Program Managers: Linda Engelman, Hilary Long
Project Editor: Lynn Finnel
Technical Editor: Eric Dettinger
Indexer: Bill Meyers
Instructional Designer: Emily Springfield

Sub Assy Part No. X10-23986
Body Part No. X10-23991

ISBN 13: 978-0-470-64115-6

CONTENTS AT A GLANCE

CONTENTS

PART 2: MANAGING AND MAINTAINING USERS, GROUPS, AND COMPUTERS

ABOUT THIS BOOK

Welcome to *Managing and Maintaining a Microsoft Windows Server 2003 Environment (70-290)*, a part of the Microsoft Official Academic Course (MOAC) series. Through lectures, discussions, demonstrations, textbook exercises, and classroom labs, this course teaches students the skills and knowledge necessary to take Microsoft certification exam 70-290: Managing and Maintaining a Microsoft Windows Server 2003 Environment and to become a Microsoft Certified Professional (MCP), a Microsoft Certified Systems Engineer (MCSE) on Windows Server 2003, or a Microsoft Certified Systems Administrator (MCSA) on Windows Server 2003.

This course is for anyone who wants to learn how to install, configure, administer, and support the primary services in the Windows Server 2003 operating system, as well as those seeking Microsoft certification. The course begins by examining basic system administration procedures. Subsequent chapters are devoted to creating and managing Windows Server 2003 user, group, and computer accounts; sharing system resources; and installing and maintaining system hardware.

TARGET AUDIENCE

Students in this course typically aspire to careers as Windows Server 2003 system administrators or support technicians, and they want an objective assessment and certification of their skills. The audience for this book consists of IT professionals who work in the typically complex computing environment of medium-size to large companies. Students should have 6 to 12 months of experience administering client and network operating systems in environments with the following characteristics:

- 250 to 5000 or more users
- Three or more physical locations
- Three or more domain controllers
- Network services and resources such as messaging, database, file and print, proxy server, firewall, Internet, intranet, remote access, and client computer management
- Connectivity requirements such as connecting branch offices and individual users in remote locations to the corporate network and connecting corporate networks to the Internet

PREREQUISITES

There are no official prerequisites for taking the 70-290 exam, but students taking this course should have the following background:

- CompTIA A+ certification or equivalent knowledge and skills
- CompTIA Network+ certification or equivalent knowledge and skills

THE TEXTBOOK

The textbook content has been crafted to provide a meaningful learning experience to students in an academic classroom setting.

Key features of the Microsoft Official Academic Course (MOAC) textbooks include the following:

- Learning objectives for each chapter that prepare the student for the topic areas covered in that chapter

- Chapter introductions that explain why the content is important

- An inviting design with screen shots, diagrams, tables, bulleted lists, and other graphical formats that makes the book easy to comprehend and supports a number of different learning styles

- Clear explanations of concepts and principles, and frequent exposition of step-by-step procedures

- A variety of reader aids that highlight a wealth of additional information, including:

  - ❏ Note – Real-world application tips and alternative procedures, and explanations of complex procedures and concepts

  - ❏ Caution – Warnings about mistakes that can result in loss of data or are difficult to resolve

  - ❏ Important – Explanations of essential setup steps before starting a procedure, and other instructions

- Short, optional, hands-on exercises that break up lectures and provide a warm-up for more complex lab exercises.

- End-of-chapter review questions that assess knowledge and can serve as homework, quizzes, and review activities before or after lectures. Answers to the textbook questions are available from your instructor.

- Chapter summaries that distill the main ideas in a chapter and reinforce learning.

- Case scenarios, approximately two per chapter, that provide students with an opportunity to evaluate, analyze, synthesize, and apply information learned during the chapter.

- Comprehensive glossary that defines key terms introduced in the book.

THE SUPPLEMENTAL COURSE MATERIALS CD-ROM

This book comes with a Supplemental Course Materials CD-ROM, which contains a variety of informational aids to complement the book content:

- An electronic version of this textbook (eBook). For information about using the eBook, see the section titled "eBook Setup Instructions" later in this introduction.

- The Microsoft Press Readiness Review Suite from MeasureUp. This suite of practice tests and objective reviews contains questions of varying complexity and offers multiple testing modes. You can assess your understanding of the concepts presented in this book and use the results to develop a learning plan that meets your needs.

■ Installation scripts and example files for performing the hands-on exercises in the Lab Manual. These include files that demonstrate key concepts and illustrate a specific point, as well as files included for your convenience, such as scripts that can be used to reduce the amount of time you spend setting up your system to perform a particular exercise.

■ An eBook of *Microsoft Encyclopedia of Networking*, Second Edition.

■ Microsoft PowerPoint slides based on textbook chapters, for note taking.

■ Windows System Resource Manager, a feature of Microsoft Windows, that allows administrators to control how CPU and memory resources are allocated to applications, services, and processes. For more information or to install Windows System Resource Manager, open the Readme.htm file in the \WSRM folder.

■ Microsoft Word Viewer and PowerPoint Viewer

■ A second CD contains a 180-day evaluation edition of Windows Server 2003 Enterprise Edition.

CAUTION   The 180-day evaluation edition of Windows Server 2003 Enterprise Edition provided with this book is not the full retail product; it is provided only for the purposes of training and evaluation. Microsoft Technical Support does not support this evaluation edition.

Readiness Review Suite Setup Instructions

The Readiness Review Suite includes a practice test of 300 sample exam questions and an objective review with an additional 125 questions. Use these tools to reinforce your learning and to identify areas in which you need to gain more experience before taking the exam.

▶ **Installing the Practice Test**

1. Insert the Supplemental Course Materials CD into your CD-ROM drive.

   NOTE   If AutoRun is disabled on your machine, refer to the Readme.txt file on the Supplemental Course Materials CD.

2. On the User Interface menu, select Readiness Review Suite and follow the prompts.

eBook Setup Instructions

The eBook is in Portable Document Format (PDF) and must be viewed using Adobe Acrobat Reader.

▶ **Using the eBook**

1. Insert the Supplemental Course Materials CD into your CD-ROM drive.

   NOTE   If AutoRun is disabled on your machine, refer to the Readme.txt file on the CD.

2. On the User Interface menu, select Textbook eBook and follow the prompts. You also can review any of the other eBooks provided for your use.

NOTE You must have the Supplemental Course Materials CD in your CD-ROM drive to run the eBook.

THE LAB MANUAL

The Lab Manual is designed for use in a combined lecture and lab situation, or in a separate lecture and lab arrangement. The exercises in the Lab Manual correspond to textbook chapters and are intended for use in a classroom setting under the supervision of an instructor. However, they are also suitable for independent study under the supervision of an instructor.

The Lab Manual presents a rich, hands-on learning experience that encourages practical solutions and strengthens critical problem-solving skills:

- Lab Exercises teach procedures by using a step-by-step format. Questions interspersed throughout Lab Exercises encourage reflection and critical thinking about the lab activity.

- Lab Review Questions appear at the end of each lab and ask questions about the lab. They are designed to promote critical reflection.

- Lab Challenges are review activities that ask students to perform a variation on a task they performed in the Lab Exercises, but without detailed instructions.

- Troubleshooting Labs appear after a number of regular labs and consist of mid-length review projects based on true-to-life scenarios. These labs challenge students to think like an expert to solve complex problems.

- Labs are based on realistic business settings and include an opening scenario and a list of learning objectives.

Students who successfully complete the Lab Exercises, Lab Review Questions, Lab Challenges, and Troubleshooting Labs in the Lab Manual will have a richer learning experience and deeper understanding of the concepts and methods covered in the course. They will be better able to answer and understand the testbank questions, especially the knowledge application and knowledge synthesis questions. They will also be better prepared to pass the associated certification exams if they choose to do so.

NOTATIONAL CONVENTIONS

The following conventions are used throughout this texbook and the Lab Manual:

- Characters or commands that you type appear in **bold** type.

- Terms that appear in the glossary also appear in **bold** type.

- *Italic* in syntax statements indicates placeholders for variable information. *Italic* is also used for book titles and terms defined in the text.

- Names of files and folders appear in Title caps, except when you are to type them directly. Unless otherwise indicated, you can use all lowercase letters when you type a filename in a dialog box or at a command prompt.

- Filename extensions appear in all lowercase.

- Acronyms appear in all uppercase.

- `Monospace` type represents code samples, examples of screen text, or entries that you might type at a command prompt or in initialization files.

- Square brackets [ ] are used in syntax statements to enclose optional items. For example, [*filename*] in command syntax indicates that you can type a filename with the command. Type only the information within the brackets, not the brackets themselves.

- Braces { } are used in syntax statements to enclose required items. Type only the information within the braces, not the braces themselves.

KEYBOARD CONVENTIONS

- A plus sign (+) between two key names means that you must press those keys at the same time. For example, "Press ALT+TAB" means that you hold down ALT while you press TAB.

- A comma (,) between two or more key names means that you must press the keys consecutively, not at the same time. For example, "Press ALT, F, X" means that you press and release each key in sequence. "Press ALT+W, L" means that you first press ALT and W at the same time, and then you release them and press L.

COURSE COVERAGE OF EXAM OBJECTIVES

The title is intended to support your efforts to prepare for the 70-290 exam. The following table correlates the exam objectives with the textbook chapters and Lab Manual lab exercises.

NOTE The Microsoft Learning Web site describes the various MCP certification exams and their corresponding courses. It provides up-to-date certification information and explains the certification process and the course options. See *http://www.microsoft.com/learning/learning/mcp* for up-to-date information about MCP exam credentials about other certification programs offered by Microsoft.

Textbook and Lab Manual Coverage of Exam Objectives

Objective	Textbook Chapter	Lab Items
Managing and Maintaining Physical and Logical Devices		

(continued)

Textbook and Lab Manual Coverage of Exam Objectives

Objective	Textbook Chapter	Lab Items
■ Manage basic disks and dynamic disks.	12	Lab 12, Exercises 1 to 5
■ Monitor server hardware. Tools might include Device Manager, the Hardware Troubleshooting Wizard, and appropriate Control Panel items.	11	Lab 11, Exercises 1 to 3
■ Optimize server disk performance.	12	Lab 12, Lab Challenge 1
■ Install and configure server hardware devices.	11	Lab 11, Exercises 1 to 3
Managing Users, Computers, and Groups		
■ Manage local, roaming, and mandatory user profiles.	6	Lab 6, Exercise 9
■ Create and manage computer accounts in an Active Directory environment.	8	Lab 8, Exercises 1 to 3
■ Create and manage groups.	7	Lab 7, Exercises 2 to 7
■ Create and manage user accounts.	6	Lab 6, Exercises 1 to 8
■ Troubleshoot computer accounts.	8	Troubleshooting Lab B
■ Troubleshoot user accounts.	6	Troubleshooting Lab A
■ Troubleshoot user authentication issues.	6	Troubleshooting Lab A
Managing and Maintaining Access to Resources		
■ Configure access to shared folders.	9	Lab 9, Exercise 1
■ Troubleshoot Terminal Services.	2	Troubleshooting Lab A
■ Configure file system permissions.	9	Lab 9, Exercise 5
■ Troubleshoot access to files and shared folders.	9	Troubleshooting Lab B
Managing and Maintaining a Server Environment		
■ Monitor and analyze events. Tools might include Event Viewer and System Monitor.	3	Lab 3, Exercises 1, 3, and 4
■ Manage software update infrastructure.	5	Lab 5, Exercises 3 and 5
■ Manage software site licensing.	5	Lab 5, Exercises 6 and 7
■ Manage servers remotely.	2	Lab 2, Exercises 4 and 5, and Lab Challenge 1
■ Troubleshoot print queues.	10	Lab 10, Exercises 5 and 6
■ Monitor system performance.	3	Lab 3, Exercise 2
■ Monitor file and print servers. Tools might include Task Manager, Event Viewer, and System Monitor.	3	Lab 10, Exercise 6

(continued)

Textbook and Lab Manual Coverage of Exam Objectives

Objective	Textbook Chapter	Lab Items
■ Monitor and optimize a server environment for application performance.	3	
■ Manage a Web server.	9	Lab 9, Exercise 7, and Lab Challenge 1
■ Manage Internet Information Services (IIS).	9	Lab 9, Exercise 7, and Lab Challenge 1
■ Manage security for IIS.	9	Lab 9, Exercise 7, and Lab Challenge 1
Managing and Implementing Disaster Recovery		
■ Perform system recovery for a server.	4	
■ Manage backup procedures.	4	Lab 4, Exercises 1 to 4, and Lab Challenge 1
■ Recover from server hardware failure.	4	
■ Restore backup data.	4	Lab 4, Exercises 1 to 3
■ Schedule backup jobs.	4	Lab 4, Exercise 4

THE MICROSOFT CERTIFIED PROFESSIONAL PROGRAM

The MCP program is the best way to prove your proficiency with current Microsoft products and technologies. The exams and corresponding certifications are developed to validate your mastery of critical competencies as you design and develop, or implement and support, solutions using Microsoft products and technologies. Computer professionals who become Microsoft certified are recognized as experts and are sought after industrywide. Certification brings a variety of benefits to the individual and to employers and organizations.

> **MORE INFO** For a full list of MCP benefits, go to http://www.microsoft.com/learning/itpro/.

Certifications

The MCP program offers multiple certifications, based on specific areas of technical expertise:

- **Microsoft Certified Professional (MCP)** In-depth knowledge of at least one Windows operating system or architecturally significant platform. An MCP is qualified to implement a Microsoft product or technology as part of a business solution for an organization.

- **Microsoft Certified Systems Engineer (MCSE)** Qualified to effectively analyze the business requirements for business solutions and design and implement the infrastructure based on the Windows and Windows Server 2003 operating systems.

- **Microsoft Certified Systems Administrator (MCSA)** Qualified to manage and troubleshoot existing network and system environments based on the Windows and Windows Server 2003 operating systems.

- **Microsoft Certified Database Administrator (MCDBA)** Qualified to design, implement, and administer Microsoft SQL Server databases.

MCP Requirements

Requirements differ for each certification and are specific to the products and job functions addressed by the certification. To become an MCP, you must pass rigorous certification exams that provide a valid and reliable measure of technical proficiency and expertise. These exams are designed to test your expertise and ability to perform a role or task with a product, and are developed with the input of industry professionals. Exam questions reflect how Microsoft products are used in actual organizations, giving them real-world relevance.

- Microsoft Certified Professional (MCP) candidates are required to pass one current Microsoft certification exam. Candidates can pass additional Microsoft certification exams to validate their skills with other Microsoft products, development tools, or desktop applications.

- Microsoft Certified Systems Engineer (MCSE) candidates are required to pass five core exams and two elective exams.

- Microsoft Certified Systems Administrator (MCSA) candidates are required to pass three core exams and one elective exam.

- Microsoft Certified Database Administrator (MCDBA) candidates are required to pass three core exams and one elective exam.

ABOUT THE AUTHORS

Craig Zacker, the author of the textbook, is a writer, editor, and networker whose computing experience began in the days of teletypes and paper tape. After making the move from minicomputers to PCs, he worked as an administrator of Novell Net-Ware networks and as a PC support technician while operating a freelance desktop publishing business. After earning a masters degree in English and American literature from New York University, Craig worked extensively on the integration of Windows NT into existing internetworks, supported fleets of Windows workstations, and was employed as a technical writer, content provider, and Webmaster for a large software company. Since devoting himself to writing and editing full time, Craig has authored or contributed to many books on networking topics, operating systems, and PC hardware, including *MCSE Self-Paced Training Kit (Exam 70-293): Planning and Maintaining a Microsoft Windows Server 2003 Network Infrastructure*, and *MCSA Training Kit: Managing a Microsoft Windows 2000 Network Environment*. He has also developed educational texts for college courses and online training courses for the Web, and he has published articles in top industry publications. For more information on Craig's books and other works, see *http://www.zacker.com*.

Mark Fugatt, the author of the Lab Manual, is a Microsoft Certified Trainer and the owner of Pentech Office Solutions, Inc., a consulting/training organization specializing in delivering certified technical training to small- and medium-sized business,

Mark has been delivering certified training since 1995 and holds MCSE, MCSA, and MCT certifications and is also a Microsoft Exchange MVP.

Drew Bird, the author of the Pretest and Testbank questions and the PowerPoint slides, has been working in the IT industry for over 14 years. In addition to his 400-plus days of classroom teaching as a Microsoft Certified Trainer and Master Certified Novell Instructor, he has performed the roles of network manager, network system analyst, and networking consultant to some of the world's most prestigious organizations. Drew is the author of numerous certification study guides, including Microsoft's *Faster Smarter A+ Certification*. He is also a contributor to a number of technical Web sites and journals, with over 100 articles published.

MOAC SUPPORT

Every effort has been made to ensure the accuracy of the material in this book and the contents of the CD-ROM. Microsoft Learning provides corrections for books through the World Wide Web at the following address:

http://www.microsoft.com/learning/support/

If you have comments, questions, or ideas regarding this book or the companion CD-ROM, please send them to Microsoft Learning via e-mail at moac@microsoft.com or at the following postal address:

Microsoft Learning

Attn: *MOAC: Managing and Maintaining a Microsoft Windows Server 2003 Environment (70-290)* editor

One Microsoft Way

Redmond, WA 98052-6399

Please note that product support is not offered through the above addresses.

EVALUATION EDITION SOFTWARE SUPPORT

The 180-day evaluation edition of Windows Server 2003 Enterprise Edition provided with this textbook is not the full retail product and is provided only for training and evaluation purposes. Microsoft and Microsoft Technical Support do not support this evaluation edition. For information about issues relating to the use of the evaluation edition, go to the Support section of the Microsoft Learning Web site (*http://www.microsoft.com/learning/support/*).

For online support information relating to the full version of Windows Server 2003 Enterprise Edition that might also apply to the evaluation edition, go to *http://www.microsoft.com/learning/support/*. For information about ordering the full version of any Microsoft software, call Microsoft Sales at (800) 426-9400 or visit *http://www.microsoft.com*.

> **CAUTION** The evaluation edition of Windows Server 2003 Enterprise Edition should not be used on a primary work computer.

PART 1
MANAGING AND MAINTAINING THE OPERATING SYSTEM

CHAPTER 1

INTRODUCING MICROSOFT WINDOWS SERVER 2003

The purpose of this course is to teach you to manage and maintain a Microsoft Windows Server 2003 environment and to prepare you for the 70-290 certification examination. The course assumes that you have some experience with Microsoft Windows, but the Windows Server 2003 family might be new to you. The goal of this chapter, therefore, is to introduce you to the various editions of Windows Server 2003 so you can identify the key differences among them and select the appropriate product to satisfy the needs of your organization.

The chapter then guides you through the process of installing Windows Server 2003 on a computer and configuring it to function as an Active Directory domain controller. Your instructor might not require you to install the operating system on your classroom computer, but if you want to work with Windows Server 2003 at home or elsewhere outside of class, you must be familiar with this installation and configuration process.

Upon completion of this chapter, you will be able to:

- Identify the key differences among the Windows Server 2003 editions

- Install Windows Server 2003

- Create a domain controller

- Identify the logical components and concepts of Active Directory

3

THE WINDOWS SERVER 2003 FAMILY

Windows Server 2003 is the latest incarnation of the Windows server operating system and provides substantial improvements over previous versions: it is more secure, more reliable, and easier to administer. This section provides a brief overview of the Windows Server 2003 family, focusing on the similarities and differences among the four product editions: Web Edition, Standard Edition, Enterprise Edition, and Datacenter Edition.

Windows Server 2003 Editions

Windows Server 2003 is an update to the platform and technologies introduced in Windows 2000. If you are coming to Windows Server 2003 with experience from Windows 2000 servers, you will find the transition to be relatively easy. If your only experience is with Windows NT 4, your learning curve will be much steeper.

Although the basic appearance of Windows Server 2003 is similar to that of Windows 2000, the operating system includes a great many improvements and new features that add security and reliability and enhance the administrative toolset. When you consider an upgrade or migration to Windows Server 2003, you might be drawn to the significant new features and improvements in Active Directory, the new tools to support **group policy objects (GPOs)**, the enhancements to enterprise security, the improvements to Terminal Services, or a number of other enhanced capabilities of the new operating system.

> **MORE INFO**   New Features in Windows Server 2003   For a complete list of new features and capabilities in the Windows Server 2003 platform, see the Microsoft Web site at http://www.microsoft.com/windowsserver2003.

The different editions of Windows Server 2003 are designed to support various hardware platforms and server roles. In addition to the four basic editions of Windows Server 2003—Web, Standard, Enterprise, and Datacenter—the operating system is also available in versions that support 64-bit processor platforms and embedded systems. The following sections discuss the editions in greater detail.

System Requirements

The four main operating system editions differ in the hardware they support. Table 1-1 lists the system requirements for each, as well as hardware recommendations.

Table 1-1   **Windows Server 2003 System Requirements**

	Web Edition	Standard Edition	Enterprise Edition	Datacenter Edition
Minimum Processor Speed	133 MHz	133 MHz	133 MHz	400 MHz
Recommended Processor Speed	550 MHz	550 MHz	733 MHz	733 MHz
Minimum RAM	128 MB	128 MB	128 MB	512 MB
Recommended Minimum RAM	256 MB	256 MB	256 MB	1 GB
Maximum RAM	2 GB	4 GB	32 GB	64 GB

Table 1-1 Windows Server 2003 System Requirements

	Web Edition	Standard Edition	Enterprise Edition	Datacenter Edition
Symmetric Multiprocessing (SMP) Support	Up to 2 processors	Up to 4 processors	Up to 8 processors	Up to 32 processors
Minimum Disk Space	1.5 GB	1.5 GB	1.5 GB	1.5 GB

Web Edition

To position Windows Server 2003 more competitively against other Web servers, Microsoft has released a special-purpose edition of Windows Server 2003 that was designed specifically to function as a Web server. The Web Edition is a subset of the standard operating system that enables customers to deploy Web sites, Web applications, and Web services with a minimum of expense and administrative overhead. The operating system supports a maximum of 2 GB of memory and up to two processors—half the capacity of the Standard Edition.

The Web Edition does not contain any features that are not found in the other Windows Server 2003 editions, but it does omit some of the components that are typically not needed on a Web server, such as the following:

- A computer running the Web Edition can be a member of an Active Directory **domain**, but it cannot function as a domain controller.

- The standard Client Access License model does not apply to computers running the Web Edition. The operating system supports an unlimited number of Web connections, but it is limited to 10 simultaneous Server Message Block (SMB) connections. This means that no more than 10 internal network users can access the server's file and print resources at any one time.

- The Internet Connection Firewall (ICF) and Internet Connection Sharing (ICS) features are not included with the Web Edition, which prevents the computer from functioning as an Internet gateway.

- A computer running the Web Edition cannot function as a Dynamic Host Configuration Protocol (DHCP) server, fax server, Microsoft SQL Server, or terminal server, although Remote Desktop for Administration is supported.

- The Web Edition cannot run non–Web serving applications.

However, the Web Edition does include all of the standard components that a Web server would need, including Microsoft Internet Information Services (IIS) 6, Network Load Balancing (NLB), and Microsoft ASP.NET.

Obviously, the Web Edition is not a suitable platform for a general purpose network server, nor is it intended to be one. However, it does enable organizations to deploy dedicated Web servers without having to provide support for a lot of components that the computer doesn't need to fulfill its role.

NOTE Purchasing the Web Edition   The Web Edition is not sold through retail channels. The product is available only to Microsoft customers with Enterprise and Select licensing agreements, to service providers with a service provider licensing agreement (SPLA), and through Microsoft original equipment manufacturers (OEMs) and System Builder partners.

Standard Edition

The Standard Edition is a multipurpose server platform that can provide directory, file, print, application, multimedia, and Internet services for small to medium-sized businesses. Among the many features included with the operating system are:

- **Directory services**   The Standard Edition includes full Active Directory support, enabling the computer to function as a member server or a domain controller. Administrators can therefore use the tools included with the operating system to deploy and manage Active Directory objects, group policies, and other Active Directory–based services.

- **Internet services**   The Standard Edition includes IIS 6, which provides Web and FTP services as well as other components used by Web server deployments, such as NLB, which enables multiple Web servers to host a single Web site, sharing the incoming client requests among up to 32 servers and providing fault tolerance.

- **Infrastructure services**   The Standard Edition includes the Microsoft DHCP Server, Domain Name System (DNS) Server, and Windows Internet Name Service (WINS) server, which provide important services for internal network and Internet clients.

- **TCP/IP routing**   A computer running the Standard Edition can function as a router in a variety of configurations, including local area network (LAN) and wide area network (WAN) routing, Internet access routing, and remote access routing. To facilitate these roles, the operating system's Routing and Remote Access service (RRAS) also includes support for network address translation (NAT), Internet Authentication Service (IAS), Routing Information Protocol (RIP), and the Open Shortest Path First (OSPF) routing protocol.

- **File and print services**   Users on the network can access shared drives, folders, and printers on a Standard Edition server. A Client Access License (CAL) is needed for each client that attempts to access server shares. The Standard Edition is typically sold with a package of 5, 10, or more CALs. To add more users, you must purchase additional CALs.

- **Terminal Server**   A computer running the Standard Edition can function as a terminal server, enabling computers and other devices to access the Windows desktop and applications running on the server. Terminal Server is essentially a remote control mechanism that enables clients to access a Windows session on the server. All application execution takes place on the server, and only keyboard, mouse, and display information is transmitted over the network. Terminal Server clients require a license that is separate from the standard Windows Server 2003 CAL, although Standard Edition does include a two-user license for Remote Desktop for Administration, which is a Terminal Server–based remote administration tool.

- **Security services**   The Standard Edition includes a variety of security features that administrators can deploy as needed, including Encrypting File System (EFS), which protects files on server drives by storing them in an encrypted format, IP Security extensions (IPsec), which digitally sign and encrypt data before transmitting them over the network, ICF, which regulates the traffic admitted onto the network from the Internet, and the Public Key Infrastructure (PKI), which provides security based on public key encryption and digital certificates.

Enterprise Edition

The Enterprise Edition is designed to be a powerful server platform for medium- to large-sized businesses. The Enterprise Edition differs from the Standard Edition primarily in terms of degree. For example, the Enterprise Edition supports up to eight processors, compared to the Standard Edition's four, and up to 32 GB of memory, compared to the Standard Edition's 4 GB.

The Enterprise Edition also includes some important additional features that are not supplied with the Standard Edition, including the following:

- **Microsoft Metadirectory Services (MMS)** A *metadirectory* is essentially a directory of directories—a means of integrating multiple information sources into a single, unified directory. MMS makes it possible to combine Active Directory information with other directory services, to create a unified view of all available information about a given resource. The Enterprise Edition includes support only for MMS, not the actual MMS software, which you must obtain from a Microsoft Consulting Service (MCS) or via an MMS partner engagement.

- **Server clustering** A *server cluster* is a group of servers that function as a single entity, providing high availability for a particular set of applications. High availability in this case means that application processing is distributed among the servers in the cluster, reducing the load on each computer and providing fault tolerance if any of the servers fails. The servers in a server cluster, which are called *nodes*, have shared access to a common data source, usually in the form of a storage area network (SAN), enabling all of the nodes to maintain a current information base. The Enterprise Edition supports server clusters of up to eight nodes.

- **Hot Add Memory** The Enterprise Edition includes software support for a hardware feature called Hot Add Memory, which enables administrators to add or replace memory in the computer without powering it down or restarting. To use this capability, the computer must have the appropriate hardware support.

- **Windows System Resource Manager (WSRM)** This feature enables administrators to allocate system resources to specific applications or processes, based on the needs of the computer's users, and maintain accounting records of the resources used by those applications or processes. This enables businesses to set resource limits for specific processes or to bill customers based on their resource usage.

Datacenter Edition

The Datacenter Edition is designed for high-end, high-traffic application servers that require huge amounts of system resources. The Datacenter Edition is nearly identical to the Enterprise Edition in its feature set but provides even greater hardware scalability, supporting up to 64 GB of RAM and up to 32 processors. The Datacenter Edition does omit a few Enterprise Edition features, such as ICS and ICF, primarily because a high-end server such as those supporting the Datacenter Edition are not expected to serve in the roles that use these features.

> **NOTE** **Purchasing the Datacenter Edition** Like the Web Edition, the Datacenter Edition is not available through standard retail channels. You can obtain the operating system only through an OEM as part of a high-end server hardware package.

64-Bit Editions

Both the Enterprise Edition and the Datacenter Edition are available in versions that support computers equipped with Intel Itanium processors. Itanium is a processing platform that provides 64-bit addressing (while Intel's standard x86 processors are 32-bit), a greatly enlarged virtual address space and paged pool area, and enhanced floating point performance. It is specifically designed for processor-intensive tasks, such as massive database applications, scientific analysis, and heavily accessed Web servers.

The system requirements for the Itanium versions of the Enterprise Edition and the Datacenter Edition are slightly different from those of the x86 versions, as summarized in Table 1-2. Also, some features of the x86 editions are not available in the Itanium editions. Most notably, the Itanium editions do not support 16-bit Windows applications, real-mode applications, POSIX applications, or print services for Apple Macintosh clients.

Test your knowledge of the Windows Server 2003 operating system versions by doing Exercise 1.1, "Selecting an Operating System," now.

Table 1-2   **Special System Requirements for Windows Server 2003 Itanium Versions**

	Enterprise Edition	Datacenter Edition
Minimum Processor Speed	733 MHz	733 MHz
Maximum RAM	64 GB	512 GB
Minimum Disk Space	2 GB	2 GB

INSTALLING WINDOWS SERVER 2003

Before you can learn to manage and maintain Windows Server 2003, you must be able to install the operating system and configure it to perform the tasks demanded of it. Although this course does not cover advanced topics such as Active Directory design, it does cover the administration of Active Directory objects, such as users, computers, and groups. Before you can perform some of the exercises in this textbook and in the accompanying Lab Manual, you must have a computer with Windows Server 2003 installed that is configured to function as an Active Directory domain controller.

Installation Phases

If you have experience installing Windows 2000, the Windows Server 2003 installation process will be familiar. It has two distinct phases:

- **Text mode**   The initial phase of the installation begins when the computer boots from the Windows Server 2003 distribution CD and runs the Winnt.exe program. Unlike Windows 2000 and earlier, there is no support for starting the installation using floppy disks in Windows Server 2003. The Winnt.exe program loads the Windows Server 2003 operating system files from the CD. This is a limited, character-based version of the operating system because the files needed for the graphical user interface (GUI) have not been installed yet. The program then formats the partition that will become the system drive, creates the system root directory structure, and copies the operating system files from the temporary directories to their final locations. The program also begins to build the registry during this phase, creating keys containing basic operating system information, as well as information about the hardware detected in the computer thus far. The computer then restarts.

■ **Graphical mode**   When the system starts for the second time, it uses the boot and operating system files, which are now in their final, permanent locations on the system drive. The familiar Windows interface appears for the first time, using a low-resolution VGA display driver. After the system starts, the graphical mode phase begins, with the operating system executing its primary hardware detection routine. When the hardware is detected and drivers installed, the program begins to gather information from the user that is needed to complete the installation and installs various nonessential operating system components. If a network interface adapter is detected, the installation program installs the required networking components and binds them to the network adapter driver. Finally, the program builds the Start menu, sets system security parameters, deletes any temporary files it has created, and saves the system configuration before restarting the computer for the final time.

Installation Procedure

This section contains a detailed account of the Windows Server 2003 installation process. It assumes that you are using a computer that meets the Windows Server 2003 system requirements, that you are installing the operating system from the original distribution CD, and that the computer's primary hard drive is completely empty.

> **NOTE**   **Installation Variations**   This installation procedure assumes the use of a computer with a basic hardware configuration. The presence of certain hardware devices in the computer can cause variations in the installation process (such as additional configuration steps) that are not mentioned here.

▶ **Windows Server 2003 Installation**

To install Windows Server 2003, use the following procedure:

1. Insert the Windows Server 2003 installation CD into the CD-ROM drive and restart the computer.

   If you are prompted to do so, press a key to boot from the CD.

2. After the computer starts, a brief message appears, stating that Setup is inspecting your computer's hardware configuration. The Windows Setup screen appears.

3. If your computer requires special mass storage drivers that are not part of the Windows Server 2003 driver set, press F6 when prompted and provide the appropriate drivers.

4. The system prompts you to press F2 if you want to perform an Automated System Recovery (ASR). Do not press F2 at this time. The setup continues.

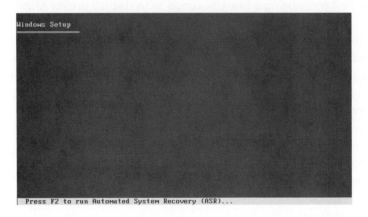

```
Windows Setup
```
```
Press F2 to run Automated System Recovery (ASR)...
```

NOTE   Automated System Recovery   ASR is a new feature in Windows Server 2003 that replaces the Emergency Repair Disk feature of previous Windows versions. For more information on using ASR, see Chapter 4 in this textbook.

The gray status bar at the bottom of the screen indicates that Setup is loading files. This is required to start a minimal version of the operating system. At this point, the hardware in the computer has not been specifically identified, so after loading the operating system kernel, the setup program loads a series of drivers that support a wide range of mass storage, keyboard, pointer, and video devices, in an attempt to create a functional input/output (I/O) configuration that will allow the installation to proceed.

```
Windows Setup
```
```
Setup is loading files (Video Driver)...
```

NOTE   Locating Storage Drivers   If appropriate drivers for your mass storage devices are not included with Windows Server 2003, you must obtain them, restart the installation, and press F6 to supply them to the setup program.

5. If you are installing an evaluation version of Windows Server 2003, the Setup Notification screen appears, informing you of this. Read the Setup Notification message, and then press ENTER to continue. The Welcome To Setup screen appears.

```
Windows Server 2003, Standard Edition Setup

Welcome to Setup.

This portion of the Setup program prepares Microsoft(R)
Windows(R) to run on your computer.

    •  To set up Windows now, press ENTER.
    •  To repair a Windows installation using
       Recovery Console, press R.
    •  To quit Setup without installing Windows, press F3.








ENTER=Continue   R=Repair   F3=Quit
```

6. Read the Welcome To Setup message, and then press ENTER to continue. The License Agreement screen appears.

```
Windows Licensing Agreement

    END-USER LICENSE AGREEMENT FOR 180-DAY
    EVALUATION OF MICROSOFT SOFTWARE

    MICROSOFT WINDOWS SERVER 2003, STANDARD EDITION
    EVALUATION VERSION
    MICROSOFT WINDOWS SERVER 2003, ENTERPRISE EDITION
    EVALUATION VERSION

    PLEASE READ THIS END-USER LICENSE AGREEMENT
    ("EULA") CAREFULLY.  BY INSTALLING OR USING
    THE SOFTWARE THAT ACCOMPANIES THIS EULA
    ("SOFTWARE"), YOU AGREE TO THE TERMS OF THIS
    EULA.  IF YOU DO NOT AGREE, DO NOT USE THE
    SOFTWARE AND, IF APPLICABLE, RETURN IT TO THE
    PLACE OF PURCHASE.

    THE SOFTWARE CONTAINS FUNCTIONALITY THAT
    IS TIME-SENSITIVE AND DESIGNED TO CEASE
    FUNCTIONING AFTER A CERTAIN PERIOD.  PLEASE
    REFER TO SECTION 2.e FOR DETAILS.

    THIS SOFTWARE DOES NOT TRANSMIT ANY
    PERSONALLY IDENTIFIABLE INFORMATION FROM YOUR
    SERVER TO MICROSOFT COMPUTER SYSTEMS WITHOUT
    YOUR CONSENT.

     1. GENERAL.  This EULA is a legal agreement between you (either

    F8=I agree   ESC=I do not agree   PAGE DOWN=Next Page
```

7. Read the license agreement and press F8 to accept it. A screen appears, containing a list of the partitions on the computer's available disk drives as well as any unpartitioned space. From this screen, you can also create and delete partitions on the computer's drives as needed. Selecting an Unpartitioned Space entry in the list creates a new partition using all of that space. If you want to create a partition using only part of the unpartitioned space, press C and specify the size of the partition you want to create. To complete the exercises in this book, a partition of at least 3 GB is recommended. In addition, you must leave at least 1 GB of unpartitioned space on the drive for exercises that involve the creation of new partitions.

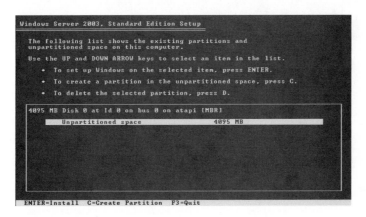

```
Windows Server 2003, Standard Edition Setup

    The following list shows the existing partitions and
    unpartitioned space on this computer.

    Use the UP and DOWN ARROW keys to select an item in the list.

    •  To set up Windows on the selected item, press ENTER.
    •  To create a partition in the unpartitioned space, press C.
    •  To delete the selected partition, press D.

 ┌─────────────────────────────────────────────────────────────┐
 │ 4095 MB Disk 0 at Id 0 on bus 0 on atapi [MBR]                │
 │      Unpartitioned space                    4095 MB           │
 │                                                               │
 │                                                               │
 │                                                               │
 │                                                               │
 └─────────────────────────────────────────────────────────────┘

 ENTER=Install   C=Create Partition   F3=Quit
```

8. Select an area of unpartitioned disk space at least 4 GB in size, and then press C and specify 3072 as the size of the new partition. Then press ENTER.

9. A screen appears, prompting you to select the file system to use when formatting the selected partition. Select the Format The Partition Using The NTFS File System option and press ENTER to continue.

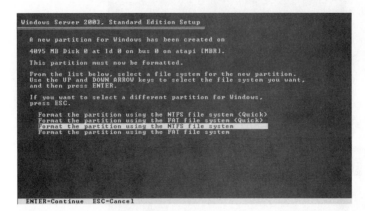

Setup formats the partition using NTFS, examines the hard disk for physical errors that might cause the installation to fail, and begins copying files from the CD to the hard disk. This process takes several minutes.

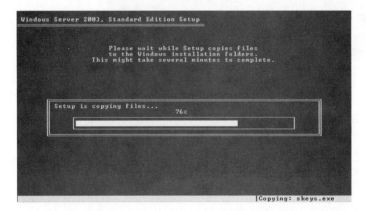

10. Setup initializes the Windows configuration and then displays a screen with a red status bar that counts down for 15 seconds before the computer restarts and enters the GUI mode phase of the installation process.

Windows Setup launches and produces a graphical user interface that tracks the progress of installation in the left pane. The Collecting Information, Dynamic Update, and Preparing Installation options are selected, indicating these steps have been completed. Collecting Information was completed before the GUI appeared, and Dynamic Update is not used when starting from the CD.

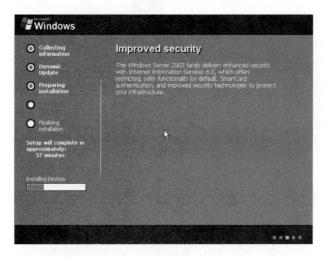

The Preparing Installation step occurred when the Setup program copied the operating system files to the local disk drive. The Installing Windows step begins with Setup's hardware detection process, which might take several minutes. Unlike the text mode hardware detection routine, which identifies hardware components by loading drivers using trial and error, this process identifies the specific components in the computer, writes information about them to the registry, and configures the operating system to load the correct drivers for the hardware. Eventually, the Windows Setup Wizard loads and the Regional And Language Options page appears.

11. Modify the default regional and language option settings if necessary, by clicking the Customize button or the Details button. Then click Next. The Personalize Your Software page appears.

![Windows Setup - Personalize Your Software dialog box. Setup uses the information you provide about yourself to personalize your Windows software. Type your full name and the name of your company or organization. Name: [ ] Organization: [ ]. Buttons: < Back, Next >]

12. In the Name text box, type your name; in the Organization text box, type the name of an organization, and then click Next. The Your Product Key page appears.

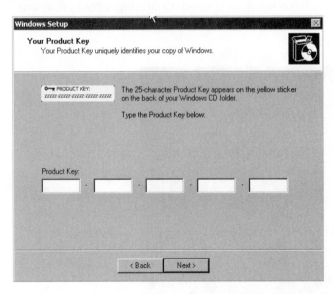

13. Enter the product key included with your Windows Server 2003 installation CD in the Product Key text boxes, and then click Next. The Licensing Modes page appears.

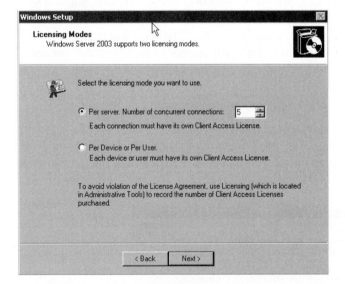

14. Leave the default value of 5 in the Per Server Number Of Concurrent Connections option, and then click Next. The Computer Name And Administrator Password page appears.

NOTE **Windows Server 2003 Licensing** If you are using an evaluation version of Windows Server 2003, the default value of 5 servers is sufficient to complete this course. However, if you are using a licensed copy of Windows Server 2003, you should specify a legal number of concurrent connections based on the actual licenses that you own.

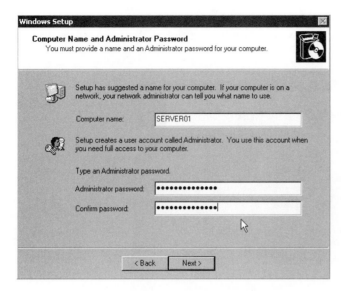

15. In the Computer Name text box, type **Server*xx*,** where *xx* is a unique number assigned to you by your instructor.

CAUTION   Avoiding Name Conflicts   If your computer is connected to a LAN, check with the network administrator before assigning a name to your computer.

16. In the Administrator Password text box and the Confirm Password text box, type a password for the Administrator account, and then click Next. The Date And Time Settings page appears.

IMPORTANT   Specifying a Password   In a manual installation, Windows Server 2003 will not let you progress to subsequent steps until you enter an Administrator password that meets complexity requirements. By default, Windows Server 2003 requires complex passwords that are at least seven characters long. A complex password is one that contains at least three of the following four component elements: uppercase letters, lowercase letters, numbers, and symbols. You are allowed to enter a blank password, although this practice is strongly discouraged.

17. Specify the correct date and time, and select the correct time zone for your location. Then click Next. After a brief delay, the Network Settings page appears.

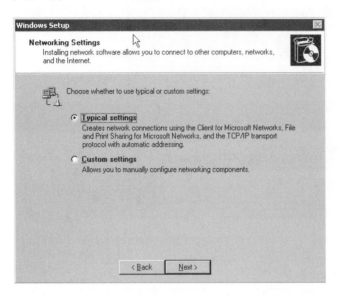

18. Leave the default Typical Settings option selected, and then click Next. The Workgroup Or Computer Domain page appears.

NOTE   Typical Networking Settings   Selecting the Typical Settings option on the Network Settings page causes the setup program to install the Client for Microsoft Networks, Network Load Balancing, File and Printer Sharing for Microsoft Networks, and Internet Protocol (TCP/IP) components (although the Network Load Balancing module is disabled) and configure TCP/IP to obtain an IP address from a DHCP server. If you are connected to a network with no DHCP server, you must obtain an IP address and other TCP/IP configuration settings from your network administrator and select the Custom Settings option to apply them before your computer can communicate with the LAN.

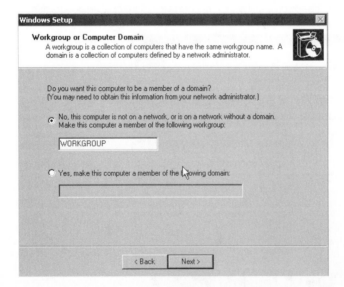

19. Leave the default No option selected and the default workgroup name of WORKGROUP in place, and then click Next.

The setup program installs and configures the remaining operating system components by copying files, installing Start menu items, registering components, saving settings, and removing temporary files. When the installation is complete, the computer restarts automatically and the Welcome To Windows dialog box appears.

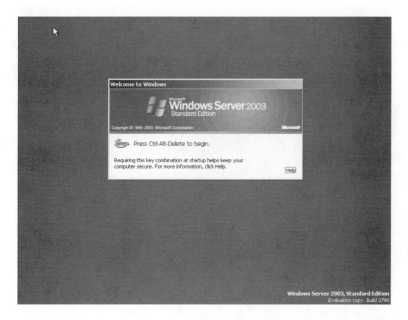

In a business environment, such as a large enterprise network, the operating system installation process is often substantially different from this procedure. Network administrators who are responsible for large fleets of computers usually do not have the time to perform lengthy manual operating system installations such as the one described here. They can use a number of methods to streamline or automate the Windows Server 2003 installation process, including the following:

- **Answer files** An *answer file* is a script that contains settings for all of the options presented to the user during a Windows Server 2003 installation. With a properly configured answer file, it is possible to start an operating system installation and let it proceed unattended, with responses to all prompts supplied by the answer file. The main drawback of using answer files for a mass operating system deployment is that each computer requires its own file. Some of the settings supplied during the installation must be unique, such as computer names and IP addresses.

- **Disk images** When you deploy a large number of identical computers, you can bypass much of the operating system installation process by using a *disk image*. A disk image is a bit-for-bit copy of the hard drive in a computer that has the operating system already installed. Transferring the image to another computer with the same hardware configuration enables the operating system to run on that computer with no interactive installation. Windows Server 2003 includes a tool called Remote Installation Services that administrators can use to deploy disk images to other computers over the network.

Practice
logging on to
Windows
Server 2003
for the first
time by doing
Exercise 1.2,
"Logging On

to Windows,"
now.

Activating Windows Server

Some editions of Windows Server 2003, including the evaluation edition provided with this book, require that you activate the operating system after installation. Depending on the version you are using, you might have 14 days or 30 days to activate Windows Server 2003. Activation is a simple, one-time process that can be completed over the Internet or by telephone. To begin the activation process, click Start, point to All Programs, and click Activate Windows. The Let's Activate Windows page of the Activate Windows Wizard appears (as shown in Figure 1-1).

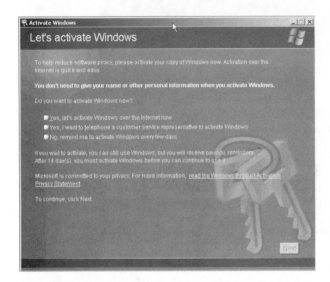

Figure 1-1   The Let's Activate Windows page of the Activate Windows Wizard

> **NOTE   Volume Licensing**   If you acquired your Windows Server 2003 license through one of the Microsoft volume licensing programs, you are not required to activate the license.

To activate Windows over the Internet, you must have your computer connected to the Internet when you begin the activation procedure. This means that the computer must either be equipped with a modem and configured to connect to an Internet service provider (ISP) or be configured with appropriate TCP/IP configuration parameters (including IP Address, Subnet Mask, Preferred DNS Server, and Default Gateway settings) and connected to a LAN that provides Internet access. If the computer cannot access the Internet, you must activate Windows by telephone.

CONFIGURING WINDOWS SERVER 2003

After installing and activating Windows, you can configure the server using the Manage Your Server page, as shown in Figure 1-2. This page launches after you log on, or you can launch it at any time by selecting Manage Your Server from the Start menu. This page enables you to install specific services, tools, and configurations based on the roles that the server can perform.

Figure 1-2   The Manage Your Server page

When you click the Add Or Remove A Role hyperlink, the Configure Your Server Wizard appears. After scanning for network connections, the wizard enables you to select any of the following server roles:

- **File Server**   Provides centralized access to files and folders for individual users, departments, and entire organizations. Choosing this role enables you to manage user disk space by enabling and configuring disk quotas and to provide improved file system search performance by enabling the Indexing service.

- **Print Server**   Provides centralized and managed access to printing devices by serving shared printers and printer drivers to client computers. Choosing this role starts the Add Printer Wizard, enabling you to install printers and their associated Windows printer drivers. Selecting the Print Server role also installs IIS 6, configures the Internet Printing Protocol (IPP), and installs the Web-based printer administration tools.

- **Application Server (IIS, ASP.NET)**   Provides infrastructure components required to support the hosting of Web applications. Selecting this role installs and configures IIS 6 as well as Microsoft ASP.NET and COM+.

- **Mail Server (POP3, SMTP)**   Installs Post Office Protocol version 3 (POP3) and Simple Mail Transfer Protocol (SMTP) so the server can function as an incoming and outgoing e-mail server for network clients.

- **Terminal Server**   Provides multiple network clients with access to server applications and resources as if those applications and resources were installed on their own computers. Users connect to the server with the Terminal Services client or the Remote Desktop client.

- **Remote Access / VPN Server**   Provides multiple-protocol routing and remote access services for dial-in, LAN, and WAN connections. Virtual private network (VPN) connections enable remote sites and users to connect securely and inexpensively to the network using the Internet as a network medium.

- **Domain Controller (Active Directory)**   Provides directory services to clients on the network. Choosing this role runs the Active Directory Installation Wizard, which configures the server to function as a domain controller for a new or existing domain and, if there is not already a DNS server on the network, installs the Microsoft DNS Server service.

- **DNS Server**   Provides host name resolution by translating host names to IP addresses (forward lookups) and IP addresses to host names (reverse lookups). Choosing this role installs the Microsoft DNS Server service and then starts the Configure A DNS Server Wizard.

- **DHCP Server**   Provides automatic IP addressing services to clients configured to use dynamic IP addressing. Choosing this role installs the DHCP Server service and then starts the New Scope Wizard so you can define one or more IP address scopes in the network.

- **Streaming Media Server**   Choosing this role installs Windows Media Services (WMS), which enables the server to stream multimedia content over an intranet connection or the Internet. Content can be stored and delivered on demand or delivered in real time.

- **WINS Server**   Provides computer name resolution by translating NetBIOS names to IP addresses. It is not necessary to install WINS unless you are supporting legacy operating systems such as Windows 95 or Windows NT, which are based on NetBIOS names. The Windows Server 2003, Windows 2000, and Windows XP operating systems do not require WINS, although legacy applications on those platforms might very well require NetBIOS name resolution. Choosing this option installs the WINS service.

CREATING A DOMAIN CONTROLLER

To complete the exercises in this book and in the Lab Manual, you must have a Windows Server 2003 computer that is configured as a domain controller.

▶ **Active Directory Installation**

To configure your Server01 computer to function as a domain controller, use the following procedure:

> **NOTE**   Active Directory Installation Options   When the Active Directory Installation Wizard runs, the prompts that the wizard displays differ depending on whether it detects another domain on the network. The steps presented below assume that you are running the wizard on an isolated network. If you are connected to a network with another domain, the steps might vary, and you might have to modify your selections or disconnect from the network before performing the exercise.

1. Log on to Windows Server 2003 as Administrator.

2. If it is not already open, open the Manage Your Server page from the Administrative Tools program group.

3. Click the Add Or Remove A Role hyperlink. The Configure Your Server Wizard loads and the Preliminary Steps page appears.

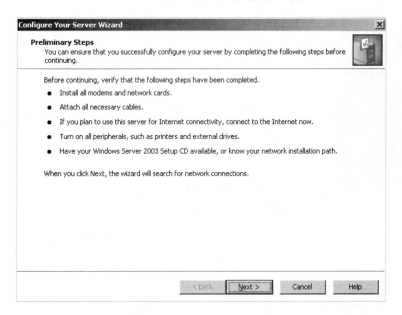

4. Verify that all of the steps listed on the page have been completed, and then click Next. After a brief delay while the wizard scans the network, the Server Role page appears.

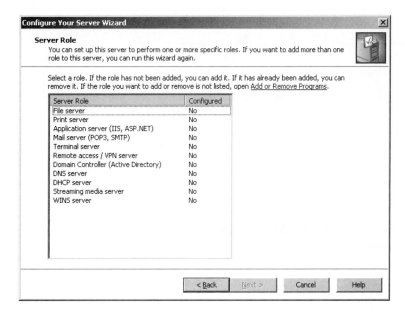

5. Select Domain Controller (Active Directory) from the list of server roles and click Next. The Summary Of Selections page appears.

6. Click Next. The Active Directory Installation Wizard launches.

7. Click Next to bypass the Welcome page. The Operating System Compatibility page appears.

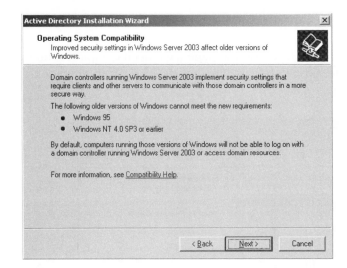

8. Read the information on the page and click Next. The Domain Controller Type page appears.

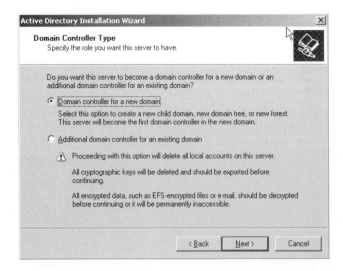

9. Leave the default Domain Controller For A New Domain option selected, and click Next. The Create New Domain page appears.

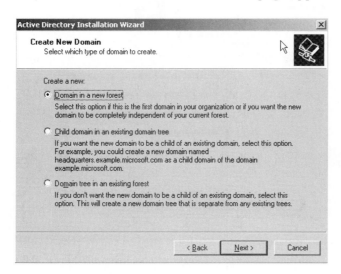

10. Leave the default Domain In A New Forest option selected, and click Next. The New Domain Name page appears.

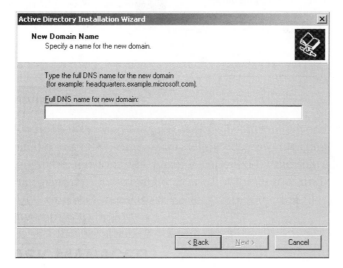

11. In the Full DNS Name For New Domain text box, type **contosoxx.com,** where ***xx*** is a number assigned to you by your instructor, and then click Next. The NetBIOS Domain Name page appears.

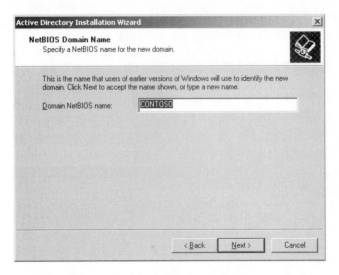

12. Verify that the Domain NetBIOS Name text box reads *CONTOSOXX*, and then click Next. The Database And Log Folders page appears.

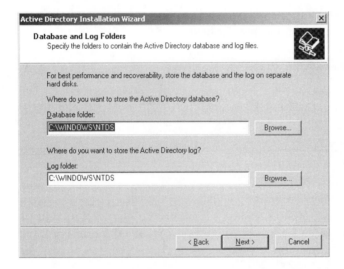

13. Click Next to accept the default database and log folder locations. The Shared System Volume page appears.

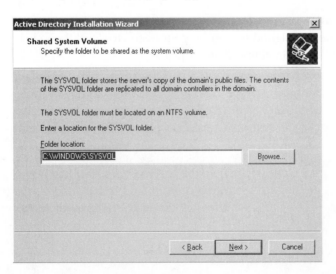

14. Click Next to accept the default shared system volume location. The DNS Registration Diagnostics page appears.

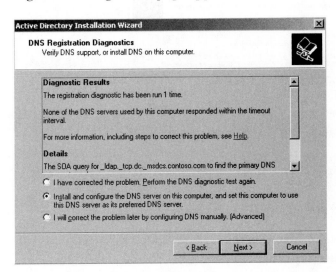

At this time, the wizard attempts to connect to the DNS servers specified in the computer's TCP/IP configuration to determine whether they are capable of hosting the records required for an Active Directory domain.

15. Select the Install And Configure The DNS Server On This Computer option, and then click Next. The Permissions page appears.

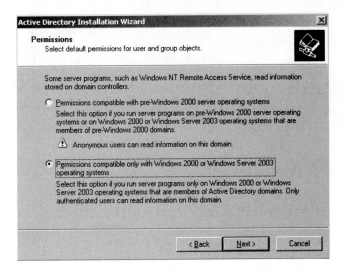

16. Click Next to accept the default permissions option, and then click Next. The Directory Services Restore Mode Administrator Password page appears.

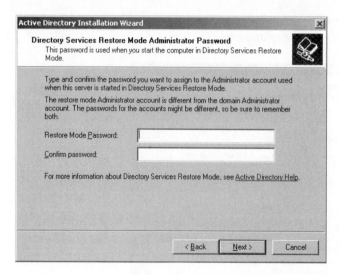

17. Type an appropriate password in the Restore Mode Password and Confirm Password text boxes, and then click Next. The Summary page appears.

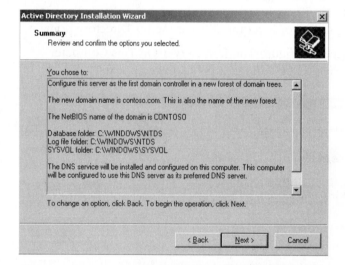

18. Review the options you have selected in the wizard, and then click Next. The wizard proceeds to install the Active Directory and DNS Server services.

19. When the configuration process is finished, the Completing The Active Directory Installation Wizard page appears. Click Finish.

20. An Active Directory Installation Wizard message box appears, prompting you to restart the computer. Click Restart Now.

21. After the system has restarted, log on as Administrator. The Configure Your Server Wizard reappears, displaying the This Server Is Now A Domain Controller page.

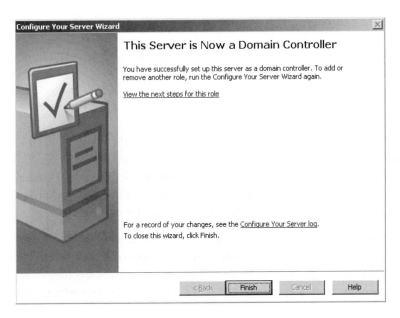

22. Click Finish.

AN ACTIVE DIRECTORY PRIMER

Although the Active Directory directory service is not the primary focus of this course, some exposure to Active Directory is unavoidable for every Windows Server 2003 system administrator. The upcoming chapters will not cover advanced topics such as Active Directory design and schema administration, but you will work with the Active Directory management tools supplied with Windows Server 2003 and learn to manipulate the properties of Active Directory objects, such as users, groups, and computers.

> **NOTE   Active Directory**   To study the more advanced Active Directory topics, consider taking the course for exam 70-294: Planning, Implementing, and Maintaining a Microsoft Windows Server 2003 Active Directory Infrastructure.

What Is a Directory Service?

The first commercial local area networking products that appeared in the early 1990s were geared toward small collections of computers, commonly called *workgroups*. A workgroup network enabled a handful of users working together on the same project to share resources such as documents and printers. As the value of data networking was recognized by the business world, networks grew larger. Today it is not uncommon for organizations to have networks consisting of thousands of nodes.

As networks grew larger, so did the number of shared resources available on them, and it became increasingly difficult to locate and keep track of the available resources. When you work in a company with 12 employees, it is usually not a problem to memorize everyone's telephone extension. However, when you work for a company with 1200 employees, memorizing everyone's extension is virtually impossible. To find out the number of the person you want to reach, most large companies provide a list of employees and their numbers—that is, a directory. A **directory service** is a digital resource that functions in exactly the same way, except that it contains a list of the resources available on a data network.

A directory service can contain information about the computers on the network, the network users, and other hardware and software devices, such as printers and applications. By storing the information in a central directory, it is available to anyone at any time.

Domains and Domain Controllers

Windows networks support two directory service models: the workgroup and the domain, with the domain model being far more common in organizations implementing Windows Server 2003. The workgroup directory service is a flat database of computer names, designed to support a small network. This is the original directory service that was introduced in Windows NT 3.1 in the early 1990s.

The domain model is a hierarchical directory of enterprise resources—Active Directory—that is trusted by all systems that are members of the domain. These systems can use the user, group, and computer accounts in the directory to secure their resources. Active Directory thus acts as an identity store, providing a single trusted Who's Who list for the domain.

Active Directory itself is more than just a database, though. It is also a collection of supporting components, including transaction logs and the system volume, or Sysvol, that contains logon scripts and group policy information. It is the services that support and use the database, including Lightweight Directory Access Protocol (LDAP), the Kerberos security protocol, replication processes, and the File Replication Service (FRS). Finally, Active Directory is a collection of tools that administrators use to manage the directory service.

The Active Directory database and its services are installed on one or more **domain controllers**. A domain controller is a server that has been promoted by running the Active Directory Installation Wizard, as described earlier in the "Creating a Domain Controller" section. Once a server has been promoted to a domain controller, it hosts a copy, or replica, of the Active Directory database.

Because Active Directory is such a vital network resource, it is critical that it be available to users at all times. For this reason, Active Directory domains typically have at least two domain controllers, so that if one fails, the other can continue to support clients. These domain controllers continually replicate their information with each other, so that each one has a database containing current information. When an administrator makes a change to an Active Directory database record on any domain controller, the change is replicated to all of the other domain controllers within the domain. This is called multiple-master replication, because it is possible to make changes to any one of the domain controllers.

> **NOTE   Single-Master Replication**   Windows NT's domain model uses a technique called single-master replication, in which all changes to the domain records have to be made to a primary domain controller (PDC), which then replicates them to one or more backup domain controllers (BDCs). Multiple-master replication is better suited to a large enterprise network because administrators can update the Active Directory database from any domain controller, not just a designated PDC.

Domains, Trees, and Forests

The domain is the fundamental administrative unit of the Windows Server 2003 directory service. However, an enterprise might have more than one domain in its Active Directory. Multiple domain models create logical structures called **trees** when they share contiguous DNS names. For example, contoso.com, us.contoso.com, and europe.contoso.com share contiguous DNS namespaces and would together be considered a tree (as shown in Figure 1-3). The contoso.com domain is the parent in which the child domains are created and is therefore called the *root domain*.

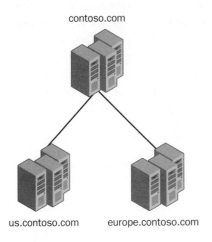

contoso.com

us.contoso.com   europe.contoso.com

Figure 1-3   An Active Directory tree

If domains in an Active Directory do not share a common root domain, they exist as multiple trees. An Active Directory that consists of multiple trees is naturally called a **forest** (as shown in Figure 1-4). The forest is the largest structure in an Active Directory. When you promote the first domain controller on a Windows Server 2003 network, you create a forest, a tree within that forest, and a domain within that tree, all at the same time. A forest might contain multiple domains in multiple trees, or just one domain.

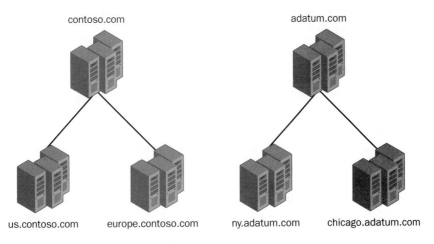

contoso.com   adatum.com

us.contoso.com   europe.contoso.com   ny.adatum.com   chicago.adatum.com

Figure 1-4   An Active Directory forest

When an Active Directory installation consists of more than one domain, a component of Active Directory called the global catalog enables clients in one domain to find information in other domains. The *global catalog* is essentially a subset of the information in all of the domain databases combined. When you search for a user in another domain, for example, the global catalog might not contain all of the available information about the user, but it will contain enough information to tell you where to look for greater detail.

Objects and Attributes

All databases are made up of records, and in Active Directory the records are called **objects**. An object is a component that represents a specific network resource. An Active Directory can contain objects representing physical resources, such as computers and printers; human resources, such as users and groups; software resources, such as applications and DNS zones; and administrative resources, such as organizational units (OUs) and sites. After promoting a server to a domain controller, administrators can populate the domain by creating objects.

The most commonly used Active Directory objects are as follows:

- **Domain**   The root object that contains all of the other objects in the domain.

- **Organizational unit**   A **container object** that is used to create logical groupings of computer, user, and group objects.

- **User**   Represents a network user and functions as a repository for identification and authentication data.

- **Computer**   Represents a computer on the network and provides the machine account needed for the system to log on to the domain.

- **Group**   A container object representing a logical grouping of users, computers, and/or other groups that is independent of the Active Directory tree structure. Groups can contain objects from different OUs and domains.

- **Shared Folder**   Provides Active Directory–based network access to a shared folder on a Windows computer.

- **Printer**   Provides Active Directory–based network access to a shared printer on a Windows computer.

Every Active Directory object consists of a set of **attributes**, which are pieces of information about that object. A user object, for example, contains attributes specifying the user's account name, password, address, telephone number, and other identifying information. A group object has an attribute containing a list of the users who are members of that group. Administrators can use Active Directory to store virtually any information about the organization's users and other resources. In addition to purely informational attributes, objects also have attributes that perform administrative functions, such as an access control list (ACL) that specifies who has permission to access each object.

View the objects created in an Active Directory domain by default by doing Exercise 1.3, "Viewing Active Directory Objects," now.

The Active Directory component that specifies what types of objects administrators can create and what attributes each object has is called the *schema*. By default, the Active Directory schema contains a large collection of object types and attributes, but it is sometimes necessary to add new object types or new attributes to existing object types. This is possible because the Active Directory schema is extensible. Administrators can extend the schema manually using the Active Directory Schema snap-in, or applications can automatically extend the schema to create object types or attributes specific to their needs. For example, when you install Microsoft Exchange, the application modifies the schema to add additional attributes to every user object in the Active Directory database.

Containers and Leaves

Active Directory is capable of hosting millions of objects, and consequently there must be a means of organizing those objects into units smaller than the domain. To make this organization possible, Active Directory uses a hierarchical structure. A domain is called a **container object** because other objects can exist beneath it in the hierarchy. OUs are another type of container that administrators can use to create a hierarchy of objects within a domain. An object that cannot contain another object, such as a user or computer, is called a **leaf object**.

One of the more complicated tasks in Active Directory administration is creating an effective hierarchy of OUs. Administrators use various organizational structures when designing the OU hierarchy, such as geographical locations, departmental divisions, or a combination of the two. For example, Figure 1-5 shows an Active Directory hierarchy in which the first layer of OUs represents the cities in which the organization has branch offices, and the second layer represents the departments in each branch. By creating a logical Active Directory hierarchy, users and administrators can locate the objects they need more easily.

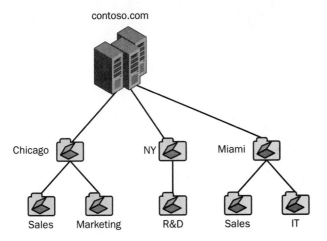

Figure 1-5   An Active Directory OU hierarchy

Group objects are also containers, but they are not elements of the hierarchy because they can contain members located anywhere in the domain. In addition to their purely organizational function, container objects also perform a crucial role in object administration. As in a file system, permissions flow downward in the Active Directory hierarchy. If you grant an OU object permission to access a specific share, for example, all of the objects in that container will inherit that permission. This is one of the fundamental characteristics that makes a hierarchical directory service so useful to administrators. Instead of granting rights and permissions to individual users, administrators are more likely to grant them to containers and let them flow down to the leaf objects in the container.

Group Policies

Because of the way objects inherit settings from their parent containers, administrators typically use OUs to collect objects that are configured similarly. Just about any configuration setting that you can apply to an individual Windows computer can also be managed centrally using a feature of Active Directory called *group policies*. Group policies enable you to specify security settings, deploy software, and configure operating system and application behavior on a computer without ever having to touch it directly. Instead, you implement the desired configuration settings in a special Active Directory object called a **group policy object** (GPO) and then link the GPO to an Active Directory object containing the computers or users you want to configure.

GPOs are collections of hundreds of possible configuration settings, from user logon rights and privileges to the software that is allowed to be run on a system. You can link a GPO to any domain, site, or OU container object in Active Directory, and all the users and computers in that container will receive the settings in the GPO. In most cases, administrators design the Active Directory hierarchy to accommodate the configuration of users and computers using GPOs. By placing all of the computers performing a specific role into the same OU, for example, you can assign a GPO containing role-specific settings to that OU and configure all of the computers at once.

SUMMARY

- Windows Server 2003 is available in four main editions—Web Edition, Standard Edition, Enterprise Edition, and Datacenter Edition—which differ primarily in the hardware they support and the features they provide.

- The Enterprise Edition and Datacenter Edition are available in 64-bit as well as 32-bit versions.

- Windows Server 2003 retail and evaluation versions require a product key and product activation within 14 or 30 days of installation.

- The Manage Your Server page and the Configure Your Server Wizard enable you to configure a computer running Windows Server 2003 to perform specific roles.

- Active Directory is a domain-based enterprise directory service that consists of objects, which are themselves composed of attributes.

- The Active Directory hierarchy is made up of forests, trees, domains, and organizational units. Permissions, rights, and group policy settings all flow downward in the hierarchy.

- To install Active Directory, you promote one or more servers to be domain controllers, using the Active Directory Installation Wizard. A domain controller stores a copy of the Active Directory database and is responsible for responding to requests for Active Directory information from clients.

EXERCISES

Exercise 1-1: Selecting an Operating System

For each of the Windows Server 2003 versions in the left column, specify which description (or descriptions) in the right column apply.

1. Web Edition	a. Supports 512 GB of memory
2. Standard Edition	b. Supports eight-node server clusters
3. Enterprise Edition	c. Cannot run 16-bit Windows applications
4. Datacenter Edition	d. Supports 32-node NLB clusters
5. Datacenter Edition (64-bit)	e. Supports computers with four processors

Exercise 1-2: Logging On to Windows

Once you have completed the Windows Server 2003 operating system installation, the computer restarts and displays the Welcome To Windows dialog box. To log on to the computer for the first time, use the following procedure:

1. In the Welcome To Windows dialog box, press CTRL+ALT+DELETE. The Log On To Windows dialog box appears.

2. In the Password text box, type the password you specified for the Administrator account in the operating system installation procedure. The Windows desktop appears.

Exercise 1-3: Viewing Active Directory Objects

When you create a new Active Directory domain, the operating system creates a number of container and leaf objects by default. To view some of these objects, use the following procedure:

1. Log on to a Windows Server 2003 domain controller as Administrator.

2. Click Start, point to Administrative Tools, and click Active Directory Users And Computers. The Active Directory Users And Computers console appears.

3. Expand the contoso*xx*.com domain icon in the scope pane (on the left) and select the Users container beneath the domain. The user and group objects in the Users container appear in the details pane (on the right).

REVIEW QUESTIONS

1. You are planning the deployment of Windows Server 2003 computers for a department of 250 employees. The server will host the home directories and shared folders for the department, and it will serve several printers to which departmental documents are sent. Which edition of Windows Server 2003 will provide the most cost-effective solution for the department? Explain your answer.

2. Which of the following versions of Windows Server 2003 require product activation? (Select all that apply.)

   a. Standard Edition, retail version

   b. Enterprise Edition, evaluation version

   c. Enterprise Edition, Open License version

   d. Standard Edition, Volume License version

3. What is the primary distinction between an Active Directory tree and an Active Directory forest?

4. Which of the following types of Active Directory objects are not container objects?

   a. User

   b. Group

   c. Computer

   d. Organizational unit

5. Which of the following is true about setup in Windows Server 2003? (Select all that apply.)

   a. Setup can be launched by booting from the CD.

   b. Setup can be launched by booting from setup floppy disks.

   c. Setup requires an Administrator password that is not blank to meet complexity requirements.

   d. Setup requires you to activate the product license before it installs the operating system.

CASE SCENARIOS

Scenario 1-1: Windows Server 2003, Web Edition Capabilities

You are a network administrator who has been assigned the task of deploying the Windows Server 2003 servers for your company's new e-commerce Web site, which is being designed by an outside consultant. The site will require four Web servers, configured as a four-node NLB cluster, and a single database server, running SQL Server. The consultant's deployment plan calls for the use of Windows Server 2003 Web Edition on all five of the servers. Which of the following statements regarding this proposed deployment is true?

1. The Web Edition is a suitable operating system for all five servers.

2. The Web Edition is a suitable operating system for the database server, but not for the Web servers, because it does not support NLB clusters.

3. The Web Edition is a suitable operating system for the Web servers, but not for the database server, because it cannot run SQL Server.

4. The Web Edition is not a suitable operating system for either the database or the Web servers.

Scenario 1-2: Selecting a Windows Server 2003 Edition

You are planning the deployment of Windows Server 2003 computers for a new Active Directory domain in a large corporation that includes multiple separate Active Directories maintained by each of the corporation's subsidiaries. The company has decided to roll out Exchange Server 2003 as a unified messaging platform for all the subsidiaries and plans to use Microsoft Metadirectory Services (MMS) to synchronize appropriate properties of objects throughout the organization. Which edition of Windows Server 2003 will provide the most cost-effective solution for this deployment? Explain your answer.

CHAPTER 2
ADMINISTERING MICROSOFT WINDOWS SERVER 2003

A large part of a Windows Server 2003 system administrator's daily work consists of configuring Active Directory objects, modifying computer software and service settings, installing new hardware and software, and performing many other tasks, using tools supplied with the operating system. As the computing environment expands to include more computers, the amount of work to be done increases as well. Microsoft Management Console (MMC) is the primary Windows Server 2003 system administration tool. MMC makes it possible to consolidate your most commonly used tools into a single interface and use them to manage Windows computers anywhere on the network. Understanding the capabilities of MMC is essential to efficient system administration.

When more comprehensive control of a computer at a remote location is required, beyond what can be accomplished remotely using MMC, two other key tools make administration of remote computers possible: Remote Desktop for Administration and Remote Assistance. Remote Desktop for Administration is a client/server application that displays the local console of a remote server in a window on your desktop, enabling you to control the keyboard and mouse functions as if you were logged on to that computer locally. Remote Assistance is similar in function but is designed to enable a Windows Server 2003 or Windows XP user to request help from another user on the network. Once the user issues a request for assistance, an expert elsewhere on the network can establish a remote connection to the user's desktop.

Upon completion of this chapter, you will be able to:

- Use a preconfigured MMC console
- Create a new MMC console
- Administer both local and remote computers using an MMC console
- Troubleshoot Terminal Services
- Configure a server to enable Remote Desktop for Administration
- Enable a computer to accept requests for Remote Assistance
- Use one of the available methods to request and establish a **Remote Assistance** session

USING MICROSOFT MANAGEMENT CONSOLE

MMC is a shell application that Windows Server 2003 uses to provide access to most of its system and network management tools. MMC provides a standardized, common interface for one or more application modules (called **snap-ins**) that are used to configure your system environment. These snap-ins are individualized to specific tasks and can be combined, ordered, and grouped within the MMC shell to your administrative preference. An instance of MMC with one or more snap-ins installed is referred to as a *console*. Most of the primary administrative tools in Windows Server 2003 are MMC consoles with collections of snap-ins installed that are suited to a specific purpose. With only a few exceptions, all of the shortcuts in the Administrative Tools program group on a computer running Windows Server 2003 are links to preconfigured MMC consoles.

For example, when you promote a Windows Server 2003 computer to a domain controller, the Active Directory Installation Wizard creates shortcuts to the following three primary management tools for Active Directory:

- Active Directory Domains and Trusts

- Active Directory Sites and Services

- Active Directory Users and Computers

Each of these shortcuts opens an MMC console containing a single snap-in, as shown in Figure 2-1. The Active Directory Users and Computers snap-in, for example, is specifically designed to administer the user, group, and computer objects in a domain. It is the snap-ins within the MMC shell, not MMC itself, that provide the administrative tools you use.

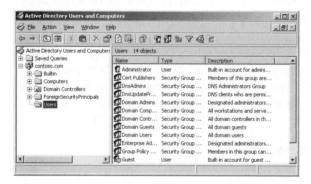

Figure 2-1   The Active Directory Users and Computers console

The three Active Directory consoles listed earlier all consist of a single snap-in, but an MMC console is not limited to using one snap-in at a time. When you open the Computer Management console found in the Administrative Tools program group on any Windows Server 2003 computer, you see a console containing many snap-ins, all combined into a single, convenient interface, as shown in Figure 2-2.

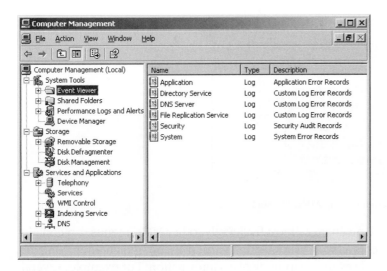

Figure 2-2   The Computer Management console

> **NOTE**   **MMC Interoperability**   MMC consoles can run on Windows Server 2003, Windows XP, Windows 2000, Windows NT 4, and Windows 98.

Using the MMC Interface

MMC uses a two-pane design, much like Windows Explorer. The left pane, called the **scope pane**, contains a hierarchical list of the snap-ins installed in the console and any subheadings that the snap-ins provide. This hierarchy is sometimes called the **console tree**. You can expand and contract the elements in the scope pane to display more or less information, just as you can expand and contract folders in Windows Explorer. Selecting an element in the scope pane displays its contents in the console's right pane, called the **details pane**. What you see in the details pane is wholly dependent on the function of the snap-in you are using.

Using MMC Menus

Above the two panes, MMC has a standard Windows menu and toolbar. The commands on the menus and the tools on the toolbar vary depending on the snap-in that is currently selected in the scope pane. For example, when you open the Computer Management console and click each snap-in in the scope pane in turn, you see the contents of the toolbar change with each one, as well as some of the menu contents.

The primary menu for context-specific functions in an MMC console is the Action menu. When you select a snap-in element in either the scope or the details pane, the Action menu changes to include commands specific to that element. Most Action menus contain an All Tasks submenu that lets you select any of the possible tasks to perform on the selected element (as shown in Figure 2-3). It is also common to find a New submenu under Action, which enables you to create subelements beneath the selected element. In most cases, the Action menu commands for a selected element are also available from a context menu, which is accessible by clicking the secondary mouse button on the element.

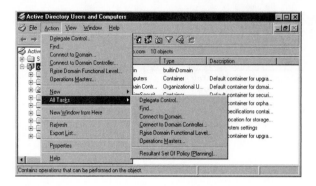

Figure 2-3   The Action menu in an MMC console

Although the Action menu changes most frequently, other MMC menus can contain context-specific elements as well, particularly the View menu, which often contains commands that control how the snap-in displays information. For example, several MMC snap-ins display a subset of their available information by default. When an Advanced Features command appears on the View menu, selecting it switches the console to the full display (as shown in Figure 2-4).

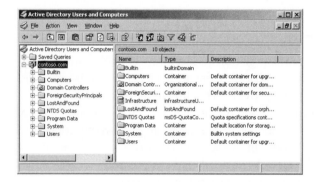

Figure 2-4   The Active Directory Users and Computers console with Advanced Features displayed

Using Multiple Windows

If you look carefully at the upper-right corner of one of the predefined MMC consoles, you'll see two sets of window manipulation buttons, because the snap-ins installed in that console are actually in a separate window that is maximized by default. When you click the Restore Down button (the middle one of the three), the snap-ins revert to a floating window, as shown in Figure 2-5.

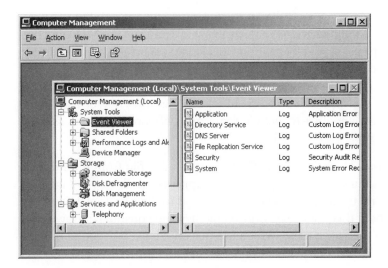

Figure 2-5   An MMC console with a floating window

Practice
creating a new
window in an
MMC console
by doing
Exercise 2.1,
"Opening an
MMC
Window," now

You can create additional windows in the console by selecting New Window from the Window menu. This enables you to create two different views of a single snap-in or to work with two different snap-ins in one console at the same time (as shown in Figure 2-6). You can also select an element in the scope pane and select New Window From Here from the Action menu to create a new window with the selected element at its root.

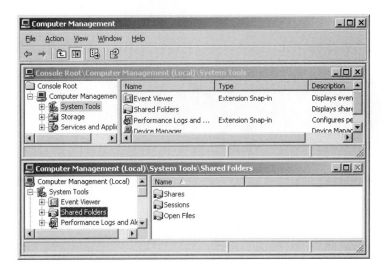

Figure 2-6   An MMC console with two open windows

NOTE   *Opening Multiple Windows*   *Not all MMC consoles enable you to open multiple windows. It is possible to configure a console to operate in a user mode that prevents the creation of new windows. For more information, see "Setting Console Options" later in this chapter.*

Creating Customized MMC Consoles

Windows Server 2003 includes a large collection of MMC snap-ins, not all of which are immediately accessible using the default shortcuts on the Start menu. Some extremely powerful tools are included with the operating system that you must seek out yourself. Third-party software developers can also create their own MMC snap-ins and include them with their products.

This leads to one of the most powerful MMC features, which is the ability to create customized consoles containing whatever snap-ins you want to use. You can combine one or more snap-ins or parts of snap-ins in a single console to create a single interface in which you can perform all of your administrative tasks. By creating a custom MMC, you do not have to switch between different programs or individual consoles. Customized consoles can contain any of the Windows Server 2003 snap-ins, whether or not they are already included in a preconfigured console, as well as any third-party snap-ins you might have.

The executable file for MMC is Mmc.exe. When you run this file from the Run dialog box or a command prompt, an empty console appears, as shown in Figure 2-7. This is a console with no snap-ins, so the menus and toolbar buttons have their default MMC functions at this point. The only element in the console window is the console root object in the scope pane, which is a placeholder representing the top of the console hierarchy. Before you can perform any administrative tasks using the console, you must add one or more snap-ins to it.

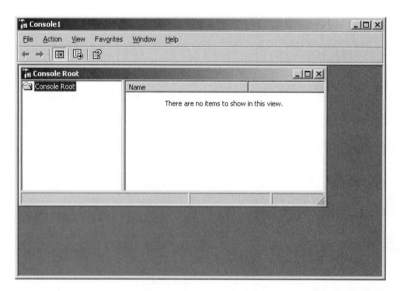

Figure 2-7   A blank MMC console

Adding Snap-Ins

There are two types of MMC snap-ins, as follows:

- **Standalone**   A standalone snap-in is a single tool that you can install directly into an empty MMC console. Stand-alone snap-ins appear in the first level directly beneath the console root in the console's scope pane.

- **Extension**   An extension snap-in provides additional functionality to specific stand-alone snap-ins. You cannot add an extension snap-in to a console without adding an appropriate stand-alone snap-in first. Extension snap-ins appear beneath the associated stand-alone snap-in in the console's scope pane.

Some snap-ins offer both stand-alone and extension functionality. For example, the Event Viewer snap-in is used to display the contents of a computer's event logs. In the Computer Management console, the Event Viewer snap-in appears as an extension, beneath the System Tools object in the scope pane. However, you can also add the Event Viewer snap-in to a custom console as a stand-alone snap-in, so that it appears directly beneath the console root.

To add snap-ins to a custom console, you select Add/Remove Snap-in from the File menu to display the Add/Remove Snap-in dialog box (as shown in Figure 2-8). By default, the Standalone tab in this dialog box is selected, and you click Add to display a list of the available stand-alone snap-ins on the computer.

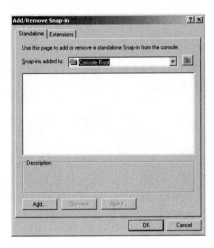

Figure 2-8   The Add/Remove Snap-in dialog box

You can select and add as many stand-alone snap-ins to a console as you like. Once you have added a stand-alone snap-in, you can select it in the Add/Remove Snap-in dialog box and click the Extensions tab to display a list of the extension snap-ins associated with the stand-alone snap-in you selected (as shown in Figure 2-9). After clearing the Add All Extensions check box, you can select which extensions you want to appear in the console. Using the Snap-ins Added To drop-down list, you can specify whether an extension snap-in is added to the console root or to a lower element in the tree.

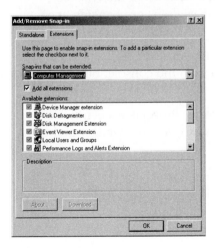

Figure 2-9   The Extensions tab of the Add/Remove Snap-in dialog box

Creating a Taskpad

Create a custom MMC console by doing Exercise 2.2, "Creating a Custom MMC Console," now.

Once you have added snap-ins to your custom console, you can create a customized taskpad, if you wish. The taskpad is an area of the details pane for a particular snap-in that contains links to frequently used functions from that snap-in (as shown in Figure 2-10). To create a taskpad, you select a snap-in in the scope pane and then select New Taskpad View from the Action menu. The New Taskpad View Wizard then takes you through the process of specifying how and where you want the taskpad to appear. After creating the taskpad view, you can run the New Task Wizard to create links in the taskpad.

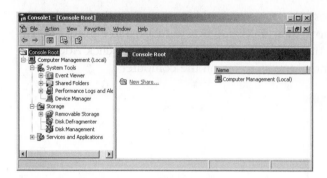

Figure 2-10   A custom MMC console with a taskpad

Setting Console Options

Once you add the snap-ins you want to have appear in your custom MMC console, you can set options that determine what changes other users can make to the console's configuration. Select Options from the File menu to display the Options dialog box, in which you can specify the name that should appear in the console's title bar, and select the console mode.

By default, all new consoles you create are configured to use Author mode, which provides full access to all console functions. The available modes you can choose from are as follows:

- **Author Mode**   Provides full console access, including adding or removing snap-ins, creating windows, creating taskpad views and tasks, viewing portions of the console tree, changing the options on the console, and saving the console.

- **User Mode: Full Access**   Allows users to navigate between snap-ins and between open windows and to access all portions of the console tree. Prevents users from adding or removing snap-ins or changing console properties.

- **User Mode: Limited Access, Multiple Windows**   Allows users to create new windows and view multiple windows in the console, but prevents them from closing existing windows.

- **User Mode: Limited Access, Single Window**   Prevents users from opening new windows and allows them to view only one window in the console.

Console modes enable you to create consoles for other users that have limited capabilities and that the users cannot alter. Console mode settings are why you can't add snap-ins to the preconfigured consoles supplied with Windows Server 2003.

Saving MMC Consoles

Once you have configured a custom console the way you want it, you must save it as a file so you can access it again later. MMC console files have an .msc extension, which is associated with the Mmc.exe application, so executing a console file launches MMC with that console module. By default, consoles are saved in the Administrative Tools folder in the users' profiles and therefore appear as shortcuts in the Start menu's Administrative Tools program group.

> **NOTE**   **Console Shortcuts**   The shortcuts for your custom consoles appear only in the All Programs/Administrative Tools program group, not in the Administrative Tools group on the Start menu itself.

Connecting to Remote Computers

The MMC consoles that appear on the Start menu of a computer running Windows Server 2003 are all configured to manage resources on the local system. However, with most of the snap-ins supplied with Windows Server 2003, you can manage other Windows computers on the network as well. This is one of MMC's most useful features because it enables administrators to manage computers anywhere on the network from their own desktops.

> **NOTE** **Exam Objectives**   The objectives for Exam 70-290 state that a student should be able to "manage servers remotely" and "manage a server by using available support tools."

You can access a remote computer using an MMC snap-in in two ways:

- Redirect an existing snap-in to another system

- Create a custom console with snap-ins directed to other systems

To connect to and manage another system using an MMC snap-in, you must launch the console with an account that has administrative credentials on the remote computer. The exact permissions required depend on the functions performed by the snap-in. If your credentials do not provide the proper permissions on the target computer, you will be able to load the snap-in but you will not be able to read information from or modify settings on the target computer.

> **NOTE**   **Using Run As**   If you know that the credentials you are currently using do not have the permissions needed to manage a remote computer, you can use Run As, or secondary logon, to launch a console with credentials other than those with which you are currently logged on.

Redirecting a Snap-In

A snap-in that is directed at a specific system has a Connect To Another Computer command on its Action menu. Selecting this command opens a Select Computer dialog box (as shown in Figure 2-11), in which you can type the name of or browse to another computer on the network. Once you specify the name of the computer you want to manage and click OK, the snap-in element in the scope pane changes to reflect the name of the computer you selected.

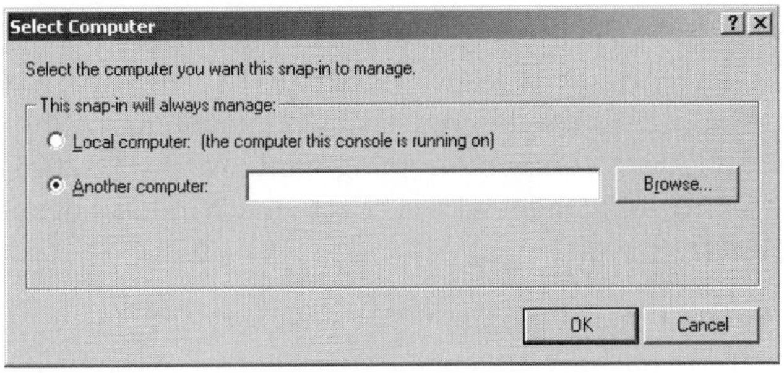

Figure 2-11   The Select Computer dialog box

Not every snap-in has the ability to connect to a remote computer because some do not need it. The Active Directory management consoles, for example, automatically locate a domain controller on the network and access the Active Directory database there. There is no need to specify a computer name.

Creating a Remote Console

Connecting to a remote computer by redirecting an existing console is convenient for impromptu management tasks, but it is limited by the fact that you can access only one computer at a time. You also have to open the console and redirect it every time you want to access the remote system. A more permanent solution is to create a custom console with snap-ins that are already directed at other computers.

When you add a snap-in to a custom console by selecting it in the list of available snap-ins and clicking the Add button, you might see a dialog box in which you can select what computer you want to manage with that snap-in, as shown in Figure 2-12. This adds a whole new dimension to MMC's functionality. Not only can you create custom consoles containing a variety of tools, but you can also create consoles containing tools for a variety of computers. For example, you can create a single console containing multiple instances of the Computer Management snap-in, with each one pointing to a different computer. This enables you to manage Windows Server 2003, Windows XP, and Windows 2000 computers all over the network from a single console.

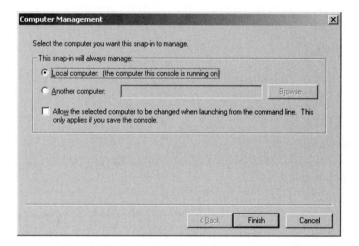

Figure 2-12   The Computer Management dialog box

MANAGING SERVERS WITH REMOTE DESKTOP FOR ADMINISTRATION

In Windows 2000, Terminal Services was a separate component that had to be installed manually. Now it is an integral part of Windows Server 2003 that is installed by default with the operating system. By purchasing and configuring the appropriate licenses, you can configure a computer running Windows Server 2003 to host Terminal Services clients, providing them with access to the Windows desktop and applications running on the server.

Terminal Services has functions other than supporting Terminal Services clients, however. You can also use the Terminal Services engine to access a remote computer for administrative purposes, without the application-sharing capabilities. Windows Server 2003 calls this feature Remote Desktop for Administration. The operating system allows two concurrent Remote Desktop connections without the need for any additional licensing and with little additional system overhead.

> **NOTE   Exam Objectives**   The objectives for Exam 70-290 state that a student should be able to "manage a server by using Terminal Services remote administration mode."

Using MMC consoles, you can connect to a remote computer and perform many administrative tasks, but sometimes an administrator needs full access to the computer. Terminal Services in Windows Server 2003 enables a client program called Remote Desktop Connection running on another computer to connect to the server and access virtually any part of the system. The client window shows the server's desktop, making it possible for the user to access all of the standard controls and tools and even run applications on the server (as shown in Figure 2-13).

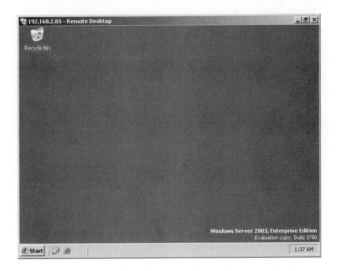

Figure 2-13   A Remote Desktop session

Enabling and Configuring the Remote Desktop Server

Because all of the components needed to support Remote Desktop for Administration connections are installed by default with the Windows Server 2003 operating system, activating the server side of the application is simplicity itself. In the Remote tab of the System Properties dialog box (accessible using the System icon in Control Panel), select the Allow Users To Connect Remotely To This Computer check box (as shown in Figure 2-14). By default, members of the local Administrators group are granted remote access permission. To allow other users to access the computer using Remote Desktop, you must click Select Remote Users and add them to the list of remote desktop users.

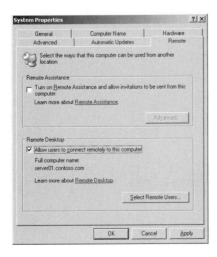

Figure 2-14   The Remote tab of the System Properties dialog box

Practice
enabling
Remote
Desktop for
Administratio
n on your
computer by
doing Exercise
2.3, "Enabling
Remote
desktop for
Administratio
n," now.

Selecting this one check box is all you have to do to enable the Remote Desktop server in Windows Server 2003. However, you can also configure the Remote Desktop server properties using the Terminal Services Configuration snap-in for MMC (as shown in Figure 2-15).

> **NOTE**   **Terminal Services and Domain Controllers**   By default, Windows Server 2003 domain controllers are configured to accept Terminal Services connections only from members of the Administrators group. Even users you have explicitly added to the Remote Desktop Users group are not permitted access. To override this behavior, you must change the effective value of the Allow Log On Through Terminal Services group policy, which lists the Administrators group only, by default. To do this, you can either modify the domain controller's local computer policy or define the same policy in the group policy object (GPO) for an Active Directory object containing the computer, such as the Default Domain Controllers Policy GPO.

Figure 2-15   The Terminal Services Configuration snap-in

To configure the Remote Desktop server properties, add the Terminal Services Configuration snap-in to an MMC console. Click the Connections folder in the scope pane, select the RDP-Tcp connection listed in the details pane, and, from the Action menu, select Properties. The RDP-Tcp Properties dialog box appears.

Using the tabs in this dialog box, you can configure various properties of the server, as follows:

■ **General**   Sets the encryption level and authentication mechanism for connections to the server.

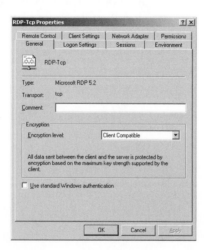

■ **Logon Settings**   Enables you to specify static credentials to be used by Remote Desktop connections rather than those provided by the client.

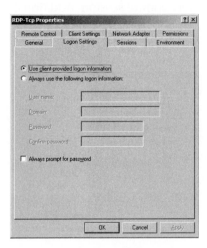

■ **Sessions**   Contains settings that override the client values, specifying when to end a disconnected session, session time limits and idle time-outs, and whether reconnection is allowed.

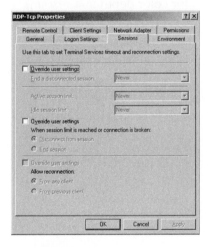

■ **Environment**   Overrides the client and user profile settings for starting a program upon connection to the server.

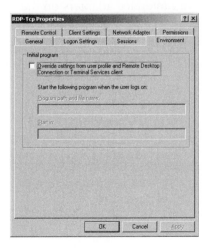

- **Remote Control**   Specifies whether remote control of a Remote Desktop Connection session is possible and, if it is, whether the user must grant permission at the initiation of the remote control session. Additional settings can restrict the remote control session to viewing only or allow full interactivity with the Remote Desktop client session.

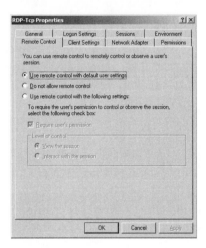

- **Client Settings**   Overrides client settings for color depth and resource mapping.

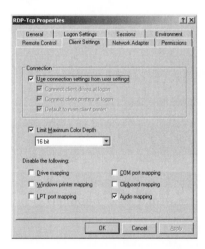

- **Network Adapter**   Specifies which network interface adapters on the server can accept Remote Desktop for Administration connections.

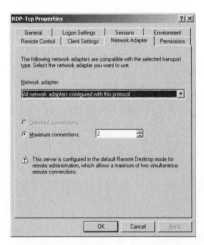

■ **Permissions**   Specifies permissions for Remote Desktop connections.

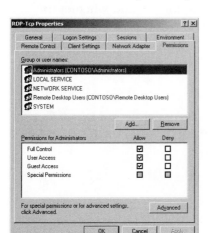

Installing and Configuring Remote Desktop Connection

For a computer to connect to a Remote Desktop server, it must run a client program called Remote Desktop Connection. This client program is installed by default with the Windows Server 2003 and Windows XP operating systems, but it can also run on any other 32-bit version of Windows. Windows Server 2003 includes the Remote Desktop Connection files on the installation CD and also copies them to the *Systemroot*\System32\Clients\Tsclient\Win32 folder. You can install the client on another computer from either location by using the following procedures:

■ **From the CD**   Insert the Windows Server 2003 CD into the drive. When the Welcome to Microsoft Windows Server 2003 screen appears, click the Perform Additional Tasks hyperlink, and then click Set Up Remote Desktop Connection. Follow the instructions displayed by the Remote Desktop Connection – InstallShield Wizard.

■ **From the network**   Create a share out of the *Systemroot*\System32\Clients\Tsclient\Win32 folder. Connect to the share from the client computer and run the Setup.exe file. Follow the instructions displayed by the Remote Desktop Connection – InstallShield Wizard.

   TIP   Client Updates   It is recommended that you update computers running previous versions of the Terminal Services client to the latest version of Remote Desktop Connection to take advantage of improvements such as a revised user interface, 128-bit encryption, and alternate port selection.

Once the client is installed, you connect to a server by running the program using the Remote Desktop Connection shortcut in the Start menu and configuring the client using the Remote Desktop Connection dialog box. The tabs in this dialog box enable you to configure client parameters, as follows:

   NOTE   Viewing Client Options   Click the Options button to display the entire Remote Desktop Connection dialog box.

■ **General** Allows you to specify the computer to which the client should connect, the credentials the client should use to log on, and whether to save the configuration settings for the connection.

■ **Display** Allows you to specify the size of the Remote Desktop client window, its color depth, and whether the connection bar is available in full-screen mode.

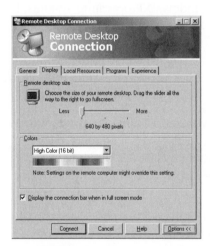

■ **Local Resources** Allows you to specify whether the client should bring the server's sound events to the local computer, how Windows key combinations should be interpreted by the remote computer, and whether local disk, printer, and serial port connections should be available within the remote session. For example, selecting the Disk Drives option causes the local drives on the client computer to appear in the Remote Desktop session as if they were local drives on the server.

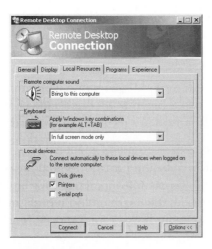

- **Programs**   Allows you to specify the name and the starting folder for an application to launch as soon as a connection with the server is established.

- **Experience**   Allows you to specify the speed of the connection between the client and the server and to disable the display of certain server desktop characteristics to conserve bandwidth and increase the client/server response time.

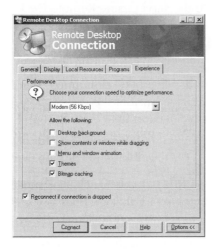

> **NOTE   Remote Desktop and Terminal Services**   *Remote Desktop for Adminis-tration and Terminal Services use many of the same components. With the appro-priate licenses in place, network users can run the same client to access a terminal server for application-sharing purposes that they use for Remote Desk-top for Administration.*

Terminal Services Troubleshooting

When you use Remote Desktop for Administration, you create a connection between a client program and a server. Remote Desktop for Administration uses the same type of connection as a Terminal Services connection used for application sharing, and the possible causes of a connection failure are the same as well. In the event of a failed connection or problematic session, some of the potential causes that you should investigate are as follows:

> **NOTE   Exam Objectives**   *The objectives for Exam 70-290 state that a student should be able to "troubleshoot Terminal Services," "diagnose and resolve issues related to Terminal Services security," and "diagnose and resolve issues related to client access to Terminal Services."*

- **Network failures**   With any application that relies on client/server com-munications, failures are commonly caused by network problems, such as incorrectly configured TCP/IP settings, name resolution failures, rout-ing problems, or networking hardware malfunctions. You can check for network communication problems by testing to see if other network applications are functioning, trying to connect using an IP address instead of a DNS name, and determining whether other users are experiencing the same problem. Check to see that the TCP/IP configuration settings on the client and server are correct, that DNS servers are operating properly, and that networking hardware is intact.

- **Port settings**   Terminal Services uses TCP and UDP port number 3389 for all of its client/server communications, by default. If either the client or the server has been configured to use a different port number, or if that port is somehow being blocked (such as by a firewall), a Terminal Ser-vices client/server connection will not be possible.

- **Credentials**   Users must belong to the Administrators or Remote Desk-top Users group to successfully connect to the server using Remote Desk-top for Administration. In addition, you can block client access for a specific user or group by enabling the Deny Logon Through Terminal Services user right, either on the local system or by using group policies.

- **Number of connections**   If client sessions have been disconnected without the users logging off, the server might consider the connections still open and might reach its concurrent connection limit even though two human users are not connected at the time. Remote Desktop for Administration allows only two concurrent connections.

USING REMOTE ASSISTANCE

Remote Desktop is designed to provide administrative access to a computer, but end users can sometimes benefit from this capability as well. Many users, but par-ticularly those without much technical expertise, have configuration problems or usage questions that are difficult for a support professional or even a friend or fam-ily member to diagnose and fix over the telephone. Remote Assistance is another permutation of the Terminal Services model that enables a user to request help from another user at a remote location and receive that help in the form of on-screen guidance or demonstration, with neither party having to travel to the other. Remote Assistance enables helpers (or, as the application refers to them, experts) to offer technical support, troubleshooting help, and even training to users whenever they need it, with minimal expense and delay.

> **NOTE** **Exam Objectives** *The objectives for Exam 70-290 state that a student should be able to "manage a server by using Remote Assistance."*

Enabling Remote Assistance

Before you can receive remote assistance, you must enable the feature, in one of the following ways:

- **Using Control Panel** Open the System Properties from Control Panel and select the Remote tab. Select the Turn On Remote Assistance And Allow Invitations To Be Sent From This Computer check box. By clicking the Advanced button, you can specify whether to let the expert take control of the computer or simply view activities on the computer, as well as specify the amount of time that the invitation for remote assistance will remain valid.

- **Using group policies** Use the Group Policy Object Editor console (gpedit.msc) to open a GPO for a domain or organizational unit object containing the client computer. Browse to the Computer Configuration\Administrative Templates\System\Remote Assistance container and enable the Solicited Remote Assistance policy. This policy also enables you to specify the degree of control the expert will receive over the client computer, the duration of the invitation, and the method for sending e-mail invitations. The Offer Remote Assistance policy enables you to specify the names of users or groups that can function as experts and whether those experts can perform tasks or just observe.

Creating an Invitation

To receive remote assistance, a client must issue an invitation and send it to a particular expert. The client can send the invitation using any of the following methods:

- **Microsoft Windows Messenger** To use the Windows Messenger service for your Remote Assistance connection, you must have the expert's Windows Messenger username in your contact list and make the request from a Windows Messenger client. Remote Assistance can be requested directly only when the expert is online.

- **E-mail** To send an invitation using e-mail, both computers must be using a MAPI-compliant e-mail client.

- **File** When you save the invitation to a file, you can use any method to send it to an expert, such as a non-MAPI e-mail message, an FTP transfer, or a floppy disk.

To issue an invitation, you select Help And Support from the Start menu to open the Help and Support Center screen and then click the Remote Assistance hyperlink to display the screen shown in Figure 2-16.

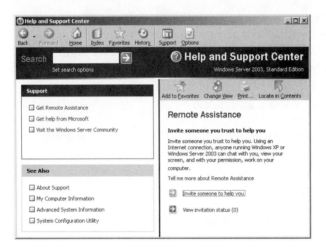

Figure 2-16   The Remote Assistance screen

When you click the Invite Someone To Help You link, you see the interface shown in Figure 2-17. You then follow the instructions for the contact method of your choice.

Figure 2-17   The Remote Assistance page of the Help And Support Center

> **TIP**   **Using Passwords**   When users create invitations, they can specify a password that experts have to supply to connect to their computers. You should urge your users to always require passwords for Remote Assistance connections and instruct them to supply the expert with the correct password using a different medium from the one they are using to send the invitation.

The expert who receives the invitation can invoke it to launch the Remote Assistance application, which enables the expert to connect to the remote computer, as shown in Figure 2-18. Using this interface, the user and the expert can talk or type messages to each other and, by default, the expert can see everything that the user is doing on the computer. If the client computer is configured to allow remote control, the expert can also click the Take Control button and operate the client computer interactively.

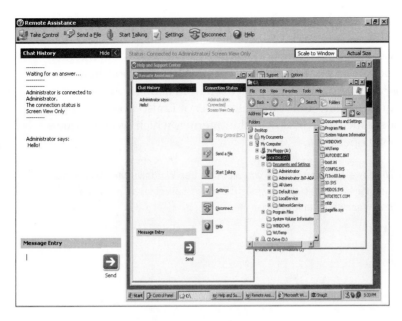

Figure 2-18   The expert's Remote Assistance interface

Securing Remote Assistance

Because an expert offering remote assistance to another user can perform virtually any activity on the remote computer that the local user can, this feature can be a significant security hazard. An unauthorized user who takes control of a computer using Remote Assistance can cause almost unlimited damage. However, Remote Assistance is designed to minimize the dangers. Some of the protective features of Remote Assistance are as follows:

- **Invitations**   No person can connect to another computer using Remote Assistance unless that person has received an invitation from the client. Clients can configure the effective lifespan of their invitations in minutes, hours, or days to prevent experts from attempting to connect to the computer later.

- **Interactive connectivity**   When an expert accepts an invitation from a client and attempts to connect to the computer, a user must be present at the client console to grant the expert access. You cannot use Remote Assistance to connect to an unattended computer.

- **Client-side control**   The client always has ultimate control over a Remote Assistance connection. The client can terminate the connection at any time by pressing the Esc key or clicking Stop Control (ESC) in the client-side Remote Assistance page.

- **Remote control configuration**   Using the System Properties dialog box or Remote Assistance group policies, users and administrators can specify whether experts are permitted to take control of client computers. An expert who has read-only access cannot modify the computer's configuration in any way using Remote Access. The group policies also enable administrators to grant specific users expert status so no one else can use Remote Access to connect to a client computer, even with the client's permission.

- **Firewalls**   Remote Assistance uses Transmission Control Protocol (TCP) port number 3389 for all its network communications. For networks that use Remote Assistance internally and are also connected to the Internet, it is recommended that network administrators block this port in their firewalls to prevent users outside the network from taking control of computers that request remote assistance. However, it is also possible to provide remote assistance to clients over the Internet, which would require leaving port 3389 open.

NOTE   **Using Windows Messenger**   If you elect to use Windows Messenger to send Remote Assistance invitations, port 1863 must be left open as well, to permit Windows Messenger communications.

SUMMARY

- Microsoft Management Console is the primary system administration tool for Windows Server 2003.

- MMC is a shell application that you use to run snap-ins, which are individual tools that load into an MMC console.

- There are two types of snap-ins, stand-alone and extension, with extensions appearing and behaving within the MMC based on the context of their placement.

- Some snap-ins can be used to configure both local and remote computers; others are limited to local computer access only.

- MMC consoles can be saved in either Author mode, granting users full access to the console configuration, or User mode, granting limited access.

- Remote Desktop for Administration allows you to administer a remote server as if you were logged on locally to the server as an administrator.

- Remote Assistance is a tool that enables users to request assistance from an expert, who can then connect to the user's computer and either view the user's actions or take over operation of the system.

- Remote Assistance is a mutual arrangement: the user can ask an expert for help, or the expert, if properly configured through Group Policy, can initiate a help session. In either case, the user must actively agree to the establishment of the connection and is always in control of the session. At no time can the expert take control of the user's desktop unannounced.

- The Remote Desktop Connection client, a default component of Windows XP and Windows Server 2003, can be installed on any 32-bit Windows platform from the Windows Server 2003 installation CD or (after sharing the directory) from any Windows Server 2003 computer.

- Both Remote Desktop for Administration and Remote Assistance use the Terminal Services service for their communications, but neither requires a special Terminal Services license.

EXERCISES

Exercise 2-1: Opening an MMC Window

In this exercise, you open a second window in an MMC console.

1. Click Start, point to Administrative Tools, and click Computer Management. The Computer Management console appears.

2. From the Window menu, select New Window. A second window appears on top of the first one.

3. From the Window menu, select Tile Horizontally. The console display changes to show both windows at once. Notice that you can navigate in each window independently.

Exercise 2-2: Creating a Custom MMC Console

In this exercise, you create a new, custom MMC console.

1. Click Start, and then click Run. The Run dialog box will appear.

2. In the Open text box, type **mmc** and click OK. A Console1 window appears.

3. From the File menu, select Add/Remove Snap-in. The Add/Remove Snap-in dialog box appears.

4. Click Add. The Add Standalone Snap-in dialog box appears.

5. In the Available Standalone Snap-ins list, select Device Manager and then click Add. The Device Manager dialog box appears.

6. Click Finish to accept the default settings, click Close, and then click OK. The Device Manager snap-in now appears in the console's scope pane.

7. From the File menu, select Save As, and save the console in the default Administrative Tools folder using the filename DevMgr.msc.

Exercise 2-3: Enabling Remote Desktop for Administration

In this exercise, you configure your client computer to accept Remote Desktop connections.

1. Click Start, point to Control Panel, and then click System. The System Properties dialog box appears.

2. Select the Remote tab, and then select the Allow Users To Connect Remotely To This Computer check box.

3. Click OK.

REVIEW QUESTIONS

1. What is the default mode when you create a new MMC console?

2. Can a snap-in have focus on both the local computer and a remote computer simultaneously?

3. What credentials are required for administration of a remote computer using MMC?

4. Can an existing MMC snap-in be changed from local to remote context, or must a snap-in of the same type be loaded into the console for a remote connection?

5. Are all of the functions in a snap-in always available for use when you are connected to a remote computer?

6. How many simultaneous connections are possible to a terminal server running in Remote Administration mode? Why?

7. What tool is used to enable Remote Desktop on a server?

    a. Terminal Services Manager

    b. Terminal Services Configuration

    c. System Properties in Control Panel

    d. Terminal Services Licensing

CASE SCENARIOS

Scenario 2-1: Using Remote Assistance

Your company has enabled Remote Assistance on each computer in the enterprise. The company's sales representatives travel frequently and use laptops to perform their work while on the road. On your internal network, you use Windows Messenger for spontaneous communication with your clients and for Remote Assistance. However, you disallow Instant Messenger traffic across the Internet by closing port 1863 at the firewall. You want to perform Remote Assistance for your remote users, but you cannot connect to them with Windows Messenger to determine whether they are online. Describe two alternative methods that traveling sales representatives can employ to send a Remote Assistance invitation to an expert in the home office.

Scenario 2-2: Using Remote Desktop Connection

You are trying to connect to a Windows Server 2003 server in your environment with Remote Desktop Connection, but you consistently get the following message when you attempt to connect:

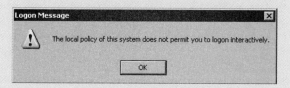

You have checked settings on the server and confirmed the following:

- You are a member of the Remote Desktop Users group.

- You are not a member of the Administrators group.

- You are able to connect to share points on the Terminal Server computer, and the computer responds affirmatively to a ping.

What other settings should you check on the Terminal Server computer to troubleshoot this problem?

CHAPTER 3
MONITORING MICROSOFT WINDOWS SERVER 2003

Keeping the network servers running smoothly and efficiently is one of the primary jobs of a system administrator, and Microsoft Windows Server 2003 includes a collection of tools that enable you to do this. Although a server might be running at peak capacity immediately after installation, performance can degrade over time for a variety of reasons. A good system administrator must monitor the server's performance on a regular basis to identify trends and detect problems that can affect performance. Learning to use the Windows Server 2003 monitoring tools properly is an important skill to acquire so you can recognize changes in a server's performance before the situation turns into a catastrophe.

Upon completion of this chapter, you will be able to:

- Use Event Viewer to monitor system logs
- Configure Task Manager to display performance data
- Use System Monitor to display real-time performance data
- Create counter logs and alerts

SERVER MONITORING PRACTICES

The performance monitoring tools included with Windows Server 2003 enable an administrator to examine a variety of system parameters in a number of ways. How you use the tools depends on the resources that you want to monitor as well as your personal preferences. The two basic types of system monitoring are as follows:

- **Real-time monitoring** Real-time monitoring uses tools that display a continuous stream of statistics about what the system is doing right now. The statistics can be displayed numerically or in the form of a graph. Obviously, this method provides the most current information, but few system administrators have the time or the inclination to watch a graph of system performance parameters all day long.

- **Logged monitoring** Logged monitoring typically produces the same information as real-time monitoring but stores it on a permanent medium instead of (or in addition to) displaying it immediately. This method enables administrators to observe trends that develop over longer periods of time than those observed in a typical real-time monitoring session. When using logged monitoring, administrators must be sure to provide sufficient storage space for the captured data, and, of course, they must examine the captured information on a regular basis.

The uses of real-time and logged monitoring are not mutually exclusive. Each method has its value, and indeed some of the Windows Server 2003 monitoring tools support both.

Monitoring Subsystems

Windows Server 2003 system performance can be broken down into four basic subsystems, each of which must function properly for the computer to perform satisfactorily. These four subsystems are as follows:

- **Processor** A computer's microprocessor performs millions of individual computations using clock cycles, with each computation devoted to a particular task. The processor's available clock cycles are divided between the many different processes running on the computer. The faster the processor, the more clock cycles there are to go around in a given period of time. Monitoring processor performance typically involves checking the burden on the processor as it performs its regular tasks. If the processor's clock cycle utilization consistently approaches 100 percent, system performance might be suffering due to insufficient processing power.

- **Memory** Random access memory (RAM) is the temporary storage space that a computer uses as a staging area for the data passing to and from the processor. When insufficient RAM is available to complete a particular task, Windows uses hard disk space instead of RAM, in a process called memory paging. Because accessing hard disks is much slower than accessing RAM, performance degrades when too much paging occurs. Monitoring memory performance is a matter of ensuring that the computer has sufficient memory to complete its designated tasks.

- **Disk**   The computer's hard disk drives provide permanent storage for operating system and application files, as well as for the data used and produced by the applications. Monitoring disk storage subsystem performance typically involves checking the number of disk access requests that are waiting to be processed at a given time. If large amounts of data are waiting to be read from or written to the disks, the overall performance of the computer can suffer.

- **Network**   Network subsystem monitoring differs slightly from that of the other three subsystems because the performance of the network can be affected by external factors as well as internal ones. A large number of queued network transmission requests can degrade a server's performance as perceived by its users on the network, even though the computer itself is functioning properly.

Determining which subsystems in the computer require the most careful monitoring depends on the applications that the computer is running. Different applications require different degrees of performance from each subsystem, and a problem with one particular subsystem can have a different effect on various applications.

Establishing a Baseline

When you monitor a server's performance characteristics, the actual subsystem performance values themselves are not as important as the changes that occur in the performance values over time. For example, if you examine the processor performance of a server that was first installed a year ago and discover that processor utilization is at 100 percent, you have no way of knowing whether this has always been the case or something has changed recently to affect the processor's performance.

For this reason, one of the most important parts of monitoring server performance is establishing a baseline of performance levels that you can refer to later. This is why the introduction to this chapter states that you should learn to use the Windows Server 2003 monitoring tools before something goes wrong. A **baseline** is a collection of performance levels taken when the computer is functioning normally, preferably soon after it is fully installed and configured. By comparing later levels with the baseline, you can determine whether the performance of the various subsystems is degrading. You'll learn more about creating a baseline later in this chapter, in the discussions of the various Windows Server 2003 monitoring tools.

USING EVENT VIEWER

Windows Server 2003 maintains a variety of logs that contain information about its ongoing processes. To view these logs, you use the Event Viewer MMC snap-in. Event Viewer can function as either a standalone or an extension snap-in. The Windows Server 2003 Administrative Tools program group has a shortcut to an Event Viewer console, but the snap-in is also included with many other tools in the Computer Management console.

> **NOTE**   *Exam Objectives*   *The objectives for the 70-290 exam state that a student should be able to "monitor and analyze events. Tools might include Event Viewer and System Monitor."*

Event Viewer Logs

When you launch Event Viewer (shown in Figure 3-1), the scope pane contains a list of the logs maintained by the system. The three base logs that appear on all Windows Server 2003 computers are as follows:

- **Application**   Contains information about specific programs running on the computer, as determined by the application developer.

- **System**   Contains information about events generated by Windows Server 2003 components, such as services and device drivers. For example, a failure of a service to start or a driver to load during system startup is recorded in the System log. The types of events recorded in this log are preconfigured by the operating system and cannot be changed. This is the primary Windows Server 2003 log; you should always view this log first when looking for information about system problems.

- **Security**   Can contain information about security-related events, such as failed logons, attempts to access protected resources (such as shares and file system elements), and success or failure of audited events. Windows Server 2003, in its default configuration, does not record information in the Security log. The events recorded in this log are determined by audit policies, which you can enable using either local computer policies or group policies. By default, only members of the Administrators group can view this log.

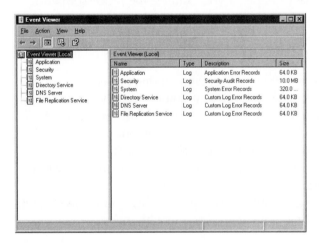

Figure 3-1   The Event Viewer console

When the computer is promoted to a domain controller, the following two logs are added to Event Viewer:

- **Directory Service**   Contains information about the Active Directory directory service, such as irreconcilable object replications or other significant events within the directory.

- **File Replication Service**   Contains information about the success or failure of the replication activities that occur between Active Directory domain controllers.

Finally, when the computer has the Microsoft DNS Server service installed, Event Viewer contains one more log:

- **DNS Server**   Contains information about the status and operations of the DNS Server service.

Although Event Viewer contains the most important Windows Server 2003 logs, it does not contain all of them. A number of services are included with the operating system that maintain their own separate logs. In nearly all cases, these logs are simple text files that you can open with any text editor, such as the Windows Notepad application. Some of the separate logs you might find on a computer running Windows Server 2003 are as follows:

- DHCP auditing

- Dr. Watson (program errors)

- Fax activity

- Internet Connection Firewall (ICF)

- Microsoft Internet Information Services (IIS)

- Windows Media Services clients

- WINS database transactions

Understanding Event Types

When you select one of the logs listed in the scope pane of the Event Viewer snap-in, you see a list of individual events in the details pane. The most immediately apparent element in each event is its type, which is identified with an icon. The type indicates the importance of the event, and whether it is the result of a normal process or a problem of some sort. The event types used in the Event Viewer snap-in are listed in Table 3-1. Obviously, errors and warnings are the most significant types of events to a system administrator, because they indicate that a significant event has occurred.

Table 3-1 **Windows 2000 Event Types**

Event Type	Icon	Description
Error		A significant problem, such as loss of data or loss of functionality
Warning		An event that might not be significant but might indicate a future problem
Information		An event that describes the successful operation of an application, driver, or service
Success audit		An audited security access attempt that succeeds
Failure audit		An audited security access attempt that fails

Double-clicking an entry in the Event Viewer's details pane displays an Event Properties dialog box like the one shown in Figure 3-2. This dialog box contains more information about the event, including:

- **Date**   The date on which the event occurred

- **Time**   The time at which the event occurred

- **Type**   The type of event that occurred (error, warning, information, success audit, or failure audit)

- **User**   The name of the user account associated with the process that generated the event

- **Computer**   The name of the computer on which the event occurred

- **Source**   The software module that generated the event

- **Category**   A classification of the event, as defined by the source process

- **Event ID**   A unique value identifying this particular event

- **Description**   A text message describing the nature of the event, generated by the source process

- **Data**   Binary data generated by the event

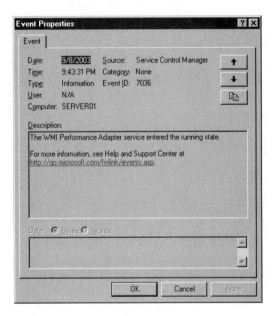

Figure 3-2   An Event Properties dialog box

Configuring Event Viewer Logs

Practice using Event Viewer by doing Exercise 3.1, "Using Event Viewer," now.

Each log in the Event Viewer snap-in has its own Properties dialog box, which you can use to configure the log's retention parameters and control what information is displayed in the log. These settings are discussed in the following sections.

Event Log Retention Settings

On the general tab of each log's Properties dialog box (shown in Figure 3-3), you can specify the maximum size of the log and its behavior when the log reaches its maximum size. The available log retention options are as follows:

- **Overwrite Events As Needed**   The log erases the oldest individual entries as needed once the log file has reached the specified maximum size.

- **Overwrite Events Older Than *X* Days**   The log retains all entries for the number of days (from 1 to 365) specified by this option and overwrites older entries as needed. If the log reaches its specified maximum size and there are no entries older than the number of days specified, the system stops writing new events to the log.

- **Do Not Overwrite Events (Clear Log Manually)**   The system retains all log entries until they are manually erased by an administrator. Once the log reaches its specified maximum size, the system stops writing new events to the log.

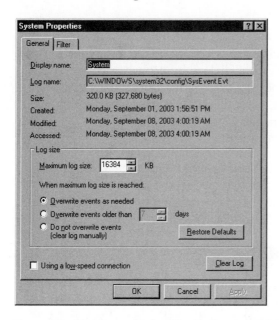

Figure 3-3   The General tab of the System event log's Properties dialog box

The default settings for the event logs on a Windows Server 2003 domain controller running the Microsoft DNS Server service are shown in Table 3-2. The Directory Service and File Replication Service logs have small maximum sizes (512 KB) because entries to these logs are relatively rare. The Security log, however, has an extremely large maximum size (128 MB). This is because the computer has been promoted to a domain controller, and part of the default configuration for Windows Server 2003 domain controllers is the activation of several audit policies, which cause large numbers of events to be written to the Security log. The default maximum size for the Security log on a Windows Server 2003 computer that is not a domain controller is 16 MB.

Table 3-2   Default Event Log Retention Settings

Event Log	Maximum Log Size	Log Retention Setting
Application	16,384 KB (16 MB)	Overwrite events as needed
Directory Service	512 KB	Overwrite events as needed
DNS Server	16,384 KB (16 MB)	Overwrite events older than 7 days
File Replication Service	512 KB	Overwrite events as needed
Security	131,072 KB (128 MB)	Overwrite events as needed
System	16,384 KB (16 MB)	Overwrite events as needed

NOTE   Configuring Retention Settings Using Group Policies   In addition to configuring the retention settings for the event logs manually by using the Event Viewer snap-in, you can configure the same parameters for the Application, System, and Security logs by enabling the Event Log policies in a group policy object (GPO) and applying it to an individual computer or to an Active Directory container object.

On a domain controller, leaving the default setting of Overwrite Events As Needed on the Security log could overwrite important resource access or other security-related data if an administrator does not archive the log entries on a regular basis. To ensure that no Security log entries are lost, Windows Server 2003 has a drastic measure available in the form of a Security Option group policy called Audit: Shut Down System Immediately If Unable To Log Security Audits.

Using Filters

When you first start Event Viewer, the snap-in displays all of the events that are recorded in the selected log, chronologically. Depending on the size of the log and the retention settings, the list could be extremely lengthy. However, many of the event entries are of the Information type, which result from normal, everyday activities. To locate specific entries in the list, you can modify its order by clicking one of the column headings, or you can limit the display of what appears in the log to focus on the important events, by using the Filter or the Find command.

To implement a filter on a log in Event Viewer, from the View menu, select Filter to display the Filter tab of the event log's Properties dialog box, as shown in Figure 3-4. In this dialog box, you can specify the event types you want to display and select other event criteria to reduce the event list to a manageable size.

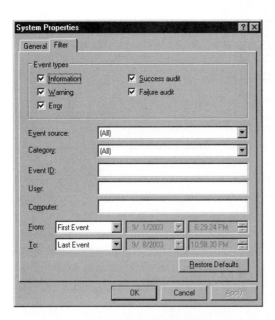

Figure 3-4   The Filter tab of an event log's Properties dialog box

To search for specific items in the event list, you can select Find from the View menu to display the Find dialog box (shown in Figure 3-5).

Both the Filter tab and the Find dialog box enable you to select from the event criteria listed in "Windows 2000 Event Types," earlier in this chapter, to locate specific entries.

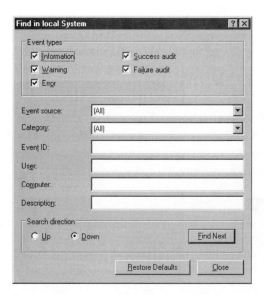

Figure 3-5 Event Viewer's Find dialog box

Accessing Remote Event Logs

As with many MMC snap-ins, you can use Event Viewer to view the logs on other Windows computers as well as the computer on which you are working. To perform this task, in the scope pane, select the Event Viewer (Local) object and select Connect To Another Computer from the Action menu. In the Select Computer dialog box, specify the name of the computer whose event logs you want to see.

Archiving Event Logs

The Event Viewer snap-in can save logs to files in several formats, including tab-delimited text (.txt) files, comma-delimited (.csv) files, and an Event Log format with an .evt extension, which can be opened by the snap-in. Once you save a log to a file, you have a permanent record of the entries and you can safely clear the log. Archiving on a regular basis ensures that the log files never grow too large, causing entries to be lost.

USING TASK MANAGER

Task Manager is an important Windows application that you can use to display information about the computer's current performance levels as well as manage the programs and processes running on the system. You can open Task Manager by right-clicking an open area of the taskbar and then selecting Task Manager from the context menu, or by pressing Ctrl+Alt+Del and then clicking the Task Manager button. The Windows Task Manager dialog box contains five tabs by default:

- Applications
- Processes
- Performance
- Networking
- Users

The functions found on these tabs are described in the following sections.

> **NOTE   Exam Objectives**   The objectives for the 70-290 exam state that a student should be able to "monitor file and print servers. Tools might include Task Manager, Event Viewer, and System Monitor."

Working with Applications

The Applications tab (shown in Figure 3-6) shows the status of the user-level programs currently running on the computer. Services and system applications running in different contexts from the logged-on user are not displayed. For each application listed, the Status column indicates whether the application is running or not responding.

Figure 3-6   Task Manager's Applications tab

By selecting an application from the list and clicking Switch To, you can make the selected application the active window, leaving Task Manager open in the background. You can also select an entry in the list and click End Task to close the application.

> **NOTE   Ending Tasks**   Closing applications by using Task Manager is not a recommended practice unless the application has a status of Not Responding and cannot be terminated any other way. When you end a task in this way, you usually lose any data that has not been saved to disk.

When you right-click an application in the list and select Go To Process from the context menu, the dialog box switches to the Processes tab and highlights the process associated with the application. This is a helpful feature when you are trying to locate the process for a particular application and the process name is less than intuitive.

When you click the New Task button, a Create New Task dialog box appears, in which you can enter or browse for the name of any standard executable file or command. This dialog box is the functional equivalent of the Run dialog box, which is accessible from the Start menu.

Monitoring Processes

The Processes tab (shown in Figure 3-7) lists all of the current user's processes running on the computer. When you select the Show Processes From All Users check box, the list includes all services and other system processes, in addition to user-level applications. By default, the list includes the following information about each process:

- **Image Name** The name of the executable file for the process
- **User Name** The user account that owns the process
- **CPU** The current processor utilization percentage for the process
- **Mem Usage** The amount of memory utilized by the process

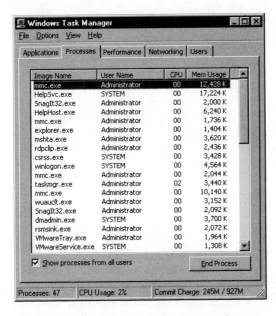

Figure 3-7 Task Manager's Processes tab

By selecting Select Columns from the View menu, you open the Select Columns dialog box (shown in Figure 3-8), which you can use to add or remove data columns from the display. Task Manager provides a large selection of counters, enabling you to display detailed information about the processor, memory, and I/O utilization of each process in the list. You can also sort the list using any of the displayed counters by clicking the column heading.

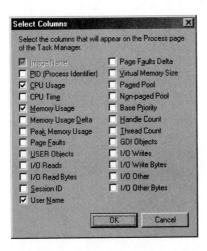

Figure 3-8 The Select Columns dialog box

In addition to simply monitoring information about system processes, you can also manipulate them with Task Manager. By right-clicking any process in the list, you can perform any of the following actions:

- **Set Priority**   Modifies the amount of processor time allocated to the process in relation to the other processes running on the system.

- **Set Processor Affinity**   Specifies which processor on a multiprocessor computer you want to use to run the process.

- **End Process**   Halts the process immediately. All unsaved data is lost.

- **End Process Tree**   Halts the process and any child or related processes immediately. All unsaved data is lost.

- **Debug**   Causes an exception to halt a process and attach it to the debugger, if one is installed on the system.

> **WARNING**   Manipulating Processes   Changing the settings of a process such as priority or processor affinity can have an adverse effect on the performance of other applications running on the computer. Ending a process, and especially a process tree, should be done only after normal termination procedures have failed. Windows Server 2003 safeguards its operating system processes from termination through Task Manager, but they are still susceptible to resource starvation through inappropriate priority adjustment of other processes.

Monitoring Performance Levels

The Performance tab (shown in Figure 3-9) displays a real-time view of the computer's processor and memory utilization. There are graphs displaying the current usage for each processor and the memory page file usage, as well as historical graphs for both statistics. Double-clicking one of the graphs expands it vertically to show the values with greater precision. Numerical displays show physical, kernel, and **commit memory** utilization, as well as the number of handles, threads, and active processes.

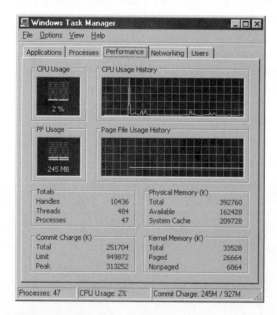

Figure 3-9   Task Manager's Performance tab

Monitoring Network Activity

The Networking tab (shown in Figure 3-10) shows all active network connections by name, with their connection speed, bandwidth utilization percentage, and operational status. There is also a graph displaying the bandwidth utilization for the currently selected network connection. Here again, double-clicking the graph displays a larger version with more precise y-axis gradations.

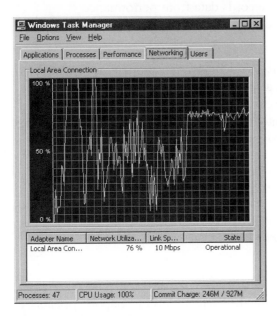

Figure 3-10   Task Manager's Networking tab

Monitoring Users

The Users tab (shown in Figure 3-11) lists all of the users who are currently logged on to the computer. Logged-on users can be working locally at the computer's console or remotely connected over the network. Using the controls on this tab, you can log off a user, forcibly disconnect a user from the computer, or send a message to a user.

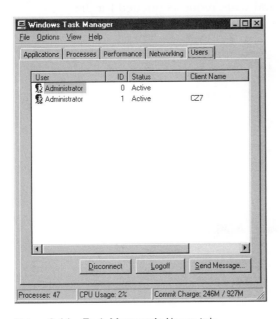

Figure 3-11   Task Manager's Users tab

USING THE PERFORMANCE CONSOLE

Practice using Task Manager by doing Exercise 3.2, "Using Task Manager," now.

The Performance console is one of the most powerful monitoring tools in Windows Server 2003. The console consists of the following two snap-ins:

- **System Monitor** Displays real-time performance data as collected from configurable components called **performance counters**

- **Performance Logs and Alerts** Records data from performance counters over a period of time and executes specific actions when counters reach a certain value

Performance is an MMC console that is accessible from a shortcut in the Administrative Tools program group. You can also add the individual snap-ins to custom consoles. By default, the Performance console monitors the current computer, but you can configure the snap-ins to monitor the performance of any computer on the network for which you have the appropriate permissions.

> **MORE INFO** Using MMC Snap-Ins For more information on creating custom MMC consoles, see Chapter 2 in this textbook.

> **NOTE** Exam Objectives The objectives for the 70-290 exam state that a student should be able to "monitor system performance."

Using System Monitor

When you open the Performance console, the System Monitor snap-in appears by default, as shown in Figure 3-12. The details pane of the snap-in contains a line graph, updated in real time, showing the current levels for the following three performance counters:

- **Memory: Pages/Second** The rate at which pages are read from or written to disk to resolve hard page faults. This counter is a primary indicator of the kinds of faults that cause system-wide delays.

- **PhysicalDisk(_Total): Average Disk Queue Length** The Length counter average number of read and write requests queued for the selected disk during the sample interval.

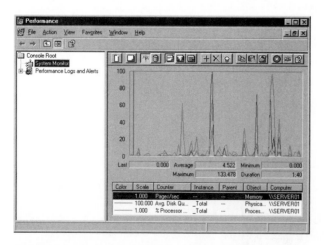

Figure 3-12 The default System Monitor display

■ **Processor(_Total): % Processor Time**   The percentage of elapsed time that the processor spends to execute a nonidle thread. This counter is the primary indicator of processor activity and displays the average percentage of busy time observed during the sample interval.

Modifying the Graph View

The legend beneath the graph specifies the line color for each of the three counters, the scale of values for each counter, and other identifying information about the counter. When you select one of the counters in the legend, its current values appear in numerical form at the bottom of the graph. Click the Highlight button in the toolbar (or press Ctrl+H) to change the selected counter to a broad, white line that is easier to distinguish in the graph (as shown in Figure 3-13).

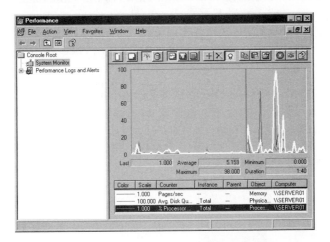

Figure 3-13   A System Monitor graph with a highlighted counter

If your computer is otherwise idle, you will probably notice that the lines in the default graph are all hovering near the bottom of the scale, making it difficult to see their values. You can address this problem by modifying the scale of the graph's y (vertical) axis. Click the Properties button on the toolbar (or press Ctrl+Q) to display the System Monitor Properties dialog box, and then select the Graph tab (as shown in Figure 3-14). In the Vertical Scale box, you can reduce the maximum value for the y axis, thereby using more of the graph to display the counter data.

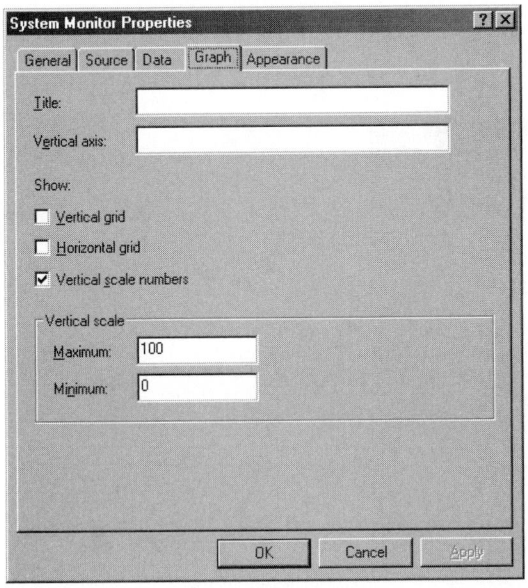

Figure 3-14   The Graph tab of the System Monitor Properties dialog box

In the General tab of the System Properties dialog box, you can also modify the sample rate of the graph. By default, the graph updates the counter values every 1 second, but you can increase this value to display data for a longer period of time on a single page of the graph. This can make it easier to detect long-term trends in counter values.

> **NOTE**   **Modifying Graph Properties**   The System Monitor Properties dialog box contains a number of other controls that you can use to modify the appearance of the graph. For example, on the Graph tab, you can add axis titles and gridlines, and in the Appearance tab, you can control the graph's background color and select a different font.

Using Other Views

In addition to the line graph, System Monitor has two other views of the same data: a histogram view and a report view. You can change the display to one of these views by clicking the View Histogram or View Report toolbar button, or by pressing Ctrl+B or Ctrl+R. To change back to the original line graph view, click View Graph or press Ctrl+G.

The histogram view is a bar graph with a separate vertical bar for each counter, as shown in Figure 3-15. In this view, it is easier to monitor large numbers of counters because the lines do not overlap.

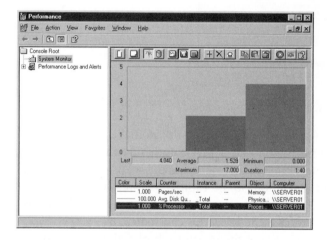

Figure 3-15   The System Monitor histogram view

The report view (as shown in Figure 3-16) displays the numerical value for each of the performance counters.

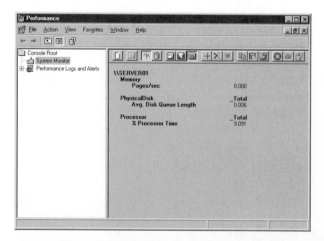

Figure 3-16   The System Monitor report view

As with the line graph, the histogram and report views both update their counter values at the interval specified in the General tab of the System Properties dialog box. The main drawback of these two views, however, is that they do not display a history of the counter values, only the current value. Each new sampling overwrites the previous one in the display, unlike the line graph, which displays the previous values as well.

Adding Counters

The three performance counters that appear in System Monitor by default are useful gauges of the computer's performance, but the snap-in includes dozens of other counters that you can add to the display. To add counters to the System Monitor details pane, click the Add button in the toolbar or press Ctrl+I to display the Add Counters dialog box (as shown in Figure 3-17).

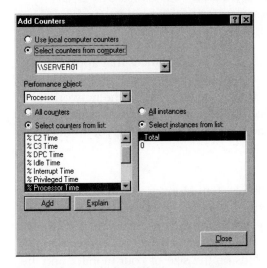

Figure 3-17   The Add Counters dialog box

NOTE   **Accessing System Monitor Functions**   Unlike most MMC snap-ins, System Monitor does not insert its most commonly used functions into the MMC console's Action menu. The only methods of accessing System Monitor functions are the toolbar buttons, hotkey combinations, and the context menu that appears when you right-click the display.

In this dialog box, you have to specify the following four pieces of information to add a counter to the display:

■ **Computer**   The name of the computer you want to monitor with the selected counter. Unlike with most MMC snap-ins, you cannot redirect the entire focus of System Monitor to another computer on the network. Instead, you specify a computer name for each counter you add to the display. This enables you to create a display showing counters for various computers on the network, such as a single graph of processor activity for all of your servers.

■ **Performance object**   A category representing a specific hardware or software component in the computer. Each **performance object** contains a selection of performance counters related to that component.

■ **Performance counter**   A statistic representing a specific aspect of the selected performance object's activities.

■ **Instance**   An element representing a specific occurrence of the selected performance counter. For example, on a computer with two network interface adapters, each counter in the Network Interface performance object would have two instances, one for each adapter, enabling you to track the performance of each adapter individually. Some counters also have instances such as Total or Average, enabling you to track the performance of all instances combined or the median value of all instances.

Once you have selected a computer name, a performance object, a performance counter in that object, and an instance of that counter, click Add to add the counter to the display. The dialog box remains open so you can add more counters. Click Close when you are finished.

> **NOTE   Understanding Counters**   Clicking the Explain button opens an Explain Text message box that contains a detailed description of the selected performance counter.

The performance objects, performance counters, and instances that appear in the Add Counters dialog box depend on the computer's hardware configuration, the software installed on the computer, and the computer's role on the network. For example, installing the DNS Server service on the computer adds the DNS performance object, which consists of a collection of counters enabling you to track the DNS server's activities.

Creating an Effective Display

Practice creating a System Monitor console by doing Exercise 3.3, "Creating a System Monitor Console," now.

In most cases, when users first discover the System Monitor snap-in, they see the embarrassment of riches that the hundreds of available performance counters provide, and they proceed to create a graph containing dozens of different counters. In most cases, the result is a graph that is crowded and incoherent. The number of counters you can display effectively depends on the size of your monitor and the resolution of your video display.

Consider the following tips when selecting counters:

■ **Limit the number of counters**   Too many counters make the graph more difficult to understand and negatively affect system performance. To display a large number of statistics, you can display multiple windows in the console and select different counters in each window, or use the histogram or report view to display a large number of counters in a more compact form (as long as you are willing to give up the value history shown in the graph view).

■ **Modify the counter display properties**   Depending on the size and capabilities of your monitor, the default colors and line widths that System Monitor uses in its graph might make it difficult to distinguish counters from each other. In the Data tab of the System Monitor Properties dialog box for each counter, you can modify the color, style, and width of that counter's line in the graph to make it easier to distinguish.

■ **Choose counters with comparable values**   System Monitor imposes no limitations on the combinations of counters you can select for a single graph, but some statistics are not practical to display together because of their disparate values. When a graph contains a counter with a typical value that is under 20 and another counter with a value in the hundreds, it is difficult to arrange the display so that both counters are readable. Choose counters with values that are reasonably comparable so you can display them legibly. Here again, if you must display counters with different value ranges, you might use the report view instead of graph view.

Saving a System Monitor Console

Once you are satisfied with the display you have created, you can save it as a console file by selecting Save As from the File menu and specifying a filename with an .msc extension. Launching this console file opens the Performance console and displays the System Monitor snap-in, with all of the counters and display properties you configured before saving it.

Monitoring Server Performance

Once you understand how to use System Monitor, the next step is to decide which of the hundreds of performance counters you should choose to monitor your server's performance most efficiently. There is, of course, no single answer to this question. You might want to create several consoles to monitor different aspects of server performance or the same performance aspects on several different computers. The best practice is to create a server-monitoring strategy as soon as possible after the computer is fully installed and configured. This way, you can establish a performance-level baseline for the server in normal, idle, and peak performance states. When problems occur during later monitoring, measurement against the baseline can help you to find a solution.

> **NOTE** Monitoring Overhead   It is important to remember that in some cases, the performance levels measured by System Monitor include resources utilized by the monitoring process itself. For example, the System Monitor snap-in utilizes some memory and processor time, just like any other program, and if you are monitoring counters on another computer, the process generates some network traffic as well. Be sure to account for this overhead when you are interpreting your System Monitor results.

The primary reasons for monitoring server performance using System Monitor are to ensure that the applications running on the server are functioning properly and to detect system bottlenecks that are affecting server efficiency. It is not uncommon for system administrators to be faced with server performance problems that are not immediately attributable to an obvious cause, such as a service failure. Users might complain that a server is slow at certain times of the day or that performance has been declining gradually over the course of weeks or months. When this occurs, one of the most common causes is a bottleneck somewhere in the path between the client and the data on the server that the client needs to use.

A **bottleneck** is a component that is not providing an acceptable level of performance compared to the other components in the system. For example, users might complain that their file server performance is slow, and you might spend a great deal of time and money upgrading your local area network (LAN) from 10Base-T to 100Base-TX, expecting to see a dramatic improvement. However, if your server is an old computer using a first-generation Pentium processor, the improvement is likely to be minimal because it is probably the server's processor, not the LAN technology, that is the bottleneck. All the other components are running well, but the processor cannot keep up with the data flow provided by the new, faster network.

> **NOTE**   *Exam Objectives*   *The objectives for the 70-290 exam state that a student should be able to "monitor server hardware for bottlenecks" and "monitor and optimize a server environment for application performance" by monitoring memory, network, processor, and disk performance objects.*

Bottlenecks can appear for a variety of reasons, including the following:

- **Increased server load**   A server might function adequately in a particular role at first, but as you increase the server's load by adding more users or more tasks, the inadequacy of one or more components might become more pronounced. For example, a Web server might be sufficient for a company's Web site at first, but then the company introduces a new product and traffic to the site triples. Suddenly, you find that the Web server's disk performance is insufficient to handle the additional traffic.

- **Hardware failure**   Hardware failures do not always manifest themselves as catastrophic stoppages. A component might malfunction intermittently for a long period of time, causing degraded server performance that is maddeningly inconsistent. For example, a faulty network cable connecting a server to a hub can cause occasional traffic interruptions that show up as degraded performance in the server.

- **Changed server roles**   Different applications have different resource requirements. You might have a computer that functions adequately as a Web server, but when you change the computer's role to that of a database server, you find that the processor is not fast enough to handle the load that the new application places on it.

Locating a bottleneck that is hindering performance can be a complicated task, but monitoring the correct performance counters in System Monitor is usually a good way to begin. In many cases, the cause of the bottleneck can be narrowed down to one of the four major subsystems listed at the beginning of this chapter (processor, memory, disk, or network).

When you monitor server performance levels, the best practice is to start from the top down—that is, you start with the broadest monitoring configuration for each subsystem to determine which one is the most likely cause of the problem. Once you have determined the general problem area, you can then look at the particular services and applications that make the heaviest use of that subsystem, and at protocol and thread levels, if needed. Usually, the problem is caused by either one device or one application, or a global lack of resources on the system. Single devices can be reconfigured or replaced, and global resources can be augmented (such as by adding more memory or an additional processor) as appropriate.

The following sections discuss the problems to look for and the performance counter to use when monitoring each of the four main subsystems.

Monitoring Processor Performance

An inadequate or malfunctioning processor array can cause a server to queue incoming client requests, preventing the server from fulfilling them promptly. For general monitoring of the processor subsystem, use the following performance counters:

> **NOTE**   *Locating Counters*   *The performance counters in this and the following sections are notated using the format* performance object: performance counter.

- **Processor: % Processor time**   Specifies the percentage of time that the processor is busy. This value should be as low as possible, with anything below 85 percent being acceptable. If this value is consistently too high, you should attempt to determine which process is using too much processor time, upgrade the processor, or add another processor, if possible.

- **System: Processor Queue Length**   Specifies the number of program threads waiting to be executed by the processor. This value should be as low as possible, with values less than 10 being acceptable. If the value is too high, upgrade the processor or add another processor.

- **Server Work Queues: Queue Length**   Specifies the number of requests waiting to use a particular processor. This value should be as low as possible, with values less than 4 being acceptable. If the value is too high, upgrade the processor or add another processor.

- **Processor: Interrupts/sec**   Specifies the number of hardware interrupts the processor is servicing each second. The value of this counter can vary greatly and is significant only in relation to an established baseline. A hardware device that is generating too many interrupts can monopolize the processor, preventing it from performing other tasks. If the value increases precipitously, examine the various other hardware components in the system to determine which one is generating too many interrupts.

Monitoring Memory Performance

An inadequate amount of memory in a server can prevent the computer from caching frequently used data aggressively enough, causing processes to rely on disk reads more than memory reads and slowing down the entire system. Memory is the single most important subsystem to monitor because memory problems can affect all of the other subsystems. For example, when a memory condition causes excessive disk paging, the system might appear to have a problem in the storage subsystem when memory is actually the culprit.

One of the most common conditions that can cause memory-related problems is a memory leak. A **memory leak** is the result of a program allocating memory for use but not freeing up that memory when it is finished using it. Over time, the computer's free memory can be totally consumed, degrading performance and ultimately halting the system. Memory leaks can be fast, causing an almost immediate degradation in overall server performance, but they can also be slow and difficult to detect, gradually degrading system performance over a period of days or weeks. In most cases, memory leaks are caused by third-party applications, but operating system leaks are not unheard of.

To monitor basic memory performance, use the following counters:

- **Memory: Page Faults/Sec**   Specifies the number of times per second that the code or data needed for processing is not found in memory. This value should be as low as possible, with values below 5 being acceptable. This counter includes both soft faults (in which the required page is found elsewhere in memory) and hard faults (in which the requested page must be accessed from a disk). Soft faults are generally not a major problem, but hard faults can cause significant delays because disk accesses are much slower than memory accesses. If this value is too high, you should determine whether the system is experiencing an inordinate number of hard faults by examining the Memory: Pages/Sec counter. If the number of hard page faults is excessive, you should either determine what process is causing the excessive paging or install more random access memory (RAM) in the system.

- **Memory: Pages/Sec**   Specifies the number of pages per second that were not in RAM and had to be accessed from disk or that had to be written to disk to make room in RAM. This value should be as low as possible, with values from 0 to 20 being acceptable. If the value is too high, you should either determine what process is causing the excessive paging or install more RAM in the system.

- **Memory: Available Bytes**   Specifies the amount of available physical memory in bytes. (Other counters are available that show the same value in kilobytes and megabytes.) This value should be as high as possible and should not fall below 5 percent of the system's total physical memory, as this might be an indication of a memory leak. If the value is too low, consider installing additional RAM in the system.

- **Memory: Committed Bytes**   Specifies the amount of virtual memory that has space reserved on the disk-paging files. This value should be as low as possible and should always be less than the amount of physical RAM in the computer. If the value is too high, this could be an indication of a memory leak. Consider installing additional RAM in the system.

- **Memory: Pool Non-Paged Bytes**   Specifies the size of an area in memory used by the operating system for objects that cannot be written to disk. This value should be a stable number that does not grow without a corresponding growth in server activity. If the value increases over time, this could be an indication of a memory leak.

Monitoring Disk Performance

A storage subsystem that is overburdened with read and write commands can slow down the rate at which the system processes client requests. The server's hard disk drives carry a greater physical burden than the other three subsystems because in satisfying the I/O requests of many clients, the drive heads must continually move to different locations on the drive platters. The drive head mechanism can move only so fast, however, and once the drive reaches its maximum read/write speed, additional requests can begin to pile up in the queue, waiting to be processed. For this reason, the storage subsystem is a prime location for a bottleneck.

- **PhysicalDisk: Disk Bytes/sec**   Specifies the average number of bytes transferred to or from the disk each second. This value should be equivalent to the levels established in the original baseline readings or higher. A decrease in this value could indicate a malfunctioning disk that could eventually fail. If this is the case, consider upgrading the storage subsystem.

- **PhysicalDisk: Avg. Disk Bytes/Transfer**   Specifies the average number of bytes transferred during read and write operations. This value should be equivalent to the levels established in the original baseline readings or higher. A decrease in this value indicates a malfunctioning disk that could eventually fail. If this is the case, consider upgrading the storage subsystem.

- **PhysicalDisk: Current Disk Queue Length** Specifies the number of pending disk read or write requests. This value should be as low as possible, with values less than 2 being acceptable per disk spindle. High values for this counter can indicate that the drive is malfunctioning or that it is incapable of keeping up with the activities demanded of it. If this is the case, consider upgrading the storage subsystem.

- **PhysicalDisk: % Disk Time** Specifies the percentage of time that the disk drive is busy. This value should be as low as possible, with values less than 80 percent being acceptable. High values for this counter can indicate that the drive is malfunctioning, that it is incapable of keeping up with the activities demanded of it, or that a memory problem is causing excess disk paging. Check for memory leaks or related problems and, if none are found, consider upgrading the storage subsystem.

- **LogicalDisk: % Free Space** Specifies the percentage of free space on the disk. This value should be as high as possible, with values greater than 20 percent being acceptable. If the value is too low, consider adding more disk space.

Most storage subsystem problems, when not caused by malfunctioning hardware, are resolvable by upgrading the storage system. These upgrades can include any of the following measures:

- Install faster hard disk drives.

- Install additional hard disk drives and split your data among them, reducing the I/O burden on each drive.

- Replace standalone drives with a RAID (redundant array of independent disks) array.

- Add more disk drives to an existing RAID array.

Monitoring Network Performance

Monitoring network performance is more complicated than monitoring the other three subsystems because many factors outside the computer can affect network performance. You can use the following counters to try to determine if a network problem exists, but if you suspect one, you should begin looking for causes external to the computer:

- **Network Interface: Bytes Total/sec** Specifies the number of bytes sent and received per second by the selected network interface adapter. This value should be equivalent to the levels established in the original baseline readings or higher. A decrease in this value could indicate malfunctioning network hardware or other network problems.

- **Network Interface: Output Queue Length** Specifies the number of packets waiting to be transmitted by the network interface adapter. This value should be as low as possible, and preferably zero, although values of two or less are acceptable. If the value is too high, the network interface adapter could be malfunctioning or another network problem might exist.

- **Server: Bytes Total/Sec** Specifies the total number of bytes sent and received by the server over all of its network interfaces. This value should be no more than 50 percent of the total bandwidth capacity of the network interfaces in the server. If the value is too high, consider migrating some applications to other servers or upgrading to a faster network.

The bandwidth of the network connections limits the amount of traffic reaching the server through its network interfaces. If these counter values indicate that the network itself is the bottleneck, there are two ways to upgrade the network, and neither one is a simple fix:

- **Increase the speed of the network**   This means replacing the network interface adapters in all the computers, hubs, routers, and other devices on the network, and possibly replacing the cabling as well.

- **Install additional network adapters in the server and redistribute the network**   If traffic frequently saturates the network interfaces already in the server, the only way to increase the network throughput without increasing the network's speed is to install more network interfaces. However, connecting more interfaces to the same network will not permit any more traffic to reach the server. Instead, you must create additional subnets on the network and redistribute the computers among them, so that there is less traffic on each subnet.

Monitoring Server Roles

When you monitor server performance and look for bottlenecks, it is important that you understand the implications of the roles that the server is performing. Applications and services make different demands on system resources, and your monitoring strategy for each server should concentrate on the performance objects and counters for the resources that are most heavily affected on that server. Table 3-3 lists some of the most common server roles, the resources most important to each role, and the performance objects you should monitor.

Table 3-3   Server Roles and Objects to be Monitored

Server Role	Resources Used	Performance Objects to Monitor
Application server	Memory, network, and processor	Memory, Processor, Network Interface, and System
Backup servers	Processor and network	System, Server, Processor, and Network Interface
Database servers	Storage, network, and processor	PhysicalDisk, LogicalDisk, Processor, Network Interface, and System
Domain controllers	Memory, processor, network, and disk	Memory, Processor, System, Network Interface, protocol objects (network-dependent, but can include TCPv4, UDPv4, ICMP, IPv4, NBT Connection, NWLink IPX, NWLink NetBIOS, and NWLink SPX), PhysicalDisk, and LogicalDisk
File and print servers	Memory, disk, and network components	Memory, Network Interface, PhysicalDisk, LogicalDisk, and Print Queue
Mail/messaging servers	Processor, disk, network, and memory	Memory, Cache, Processor, System, PhysicalDisk, Network Interface, and LogicalDisk
Web servers	Disk, cache, and network components	Cache, Network Interface, PhysicalDisk, and LogicalDisk

Using Performance Logs and Alerts

As useful as the System Monitor snap-in is, few system administrators have the time or inclination to sit around watching a graph crawl across their screens, looking for signs of trouble on their servers. Performance Logs and Alerts eliminates the need to do this. Performance Logs and Alerts is an MMC snap-in that provides logged monitoring capabilities using the same performance objects and counters as System Monitor. With this snap-in, you can collect performance data automatically from local or remote computers, store it in a variety of formats, and generate alerts when a particular counter level reaches a specified threshold.

When you select the Performance Logs And Alerts snap-in in the Performance console, you see three subheadings, as follows:

- **Counter Logs**   Enables the Performance console to capture statistics for specific counters to a log file at regular intervals over a specified time

- **Trace Logs**   Enables the Performance console to record information about system applications when certain events occur, such as disk I/O operations or page faults

- **Alerts**   Enables the Performance console to monitor the values of a specific counter at regular intervals and perform an action when the counter reaches a specified value

One of the main benefits of Performance Logs and Alerts is that it enables you to capture performance counter information for later study. The snap-in supports a variety of file formats that enable you to import the captured information into spreadsheet and database programs. You can use counter logs to establish a baseline for network performance, and then periodically check the logs for deviation from that baseline. You can also create alerts to warn you when specific network conditions deviate too far from the norm.

> **NOTE   Unattended Logging**   Performance Logs and Alerts runs as a service. This means that you can configure the snap-in to monitor certain performance counters, and the service will load during system startup and continue to operate even if no user is logged on to the system.

Creating a Counter Log

To create a counter log in the Performance Logs and Alerts snap-in, you select the Counter Logs object in the scope pane and select New Log Settings from the Action menu. After you specify a name for the new log, you see a dialog box (shown in Figure 3-18) in which you specify the following information:

- **Performance objects and counters**   The same performance objects and counters, and the same interface you use to select them, as those for System Monitor.

- **Sample interval**   The time interval at which the snap-in should log the values of the counters you selected. Keep in mind that short sample intervals produce larger log files and also generate more system overhead. The value you choose should depend largely on how long you plan to let the counter log run.

- **Run As credentials**   A user name and password that the Performance Logs and Alerts service will use to log on to the system before capturing information to the counter log.

- **Log file type**   The file format you want to use for the counter log and the folder you want to save it in. You can choose to save the log as a comma- or tab-delimited text file, a regular or circular binary file (viewable in System Monitor), or a SQL database file. You can also specify a maximum size for the log file and a naming convention for the file.

> **NOTE   Using Circular Files**   A circular binary file is one in which the snap-in continuously logs information to the same file, overwriting the oldest data as it does so.

- **Scheduling information**   You can configure the counter log to start and stop at particular dates and times, or you can choose to start and stop the logging process manually from the snap-in.

- **Close command**   Enables you to specify a command that the snap-in should run when the log file closes.

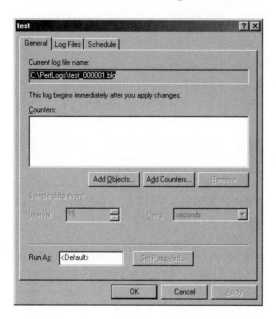

Figure 3-18   A counter log's configuration dialog box

Once you configure the counter log, it appears in the snap-in scope pane with an icon, the color of which indicates the log's current status. A red icon is stopped and a green icon is running.

Creating a Trace Log

The process of creating a trace log is similar to that of creating a counter log, except that instead of selecting performance counters, you select the system events that you want to monitor, using the interface shown in Figure 3-19.

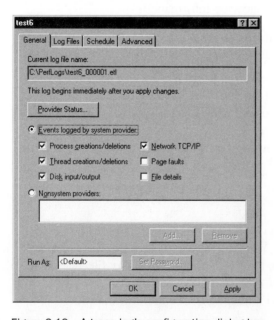

Figure 3-19   A trace log's configuration dialog box

Viewing a Counter Log

When you choose to save a counter log as a binary file, it appears in its destination folder with a .blg extension. To open one of these files and view its contents, you go to the System Monitor snap-in and click the View Log Data toolbar button or press Ctrl+L. In the System Monitor Properties dialog box that appears (as shown in Figure 3-20), you must configure the following elements:

- **Data source**   In the Source tab, click the Log Files option and select the log file you want to display.

- **Time range**   In the Source tab, click the Time Range button to display a slider bar containing the time period during which data was captured to the log. You can use the slider to select all or part of the log for display.

- **Counters**   In the Data tab, click Add and select the counters you want to display. In this case, the Add Counters dialog box contains only the performance objects and counters that you selected for inclusion in the log.

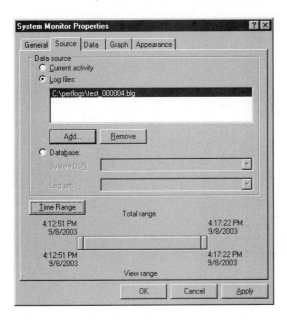

Figure 3-20   The System Monitor Properties dialog box, configured to display a log file

When you click OK to close the dialog box, the System Monitor line graph displays the data captured in the log. You can manipulate the appearance of the graph in the same way as you can when it displays the system's current activity.

Creating Alerts

Alerts enable a Windows Server 2003 computer to inform you when performance levels reach a specified threshold. To create an alert, you select the Alerts object in the scope pane of the Performance Logs and Alerts snap-in and select New Alert Settings from the Action menu to display a dialog box (as shown in Figure 3-21) in which you specify the following information:

- **Counters**   The performance object and counters that you can select for an alert, and the interface you use to select them, are the same as those for System Monitor.

- **Counter value limits**   For each counter you select, you must specify a value limit and whether you want the alert to trigger when the counter value is over or under the limit.

- **Sample interval**   The time interval at which the snap-in should monitor the values of the counters you selected.

- **Run As credential**   A username and password that the Performance Logs and Alerts service will use to log on to the system before monitoring the selected counters.

- **Action**   The action that you want the snap-in to perform when one of your selected counters reaches the limit you specified. The snap-in can create an event log entry, send a network message to a specified user, begin logging performance data for the counter, or execute a specified program or command.

- **Scheduling information**   You can configure the snap-in to start and stop monitoring the selected counters at particular dates and times, or you can choose to start and stop the monitoring process manually from the snap-in.

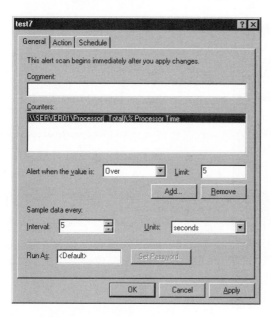

Figure 3-21   An alert's configuration dialog box

SUMMARY

- Event Viewer is an MMC snap-in that displays logs maintained by the computer. Every Windows Server 2003 computer has Application, System, and Security logs; domain controllers have two additional Directory Service and File Replication Service logs, and DNS servers have a DNS Server log.

- Individual event log entries can contain information, warnings, error messages, or auditing results.

- Task Manager displays real-time performance data for the computer's processor and memory, lists of the applications and processes running on the computer, and network and user activity information. You can also use Task Manager to end applications and processes, set process priorities, and disconnect users.

- The Performance console consists of two snap-ins: System Monitor and Performance Logs and Alerts.

- System Monitor shows real-time performance data for system hardware and software components, using graph, histogram, and report views.

- To monitor specific system characteristics using System Monitor, you choose a performance object representing a specific component, a performance counter that represents a specific aspect of the selected object, and in some cases an instance, which is a specific occurrence of the selected object.

- Performance Logs and Alerts records performance counter information to counter logs and operating system events to trace logs over scheduled periods of time, enabling you to capture large data samples for later examination.

- Performance Logs and Alerts can also monitor specific counters and perform an action when the counter values reach a specified threshold.

EXERCISES

Exercise 3-1: Using Event Viewer

In this exercise, you use the Event Viewer console to examine the computer's System log.

1. Log on to the computer as Administrator.

2. Click Start, point to Administrative Tools, and click Event Viewer. The Event Viewer console appears.

3. In the console's scope pane, click the System object. A list of System log entries appears in the details pane.

4. Double-click one of the entries in the details pane to display the Event Properties dialog box.

Exercise 3-2: Using Task Manager

In this exercise, you use Task Manager to start an application and identify its process.

1. Log on to the computer as Administrator.

2. Right-click an open section of the taskbar, and select Task Manager from the context menu. The Windows Task Manager window appears.

3. On the Applications tab, click New Task. Type **notepad**, and then click OK.

    An Untitled-Notepad window appears, and an Untitled-Notepad entry appears in the Task Manager's Applications tab.

4. In Task Manager's Applications tab, right-click the Untitled-Notepad entry and select Go To Process from the context menu. Task Manager switches to the Processes tab, with the Notepad.exe process highlighted.

Exercise 3-3: Creating a System Monitor Console

In this exercise, you create a new System Monitor console.

1. Log on to the computer as Administrator.

2. Click Start, point to Administrative Tools, and click Performance. The Performance console appears.

3. In the details pane, click the Add button in the toolbar. The Add Counter dialog box appears.

4. Leaving the default Processor object selected, click the % Idle Time counter and then click Add. Then add the % Interrupt Time and Interrupts/Sec counters in the same way, and then click Close.

5. From the File menu, select Save As. The Save As dialog box appears.

6. Save the console using the name procmon.msc.

CHAPTER REVIEW

1. You do not want data in the Security log to be overwritten, but you also do not want your Windows Server 2003 computer to stop serving the network at any time. What settings should you configure on your server?

2. Your goal is to monitor all your Windows Server 2003 servers so that they can be defragmented on a regular schedule, and as efficiently as possible. The disk defragmentation program that you use requires at least 20 percent free disk space on each volume to defragment properly. What should you do?

3. The computer that you are using to monitor the other systems on your network is overburdened with the task, so you must lighten its monitoring load. What should you do to lighten the monitoring computer's load while maintaining as much monitored data as possible?

4. You are running a database application on a computer with two processors. You want the database application to run on the second processor. How can you use Task Manager to do this?

5. Which of the following statements is true if System Monitor shows a value greater than 2 for the PhysicalDisk: Current Disk Queue Length counter on a non-RAID system?

   a. You need more disk space.

   b. You need a faster disk drive.

   c. You need additional information to determine whether the disk is the problem.

   d. You have a memory problem, not a disk problem.

6. Which of the following logs are available using Event Viewer on a member server functioning as an application server? (Choose all correct answers.)

   a. Application

   b. Directory Service

   c. System

   d. Security

   e. File Replication Service

7. Why do System Monitor performance counters sometimes have multiple instances?

8. What are two possible remedies for a disk subsystem that is the bottleneck in a server's performance?

CASE SCENARIOS

Scenario 3-1: Detecting a Bottleneck

You are a network administrator for Fabrikam, Inc., a high-technology company that has recently landed a lucrative government contract. As a result of the contract, the company will be undergoing a dramatic expansion over the next 12 months. The number of users accessing the company's client database is expected to double, and the IT director has instructed you to determine if the database server in its current configuration can keep up with the increased load, and if not, what improvements need to be made.

To accomplish this task, your first course of action is to implement a plan to monitor the server for performance bottlenecks. As the first step in the plan, you establish a baseline by using the Performance Logs and Alerts snap-in to create a counter log that tracks the values for critical counters in the Processor, Memory, PhysicalDisk, and Network Interface performance objects. After establishing the normal operational values for the counters, what should you do next to configure the Performance console to detect a bottleneck?

   a. Leave the counter log running at all times and check the values of the counters at regular intervals.

   b. Using System Monitor, create a graph of the same counters and configure the snap-in to sound an alarm when any counter value exceeds the maximum baseline value.

   c. In the Performance Logs And Alerts snap-in, create a series of alerts that send a message to your workstation when any baseline counter exceeds a certain value.

   d. In the Performance Logs And Alerts snap-in, create a trace log using the same counters as the baseline.

Scenario 3-2: Eliminating a Bottleneck

You are a network administrator who has been given the task of determining why the Windows Server 2003 file and print server on a particular LAN is performing poorly. You must also implement a remedy for the problem. After monitoring server performance counters using the Performance console, you have determined that the network itself is the bottleneck preventing peak performance. Which of the following solutions would enable you to achieve the goal of increasing the performance level of the file and print server? (Choose all correct answers.)

   a. Install a second network interface adapter in the server, and connect it to the same network.

   b. Increase the speed of the network by replacing the 10Base-T network interface adapters in the computers on the network and the hub to which the computers are connected with 100Base-TX equipment.

   c. Split the network into two separate LANs with an equal number of computers on each. Then install a second network interface adapter in the file and print server and connect the server to both LANs.

   d. Replace the network interface adapter in the file and print server with a model that has a larger memory buffer.

CHAPTER 4
BACKING UP AND RESTORING DATA

The most common analogy used to describe the relationship between a hard disk drive's platters (where the data is stored) and its heads (which read and write the data to the platters) is that of a 747 airliner flying at 600 miles an hour, five feet above the ground. When you consider this, it is amazing that hard drives work as well and as long as they do. Someday, you are going to lose a hard drive containing essential data. It might not happen today or tomorrow, but it will happen someday. The drive might be stolen along with the computer, destroyed in a fire or other catastrophe, or simply fail. Whatever the cause, the data will be gone, and it might be up to you to get it back. The day this occurs is the day you will thank yourself for all the effort you took to set up a backup strategy. If you don't have a backup strategy in place, that might be the day you start working on your résumé.

Performing regular backups is one of the most basic functions of the system and network administrator. Unlike most of the key components in a computer, hard drives have parts that move at high speeds, working at very close tolerances. As a result, hard drive failures are relatively common, and you must prepare for them by regularly saving your data on another storage medium.

Upon completion of this chapter, you will be able to:

- Describe the various types of hardware used to perform backups

- Understand the capabilities of network backup software products

- Understand the difference between full, incremental, and differential backup jobs

- List the capabilities of the Microsoft Windows Server 2003 Backup program

- Back up and restore an Active Directory database

- Use volume shadow copies

UNDERSTANDING BACKUPS

Backups are simply copies of your data that you make on a regular basis so that if a storage device fails or is damaged, and the data stored there is lost, you can restore it in a timely manner. A backup is the ultimate fault-tolerance measure. Even if you have other storage technologies in place that provide fault tolerance, such as a redundant array of independent disks (RAID) or clustered servers, you still need a backup solution.

Networks both complicate and simplify the process of making regular backups. A backup strategy for a stand-alone computer consists of a backup drive installed in the system. The network backup process is more complicated because you have data, stored on multiple devices, that must be protected, and it is not practical to install and maintain a separate backup drive for each one. However, the network backup process is simplified by the fact that you can use the network to access the devices that need backing up, enabling you to use one backup drive to protect multiple computers.

A network backup strategy specifies what data you back up, how often you back it up, and what medium you use to store the backups. The decisions you make regarding the backup hardware, software, and administrative policies you will use depend on how much data you have to back up, how much time you have to back it up, and how much protection you want to provide.

A network backup solution consists of the following two elements:

- One or more backup drives
- A backup software product

An effective backup plan specifies how to use the capabilities provided by these two items to provide the degree of protection that the organization needs. The criteria you should use when evaluating backup hardware and software products are discussed in the following sections.

> **NOTE**   **Exam Objectives**   *The objectives for the 70-290 examination state that students should be able to "manage backup procedures."*

Backup Hardware

You can perform backups using any type of storage device, although a device that uses removable media is the norm. The three main criteria used to evaluate backup hardware devices are:

- **Capacity**   One of the main objectives in developing an effective backup strategy should be to automate as much of the process as possible. Although you can back up a gigabyte of data onto 1.44-MB floppy disks, you probably don't want to be the person sitting around feeding 712 disks into a floppy drive. Therefore, you should select a device that is capable of storing as much of your data as possible without your having to change media. The ideal situation is one in which an entire backup job fits on a single tape cartridge or other medium. This enables you to schedule backup jobs to run completely unattended. This does not mean, however, that you have to purchase a drive that can hold all of the data stored on all of your network's computers. You can be selective about which data you want to back up. But it's therefore important to determine just how much of your data needs protecting, and how often, before you decide on the capacity of your backup device.

■ **Speed** Another important criterion to use when selecting a backup device is the speed at which the drive writes data to the medium. Backup drives are available in many speeds, and, not surprisingly, the faster ones are generally more expensive. It is typical for backup jobs to run during periods when the network is not otherwise in use. This ensures that all of the data on the network is available for backup. The amount of time that you have to perform your backups is sometimes called the *backup window*. The backup device that you choose should depend in part on the amount of data you have to protect and the amount of time in which you have to back it up. If, for example, you have 10 GB of data to back up and your company closes down from 5 P.M. until 9 A.M. the next morning, you have a 16-hour backup window—plenty of time to copy your data using a medium-speed backup device. However, if your company operates three shifts and leaves you only one hour, from 7 A.M. to 8 A.M., to back up 100 GB of data, you have to use a much faster device or, in this case, several devices.

■ **Cost** Cost is always a factor in selecting a hardware product. You can purchase a low-end backup drive for $100 to $200, which is suitable for backing up a home computer, where speed and capacity are not major factors. However, when you move up to the drives that have the speed and capacity that make them suitable for network backups, the prices increase dramatically. High-end backup drives can command prices that run into five figures. When you evaluate backup devices, you must be aware of the product's extended costs as well. Backup devices use a removable medium, such as a tape or disk cartridge. This enables you to store copies of your data offsite, such as in a bank's safe deposit vault. If the building where your network is located is destroyed by a fire or other disaster, you still have your data, which you can use to restart operations elsewhere. Therefore, in addition to purchasing the drive, you must purchase storage media as well. Some products might seem at first to be economical because the drive is inexpensive, but in the long run they might not be because the media are so expensive. One of the most common methods of evaluating a backup device is to determine the cost per megabyte (or gigabyte) of the storage it provides. Divide the price of the medium by the number of megabytes (or gigabytes) it can store, and use this figure to compare the relative media cost of various devices. Of course, in some cases you might need to sacrifice economy for speed or capacity.

Some of the removable storage devices used as backup drives are examined in the following sections.

CD-ROM and DVD-ROM Drives

The popularity of writable CD-ROM drives, such as compact disc-recordable (CD-R) drives and compact disc-rewritable (CD-RW) drives, has led to their increasing use as backup devices. Although the capacity of a CD is limited to approximately

650 MB, the low cost of the media can make CDs appear to be an economical solution, even if the disks can only be used once, as is the case with CD-Rs. Now that prices for DVD-ROM drives are coming down, DVD-ROMs are more suitable than CD-ROMs because of their greater capacity (over 4 GB). The biggest factor in favor of using CD-ROMs or DVD-ROMs for backup is that many computers already have the drives installed for other purposes, eliminating the need to purchase a dedicated backup drive.

For network backups, CD-ROMs are usually inadequate because most networks have many gigabytes' worth of data to back up, which would require many disc changes. DVD-ROMs reduce the number of media changes, and might be suitable for smaller networks, but they still do not have the capacity required for efficient backups of a large enterprise network. In addition, CD-ROM and DVD-ROM drives are usually not recognized by network backup software products. Although these drives often come with software that provides its own limited backup capabilities (intended for relatively small, single-system backups), this software usually does not provide the features needed to back up a network effectively.

Cartridge Drives

Another commonly used storage device that can be easily used for backups is the removable cartridge drive. Products such as Iomega's Zip and Jaz drives provide performance that approaches that of a hard disk drive, but they use removable cartridges. These drives mount into a computer's file system, which means that you can assign them a drive letter and copy files to them, just as you can with a hard drive.

Zip cartridges hold no more than 750 MB, which makes them only slightly more practical than CDs for backups. However, Jaz drives are available in 1-GB and 2-GB versions, which is sufficient for a backup device, even on a small network. The drawback of using this type of drive for backup purposes is the extremely high cost of the media. A 2-GB Jaz cartridge can cost as much as $125, which is more than 6 cents per megabyte—far more than virtually any other storage device.

Magnetic Tape Drives

The most commonly used hardware device for backing up data is the magnetic tape drive, like the one shown in Figure 4-1. Unlike hard disk, floppy disk, and CD-ROM drives, tape drives are not random access devices. This means that the drive can't move its heads to read any particular file on a tape without spooling through all of the files before it. As with other types of magnetic tape drives, such as audio and video, the drive unwinds the tape from a spool and pulls it across the heads until it reaches the point in the tape where the data you want is located. As a result, you can't mount a tape drive in a computer's file system, assign it a drive letter, and copy files to it, as you can with a hard disk drive. A special software program is required to address the drive, send the data you select to it for storage, and restore the data later. This also means that tape drives are useless for anything other than backups, whereas other types of removable storage media, such as writable CD-ROMs, can be used for other things.

Figure 4-1   An external magnetic tape drive

Magnetic tape drives are well-suited for backups. They're fast, they can hold a lot of data, they can archive that data nearly indefinitely, and their media cost per megabyte is low—often less than one-half cent per megabyte. There are many different types of magnetic tape drives that differ greatly in speed, capacity, and price. The general rule with magnetic tape drives is that you trade speed and capacity for cost. At the low end are quarter-inch cartridge (QIC) drives, which can cost as little as $200. There are many different QIC formats, with the capacity of a single QIC tape cartridge ranging from 150 MB to 20 GB. At the high end of the market are digital linear tape (DLT) and linear tape-open (LTO) drives, which can cost many thousands of dollars and store hundreds of gigabytes on a single tape. The most common magnetic tape technologies used for backups are listed in Table 4-1.

Table 4-1   **Magnetic Tape Drive Types**

Type	Tape Width	Cartridge Size	Capacity (uncompressed)	Speed
QIC, Travan	.25 inch	4 × 6 × 0.625 inches (data cartridge); 3.25 × 2.5 × 0.6 inches (minicartridge)	50 GB	600 MB/min
DAT	4 mm	2.875 × 2.0625 × 0.375 inches	20 GB	360 MB/min
8 mm	8 mm	3.7 × 2.44 × 0.59 inches	100 GB	1400 MB/min
DLT, Super DLT	.50 inch	4.16 × 4.15 × 1 inches	160 GB	960 MB/min
LTO, Ultrium	.50 inch	4.0 × 4.16 × 0.87 inches	200 GB	Up to 3600 MB/min

NOTE   Magnetic Tape Compression   The capacities of magnetic tape drives are generally specified using two figures, such as 40 GB to 80 GB. These numbers refer to the capacity of a tape without compression and with compression. Most tape drives have hardware-based data compression capabilities built into them, but the additional capacity that you achieve when using compression is based on the type of data you are storing. The capacity figures cited by drive manufacturers assume an average compression ratio of 2:1, which is the typical amount of compression achieved with executables and other types of application files. Some file types, such as image files that use uncompressed BMP or TIF formats, can compress at much higher ratios, as high as 8:1. However, files that are already compressed, such as GIF and JPG image files or ZIP archives, cannot be compressed further and are stored at a 1:1 compression ratio.

Autochangers

In some cases, even the highest-capacity magnetic tape drive isn't sufficient to back up a large network with constantly changing data. A network might have an extraordinarily large amount of data to back up or an extremely small backup window to work with. To create an automated backup solution with a greater capacity than that provided by a single drive, you can purchase a device called an **autochanger**.

An *autochanger* (shown in Figure 4-2) is a hardware device that contains one or more drives (usually magnetic tape drives, but optical disk and CD-ROM autochangers are also available), a media array, and a robotic mechanism that swaps the media in and out of the drives. Sometimes these devices are called jukeboxes or tape libraries. When a backup job fills one tape (or other storage medium), the robotic mechanism extracts it from the drive and inserts another, after which the job continues. The autochanger also retains a memory of which tapes are available, commonly called an *index*, and can automatically load the appropriate tape needed to perform a restore job.

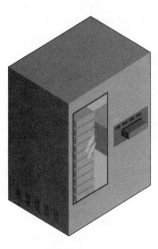

Figure 4-2 A magnetic tape autochanger

Some autochangers are small devices with a single drive and an array of four or five tapes, whereas others are enormous devices with four or more drives and an array of 100 tapes or more. If you purchase a large enough autochanger, you can create a long-term backup strategy that enables backups to run completely unattended for weeks at a time. However, before you solidify your plans to get a refrigerator-size autochanger and never load a tape into a drive by hand again, be aware that the cost of these devices can be astonishingly high, reaching well into six figures in some cases.

Drive Interface Selection

Backup devices can use any of the standard computer interfaces, such as Integrated Device Electronics (IDE), universal serial bus (USB), and Small Computer System Interface (SCSI), plus the newest interface to hit the mainstream, IEEE 1394 (FireWire). Some backup drives even connect to the computer's parallel port, although this is just a form of SCSI that uses a different port. The most common interface used in high-end network backup solutions is SCSI.

SCSI devices operate more independently than those using IDE, which means that the backup process, which might entail reading from one device while writing to another on the same interface, is more efficient. When two IDE devices share a channel, only one operates at a time. Each drive must receive, execute, and complete a command before the other drive can receive its next command. On the other hand, SCSI devices can maintain a queue of commands that they have received from the host adapter, and execute them sequentially and independently.

Magnetic tape drives, in particular, require a consistent stream of data to write to the tape with maximum effectiveness. If there are constant interruptions in the data stream, as can be the case with the IDE interface, the tape drive must repeatedly stop and start the tape (called *shoeshining*), which reduces its speed and its overall storage capacity. A SCSI drive can often operate continuously, without pausing to wait for the other devices on the channel.

A SCSI backup device is usually more expensive than a comparable IDE alternative because the drive requires additional electronics, and because you must have a SCSI host adapter installed in the computer. Most SCSI devices are available as internal or external units. The latter have their own power supplies, which also adds to the cost. However, the additional expense for SCSI is worth it for a fast, reliable network backup solution.

Backup Software

Apart from the hardware, the primary component in a network backup solution is the software that you use to perform the backups. Storage devices designed for use as dedicated backup solutions are not treated like the other storage subsystems in a computer; a specialized software product is required to gather the data that you want to back up, and to send it to the drive. Windows Server 2003 includes a backup software program that provides basic functionality for single-system back-ups, but as with most operating system backup programs, it lacks the advanced features that are required to effectively back up a complex network environment.

The primary functions of a good backup software product are examined in the following sections.

Target Selection
The most basic function of a backup software program is to let you select what you want to back up, which is sometimes called the *target*. A good backup program enables you to do this in many ways. In most cases, you can select:

- Entire computers
- Specific drives on a computer
- Specific folders on a drive
- Specific files in a folder

Using Tree Selection   Most backup programs provide a tree display that you can use to select the targets for a backup job. Figure 4-3 shows the interface that the Windows Server 2003 Backup program uses to select backup targets.

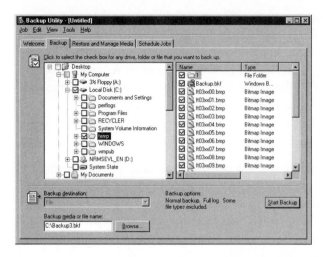

Figure 4-3 The Backup tab in the Windows Server 2003 Backup program

In nearly all cases, it is not necessary to back up all of the data on a computer's drives. If a hard drive is completely erased or destroyed, you are likely to have to reinstall the operating system before you can restore files from a backup tape, so it might not be worthwhile to back up all of the operating system files each time you run a backup job. The same is true for applications. You can reinstall an application from the original distribution media, so you might want to back up only your data files and configuration settings for that application. In addition, most operating systems today create temporary files as they run, which you do not need to back up. Windows, for example, creates a memory paging file that can be hundreds or thousands of megabytes in size. Because this file is automatically created, you can save space on your backup tapes by omitting it and files like it from your backup jobs. Judicious selection of backup targets can mean the difference between fitting an entire backup job onto one tape or staying late after work to insert a second tape into the drive.

Practice selecting files for backup by doing Exercise 4-1, "Selecting Backup Targets," now.

Using Filters Individually selecting the files, directories, and drives that you want to back up can be quite tedious on a large network installation, so many backup programs provide other ways to specify targets. One common method is to use filters that enable the software to evaluate each file and folder on a drive and decide whether to back it up. Backup software products that support filtering typically enable you to use the filters inclusively or exclusively; that is, a filter can identify the files you want to back up or the files you want to exclude from the backup.

A good backup program provides a variety of filters that enable you to select targets based on any of the following criteria:

- **File and folder name** Specifying individual file and folder names using filters is not easier than using a tree display, but the ability to use wildcard characters in file and folder names makes this a powerful feature. You can use the standard question mark (?) and asterisk (*) to represent single characters and multiple characters, respectively. For example, creating an exclude filter using the file mask *.tmp would exclude all files with a .tmp extension (which is commonly used for temporary files) from the backup job.

- **File size**   Filtering based on file size enables you to exclude zero-length files from your backups or exclude extremely large files, such as the Pagefile.sys memory paging file.

- **File dates/times**   All file systems maintain at least one date and time for each file stored, typically specifying when the file was most recently modified. Some file systems, such as the Windows NTFS file system, include multiple dates and times for each file, such as when the file was created, when it was last accessed, and when it was last modified. Filtering based on these dates enables you to back up only the files that have changed since a given date and time, or only the files that are older than a certain date.

- **File attributes**   Attributes are 1-bit flags attached to files that specify characteristics about them. Most file systems support the four standard MS-DOS attributes, which are *H* for hidden, *R* for read-only, *S* for system, and *A* for archive, but some file systems include other attributes as well. Most backup programs rely primarily on archive attribute filtering for performing backups, which enables them to back up only the files that have changed since the last backup. This type of filter is the basis for **incremental** and **differential backup** jobs.

    NOTE   Windows Server 2003 Backup Filtering   The Windows Server 2003 Backup program enables you to create custom file and folder name filters to exclude specific files from a backup job, but it does not support inclusive filters or size, date/time, and attribute filters other than those provided in the standard backup job types.

Understanding Backup Job Types   Most, if not all, backup software products include a collection of standard backup job types that are actually preset filter combinations. For example, the Windows Server 2003 Backup program enables you to select from the following five job types (as shown in Figure 4-4):

- **Normal**   Backs up all files to the storage medium and resets each file's **archive bit** to indicate that the file has been backed up

- **Copy**   Backs up all files to the storage medium and does not reset their archive bits

- **Differential**   Backs up only the files that have changed since the last normal backup and does not reset their archive bits

- **Incremental**   Backs up only the files that have changed since the last normal or incremental backup and resets their archive bits

- **Daily**   Backs up only the files that were created or modified today and does not reset their archive bits

Figure 4-4   The Backup Type tab in the Windows Server 2003 Backup program's Options dialog box

The most basic type of backup job is a *full backup* (called a *normal job* by Windows Server 2003 Backup), which copies the entire set of selected targets to the tape or other backup medium. You can perform a full backup every day, if you want to, or each time that you back up a particular computer. However, this practice can be impractical for any of the following reasons:

- **There is too much data to back up.**   The hard drives that are typically included in today's computers hold more data than ever, and on a large network, total storage capacity can easily add up to thousands of gigabytes. Unless you want to spend an enormous amount of money on tape drive and autochanger hardware, it is not feasible to back up all of the data in every computer every day.

- **There is not enough time to perform the backups.**   Most network administrators schedule network backup jobs to occur at night or whenever the organization is closed. Backing up during off hours makes it less likely for the backup to skip files because they are locked open, and it minimizes the impact of the network traffic generated by remote backup processes. For some organizations, the amount of time available to perform backups is insufficient to back up the entire network unless multiple high-speed drives are used.

- **There is too much redundant data.**   Much of the data stored on a typical computer's hard drive is static; it does not change every day. Application and operating system files never change, and some document files can go for long periods without users changing them. Backing up files such as these every day means saving the same data to tape over and over, which is a waste of time and media.

> **TIP**   *Server-Based Storage*   *Ease of backup is one of the primary reasons that many network administrators insist that users store their data files on servers rather than on their local hard drives. By giving each user a home directory on a server, it is possible to back up everyone's data files with a single server backup rather than having to configure the backup software to connect to each individual workstation every day.*

To save tape and shorten the backup time, many administrators perform full backups only once a week or even less frequently. In between the full backups, they perform special types of filtered jobs that back up only the files that have recently been modified. These types of jobs are called incremental backups and differential backups. An incremental backup is a job that backs up only the files that have changed since the last backup job of any kind. A differential backup is a job that backs up only the files that have changed since the last full backup. The backup software filters the files for these jobs using the archive attribute, also known as the *archive bit*, which every file on the computer possesses.

The archive bit does not actually modify a file's functionality, as the read-only and hidden attributes do; it is simply a marker that backup software uses to determine whether to back up each file. The state of the archive bit during a typical sequence of backup jobs is as follows:

1. When a file is written to a computer's hard disk for the first time, its archive bit is activated, meaning that it is set to a value of 1.

2. During the first full backup you perform on the computer, the software backs up the entire contents of the computer's drive and also resets (that is, sets to a value of 0) the archive bit on all of the files. At this point, you have a complete backup of the drive on tape, and none of the files on the drive has an active archive bit.

3. Whenever a file on the drive is modified by any application or process, the file system reactivates the archive bit.

4. For the next backup, you perform an incremental or differential job. The backup software scans the archive bits of all the files on the drive and backs up only the files with active bits. At this point, you have a full backup of the entire drive and a backup of all the files that have changed since that full backup. If a disaster occurs, causing the entire contents of the drive to be lost, you can return it to its current state by performing a restore from the full backup tape and then restoring the incremental or differential tape, allowing the changed versions of the files to overwrite the original versions.

Because incremental and differential jobs back up only part of the drive's contents, they run faster and take up less tape than full backups. A typical network backup strategy consists of a full backup on one day of the week and an incremental or differential job on the other days. With this arrangement, you can always restore the drive to a state no more than 24 hours old.

The difference between an incremental job and a differential job lies in the behavior of the backup software when it either resets or does not reset the archive bits of the files it copies to tape. Incremental jobs reset the archive bits, and differential jobs do not. Running incremental or differential jobs is often what makes it possible to automate your backup regimen without spending too much on hardware. If your full backup job totals 50 GB, for example, you might be able to purchase a 20-GB drive. You'll have to manually insert two additional tapes during your full backup jobs, once a week, but you should be able to run incremental or differential jobs the rest of the week using only one tape for each one, which means that the jobs can run unattended.

Using Incremental Backups This means that when you run an incremental job, you're backing up only the files that have changed since the last backup, whether it was a full backup or an incremental backup. Performing incrementals between your full backups uses the least amount of tape, but it also lengthens the restore process. If you have to restore an entire computer, you must first perform a restore from the last full backup tape, and then you must restore each of the incremental jobs you performed since the last full backup.

For example, consider the backup schedule shown in Table 4-2.

Table 4-2 **Sample Incremental Backup Schedule**

Day	Job Type	Files Included in Job
Sunday	Full	Data1.txt, Data2.txt, Data3.txt
Monday	Incremental	Data1.txt
Tuesday	Incremental	Data1.txt, Data3.txt
Wednesday	Incremental	Data1.txt, Data2.txt
Thursday	Incremental	Data1.txt, Data3.txt
Friday	Incremental	Data1.txt
Saturday	Incremental	Data1.txt

The Sunday backup is the only complete copy of the computer's drive, and each of the incrementals consists of only the files that have changed during the previous 24 hours. Because Data1.txt changes every day, it appears in every one of the incremental backups. The file's archive bit is activated each time it changes, and each incremental backup resets the bit again. Data2.txt changes only once, on Wednesday, so it appears only in the full backup job and in Wednesday's incremental. Data3.txt changes twice, on Tuesday and Thursday, so it appears in the full backup and in Tuesday's and Thursday's incrementals.

If the computer's drive were to malfunction on Friday, causing all of its data to be lost, you would begin the restoration process by restoring the most recent Sunday full backup, and then you would restore the Monday, Tuesday, Wednesday, and Thursday incrementals that followed the full backup, in that order. The results of the restorations on the three data files would be as follows:

■ **Data1.txt** The original copy from the full restore would be overwritten by a newer copy during each incremental restore, leaving the newest (Thursday) version on the drive when the restoration process is complete.

■ **Data2.txt** The original copy from Sunday's full restore would remain on the drive until the restoration of the Wednesday incremental tape, at which time the newest (Wednesday) version would overwrite the Sunday version. The Wednesday version would be left on the drive when the restoration process is complete.

■ **Data3.txt** The original copy from Sunday's full restore would be overwritten twice, first by the version on the Tuesday incremental tape and then by the Thursday version, leaving the latest (Thursday) version on the drive when the restoration process is complete.

NOTE **Restoring Incrementals** When you restore from incrementals, the order of the tapes you restore is crucial. You must restore the incrementals in the order they were written, or you might end up with old versions of files overwriting the newer versions.

Using Differential Backups If you were to perform the same sequence of backups using differential jobs instead of incrementals, the results would be like those in Table 4-3.

Table 4-3   Sample Differential Backup Schedule

Day	Job Type	Files Included in Job
Sunday	Full	Data1.txt, Data2.txt, Data3.txt
Monday	Differential	Data1.txt
Tuesday	Differential	Data1.txt, Data3.txt
Wednesday	Differential	Data1.txt, Data2.txt, Data3.txt
Thursday	Differential	Data1.txt, Data2.txt, Data3.txt
Friday	Differential	Data1.txt, Data2.txt, Data3.txt
Saturday	Differential	Data1.txt, Data2.txt, Data3.txt

Because the Data1.txt files changes every day, it appears in every differential job, just as it appeared in every incremental. However, because differential jobs do not reset the archive bits on the files they back up, once a file appears in a differential, it appears in every subsequent differential until the next full backup. Therefore, the Data2.txt file that first appears in the Wednesday incremental is also backed up on Thursday, Friday, and Saturday because its archive bit is still active. In the same way, the Data3.txt file that first appears in Tuesday's differential also appears in all of the subsequent differentials, but starting on Thursday, it is a newer version that is backed up each night. The archive bits for all three files are not reset until the next full backup, on the following Sunday.

When you use differential backups, the jobs take a bit longer and they use a bit more tape because in some cases you are backing up the same files several days in a row. However, restoring from differentials is simpler and faster because you only have to restore the last full backup and the most recent differential. If the drive in this example were to fail on a Saturday, you would only have to restore the full backup from the previous Sunday and the previous day's (Friday's) differential. The Friday tape would have the Data1.txt, Data2.txt, and Data3.txt files on it. The version of Data1.txt would be Friday's, Data2.txt would be Wednesday's version, and Data3.txt would be Thursday's version.

Test your understanding of incremental and differential backups by doing Exercise 4-2, "Incremental and Differential Backups," now.

Using Copy Jobs and Daily Jobs All backup software programs enable you to perform full, incremental, and differential backups, but Windows Server 2003 Backup includes two additional job types that are not necessarily found in all other software products. A daily job uses a filter based on the date rather than the archive bit to back up only the files that were created or changed on the day the job is run. A copy job is identical to a full backup job except that the software does not modify the archive bits of the files it copies to tape. You can use copy jobs to perform additional full backups at any time, such as for offsite storage, without disturbing your regular sequence of full and incremental or differential jobs.

NOTE   Backup Job Names   Just as the Windows Server 2003 Backup program refers to full backups as normal jobs, it is not unusual for other backup software programs to use different names when referring to the basic job types.

Job Scheduling

All backup products enable you to create a backup job and execute it immediately, but the key to automating a backup routine is being able to schedule jobs to execute unattended. Not all of the backup programs supplied with operating systems or designed for standalone computers support scheduling, but all network backup software products do.

NOTE   Exam Objectives   The objectives for the 70-290 examination state that students should be able to "schedule backup jobs."

Most organizations perform incremental or differential backups daily, and a full backup once a week. This arrangement provides a good compromise between sufficient protection and the amount of time and media devoted to backups. The ideal situation for a backup administrator is having each daily incremental or differential job fit on a single tape. This enables the administrator to schedule the job to run unattended when the office is closed and the network is idle. As a result, all resources are available for backup and user productivity is not compromised by the sudden surge of network traffic caused by the backup process, and there is no need to have someone change media. Once you have created the backup schedule, you can simply insert the correct tape into the drive each day. Full backups might require more than one tape, so someone might have to be there to change media.

TIP   Selecting Backup Hardware   The ability to create an unattended backup schedule is a key factor to consider when you evaluate backup hardware products. Before selecting a drive, you should estimate the amount of data you will have to back up each day (allowing some leeway for growth) and look at drives that can store at least that much data on a single tape.

Backup programs use various methods to automatically execute backup jobs. The Windows Server 2003 Backup program adds its jobs to the operating system's Scheduled Tasks list; other programs supply their own program or service that runs continuously and triggers the jobs at the appropriate times. Some of the higher-end network backup products can use a directory service such as Microsoft's Active Directory or Novell's eDirectory for scheduling. These programs modify the directory schema (the code that specifies the types of objects that can exist in the directory) to create an object representing a queue of jobs waiting to be executed.

No matter which mechanism the backup software uses to launch jobs, the process of scheduling them is usually the same. You specify whether you want to execute the job once or repeatedly at a specified time each day, week, or month, using an interface like the one from the Windows Server 2003 Backup program (shown in Figure 4-5). The idea of the scheduling feature is for the network administrator to create a logical sequence of backup jobs that execute by themselves at regular intervals. After the administrator does this, the only action required is to change the tape in the drive each day. If you have an autochanger, you can even eliminate this part of the job and create a backup job sequence that runs for weeks or months without any attention at all.

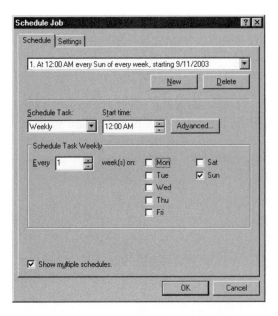

Figure 4-5   The Windows Server 2003 Backup program's Schedule Job dialog box

Maintaining Backup Logs

When a backup job runs, the software accesses the specified targets and feeds the data to the backup drive in the appropriate manner. Because of the nature of the media typically used for backups, it is important for the data to arrive at the storage device in a consistent manner and at the proper rate of speed. The software, therefore, must be designed to address specific drives in the manner appropriate for that device.

As the software feeds the data to the drive, it also keeps track of the software's activities. Most backup software products can maintain a log of the backup process as it occurs. You can often specify a level of detail for the log, such as whether it should contain a complete list of every file backed up or just record the major events that occur during the job. The Backup program in Windows Server 2003 uses the interface shown in Figure 4-6 to specify whether the program should keep a detailed log, a summary, or no log at all.

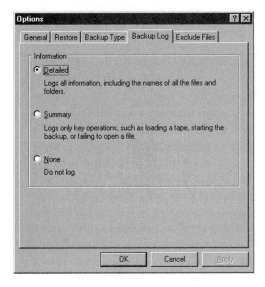

Figure 4-6   The Backup Log tab in the Windows Server 2003 Backup program's Options dialog box

In most cases, a detailed log of your backup jobs is not necessary. This type of log typically contains a list of every file that the program has backed up (as shown in Figure 4-7), and since backup jobs can consist of many thousands of files, a detailed log can be very long and the pertinent entries (such as errors) difficult to find. It is also important to keep an eye on the size of your log files, particularly when you configure them to maintain a high level of detail. These files can grow huge very quickly and can consume all of the available disk space on the drive on which they are stored.

Figure 4-7   A Windows Server 2003 backup log

Periodically checking the logs is an essential part of administering a network backup program. The logs tell you when selected files are skipped for any reason, such as when the files are locked open by an application or the computers on which they are stored are unreachable. The logs also let you know when errors occur on either the backup drive or one of the computers involved in the backup process. Some software products can generate alerts when errors occur, notifying you by sending a status message to a network management console, by sending you an e-mail message, or by other methods.

> **NOTE**   **Exam Objectives**   *The objectives for the 70-290 examination state that students should be able to "verify the successful completion of backup jobs."*

Cataloging

In addition to logging their activities, backup software programs also catalog the files they back up, thus facilitating the process of restoring files later. The catalog is essentially a list of every file that the software has backed up during each job. To restore files from the backup medium, you browse through the catalog and select the files, folders, or drives that you want to restore. Different backup software products store the catalog in different ways. Lower-end backup programs, such as those intended for stand-alone computers, store the catalog for each tape on the tape itself. The problem with this method is that you have to insert a tape into the drive to read the catalog and browse the files on that tape.

More elaborate network backup software programs take a different approach by maintaining a database of the catalogs for all of your backup media on the computer where the backup software is installed. This database enables you to browse through the catalogs for all of your tapes and select any version of any file or folder for restoration. In some cases, you can view the contents of the database in several different ways, such as by the computer, drive, and folder where the files were originally located, by the backup job, or by the tape or other media name. After you make your selection, the program specifies which tape contains the file or folder; you insert it into the drive, and the restore job proceeds.

The database feature can use a lot of the computer's disk space and processor cycles, but it greatly enhances the usability of the software, particularly in a network environment.

> **NOTE Backup Databases**   Backup software products that rely on a database typically store a copy of the database on your tapes as well as on the computer's hard drive. This is done so that if the computer you use to run the backups suffers a drive failure, you can restore the database later. Many products also enable you to rebuild the database on a computer by reading the contents of a tape and assimilating its index into a new database file.

Media Rotation

Some fastidious administrators use new tapes for every backup job and store them all permanently. However, this practice can be extremely expensive. It is more common for administrators to reuse backup tapes. To do this properly, however, you must have a carefully planned media rotation scheme so that you don't inadvertently overwrite a tape you might need later. You can always create such a scheme yourself, but some backup software products do it for you.

> **NOTE Exam Objectives**   The objectives for the 70-290 examination state that students should be able to "manage backup storage media."

One of the most common media rotation schemes is called the Grandfather-Father-Son method. In this method, the terms *grandfather*, *father*, and *son* refer to monthly, weekly, and daily tapes, respectively. For daily backups, you have one set of "son" tapes that you reuse every week. For the weekly full backup, you have "father" tapes that you reuse every month. Then, every month, you perform an additional full backup to tapes in your "grandfather" set, which you reuse every year. This method enables you to perform a complete restore at any time and maintains a year's history of your files. There are also other schemes that vary in complexity and utility, depending on the software product.

When the software program implements the rotation scheme, it provides a basic schedule for the jobs (which you can modify to have the jobs execute at specific times of the day), tells you what name to write on each tape as you use it, and once you begin to reuse tapes, tells you which tape to put in the drive for each job. The end result is that you maintain a perpetual record of your data while using the minimum number of tapes and without fear of overwriting a tape you need.

Device Configuration

Because dedicated backup drives are accessible only using specialized programs, most backup software products include an interface that enables you to manipulate the drive directly, to perform tasks such as the following:

- **Tape formatting**   All tapes must be formatted before a backup software program can write to them. Most backup software products automatically format new tapes at the beginning of a backup job, but it is also possible to format them manually. Different types of magnetic tape cartridges require different types of formatting. Some formats require the entire tape to be overwritten, while others require only a new header at the beginning of the tape. Formatting overwrites any existing data on the tape.

■ **Tape erasing** Erasing a tape is sometimes simply a matter of reformatting it because the reformatting process overwrites the entire length of the tape in the cartridge. For other types of tapes, reformatting is just the replacement of a header, which leaves the rest of the data on the tape intact. Most network backup software products enable you to erase the data from any tape, for security purposes, by overwriting its entire length. This does not necessarily mean that the data is unrecoverable by any means, but the backup software itself can't read the erased data from the tape.

■ **Tape retensioning** Some types of magnetic tapes can benefit from retensioning, in which the drive runs the tape all the way to its end and back again, to ensure that the entire length of the tape is wound onto the spool with a consistent amount of tension. Software products that are capable of retensioning tapes typically do so only for the types of tape that can benefit from the process.

■ **Drive compression** Most magnetic tape drives manufactured today include data compression capabilities implemented in their hardware, and backup software programs frequently provide the capability to select whether the drive's hardware compression circuitry is turned on or off. Some backup programs also have their own software-based compression routines for use with devices that do not support hardware compression. However, the use of hardware compression is always preferable to software compression because software compression places an additional burden on the computer's processor.

Performing Restores

Restoring data from your backups is, of course, the sole reason for making the backups in the first place. The ease with which you can locate the files you need to restore is an important feature of any backup software product. It is absolutely essential that you perform periodic test restores from your backup tapes or other media to ensure that you can get back any data that is lost. Even if all your jobs seem to complete successfully and your log files show that all of your data has been backed up, there is no more reliable test of a backup system than an actual restore. There are plenty of horror stories about administrators who dutifully performed their backups every day, only to find out when disaster struck that all their carefully labeled tapes were blank due to a malfunctioning drive.

> **NOTE** **Exam Objectives** The objectives for the 70-290 examination state that students should be able to "restore backup data."

Although performing regular backups is usually thought of as protection against a disaster that causes you to lose an entire hard drive, the majority of the restore jobs you will perform in a network environment are of one or a few files that a user has inadvertently deleted. As mentioned earlier, your backup software's cataloging capability is a critical part of the restoration process. If a user needs to have one particular file restored and you have to insert tape after tape into the drive to locate it, everyone's time is wasted. A backup program with a database that lets you search for that particular file makes your job much easier and enables you to restore any file in minutes.

Restore jobs are similar to backup jobs in that you select the files or folders that you want to restore, using an interface like that shown in Figure 4-8. When you create a restore job, a good backup software product typically enables you to configure the following parameters:

- **File selection**   You should be able to select any combination of files, folders, or drives on any tape. Some software products enable you to switch between a media view, which displays the contents of each tape in the library, and a disk view, which displays your backup targets and a list of the multiple versions of each file available on your various tapes.

- **Restore location**   You should be able to restore your selected files to their original locations automatically or specify an alternative location; you should also be able to re-create the original directory tree or dump all the files into a single folder.

- **Overwrite options**   When restoring files to their original locations, you should be able to specify rules for overwriting existing files with the same names, based on their dates or using other criteria.

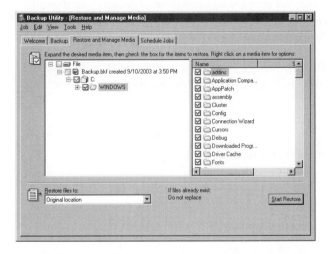

Figure 4-8   The Windows Server 2003 Backup program's Restore And Manage Media tab

Optional Network Backup Features

When you are developing a backup solution for a network, it is particularly important that you choose a backup software product that is designed for network use. The primary difference between network backup software and an application designed for standalone systems is that the former can back up other computers on the network. This means you can purchase one backup drive and use it to protect your entire network. Many standalone backup products can access drives on networked computers, but a fully functional network backup product can also back up important operating system features on other computers, such as the Windows registry and directory service databases. This type of remote backup might require you to install an additional software component on the target computer.

In many cases, network backup products also have additional components that enable you to perform specialized backup tasks, such as backing up live databases or computers running other operating systems. Some of these components are described in the following sections.

> **NOTE** **Add-On Components** In many cases, network backup software packages include only the basic components described in the previous sections. To add the greater functionality described in the following sections, you must purchase the other components as separate add-on modules that work together with the main backup engine.

Remote Backup Agents

Virtually all backup software products can back up shared drives on computers other than the one running the software, but this does not mean that they should be considered network backup software products. A true backup is one that can restore a drive that has been completely erased back to its previous state. Accessing a remote Windows computer through a drive or folder share theoretically enables you to back up everything that appears in the file system, but you cannot access elements such as the Windows registry or an Active Directory database in this way. Therefore, a backup of the share would be incomplete and could not be used to restore the remote computer to its original state.

In the Windows Server 2003 Backup program, you select a target called the System State (as shown in Figure 4-9) to back up the following elements on the local computer:

- System boot files
- System files under Windows File Protection
- Windows registry
- COM+ Class Registration database
- Active Directory directory service (domain controllers only)
- Sysvol directory (domain controllers only)
- Cluster service information (cluster nodes only)
- Internet Information Services (IIS) metadirectory (IIS servers only)
- Certificate Services database (certification authorities only)

> **NOTE** **Backing Up and Restoring the System State** You can back up and restore the System State only as a single object. You cannot, for example, restore only the Windows registry database from a System State backup and not the other elements in the object, such as the system boot files.

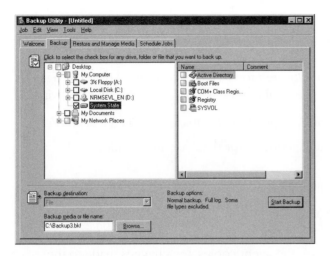

Figure 4-9   Backing up the System State object

However, in Windows Server 2003 you cannot back up the System State object on a computer other than the one running the Backup program.

Using most network backup software products, you can back up these system elements on remote computers, but in most cases, you must install a software component—typically called an *agent*—on them first. The agent enables the backup server to establish contact with the remote system and download the operating system elements needed to perform a complete backup of the computer's drives.

> **NOTE**   **Purchasing Agents**   Backup products can differ in the remote backup agents they include with the base product. For example, when you buy a product that runs the main backup engine on a Windows Server 2003 computer, the product might include the agent needed to back up other Windows computers on the network. However, if you have computers running other operating systems, you might have to purchase agents for those platforms separately.

Open File Backup

In many cases, when an application opens a document file, the file is locked open so that no other application or process can access it. This is to prevent another program from modifying the disk copy of a file that is currently in memory. One of the main reasons why administrators prefer to perform backups after hours is to prevent files from being skipped over because they are locked open by users. However, if a user leaves an application running with a file open, the backup can still fail to protect that file. To address this problem, some backup software products have open file capabilities that make it possible to back up certain types of files even when another application has them open.

Database Backup

Databases are a common backup problem, both because they often contain vital data that needs protection and because they frequently have to be left running around the clock. Databases that are running typically lock their data files open like any other application, enabling standard backup jobs to protect the database program files (that are easily replaceable) but skip the databases themselves.

▶ Backing Up a Database

To back up a database, you have to shut it down to unlock the open data files. In cases where shutting down the application is impossible because the database must remain available to users, many backup software products have specialized database agents that make it possible to back up the database using a procedure like the following:

1. The agent creates a temporary copy of the database file called a *delta file*.

2. The agent redirects all client requests for database information to the delta file.

3. The agent closes the original database file.

4. The agent communicates with the backup server and transmits the contents of the database file for backup to tape.

5. After the backup is complete, the agent copies any changes made to the delta file by clients back to the original database file.

6. The agent reopens the database file.

7. The agent directs the incoming client requests back to the original database file.

8. The agent deletes the delta file.

Disaster Recovery

As with any application, a backup software product requires an operating system in order to run. If the system drive of your backup server fails, you might have a full backup of the drive, but how do you restore it? Under normal conditions, you would have to reinstall the operating system and then reinstall the backup software before you could restore the drive back to its original condition. For an organization in which server down time means lost revenue, this delay might be intolerable.

> **NOTE   Exam Objectives**   The objectives for the 70-290 examination state that students should be able to "perform system recovery for a server" and "recover from server hardware failure."

Some backup software products can circumvent this problem by providing a disaster recovery feature. Disaster recovery software is designed to enable administrators to perform a complete restore of a computer's system drive in as little time as possible. The software creates a full backup in combination with a boot disk that contains only the operating system files needed to run the backup program and perform a restore. After booting from the disk, you can perform the restore, and the computer is back to its original condition much more quickly than if you had to install the operating system manually.

The Windows Server 2003 Backup program contains a disaster recovery feature called Automated System Recovery (ASR). The Automated System Recovery Preparation Wizard (as shown in Figure 4-10) backs up the System State data, system services, and all disks associated with the operating system components. It also creates a floppy disk, which contains information about the backup, the disk configurations (including basic and dyanmic volumes), and how to accomplish a restore.

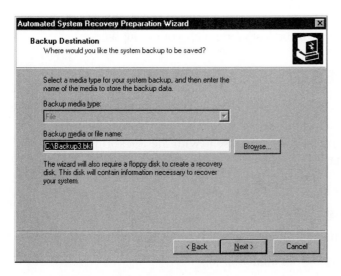

Figure 4-10   The Automated System Recovery Preparation Wizard

> **NOTE**   **Exam Objectives**   *The objectives for the 70-290 examination state that students should be able to "implement Automated System Recovery (ASR)."*

Backup Security

Backups contain copies of the same data you have stored on your hard drives, so you should take the same pains to secure the backups that you do with the original files. Network backup programs enable you to specify an account name and password that the software should use to access the backup targets. The best practice is to create a special account for this purpose that has only the privileges needed to perform the backups rather than use the Administrator account or some other, more comprehensive credentials. You can easily provide a user account with these privileges by adding it to the built-in Backup Operators group in Active Directory. This prevents unauthorized users from penetrating the security of the network using the backup software.

> **NOTE**   **Exam Objectives**   *The objectives for the 70-290 examination state that students should be able to "configure security for backup operations."*

To keep your data secure, you must also protect the files on the backup tapes themselves. Network backup software products typically enable you to password-protect your backup tapes. You specify a password during the creation of the backup job, and you must then use that same password to restore files from the backup. When password-protecting your tapes, you should use the same password requirements that you have imposed on your network, such as passwords of a specified length and complexity.

You should also physically secure your backup tapes, not only for data security but also for safekeeping. Password protection might prevent the casual intruder from restoring data on your tapes using the backup software, but the data still exists on the tape in an unprotected format, and someone with sufficient skill and equipment could still access the files. Therefore, you should always keep your backup tapes locked up, preferably in a fireproof safe or other secure storage area. You should also be sure to store copies of your backups offsite so that a theft or a disaster doesn't cause your backup tapes to be lost along with your computers.

USING WINDOWS SERVER 2003 BACKUP

The Backup program included with Windows Server 2003 is not a full-featured network backup software package as described earlier in this chapter, but it is certainly sufficient for backing up the server itself. With the Backup program, you can perform the following tasks:

- Back up local drives, network shares, and the local System State object
- Select backup targets using a tree display
- Perform normal, incremental, differential, copy, or daily backup jobs
- Exclude specific file masks from a backup job
- Back up files to a tape drive or to a file on a local disk, which you can then transfer to a CD-ROM, DVD-ROM, or other medium
- Schedule backups to occur at a specific time or at regular intervals
- Verify backups by comparing the image on the backup medium to the original target
- Restore backed-up files to their original locations or to alternate locations
- Specify when and if restored files should overwrite existing ones

Some of the other backup-related features that Windows Server 2003 provides are discussed in the following sections.

Using Volume Shadow Copy

Volume shadow copy is a Windows Server 2003 feature that maintains a library containing multiple versions of selected files. Although not a replacement for system backups, volume shadow copy enables users to access saved versions of files they have accidentally damaged or deleted. This eliminates one of the most onerous chores of the backup administrator: performing single file restores for users who have inadvertently deleted their own files.

> **NOTE   Exam Objectives**   The objectives for the 70-290 examination state that students should be able to "restore data from shadow copy volumes."

To enable volume shadow copy for a volume on your server, you display the Local Disk Properties dialog box for the volume and select the Shadow Copies tab (as shown in Figure 4-11). When you select a volume in the list and click Enable, Windows Server 2003 makes a copy of all the files in shared folders on that volume and stamps the copies with the current date and time. As long as shadow copying is enabled for that volume, Windows Server 2003 continues to make two copies of these files each weekday and saves them until the amount of space designated for volume shadow copies is full. You can modify both the frequency with which the Windows operating system makes copies and the size of the space used to store the copies.

IMPORTANT   Volume Shadow Copy Limitations   Volume shadow copy only protects the files on the volume that are stored in shared folders, and that volume must use the NTFS file system.

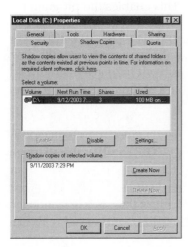

Figure 4-11   The Shadow Copies tab in a volume's Local Disk Properties dialog box

Only computers running Windows Server 2003 and Windows XP can access the shadow copies of files on your designated volumes. On Windows XP workstations, you must first install the client software that makes this possible. Then, a user can access shadow copies by displaying the Properties dialog box for a file in a shadow volume and selecting the Previous Versions tab (as shown in Figure 4-12).

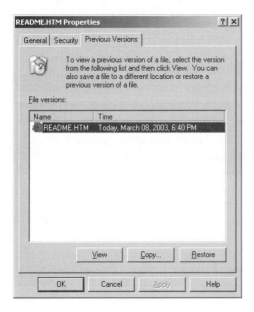

Figure 4-12   The Previous Versions tab in a file's Properties dialog box

NOTE   Volume Shadow Copy Clients   Windows Server 2003 includes the client software for volume shadow copy in its Systemroot\System32\Clients\Twclient folder. You can deploy the software by installing it manually on the Windows XP clients or by using an automated method, such as group policies.

In addition to providing users with access to multiple versions of their files, volume shadow copy also functions as an open file backup mechanism for the Windows Server 2003 Backup program. By default, Backup uses volume shadow copies of files that are locked open when performing backups. This enables the program to back up files that are in use by an application at the time the backup is performed. You can prevent Backup from using volume shadow copy during a particular backup job by selecting the Disable Volume Shadow Copy check box in the Advanced Backup Options dialog box (as shown in Figure 4-13).

Figure 4-13   The Advanced Backup Options dialog box

Backing Up and Restoring Active Directory

Practice enabling volume shadow copy on your Windows Server 2003 computer by doing Exercise 4-3, "Enabling Volume Shadow Copies," now.

As mentioned earlier in this chapter, you can back up the Active Directory database on a Windows Server 2003 domain controller using the Backup program by selecting the System State object as one of the backup targets. However, restoring Active Directory to a domain controller is not so simple. Before you can restore the Active Directory database from a System State backup, you must start the computer in Directory Services Restore Mode. You do this by pressing F8 as the system starts and selecting Directory Services Restore Mode from the Windows Advanced Options menu. This starts the computer with the Active Directory database closed, so that it is accessible to the Backup program and can be restored from a tape.

> **NOTE   Logging On**   When you restart the computer in Directory Services Restore Mode, you must log on as an Administrator by using a valid Security Accounts Manager (SAM) account name and password, not the Active Directory Administrator's name and password. This is because Active Directory is offline, and account verification cannot occur. The SAM accounts database is used to control access to Active Directory while Active Directory is offline. You specified this password when you set up Active Directory.

Once the computer is started in Directory Services Restore Mode, you can run the Backup program and restore the System State object from your tape or other medium. The Windows Server 2003 Backup program supports two types of Active Directory restores:

- **Nonauthoritative restore**   The objects in the Active Directory database are restored exactly as they appear in the System State object, with their original update sequence numbers intact. Because these sequence numbers are the same values the objects had when the backup was performed, they are outdated, and the Active Directory replication process will overwrite the objects with the newer versions from other domain controllers. You use a nonauthoritative restore when you want to rebuild a domain controller that has been damaged with the latest Active Directory information from your other domain controllers. Windows Server 2003 Backup performs nonauthoritative restores by default.

- **Authoritative restore**   The objects in the Active Directory database are restored with updated sequence numbers that prevent them from being overwritten during the next replication pass. You use an authoritative restore when you want to use a System State backup to recover Active Directory objects that have been accidentally deleted.

To perform a nonauthoritative restore, you simply restore the System State object using the Backup program while in Directory Services Restore Mode.

To perform an authoritative restore, you first perform a nonauthoritative restore, and then before restarting the computer, you use a command-line utility called Ndsutil.exe to mark specific Active Directory objects as authoritative. The Ntdsutil.exe utility can be found in the *Systemroot*\System32 folder. Marking objects as authoritative changes the update sequence number of an object so it is higher than any other update sequence number in the Active Directory replication system. This ensures that any replicated or distributed data that you have restored is properly replicated throughout your organization.

When the restored domain controller is online and connected to the network, normal replication brings the restored domain controller up-to-date with any changes from the additional domain controllers that were not overridden by the authoritative restore. Replication also propagates the authoritatively restored object(s) to other domain controllers in the forest. The deleted objects that were marked as authoritative are replicated from the restored domain controller to the additional domain controllers. Because the objects that are restored have the same object properties, security remains intact and object dependencies are maintained.

For example, suppose you back up the system on Monday and then create a new user called Jeff Smith on Tuesday, which replicates to other domain controllers in the domain. Then, on Wednesday, you accidentally delete Nancy Anderson's user object. To authoritatively restore the Nancy Anderson user without reentering information and without losing the Jeff Smith account, you perform a nonauthoritative restore of the domain controller with the backup created on Monday. Then, using Ntdsutil.exe, you mark Nancy Anderson's user object as authoritative and restart the domain controller. The result is that Nancy Anderson's object is restored without any effect on Jeff Smith.

> **NOTE Exam Objectives**   The objectives for the 70-290 examination state that students should be able to "back up files and System State data to media."

SUMMARY

■ A network backup solution consists of backup hardware, backup software, and a plan for using them.

■ When you evaluate backup hardware, higher speed and greater capacity nearly always mean higher price.

■ Magnetic tape is the most popular storage medium for backups because it is fast, inexpensive, and holds a lot of data. Tape drives are available in a variety of speeds, capacities, and price ranges to suit the needs of different installations.

■ The primary function of the backup software is to enable the administrator to select the targets for backup and then send them to the tape drive or other device.

■ Incremental and differential backup jobs save tape by backing up only the files that have changed since the last backup, based on the status of each file's archive bit.

■ A good backup software program enables you to schedule jobs to execute at any time, and it maintains both a tape version and a hard disk version of a catalog of all of the files that have been backed up.

■ Network backup software enables you to back up data from computers anywhere on the network, and it might also provide optional features such as live database backups.

■ To back up the Windows registry, the Active Directory database, and other system resources, you must back up the System State object.

■ Volume shadow copy is a Window Server 2003 feature that enables users to access multiple copies of files that they have accidentally deleted or damaged.

■ When you restore the System State data in nonauthoritative mode, any component of the System State data that is replicated with another domain controller, such as the Active Directory database, is brought up-to-date by replication after you restore the data.

■ When you restore the System State data in authoritative mode, changes that were made since the last backup operation are not restored; the deleted objects are recovered and replicated. To perform an authoritative restore, you use the Ntdsutil.exe command-line utility.

EXERCISES

Exercise 4-1: Selecting Backup Targets

In this exercise, you practice using the Backup program's tree display to select backup targets.

1. Log on to Windows Server 2003 as Administrator.

2. Click Start, point to All Programs, point to Accessories, point to System Tools, and click Backup. The Welcome To The Backup Or Restore Wizard page appears.

3. Click the Advanced Mode hyperlink. The Backup Utility window appears.

4. Select the Backup tab.

5. Expand the Local Disk (C:) object and select the check box for the Windows folder.

6. Select the System State check box.

7. From the Job menu, select Exit.

Exercise 4-2: Incremental and Differential Backups

1. If you back up your network by performing a full backup every Wednesday at 6 P.M. and differential backups in the evening on the other six days of the week, how many jobs would be needed to completely restore a computer with a hard drive that failed on a Tuesday at noon?

2. If you back up your network by performing a full backup every Wednesday at 6 P.M., how many jobs would be needed if you performed incremental backups in the evening of the other six days of the week and a hard drive failed on a Tuesday at noon?

3. For a complete restore of a computer that failed at noon on Tuesday, how many jobs would be needed if you performed full backups at 6 A.M. every Wednesday and Saturday and incremental backups at 6 A.M. every other day?

Exercise 4-3: Enabling Volume Shadow Copies

In this exercise, you enable the volume shadow copy feature for your computer's C: drive.

1. Log on to Windows Server 2003 as Administrator.

2. Click Start, point to All Programs, point to Accessories, and click Windows Explorer. The Windows Explorer window appears.

3. Expand the My Computer object in the scope pane, select Local Disk (C:), and from the File menu, select Properties. The Local Disk (C:) Properties dialog box appears.

4. Select the Shadow Copies tab, and then click Enable. The Enable Shadow Copies message box appears.

5. Read the warning message and click Yes. After a brief delay, the date and time appear in the Shadow Copies Of Selected Volume list, indicating that the system has created the first shadow copy.

REVIEW QUESTIONS

1. Why is it best to perform backups when the organization is closed?

2. Which of the following backup job types does not reset the archive bits on the files that it copies to the backup medium? (Choose all correct answers.)

   a. Full

   b. Incremental

   c. Differential

   d. Copy

3. Which of the following tape drive devices has the greatest capacity?

   a. LTO

   b. QIC

   c. DAT

   d. DLT

4. Which of the following is the criterion most commonly used to filter files for backup jobs?

   a. Filename

   b. File extension

   c. File attributes

   d. File size

5. How does an autochanger increase the overall storage capacity of a backup solution?

6. What are the three elements of the Grandfather-Father-Son media rotation system?

   a. Hard disk drives, CD-ROM drives, and magnetic tape drives

   b. Incremental, differential, and full backup jobs

   c. Monthly, weekly, and daily backup jobs

   d. QIC, DAT, and DLT tape drives

7. Network backup devices most commonly use which drive interface?

   a. IDE

   b. SCSI

   c. USB

   d. Parallel port

8. How does Windows Backup verify the data written to the backup medium?

9. When you restart the computer in Directory Services Restore Mode, what logon must you use? Why?

CASE SCENARIO

You are designing a backup solution for your company network. To make it easier to back up valuable company data, you have supplied each of the network's 125 users with a home folder on a shared server drive and have instructed the users to store all their data files in their home folder. You have also created disk quotas granting each user a maximum of 1 GB of storage space.

Because of this arrangement, you will be backing up only the network servers, not user workstations. In addition to the file servers hosting the users' home folders, there are also six Web servers, each with a 40-GB drive containing the home page files, a database server with an 80-GB drive hosting approximately 10 GB of database files, and an e-mail server with 25 GB of mail archives.

Based on this information, answer the following questions:

1. What is the approximate total amount of regularly changing data that you might have to back up each day?

    a. 60 GB

    b. 160 GB

    c. 360 GB

    d. 480 GB

2. Assuming that you decide to perform a weekly full backup and daily incremental backups, approximately how much data from the six Web servers can you expect to find on each incremental backup tape? Explain your answer.

3. Based on the information shown earlier in Table 4-1, which type of magnetic tape drive would best be suited for this network, assuming that you want to use only a single tape for your daily incremental backups?

    a. DLT

    b. 8 mm

    c. QIC

    d. DAT

CHAPTER 5
MAINTAINING THE OPERATING SYSTEM

All viable software products are in a constant state of development, and the manufacturers periodically release updates and upgrades. Operating systems are no exception, and it is important to keep your Microsoft Windows Server 2003 systems up to date. Updating a single computer is a simple task, but updating a large fleet of computers in a timely and efficient fashion is much more complicated. In this chapter, you learn about the types of operating system updates that Microsoft releases, and about some of the methods you can use to apply those updates.

Upon completion of this chapter, you will be able to:

- Understand the difference between service packs and hotfixes

- Deploy service packs using Windows Update, Automatic Updates, and group policies

- Integrate service packs and hotfixes into a Windows Server 2003 operating system installation

- Use Microsoft Baseline Security Analyzer

- Install and configure a Microsoft Software Update Services server

- Understand Per Server and Per Device or Per User licensing modes

- Configure licenses using the Choose Licensing Mode tool in Control Panel and the Licensing administrative tool

- Create license groups

WINDOWS OPERATING SYSTEM UPDATES

At one time, updating software was a relatively simple matter. If a problem arose in an application or operating system, the manufacturer released an update in the form of a patch that users applied to their computers. An *update* is a minor revision to a software product that is usually intended to address specific performance issues rather than add new features. When it came time to produce the next version of the software, the manufacturer incorporated all of the patches into an upgrade release. An *upgrade* is a major revision that might include new features as well as all of the existing patches for the previous version of the product.

> **NOTE** **Exam Objectives** *The objectives for the 70-290 exam require students to be able to "manage [a] software update infrastructure."*

As software products grew more complex, the number of programming problems tended to increase as well, and so did the number of patches. Some products, particularly operating systems, could have dozens of patch releases between upgrades. Updating applications and operating systems therefore became increasingly problematic for several reasons, including the following:

- **Number of patches** When there are a large number of patches for a software product, it becomes difficult to keep track of which patches have been applied and which versions of the product files are being used in a particular installation.

- **Patching order** When patches are applied in different orders, the resulting software configurations can be different, particularly if a product has multiple patches containing different versions of the same files.

The result of these problems is a nightmare for technical support people trying to troubleshoot an installation of the software. Determining which patches have been applied and the order in which they were applied is the only way to ascertain what versions of the program files are actually in use.

Service Packs

When faced with the hundreds of patches required for its modern operating systems, Microsoft eventually chose to use a different method of releasing its updates. Instead of many small patch releases, Microsoft creates larger interim releases called service packs. A **service pack** is a collection of patches and other updates that are tested and packaged as a single unit. A single installation program applies all of the updates at once, producing a consistent software configuration on every computer to which the service pack is applied.

Service packs simplify the update process for everyone involved. For Microsoft, releasing updates in a service pack means that it can test the entire package as a whole rather than having to test many different patch combinations. For system administrators and end users, the installation process is reduced to running a single program rather than performing many separate patch installations. For technical support personnel, the troubleshooting process is simplified because they do not have to deal with large numbers of patch releases that might have been installed in any order. It is easy to determine what service packs have been installed on a Windows 2000, Windows XP, or Windows Server 2003 computer by looking at the General tab in the System Properties dialog box (as shown in Figure 5-1).

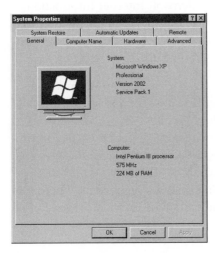

Figure 5-1   The System Properties dialog box

Microsoft service pack releases are cumulative, meaning that every service pack for a particular product contains all of the updates since the last major release of the product, including all previous service packs. Therefore, when you perform a new installation of a Windows operating system or other Microsoft product, you only have to apply the most recent service pack.

Service Pack Releases
Microsoft releases operating system service packs in three forms:

- **CD-ROM**   Service packs are available on CD-ROM directly from Microsoft for a nominal fee. The CD contains the service pack installation files and an installation program called Update.exe. The disk also contains the service pack documentation, deployment tools, and updated support tools, which aren't included as part of a downloaded installation.

- **Express download**   The express download consists only of the few files needed to begin the service pack download process. When you run the installation program, the software examines your system, accesses the Microsoft Web site, and downloads the files needed to complete the update. Because the installation program checks to see what service packs are already installed on the computer, it can download only the files it needs, which can significantly reduce the size of the download. To run an express installation, the computer must have access to the Internet.

- **Network download**   The network download option consists of the entire service pack in the form of a single executable archive file. It is intended for network administrators who have to deploy the service pack on large fleets of computers. Once you perform the initial download, you can launch the executable to install the service pack on any computer running the operating system. No additional Internet access is needed. However, because this version contains all of the service pack files, the download can be extremely large, often 100 MB or more.

One-Time Installation

When you install a service pack on a computer running one of the Windows operating systems, the installation program applies only the updates for the components installed on the system. For example, if you have Microsoft Internet Information Services (IIS) and Certificates Services installed on a computer running Windows Server 2003, installing a service pack will apply any updates for those two components but not updates for other components that are not installed.

At one time, if you modified the hardware or software configuration on a computer running Windows NT, you had to reapply the latest service pack to install the updated software for the components you just installed. However, starting with Windows 2000, this is no longer necessary. The service pack installation program now stores the location of a cabinet (.cab) file containing all of the updated drivers to the computer, as well as an information file called Layout.inf. This ensures that whenever you install a new operating system component, whether it is a device driver, an application, or a service, the system uses the latest version of the files from the service pack release.

Hotfixes

Although the schedule for service pack releases is fluid, the updates appear relatively infrequently, usually no more than once a year. However, it is not unusual for operating system issues to arise that require immediate attention and cannot wait for the next service pack release. For these occasions, Microsoft also releases individual patches, which it calls hotfixes. A **hotfix** is a software update that addresses one specific issue. Like service packs, hotfixes are released as a single executable file that installs the patch on the computer on which you run it. Microsoft typically releases hotfixes in conjunction with a Knowledge Base article that explains the problem and the circumstances in which users or administrators should apply the update.

> **MORE INFO**   **Microsoft Knowledge Base**   The Microsoft Knowledge Base is a library of articles providing support information for all Microsoft products. You can access the Knowledge Base at http://support.microsoft.com.

Unlike service packs, which Microsoft recommends that you install on all computers, hotfixes are often intended only for systems experiencing a particular problem or running a particular hardware or software configuration. You should always familiarize yourself with the function of a hotfix and the conditions of its use before installing it on a computer.

When to Update?

The question of when to apply service packs and hotfixes has been hotly debated among system administrators over the years. Not every update release has turned out to be rock solid, and some administrators are leery of applying them until they are shown to be stable. In fact, some people prefer to wait for Service Pack 3 to be released before they install Service Pack 2.

While this prudence might have once been practical, today it is not. Service packs and particularly hotfixes are often released to address specific security issues such as new viruses or other threats, and it is often important to deploy these updates in a timely fashion. However, this is not to say that everyone should immediately install every update as soon as it is released.

For a stand-alone computer, the Windows Update Web site makes the process of downloading and applying updates easy, and in most cases you can uninstall Microsoft updates when necessary. Therefore, most users can safely apply updates as they are released. However, in a network environment, the decision about which updates to install and when to install them should not be left up to the individual user. Administrators must be responsible for obtaining updates when they are released, and for deploying them on the network in a timely manner. However, network administrators should not immediately install every update that appears. It is important to test the update releases first, and this is one of the reasons why an enterprise should have a set of well-defined update policies in place.

Software update policies are designed to aid the network administrator in performing the following tasks:

- **Remain aware of new update releases.**   Microsoft frequently releases software updates that might or might not be applicable to the systems on your network. Network administrators must be aware of new releases when they occur and must understand the specific issues each release addresses.

- **Determine which computers need to be updated.**   In some cases, a new update release might apply only to computers performing a specific function, using a specific application or feature, or containing a particular hardware device. Network administrators must understand each release's specific function and determine which computers require the update.

- **Test update releases on multiple system configurations.**   A software update that causes a malfunction might be just an annoyance on a single computer, but on a large network, it can be a catastrophe. Network administrators must perform their own tests of all updates before deploying them on the entire network.

- **Deploy update releases on large fleets.**   Manually installing software updates on hundreds or thousands of computers requires enormous amounts of time, effort, and expense. To deploy updates on a large network efficiently, the process must be automated.

Microsoft offers tools that help the administrator accomplish these tasks, such as those discussed in the following sections.

Testing Security Updates

Before you deploy software updates on a network, you must test them to make sure they are compatible with all your system configurations. The amount and type of testing depends on the nature of the updates and the complexity of your network. For a major update such as a service pack, testing should be extensive. You might want to test the release on an isolated lab network first, and then do a pilot deployment on a part of your production network before proceeding with the general deployment. For smaller, minor updates, a pilot deployment might be sufficient testing, followed by a general deployment if no problems occur.

Uninstalling Service Packs

When you install a service pack, the installation program always gives you the opportunity to save backup copies of all the operating system files that the service pack replaces. This makes it possible to uninstall the service pack at a later time and restore the original system configuration, if necessary.

USING MICROSOFT BASELINE SECURITY ANALYZER

Microsoft Baseline Security Analyzer (MBSA) is a graphical tool (shown in Figure 5-2) that can check for common security lapses on a single computer or multiple computers running various Windows operating system versions. These lapses are typically due to incorrect or incomplete configuration of security features and failure to install security updates. The security faults that MBSA can detect are as follows:

- **Missing security updates**   Using a list of current update releases obtained from a Microsoft Internet server or from a local Microsoft Software Update Services (SUS) server, MBSA determines whether all the required service packs and security updates have been installed on the computer; if not, it compiles a list of the updates that need to be installed.

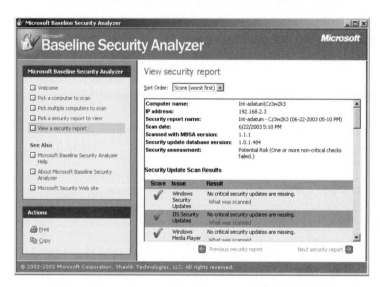

Figure 5-2   The Microsoft Baseline Security Analyzer interface

> **NOTE**   **Hfnetchk.exe**   MBSA replaces an earlier Microsoft update checking utility called Hfnetchk.exe, which operates from the command line and only checks computers for missing updates. MBSA includes all the functionality of Hfnetchk.exe, including the command-line interface, which you can activate by running the Mbsacli.exe executable with the /hf parameter. This enables administrators to continue using batch files and scripts, incorporating Htnetchk.exe commands with a minimum of modification.

- **Account vulnerabilities**   MBSA checks to see if the Guest account is activated on the computer, whether more than two accounts have Administrator privileges, whether anonymous users have too much access to system information, and whether the computer is configured to use the Autologon feature.

- **Improper passwords**   MBSA checks the passwords on all the computer's accounts to see if they are configured to expire, are blank, or are too simple. This check is not performed on domain controllers.

- **File system vulnerabilities**   MBSA checks to see whether all the disk drives on the computer are using the NTFS file system.

- **IIS and SQL vulnerabilities**   If the computer is running Internet Information Services (IIS) or Microsoft SQL Server, MBSA examines these applications for a variety of security weaknesses.

In addition, MBSA displays other information about security on the computer, such as a list of shares, the Windows operating system version number, and whether auditing is enabled.

> **NOTE   Downloading MBSA**   MBSA is not included with Windows Server 2003, but it is available without charge for download from the Microsoft Web site.

MBSA is an informational tool that can display security information about a computer, but it cannot do anything to remedy the vulnerabilities that it finds. You can use MBSA to determine which security updates to install on specific computers, but to develop effective update policies, you must implement a system to keep track of which security updates have been installed on every computer in the enterprise.

USING WINDOWS UPDATE

Windows Update is a Web site, maintained by Microsoft, that enables computers running Windows Server 2003 and most other versions of Microsoft Windows to locate and download the latest operating system and driver updates and patches. When you access the Windows Update site—by clicking Start, pointing to All Programs, and selecting Windows Update, or by using the URL *http://windowsupdate.microsoft.com*—the computer downloads an application that examines the computer's current configuration and compiles a list of all the updates and patches the system might need (as shown in Figure 5-3), in the following categories:

- Critical updates and service packs
- Version-specific Windows updates
- Driver updates

The user can then select from the list of updates, download them, and install them all at once, thereby simplifying the maintenance process.

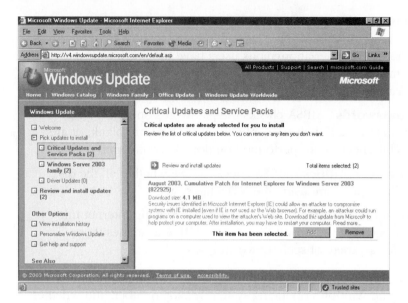

Practice using
Windows
Update by doing
Exercise 5.1,
"Using Windows
Update," now.

Figure 5-3   The Windows Update Web site interface

For a single user running a home computer, the Windows Update Web site is a great way to keep a computer current, but it is generally not suitable for use on networks, for the following reasons:

- **Bandwidth**   Each time a computer receives an update release using Windows Update, it downloads the software from a Microsoft server on the Internet. On a large network, this would mean that hundreds or thousands of computers would be downloading the same files. For small updates, this might not be a problem, but Windows service packs are usually more than 100 MB, and downloading the same file for every computer could monopolize an enormous amount of the network's Internet bandwidth.

- **Testing**   Although Microsoft tests its updates carefully before releasing them, it cannot possibly test every combination of configuration settings and software products. Therefore, it is possible for a particular update to cause problems with some or all of the computers on your network. Here again, for a single computer, this might not be a major issue, but if an update causes a problem on all a network's computers, the loss of productivity and the added burden on technical support personnel could be catastrophic.

  NOTE   **Windows Update and Software Update Services**   The drawbacks listed here to using Windows Update assume that the computer is configured to access the Windows Update Web site on the Internet. However, it is also possible to configure Windows Update to access software updates from an SUS server on the local network. This practice eliminates potential for bandwidth and testing issues. You'll learn more about SUS later in this chapter.

Using Automatic Updates

Although you can always access the Windows Update Web site manually, using Internet Explorer, it is also possible to configure Windows Server 2003 to automatically download and install software updates as they become available. This feature is called Automatic Updates, and it is available in Windows Server 2003, Windows XP with Service Pack 1 installed, and Windows 2000 with Service Pack 3 installed.

> **NOTE   Obtaining Automatic Updates**   For clients running earlier releases of the supported operating systems, you can download Automatic Updates as a standalone client from the Microsoft SUS Web site at *http://go.microsoft.com/ fwlink/?LinkID=6930.*

By default, the Automatic Updates client in Windows Server 2003 is configured to connect automatically to a Windows Update server and download updates, and then prompt the user to install them. You can modify this default behavior by opening the System Properties dialog box from Control Panel and selecting the Automatic Updates tab (as shown in Figure 5-4), or by launching the Automatic Updates Setup Wizard by clicking the Stay Current With Automatic Updates icon in the taskbar tray. You can also configure Automatic Updates using a group policy object (GPO), as described in "Configuring Automatic Updates" later in this chapter.

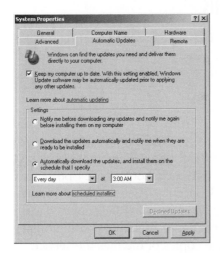

Figure 5-4   The Automatic Updates tab of the System Properties dialog box

When you configure Automatic Updates, you can select from the following three options:

- **Notify Me Before Downloading Any Updates And Notify Me Again Before Installing Them On My Computer**   When new updates are available, the computer creates an entry in the System log (which you can access using Event Viewer) and notifies the system's administrators by means of a balloon in the taskbar tray.

- **Download The Updates Automatically And Notify Me When They Are Ready To Be Installed**   The computer downloads updates from the Windows Update site as they become available, using the Background Intelligent Transfer Service (BITS) to perform the file transfer using idle network bandwidth. BITS ensures that network performance is not affected by the file transfers. The Automatic Updates client then confirms the Microsoft digital signature on the downloaded files, examines the cyclical redundancy check (CRC) on each package, and notifies the system's administrators of their presence, using a System log entry and a balloon in the taskbar tray. The administrator can then select the updates to install from a list of those downloaded.

Practice using Automatic Updates by doing Exercise 5-2, "Configuring Automatic Updates," now.

■ **Automatically Download The Updates, And Install Them On The Schedule That I Specify**   The computer downloads updates from the Windows Update site as they become available, using BITS, and installs them at a specific time each day or each week. If an administrator is logged on at the scheduled time, a countdown message appears prior to the installation, and the administrator has the option to delay the installation until the next scheduled time. If a nonadministrator is logged on, a warning dialog box appears, but the user cannot delay the installation. If no user is logged on, installation occurs automatically. If the installed updates require that the system be restarted, a five-minute countdown notification appears, informing users of the impending restart. Only an administrator can cancel the restart.

DEPLOYING UPDATES ON A NETWORK

A network administrator who decides not to have users download their own operating system updates from the Internet can use a variety of alternative methods of delivering the updates to the individual computers on the network, as described in the following sections.

Installing Service Packs Manually

When you purchase a service pack CD, you receive a disk containing all of the service pack files in expanded form. To install the service pack, you run the Update.exe program in the Update folder. This launches the Service Pack Setup Wizard (shown in Figure 5-5), which takes you through the process of installing the service pack. After you agree to the supplemental end user license agreement, the wizard prompts you to specify whether you want to create archive copies of the files the service pack replaces so you can uninstall the service pack later, if needed. After the installation is completed, you are prompted to restart the computer.

Figure 5-5   The Windows XP Service Pack 1 Setup Wizard

When you download the network version of a service pack, you receive a single executable archive file with a name that specifies the operating system for which the update is intended and the number of the service pack release. For example, the archive file for Windows XP Service Pack 1 is Xpsp1.exe. When you run the executable, the computer expands all of the files in the archive, writes them to a temporary directory on the system's drive, and then executes the Update.exe file, so the installation proceeds just as with the CD version. You can put the archive file on a network share and run it from any computer on the network. The archive program always copies the installation files to the local drive and runs the installation program from there.

The service pack's Update.exe file and the network download archive also support command-line switches that you can use to affect the installation process. You can run the executable with these switches from a command prompt or from the Run dialog box. The switches, which are the same for both Update.exe and the archive file, are as follows:

- **/D:*foldername***   By default, the installation program creates backup copies of all the files it overwrites to a folder called $ntservicepackuninstall$. This switch enables you to specify an alternate folder name for the backup files.

- **/F**   Causes the installation program to close all open applications without saving data when it restarts the computer after the installation is completed.

- **/L**   Displays a list of all hotfixes installed on the computer.

- **/N**   Prevents the installation program from creating backup copies of the files overwritten during the installation.

- **/O**   Causes the installation program to overwrite original equipment manufacturer (OEM) files during the installation without notifying the user.

- **/Q**   Runs the installation in quiet mode. In this mode, the installation program uses the default values for all options but does not display a progress indicator or any error messages.

- **/S:*foldername***   Incorporates the service pack distribution files with the operating system distribution files to create an integrated installation. This process is also known as *slipstreaming*. The foldername placeholder lets you specify the path to the operating system distribution files.

- **/U**   Runs the installation in unattended setup mode. In this mode, the installation program uses the default values for all options and displays a progress indicator, but only critical error messages stop the installation process.

- **/X**   Causes the archive executable to expand all of the files in the archive and store them in an i386 directory structure on the local drive without executing the Update.exe program.

- **/X:*foldername***   Causes the archive executable to expand all of the files in the archive and store them in the folder you specify on the local drive without executing the Update.exe program.

- **/Z**   Prevents the installation program from restarting the computer after the installation is completed. This option is most commonly used when you plan to install hotfixes immediately after the service pack and want to defer the system restart until after the hotfix installations.

Practice expanding a service pack archive by doing Exercise 5-3, "Expanding a Service Pack," now.

Installing Hotfixes Manually

As with service packs, users can download and install hotfixes through the Windows Update Web site, but it is also possible to download them as individual executables. This enables network administrators to deploy hotfixes to large numbers of computers without having to perform redundant Internet downloads. A hotfix distribution file is an executable archive file, much like the network download file for a service pack, but much smaller. The filename uses the following format:

***OperatingSystem**-KB**KnowledgeBase#-Platform-Language**.exe*

For example, one particular security update for Windows Server 2003 is named WindowsServer2003-KB823980-x86-ENU.exe. The number 823980 is that of the Knowledge Base article describing the issue the hotfix addresses, x86 is the processor platform for which the hotfix is intended, and ENU indicates that the hotfix is for the U.S. English version of Windows Server 2003.

> **NOTE** **Hotfix File Replacement**   Unlike service packs, hotfixes update only the software that is actually installed on the computer when you run the installation program. If you remove an operating system component and later reinstall it, you must also reinstall any hotfixes that apply to that component.

Running a hotfix executable extracts the files in the archive to a temporary folder on the local system and runs the Update.exe installation program, just as with a service pack. Hotfixes always make backup copies of overwritten files for uninstall purposes by default, saving them to a hidden folder beneath the system root called $NtUninstallKB######$, where ###### is the hotfix's Knowledge Base article number.

To modify the default behavior of the hotfix installation program, you can run it with any of the following switches:

- **/F**   Causes the installation program to close all open applications without saving data when it restarts the computer after the installation is completed.
- **/L**   Displays a list of all hotfixes installed on the computer.
- **/N**   Prevents the installation program from creating backup copies of the files overwritten during the installation.
- **/Q**   Runs the installation in quiet mode. In this mode, the installation program uses the default values for all options but does not display a progress indicator or any error messages.
- **/U**   Runs the installation in unattended setup mode. In this mode, the installation program uses the default values for all options and displays a progress indicator, but only critical error messages stop the installation process.
- **/X**   Causes the archive executable to expand all of the files in the archive and store them in a directory structure on the local drive without executing the Update.exe program.
- **/Z**   Prevents the installation program from restarting the computer after the installation is completed.

NOTE Hotfix Checks   When you attempt to install a hotfix, the installation program always checks to see what service packs have been installed on the computer. If the hotfix you are installing is older than the system's currently installed service pack, the installation halts because the hotfix was already applied as part of that service pack. If the hotfix is newer than the currently installed service pack, the installation proceeds.

Chaining Hotfixes

Starting with the Windows 2000 Service Pack 3 release, all hotfixes include a program called Qchain.exe that makes it possible to install multiple hotfixes one after the other without restarting the computer after each one. If you install multiple hotfixes that include different versions of the same file, Qchain.exe ensures that the system is using the correct version of that file when the installation is completed.

To chain hotfix installations, you run the hotfix installation programs with the /Z command-line switch, which prevents the programs from restarting the computer. However, you must remember to restart the system after the last hotfix is installed so the hotfixes can take effect. To automate the process of installing multiple hotfixes, you can create a batch file like the following:

```
WindowsServer2003-KB8239809-x86-ENU.exe /Z /U
WindowsServer2003-KB8239810-x86-ENU.exe /Z /U
WindowsServer2003-KB8239811-x86-ENU.exe /U
```

Notice that the first two hotfix installation commands in the batch file include the /Z switch, preventing a restart, while the last command omits this switch so the computer will restart after all of the hotfixes are installed. All three commands include the /U switch, which prevents the installations from pausing for user input.

You can also incorporate a service pack installation into the batch file, thus automating the entire postinstallation update process, as follows:

```
Update.exe /Z /U
WindowsServer2003-KB8239809-x86-ENU.exe /Z /U
WindowsServer2003-KB8239810-x86-ENU.exe /Z /U
WindowsServer2003-KB8239811-x86-ENU.exe /U
```

Slipstreaming

When you install new computers on a network, the operating system installation is not necessarily the end of the process. You might have to install a service pack and numerous hotfixes as well. While it is certainly possible to install each component separately, it is often preferable to incorporate the service pack and the hotfixes into the operating system installation. This process is called **slipstreaming**.

Slipstreaming a Service Pack

To slipstream a service pack into the Windows Server 2003 operating system installation, you must first create a distribution folder on a network share and copy the i386 folder from the Windows Server 2003 installation CD to that folder. Then, from the folder containing the service pack installation files, you run the Update.exe program or the archive executable with the /S switch, specifying the location of the distribution folder you created, as in the following examples:

```
Update.exe /s:distfolder
W2k3sp1.exe /s:distfolder
```

The installation program extracts the service pack files from the archive to a temporary directory (if necessary) and then copies the files to the appropriate places in the distribution folder. You can then start the operating system installation from the distribution folder, and the service pack files will be installed at the same time.

Using Group Policies

Another method of automating service pack installations is to use the combination of Windows Installer and the Software Installation policy in a GPO. Windows Installer is a program that installs software that has been saved as a Windows Installer Package file with an .msi extension. Service pack releases include a Windows Installer Package version of the installation program called Update.msi. Update.msi is located in the update folder on a service pack CD. If you have downloaded the network version of the service pack, you must expand the archive file by running it with the /X switch before you can use Update.msi.

To deploy a service pack using its Update.msi file and group policies, you must select an Active Directory object containing the computers you want to update. If all of the computers on your network are running the same version of Windows, you can configure the Software Installation policy in the default domain GPO associated with your Active Directory domain object. If you have computers running various versions of Windows, you can create an organizational unit (OU) object for each version and then create a GPO containing the correct Windows Installer Package for each OU, or you can create multiple Windows Installer Packages in the default domain GPO and use permissions to specify which computers should receive each package.

> **MORE INFO**   **Using GPOs**   For more information on using group policy objects, see the course for exam 70-294, "Planning, Implementing, and Maintaining a Microsoft Windows Server 2003 Active Directory Infrastructure."

▶ **Adding a Windows Installer Package**

To add the Windows Installer Package to your default domain GPO, use the following procedure:

1. Log on to Windows Server 2003 as Administrator.

2. Expand the service pack archive to a distribution folder on a network share.

3. Click Start, point to Administrative Tools, and click Active Directory Users And Computers. The Active Directory Users And Computers console appears.

4. Select the domain icon in the scope pane and, from the Action menu, select Properties. The Properties dialog box for your domain object appears.

5. Select the Group Policy tab, and then click Edit. The Group Policy Object Editor console appears.

6. In the scope pane, expand the Computer Configuration/Software Settings folder and select the Software Installation icon.

   The User Configuration heading also has a Software Settings folder and a Software Installation icon, but you cannot use them to install service packs. You must use the Computer Configuration heading.

7. On the Action menu, point to New and select Package. An Open dialog box appears.

8. Type the full path to the Update.msi Windows Installation Package file in the Update subfolder of your distribution folder. A Deploy Software dialog box appears.

   Be sure to use a Universal Naming Convention (UNC) name for the path to the package file, not a drive letter. For example, you can use \\Server01\d$\sp1\i386\update\update.msi, but not D:\sp1\i386 \update\update.msi.

9. Click OK to accept the default Assigned option. The installation package for the service pack appears in the details pane (as shown in Figure 5-6).

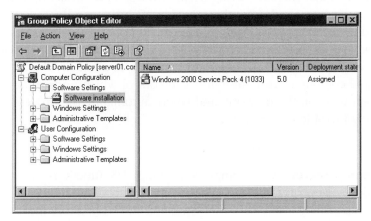

Figure 5-6   The Group Policy Object Editor console with a service pack installation package

The next time the computers in the domain restart, they will download the service pack installation files from the specified share and install them.

USING MICROSOFT SOFTWARE UPDATE SERVICES

Deploying any software on a large network is a complicated task, and operating system updates are no exception. What might be a simple task on a single computer turns into a major project when you have hundreds or thousands of computers. SUS is a free product that notifies administrators when new security updates are available, downloads the updates, and then deploys them to the computers on the network (as shown in Figure 5-7).

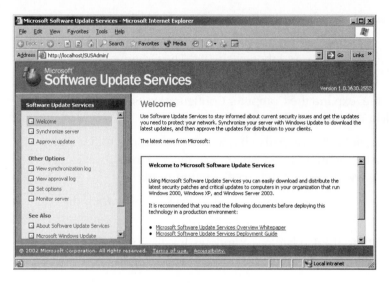

Figure 5-7   The SUS administration interface

MORE INFO   *Obtaining SUS*   SUS with Service Pack 1 (SP1) is not included with Windows Server 2003 or any of the Windows operating systems, but it is available as a free download from Microsoft's Web site at *http://www.microsoft.com/windowsserversystems/SUS/default.mspx*.

As mentioned earlier in this chapter, having users download and install their own operating system updates using the Windows Update Web site can be a waste of time and bandwidth. SUS is essentially an intranet version of the Windows Update Web site that eliminates the need for each computer to download software updates from the Internet and prevents administrators from having to manually deploy the updates on multiple computers. Administrators can control which updates are applied to the computers on the network, and when, automating the process so that it is completely invisible to the users.

SUS consists of the following components:

■ **Synchronization server**   One computer, running SUS, functions as a synchronization server, downloading software updates from the Windows Update Web site as they are released. The administrator can allow the downloads to occur as needed, schedule them to occur at specific times (such as off-peak hours), or trigger them manually. Once SUS downloads the updates, it stores them on the server. This eliminates the need for the administrator to continually check the Windows Update Web site for new releases.

■ **Intranet Windows Update server**   Once the SUS server has downloaded the updates, the administrator must decide whether the server should deploy them immediately to the network or save them for testing and later deployment. When updates are ready for deployment, SUS functions as the Windows Update server for the computers on the network, except that this server is on the intranet and does not require the clients to access the Internet.

■ **Automatic Updates** Automatic Updates is a Windows operating system feature that enables computers to download and install software updates with no user intervention. You can configure this feature on your client computers so that they retrieve the updates from an SUS server on the local network rather than from the Windows Update Web site, thereby restricting the updates to those approved by the network administrator.

PLANNING **SUS Operating System Requirements** SUS runs only on Windows Server 2003 and Windows 2000 Server with Service Pack 2 or later. SUS clients must be running Windows Server 2003, Windows 2000, or Windows XP.

▶ **Deploying SUS**

The process of deploying SUS consists of the following basic steps:

1. **Install an SUS server.** SUS is a series of Web pages and intranet applications providing client and administrator access to the service. You must have IIS installed on the server before you install SUS.

2. **Synchronize the server.** Synchronization is the process by which the SUS server downloads updates from the Windows Update Web site on the Internet and stores them on the local drive.

3. **Approve updates.** Before clients can access the updates stored on an SUS server, they must be approved, either manually by an administrator or automatically. Administrators might choose to put new updates through a testing regimen before approving them for client access.

4. **Configure Automatic Updates clients.** Using group policies, you can configure the Automatic Updates feature on your client computers to obtain updates from your SUS server rather than from the Windows Update Web site.

Installing SUS

Because SUS uses Web sites for both client and administrative access, you must install IIS on your server before you install SUS. Windows Server 2003 includes the IIS software but does not install it by default. To install IIS, open Add Or Remove Programs in Control Panel, click Add/Remove Windows Components, and select Internet Information Services (IIS) from the list of Application Server components.

Once you have installed IIS, you can execute the SUS installation program you downloaded from the Microsoft Web site, which launches the Microsoft Software Update Services Setup Wizard. After you agree to the terms of the software's end-user license agreement, the wizard leads you through configuration of the following parameters:

■ **File Locations** Each Windows Update patch consists of two components: the patch file itself and metadata that specifies the platforms and languages to which the patch applies. SUS always downloads the metadata, which you use to approve updates and which clients on your intranet retrieve from the SUS server. You can choose whether to download the files themselves and, if so, where to save the updates. If you elect to maintain the update files on Microsoft Windows Update servers, your clients will connect to the SUS server to obtain the list of approved updates but will then connect to the Windows Update Web site to download the files. If you select to store the updates locally, you must use a folder on an NTFS drive. A minimum of 6 GB of free disk space is recommended.

■ **Language Settings**   Specifies the languages for which you want to store updates on the server. If all of your clients use the English-language version of Windows, you can choose the English Only option. If you have clients using languages other than English, you can download updates in all available languages or choose specific languages. This parameter is configured only if you have selected to store updates locally.

■ **Update Approval Settings**   When SUS downloads a new version of an update that has already been approved, this setting specifies whether the new version should be approved automatically or wait for manual approval.

> **NOTE   SUS URLs**   When the wizard concludes, it displays the URL for the SUS server's administrative interface and the URL that clients must use to retrieve updates from the server. Take note of these URLs because you will need them to administer the server and when configuring your clients.

The Microsoft Software Update Services Setup Wizard installs the following three components on the server:

■ The Software Update Synchronization Service, which downloads content to the SUS server

■ An IIS Web site that services update requests from Automatic Updates clients

■ An SUS administration Web page, from which you can synchronize the SUS server and approve updates

When the installation is completed, Internet Explorer displays the SUS administration Web page.

> **NOTE   Internet Explorer Enhanced Security Configuration**   You might need to add your server to the Local Intranet trusted site list to access the site. Open Internet Explorer and select Internet Options from the Tools menu. Select the Security tab, select Trusted Sites, and click Sites. Add your server name to the trusted site list.

Synchronizing SUS

The two main administrative tasks for SUS are synchronizing the server and approving the updates. When you click the Synchronize Server hyperlink on the administrative home page, you see the interface shown in Figure 5-8. On this page, you can schedule synchronizations to occur on a regular schedule or trigger them manually.

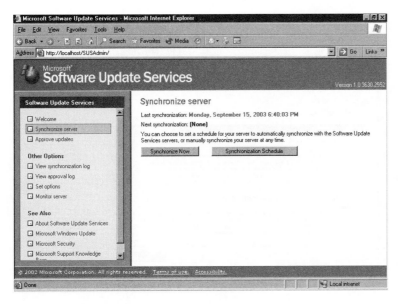

Figure 5-8   The SUS Synchronize Server page

To schedule synchronizations, you click the Synchronization Schedule button to display the Schedule Synchronization dialog box (shown in Figure 5-9). During the synchronization process, the server connects to the Windows Update Web site and downloads a catalog of all available updates. Then, depending on the settings you specified during the installation, SUS either downloads all of the new updates or incorporates the metadata into its own catalog of updates.

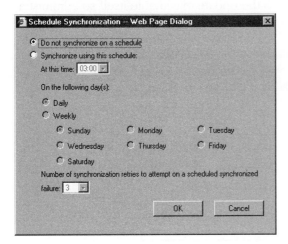

Figure 5-9   The Schedule Synchronization dialog box

Approving Updates

When the synchronization process is complete, you are taken to the Approve Updates page, shown in Figure 5-10. Here, an administrator can view the list of synchronized updates and select the ones that should be made available to clients.

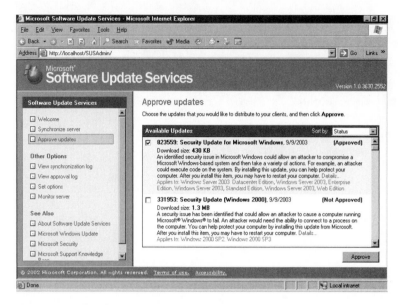

Figure 5-10   The SUS Approve Updates page

Each of the entries in the list of updates has a Details hyperlink that displays an Update Details page like that shown in Figure 5-11. This page provides information about the selected update, including the platforms for which it is intended, the languages for which it is available, its date and size, and the setup parameters that the update will use when it is installed on a client computer. The Update Details page also contains a link to the Knowledge Base article (on Microsoft's support Web site) associated with the update and a link to the update executable itself so administrators can access the updates for testing purposes.

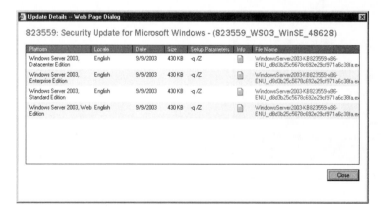

Figure 5-11   The SUS Update Details page

Configuring Automatic Updates

Once the SUS server is installed and operational, the next step is to configure the clients to make use of it. Earlier in this chapter, you learned about the Automatic Updates feature available in Windows Server 2003, Windows XP, and Windows 2000. By default, Automatic Updates downloads the update files from the Windows Update Web site, but you can also configure this client to obtain updates from an

SUS server instead. To do this, you must configure the Automatic Updates client using group policies.

To deploy these or any group policies, you must select an Active Directory domain, site, or OU object, open its Properties dialog box, select the Group Policy tab, and launch the Group Policy Object Editor console by selecting a group policy and clicking Edit. In the Group Policy Object Editor console, expand the Computer Configuration, Administrative Templates, and Windows Components folders, and then select Windows Update to display the four policies shown in Figure 5-12.

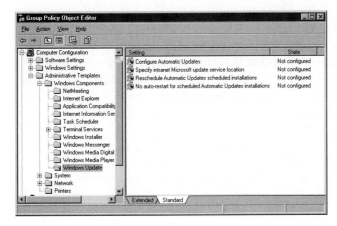

Figure 5-12   The Windows Update policies in the Group Policy Object Editor console

The policies are as follows:

- **Configure Automatic Updates**   Specifies the default behavior of the Automatic Updates client using the following three options: Notify For Download And Notify For Install, Auto Download And Notify For Install, and Auto Download And Schedule The Install. These are the same options that you can configure in the Automatic Updates tab of the client machine's System Properties dialog box.

- **Specify Intranet Microsoft Update Service Location**   Identifies the server from which the client will access Windows updates. This is the policy that enables you to redirect Automatic Updates clients to a server running SUS rather than the Windows Update Web site. In the Set The Intranet Update Service For Detecting Updates text box, you enter the client URL for your SUS server that the Microsoft Software Update Server Setup Wizard supplied to you during the installation. By default, the client logs its interactions on the SUS server from which it obtains updates. However, this policy also enables you to point clients to another IIS server for statistics logging. This makes it possible for clients to obtain updates from a local SUS server while logging their activities to a single central server for easier retrieval and analysis of the log data. The IIS logs are located in the *systemroot*\System32\Logfiles\W3svc1 folder.

- **Reschedule Automatic Updates Scheduled Installations**   If installations are scheduled and the client computer is turned off at the scheduled time, the default behavior is to wait for the next scheduled time. This policy, if set to a value between 1 and 60, causes Automatic Updates to reschedule the installation to occur the specified number of minutes after the next system startup.

- **No Auto-Restart For Scheduled Automatic Updates Installations** Causes Automatic Updates to forego a restart required by an installed update when a user is logged on to the system. Instead, the user is notified that a restart is required for installation to complete.

Once you configure the GPO and the policies take effect, the Automatic Updates clients poll their SUS server every 22 hours, minus a random offset (to prevent a surge in network traffic). After clients have downloaded the approved updates from the SUS server, they are installed and configured—manually or automatically—at the scheduled time. If an approved update is later unapproved by an administrator, that update is not uninstalled, but it will not be installed by any additional clients. Updates installed through SUS can be uninstalled manually, however, using Add Or Remove Programs in Control Panel.

> **NOTE** **Critical Updates** In some cases, an update addressing a critical security problem might be so important that you do not want to wait for your clients to poll, download, and install patches. In these cases, you should still install updates manually.

Building an SUS Topology

A single SUS server might be sufficient for a small organization, but for a large enterprise, you might want to have more than one. When you install multiple SUS servers on a network, you can configure them to interact using any one of the following topologies:

- **Multiple server topology** Each SUS server synchronizes its content from the Windows Update Web site and manages its own list of approved updates. This topology enables the administrator of each server to control that server's list of approved updates, and it also enables an organization to maintain a variety of patch and update configurations.

- **Strict parent/child topology** A parent SUS server synchronizes content from the Windows Update Web site and stores the updates in a local folder. The SUS administrator then approves the updates to be deployed to clients. Other SUS servers in the enterprise synchronize from the parent and are configured to synchronize both the update files and the list of approved updates. Clients can then retrieve updates from the closest SUS server. In this topology, administrators of child SUS servers cannot approve or disapprove updates; that task is performed on the parent SUS server only.

- **Loose parent/child topology** A parent SUS server synchronizes content from Windows Update and stores updates in a local folder. Other SUS servers in the enterprise synchronize from the parent. Unlike the strict configuration, these additional SUS servers do not synchronize the list of approved updates, so the administrator of each server can approve or disapprove updates independently. Although this topology increases administrative overhead, it is helpful when an organization wants to minimize Internet exposure and requires distributed power of update approval or a variety of client patch and update configurations.

SUS uses the multiple-server topology by default. To implement one of the parent/ child topologies, you access the Set Options page in the SUS server's administrative site and configure the Select Which Server To Synchronize Content From option. For a parent/child topology, you leave the default setting in place on the parent server and configure the child servers with the Synchronize From A Local Software Update Services Server option and the name of the parent server. For a strict parent/child topology, you also select the Synchronize List Of Approved Items Updated From This Location check box; for a loose parent/child topology, you leave the check box cleared.

SUS Monitoring

The Monitor Server page of the SUS administration Web site displays statistics that reflect the number of updates available for each platform, and the date and time of the most recent update. The information is summarized from the Windows Update metadata that is downloaded during each synchronization. Metadata information is written to disk and stored in memory to improve performance as systems request platform-appropriate updates.

You can also monitor SUS and Automatic Updates using the following logs:

- **Synchronization Log**   You can retrieve information about current or past synchronizations and the specific packages that were downloaded by clicking View Synchronization Log in the left navigation bar.

- **Approval Log**   For information about packages that have been approved, click View Approval Log in the left navigation bar.

- **Windows Update Log**   The Automatic Updates client logs activity in the *systemroot*\Windows Update.log file on the client's local hard disk.

- **Wutrack.bin**   The client's interaction with SUS is logged to the specified statistics server's IIS logs, which are typically stored in the *systemroot* \System32\Logfiles\W3svc1 folder.

SUS System Events

The synchronization service generates event log messages for each synchronization performed by the server and when updates are approved. These messages can be viewed in the System log using Event Viewer. The events relate to the following scenarios:

- **Unable to connect**   Automatic Updates could not connect to the update service (Windows Update or the computer's assigned SUS server).

- **Install ready—no recurring schedule**   Updates listed in the event were downloaded and are pending installation. An administrator must click the notification icon and click Install.

- **Install ready—recurring schedule**   Updates listed in the event are downloaded and will be installed at the date and time specified in the event.

- **Installation success**   Updates listed in the event were installed successfully.

- **Installation failure**   Updates listed in the event failed to install properly.

- **Restart required—no recurring schedule**   An update requires a restart. If installation behavior is set for notification, the restart must be performed manually. Windows cannot search for new updates until the restart has occurred.

- **Restart required—recurring schedule**   When Automatic Updates is configured to automatically install updates, an event is registered if an update requires restart. Restart will occur within five minutes. Windows cannot search for new updates until after the restart has occurred.

Troubleshooting SUS

SUS on a Windows Server 2003 computer might require the following troubleshooting steps:

- **Reloading the memory cache**   If no new updates appear since the last time you synchronized the server, it is possible that no new updates are available. However, it is also possible that memory caches are not loading new updates properly. From the SUS administration site, click Monitor Server and then click Refresh.

- **Restarting the synchronization service**   If you receive a message that the synchronization service is not running properly or if you cannot modify settings in the Set Options page of the SUS administration Web site, open the Services console from the Administrative Tools program group, right-click the Software Update Services Synchronization Service, and select Restart.

- **Restarting IIS**   If you cannot connect to the administration site or if clients cannot connect to the SUS server, restart the World Wide Web Publishing Service using the Services console.

ADMINISTERING SOFTWARE LICENSES

The End-User License Agreement (EULA) is more than just a nuisance that you must click through to begin installing a new operating system, update, or application. The EULA is a binding contract that gives you the legal right to use a piece of software. In an enterprise environment, managing software licenses is critically important, and Windows Server 2003 includes licensing tools that you use to register and monitor licenses and compliance.

> **NOTE** **Evaluation Editions**   The Evaluation Edition of Windows Server 2003 included on a supplemental CD-ROM with this book does not support licensing. You cannot follow along with the examples in this lesson without purchasing the full retail version of the product.

Obtaining a Client Access License

The server license for Windows Server 2003 enables you to install the operating system on a computer, but you need a **Client Access License (CAL)** before a user or device is legally authorized to connect to the server. CALs are typically obtained in bundles and might be included in your purchase of the operating system. For example, it is common to see Windows Server 2003 sold with a 5- or 10-user license package. However, if the operating system does not include any CALs, you must purchase them separately. Keep copies of your CAL certificates and your EULAs on file in the event that your organization is audited for licensing compliance.

> **NOTE   Upgrading Licenses**   When you upgrade a server from Windows NT 4 or Windows 2000 to Windows Server 2003, you must purchase CAL upgrades as well.

You must have a CAL for any connection to a Windows Server 2003 computer that uses server components, which include file and print services or authentication. Very few server applications run so independently that the client/server connection does not require a CAL. The most significant exception to the CAL requirement is unauthenticated access conducted through the Internet. Where there is no exchange of credentials during Internet access, such as Internet users browsing your Web site anonymously, no CAL is required. CALs are therefore not required for the Web Edition of Windows Server 2003.

There are two types of CALs: Windows Device CALs, which allow a device to connect to a server regardless of the number of users who might use that device, and Windows User CALs, which allow a user to connect to a server from a number of devices. Windows Device CALs are advantageous for an organization with multiple users per device, such as shift workers. Windows User CALs make most sense for an organization with employees who access the network from multiple or unknown devices.

> **NOTE   User and Device CALs**   The licensing tools and the user interface do not yet distinguish between Windows User and Windows Device CALs. A device CAL is registered indirectly, using license groups.

The number of CALs you require, and how you track those licenses, depends on which client access licensing mode you pursue. There are two licensing modes: Per Server licensing and Per Device or Per User licensing.

Per Server Licensing

Per Server Licensing requires a Windows User or Windows Device CAL for each concurrent connection. If a server is configured with 1,000 CALs, the 1,001st concurrent connection will be denied access. CALs are designated for use on a particular server, so if the same 1,000 users require concurrent connections to a second server, you must purchase another 1,000 CALs.

Per Server Licensing is advantageous only in limited-access scenarios, such as when a subset of your user population accesses a server product on very few servers. Per Server Licensing is less cost-effective in a situation where multiple users access multiple resources on multiple servers. If you are unsure which licensing mode is appropriate, select Per Server. The license agreement allows a no-cost, one-time, one-way conversion from Per Server to Per Device or Per User licensing when it becomes appropriate to do so.

Per Device or Per User Licensing

The **Per Device** or **Per User** licensing mode varies from the Per Seat scheme in previous versions of Windows. In this new mode, each device or user that connects to a server requires a CAL, but with that license the device or user can connect to a number of servers in the enterprise. Per User or Per Device mode is generally the mode of choice for distributed computing environments in which multiple users access multiple servers.

For example, a developer who uses a laptop and two desktops would require only one Windows User CAL. A fleet of 10 Tablet PCs that are used by 30 shift workers would require only 10 Windows Device CALs.

The total number of CALs equals the number of devices or users, or a mixture thereof, that access servers. CALs can be reassigned under certain conditions. For example, a Windows User CAL can be reassigned from a permanent employee to a temporary employee while the permanent employee is on leave. A Windows Device CAL can be reassigned to a loaner device while a device is being repaired.

The Per Server and Per Device or Per User licensing modes are illustrated in Table 5-1.

Table 5-1   CAL Licensing Modes

Per Server	Per User or Per Device

■ Traditionally licensed in Per Server mode when there are few servers and they require limited access.	■ Traditionally licensed in Per User or Per Device mode when there are many servers and they require frequent and widespread access.
■ The number of CALs needed is determined by the number of concurrent connections that are required.	■ Usually more economical when the number of CALs needed is determined by the number of users or devices, or both, that require access to the servers.

> **NOTE**   **Terminal Services Licenses**   Windows Server 2003 includes Terminal Services, which includes a two (concurrent) connection license for administrators to connect to a remote server. To have Terminal Services perform as an application server, permitting nonadministrative users to connect to hosted applications, you must acquire Terminal Services CALs, which are included in Windows XP Professional.

Licensing Tools

There are two utilities you can use to track and manage software licensing:

- **Licensing in Control Panel**   The Choose Licensing Mode tool found in Control Panel, shown in Figure 5-13, manages licensing requirements for a single computer running Windows Server 2003. You can use Licensing to add or remove CALs for a server running in Per Server mode, change the licensing mode from Per Server to Per Device or Per User, or configure licensing replication.

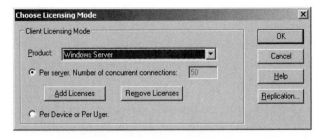

Figure 5-13   The Choose Licensing Mode tool in Control Panel

■ **Licensing in Administrative Tools**   The Licensing administrative tool, discussed in the next section, enables you to manage licensing for an enterprise by centralizing the control of licensing and license replication in a site-based model.

Administering Site Licensing

The License Logging service, which runs on each Windows Server 2003 computer, assigns and tracks licenses when clients access server resources. To ensure compliance, licensing information is replicated to a centralized licensing database on a server at the site. This server is called the site license server. A site administrator, or an administrator for the site license server, can then use the Licensing tool in the Administrative Tools program group to view and manage licensing for the entire site. This new license tracking and management capability incorporates licenses not just for file and print services, but also for IIS, Terminal Services, and other Microsoft products (such as Exchange and SQL Server).

The Site License Server
The site license server is typically the first domain controller created in a site. To find out what server is the license server for a site, open Active Directory Sites And Services, expand to select the Site node, and then right-click Licensing Site Settings and select Properties. The current site license server is displayed, as shown in Figure 5-14.

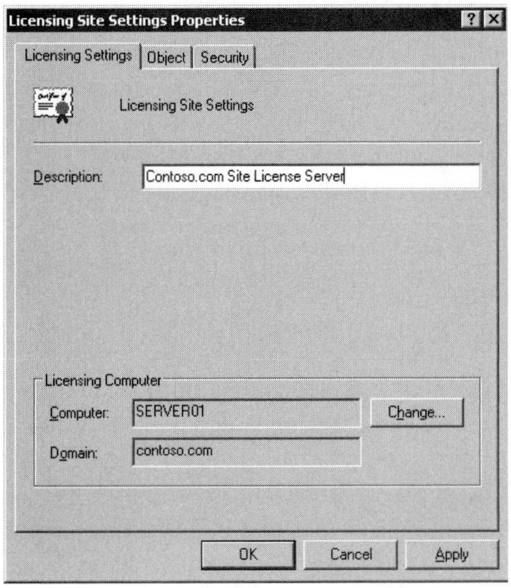

Figure 5-14   Identifying and changing the site license server with Active Directory Sites and Services

To assign the site license server role to another server or domain controller, click Change and select the desired computer. To retain the licensing history for your enterprise, you must stop the License Logging service on the new license server immediately after transferring the role, and then copy the following files from the old to the new licensing server:

- *Systemroot*\System32\Cpl.cfg, which contains the purchase history for your organization

- *Systemroot*\Lls\Llsuser.lls, which contains user information about the number of connections

- *Systemroot*\Lls\Llsmap.lls, which contains license group information

After all files have been copied, restart the License Logging service.

Administering Site Licenses

Once you have identified the site license server for a site, you can view the licensing information on that server by opening Licensing from the Administrative Tools program group. The Server Browser tab in Licensing (shown in Figure 5-15) enables you to manage licensing for an entire site or enterprise.

Figure 5-15   The Server Browser tab of the Microsoft Licensing administrative tool

The Server Browser tab of Licensing enables you to manage any server in any site or domain for which you have administrative authority. You can locate a server and, by right-clicking it and selecting Properties, manage that server's licenses. For each server product installed on that server, you can add or remove per-server licenses. You can also, where appropriate, convert the licensing mode. Remember that Per Server licensing mode issues a license when a user connects to the server product. When a user disconnects from the server product, the License Logging service makes the license available to another user.

The server properties also enable you to configure license replication, which you can configure on a server using its Licensing properties in Control Panel. By default, license information is replicated from a server's License Logging service to the site license server every 24 hours, and the system automatically staggers replication to avoid burdening the site licensing server. If you want to control replication schedules or frequency, you must manually vary the Start At time and Start Every frequency of each server replicating to a particular site license server.

To manage Per Device or Per User licensing, click Licensing from the Administrative Tools program group, and then select the New License command from the License menu. In the New Client Access License dialog box, select the server product and the number of licenses purchased. Licenses are added to the pool of licenses. As devices or users connect to the product anywhere in the site, they are allocated licenses from the pool, with one license for each device or user. After a pool of licenses is depleted, license violations occur when additional devices or users access the product.

The Purchase History tab in Licensing (shown in Figure 5-16) provides a historical overview of licenses purchased for a site, as well as the quantity, date, and administrator associated with the addition or removal of licenses.

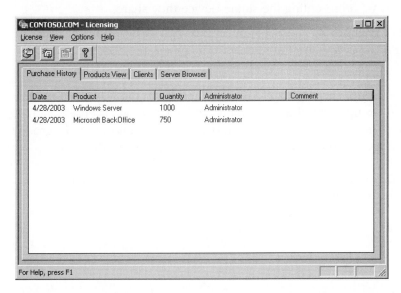

Figure 5-16   The Purchase History tab of the Microsoft Licensing administrative tool

To view cumulative information about licensing and compliance, select the Products View tab. This tab shows how many licenses have been purchased and allocated to users or devices (in Per Device or Per User mode) or the number of licenses purchased for all servers in the site and the peak connections reached to date (in Per Server mode). You can also determine compliance using the licensing status symbols shown in Table 5-2.

Table 5-2   Licensing Status Symbols

Symbol	Licensing Status
🗁	The product is in compliance with legal licensing requirements. The number of connections is less than the number of licenses purchased.
⚠	The product is not in compliance with legal licensing requirements. The number of connections exceeds the number of licenses purchased.
⬆	The product has reached the legal limit. The number of connections equals the number of licenses purchased. If additional devices or users will connect to the server product, you must purchase and log new licenses.

License Groups

Per Device or Per User licensing requires one CAL for each device. However, the License Logging service assigns and tracks licenses by username. When multiple users share one or more devices, you must create license groups, or else licenses will be consumed too rapidly. A **license group** is a collection of users who share one or more CALs. When a user connects to the server product, the License Logging service tracks the user by name but assigns a CAL from the allocation assigned to the license group. The concept is easiest to understand with examples such as the following:

- **10 users share a single handheld device for taking inventory.** You create a license group with the 10 users as members. The license group is assigned one CAL, representing the single device they share.

- **100 students occasionally use a computer lab with 10 computers.** You create a license group with the 100 students as members and allocate 10 CALs to the group.

To create a license group, click the Options menu and, from the Advanced menu, select New License Group. Enter the group name and allocate one license for each client device used to access the server. The number of licenses allocated to a group should correspond to the number of devices used by members of the group.

> **NOTE** **Exam Objectives** The objectives for the 70-290 exam require students to be able to "manage software site licensing."

SUMMARY

- Microsoft releases operating system updates in the form of service packs and hotfixes.

- A service pack is a collection of updates that have been tested together and approved for installation on all computers.

- A hotfix is a patch that addresses a single issue that is explained in an accompanying Microsoft Knowledge Base article. Hotfixes are not necessarily meant to be installed on all systems; some are intended only for computers performing certain tasks or experiencing a particular problem.

- Service packs can be obtained from Microsoft on CD for a small fee or downloaded free of charge. If the service pack is a single file, it can be extracted by executing the file with the /X switch.

- Service packs can be deployed manually on each computer, integrated into an operating system installation (slipstreamed), and automatically installed using group policies.

- Microsoft Software Update Services enables you to centralize and manage the approval and distribution of Windows critical updates and Windows security rollups. One or more SUS servers host lists of approved updates and, optionally but typically, the update files themselves. Automatic Updates clients are configured, usually through GPOs, to obtain updates from intranet SUS servers rather than directly from Microsoft Windows Update.

- Tracking and managing licenses and compliance is an important part of an administrator's job. Windows Server 2003 enables you to assign licenses based on concurrent connections to a specific server or to maintain a license for each device or user that connects to any number of servers in your enterprise.

- Licenses are replicated between servers' License Logging service and the site license server. The site license server can be identified using Active Directory Sites And Services, but site licensing is administered using the Licensing tool in the Administrative Tools programs group.

- A license group enables users to share one or more devices. The number of Windows Device CALs is assigned to the license group.

EXERCISES

Exercise 5-1: Using Windows Update

In this exercise, you use Windows Update to download the latest hotfixes for Windows Server 2003.

1. Log on to a Windows Server 2003 computer with Internet access as Administrator.

2. Connect to the Internet (if necessary).

3. Click Start, point to All Programs, and select Windows Update. The Windows Update site appears. Then a Security Warning dialog box appears, asking if you want to download and install the Windows Update application.

4. Review the security warning to ensure that the content is signed by Microsoft and then click Yes to continue.

5. Click the Scan For Updates link.

6. Click the Review And Install Updates link.

7. Review the updates listed and click Install Now. A Microsoft Windows Update dialog box appears, containing the license agreement for the updates.

8. Click Accept to agree to the terms of the license agreement. A Windows Update dialog box appears, containing a progress indicator.

9. When the installation is completed, if the installed updates require a restart, a Microsoft Internet Explorer message box appears, prompting you to restart the system. Click OK to restart the computer.

Exercise 5-2: Configuring Automatic Updates

In this exercise, you configure Automatic Updates to download updates at a scheduled time.

1. Log on to Windows Server 2003 as Administrator.

2. Click Start, point to Control Panel, and click System. The System Properties dialog box appears.

3. Select the Automatic Updates tab.

4. In the Settings box, select the Automatically Download The Updates, And Install Them On The Schedule That I Specify option.

5. In the scheduling drop-down lists, select Every Sunday and 6:00 A.M. Then click OK.

Exercise 5-3: Expanding a Service Pack

In this exercise, you expand the network version of a service pack into its component directory structure.

1. Log on to your computer as Administrator.

2. Open Windows Explorer and create a new folder on your drive C called temp.

3. Obtain a service pack for Windows Server 2003 or Windows XP from the Microsoft Web site or from your instructor and copy it to the temp folder you created on your computer.

4. Click Start, point to All Programs, point to Accessories, and click Command Prompt. A command prompt window appears.

5. In the command prompt window, type **cd\temp**. A C:\temp> prompt appears.

6. At the prompt, type the full name of the downloaded service pack file followed by a space and the /X switch, as in the following example. Then press Enter.

   xpsp1.exe /X

   A Choose Directory For Extracted Files dialog box appears.

7. Click OK to accept the default C:\temp folder. The installation program creates an i386 parent directory in the C:\temp folder containing the expanded service pack installation files.

8. Close the Command Prompt window.

REVIEW QUESTIONS

1. You are configuring a Software Update Services infrastructure using the loose parent/child topology. One server is synchronizing metadata and content from Windows Update. Other servers (one in each site) are synchronizing content from the parent SUS server. Which of the following steps is required to complete the SUS infrastructure? (Choose all correct answers.)

   a. Configure Automatic Updates clients using Control Panel on each system.

   b. Configure GPOs to direct clients to the SUS server in their sites.

   c. Configure a manual content distribution point.

   d. Approve updates using the SUS administration page on the child servers.

2. You are configuring SUS for a group of Web servers. You want the Web servers to update themselves nightly based on a list of approved updates on your SUS server. However, once in a while an administrator is logged on, performing late-night maintenance on a Web server, and you do not want the update installation and potential restart to interfere with those tasks. What Windows Update policy configuration should you use in this scenario?

   a. Notify For Download And Notify For Install

   b. Auto Download And Notify For Install

   c. Auto Download And Schedule The Install

   d. Auto Download And Install Immediately

3. You want all network clients to download and install updates automatically during night hours, and you have configured scheduled installation behavior for Automatic Updates. However, you discover that some users are turning off their machines at night and updates are not being applied. Which group policy enables you to correct this situation without changing the installation schedule?

   a. Specify Intranet Microsoft Update Service Location

   b. No Auto-Restart For Scheduled Automatic Updates Installations

   c. Reschedule Automatic Updates Scheduled Installations

   d. Configure Automatic Updates

4. What command should you use to unpack the single-file download of a service pack?

    a. Setup.exe -u

    b. Update.exe -x

    c. Update.msi

    d. *Servicepackname*.exe –x

5. What are the valid licensing modes in Windows Server 2003? (Choose all correct answers.)

    a. Per User

    b. Per Server

    c. Per Seat

    d. Per Device or Per User

6. You are hiring a team to tackle a software development project. There will be three shifts of six programmers. Each programmer uses four computers to develop and test the software, which authenticate against a Windows Server 2003 computer. What is the minimum number of CALs required if the servers involved are in Per Device or Per User licensing mode?

    a. 6

    b. 4

    c. 18

    d. 24

7. What tool enables you to identify the site license server for your site?

    a. Active Directory Domains And Trusts

    b. Licensing tool in Control Panel

    c. Active Directory Sites And Services

    d. DNS

8. You manage the network for a team of 500 telephone sales representatives. You have 550 licenses configured in Per Device or Per User licensing mode. A new campaign is launched, and you will hire another shift of 500 reps. What do you need to do to most effectively manage license tracking and compliance?

    a. Revoke the licenses from the existing clients.

    b. Delete the existing licenses, and then add 500 licenses.

    c. Create license groups.

    d. Convert to Per Server licensing.

CASE SCENARIOS

Scenario 5-1: Deploying Microsoft SUS

You are the systems administrator for a medium-sized organization that is considering implementing SUS on all Windows XP Professional workstations and Windows Server 2003 systems companywide. Before the companywide rollout can proceed, a pilot program will be implemented. You have been assigned a lab with 10 Windows XP Professional workstations, a Windows Server 2003 member server running SUS, a Windows Server 2003 domain controller, and a standalone Windows Server 2003 system. You want to configure all of the computers except the SUS server to automatically connect to the SUS server each morning at 7 A.M. to download and install new updates. Which of the following steps should you take to accomplish this goal? (Choose all correct answers.)

a. Use the Automatic Updates tab in the System Properties dialog box on every Windows XP Professional workstation computer to set the update server to the address of the SUS server. Set the Windows XP workstations to automatically download and install updates at 7 A.M. each day.

b. Use the Automatic Updates tab in the System Properties dialog box on each Windows Server 2003 system except the SUS server to set the update server to the address of the SUS server. Set these servers to automatically download and install updates at 7 A.M. each day.

c. Place the Windows XP Professional workstations and the Windows Server 2003 domain controller in a separate OU named SUStest. Edit a GPO's Windows Update properties for the SUStest OU, specifying the address of the update server as the SUS server in the Specify Intranet Microsoft Update Service Location policy. Set Configure Automatic Updates Policy to Automatic Download And Schedule The Install, and set the scheduled install day to Every Day and the time to 7 A.M. Apply this GPO to the SUStest OU.

d. On the standalone Windows Server 2003 system, edit the local GPO's Windows Update properties, specifying the address of the update server as the SUS server in the Specify Intranet Microsoft Update Service Location policy. Set Configure Automatic Updates Policy to Automatic Download And Schedule The Install, and set the scheduled install day to Every Day and the time to 7 A.M. Apply this GPO to the SUStest OU.

e. On the SUS server, edit the local GPO's Windows Update properties, specifying the address of the update server as the SUS server in the Specify Intranet Microsoft Update Service Location policy. Set Configure Automatic Updates Policy to Automatic Download And Schedule The Install, and set the scheduled install day to Every Day and the time to 7 A.M. Apply this GPO to the SUStest OU.

Scenario 5-2: Deploying a Service Pack

Fred is the systems administrator for an academic department at the local university. The department has 40 Windows XP Professional workstations and 2 Windows Server 2003 servers. One of these servers is configured as a domain controller, the other as a file and print server. All department computers are members of a single Windows Server 2003 domain. Microsoft has recently released a service pack for Windows XP and, after testing it, Fred feels confident enough to deploy it to the Windows XP Professional workstations in his department. He extracts the service pack to a directory on the file server called \\Fileshare\ newsrvpk. Which of the following methods can he use to install the service pack on all Windows XP Professional workstations? (Choose all correct answers.)

a. He can visit each Windows XP Professional workstation and manually install the service pack from the file share.

b. He can create a group called Xpwkstn and put all the Windows XP Professional workstation computer accounts in this group. He can then create a GPO in which he sets up a new package in the Computer Configuration\Software Settings node using the location of the service pack .msi file on the \\Fileshare\newsrvpk share. In the Deploy Software dialog box, he should select Assign, and then apply this GPO to the Xpwkstn group.

c. He can create a group called Xpusrs and put all who use Windows XP Professional workstations in this group. He can then create a GPO in which he sets up a new package in the Computer Configuration\Software Settings node using the location of the service pack .msi file on the \\Fileshare\newsrvpk share. In the Deploy Software dialog box, he should select Assign, and then apply this GPO to the Xpusrs group.

d. He can create an OU called Xpwkstn and put all the Windows XP Professional workstation computer accounts in this OU. He can then create a GPO in which he sets up a new package in the Computer Configuration \Software Settings node using the location of the service pack .msi file on the \\Fileshare\newsrvpk share. In the Deploy Software dialog box, he should select Assign, and then apply this GPO to the Xpwkstn OU.

PART 2
MANAGING AND MAINTAINING USERS, GROUPS, AND COMPUTERS

CHAPTER 6
WORKING WITH USER ACCOUNTS

Before any user can access a computer running Microsoft Windows Server 2003 from the console or over the network, that user must be authenticated. Authentication is the process by which the user is identified and the user's credentials are verified. In most cases, the authentication process requires the user to supply an account name and a password, which the server verifies against its records before granting the user access. Managing these user accounts and passwords is one of the most common tasks performed by network administrators. In this chapter, you learn how to create, manage, and troubleshoot user accounts, both individually and collectively.

Upon completion of this chapter, you will be able to:

■ Understand the differences between local user accounts and domain user accounts

■ Plan user account creation

■ Create and manage local user accounts

■ Create and manage domain user accounts

■ Create and manage user accounts with templates, importation, and command-line tools

■ Manage user profiles

■ Understand the differences between local, roaming, and mandatory profiles

■ Troubleshoot user authentication issues

UNDERSTANDING USER ACCOUNTS

A Microsoft Windows network can be based on one of two organizational schemes, commonly referred to as the *workgroup* and the *domain*. Both of these schemes require users to have user accounts for authentication purposes, but the nature of the accounts and the tools that you use to create and manage them are slightly different. The differences between the local user accounts used by workgroups and domain user accounts are summarized in Table 6-1.

Table 6-1   **Local and Domain User Name Characteristics**

	Local User Names	Domain User Names
Management Tool	Local Users And Groups	Active Directory Users And Computers
Account Location	Security Account Manager on each local computer	Active Directory database
Logon Location	The local computer	Active Directory domain
Provides Access To	Local computer resources only	Domain and network resources
Name Restrictions	Must be unique on the computer	Must be unique in the directory

Workgroups

A workgroup is a collection of computers that interact on an informal basis, with no centralized authority. Every computer in the workgroup has its own set of local user accounts that are stored in a local, flat-file database called the Security Accounts Manager (SAM). The computer uses these accounts to authenticate users and grant them access to resources on that computer only. If a user requires access to resources on more than one computer in a workgroup, the user must have a separate account on each computer and be authenticated by each computer before access is granted.

However, just because each computer in a workgroup has to perform its own authentications does not necessarily mean that a user has to manually supply an account name and password to connect to each computer. If every computer has an account for that user with the same account name and password, all authentications after the first one occur automatically and in the background.

To create local user accounts, you use an MMC snap-in called Local Users And Groups. To log on with a local user account, in the Log On To Windows dialog box, you specify an account name and password in the text boxes provided, and select This Computer in the Log On To drop-down list.

Although the process of creating a local user account is simple, the primary drawback of the workgroup model is the additional administrative effort required to maintain accounts for the same users on multiple computers. If, for example, a user has an account on 10 different computers, you must modify each account individually to change that user's password. For this reason, the workgroup model is impractical on anything other than a small network.

Domains

The domain model used by Windows Server 2003, Microsoft Windows XP, and Microsoft Windows 2000 is based on Microsoft's Active Directory directory service. In Chapter 1, you learned about the architecture and functions of Active Directory. Active Directory user accounts take the form of user objects, which are stored, as with all Active Directory information, on domain controllers, where they are accessible from anywhere in the domain. When users log on with domain accounts, they are actually being authenticated by a domain controller, not by the computer on which they are working or by the computer they are trying to access.

A domain user account consists of a logon name and password, as well as a unique **security identifier (SID)**. During logon, Active Directory authenticates the username and password entered by the user. The security subsystem can then build a security access token that represents that user. The access token contains the user account's SID, as well as the SIDs of groups to which the user belongs. That token can then be used to verify user rights assignments, including the right to log on locally to the system and to authorize access to resources secured by access control lists (ACLs).

In the domain model, each user has only one domain account, which greatly simplifies the task of the network administrator. This one account can be used to grant the user access to any resource on the network. Because the Active Directory database is (usually) replicated among multiple domain controllers, the user accounts are nearly always available to authenticate the user's access to a new resource. Administrators create domain user objects using the Active Directory Users And Computers MMC snap-in. To log on using a domain user account, you specify the account name and password in the Log On To Windows dialog box and then select the domain in which the account was created in the Log On To drop-down list, as shown in Figure 6-1.

Figure 6-1   The Log On To Windows dialog box

> **NOTE**   **Logging On to a Domain Controller**   When a Windows Server 2003 computer is functioning as a domain controller, there is no other choice but to log on to the domain. Local user accounts and the Local Users And Groups snap-in are not used.

PLANNING USER ACCOUNTS

Before you begin actually creating local or domain user accounts, you should consider a number of planning issues. This is particularly true when you are working with a large and complex network. Although the task of creating an account for each one of your users might seem simple at first, some preparation regarding the names you choose for the accounts, the passwords you are going to allow, and the structure of the Active Directory hierarchy can save you a great deal of trouble later.

Account Naming

When you create a user account, either local or domain, you specify the user's first and last name, but the actual name that the user employs when logging on or authenticating is the account name. Local and domain user account names can be as long as 20 characters, but for the convenience of users they are usually much shorter. The names are not case sensitive (although Windows Server 2003 does preserve the case you enter) and cannot use any of the following characters:

" / \ [ ] : ; | = , + * ? < > @

> **NOTE**   **Account Names and E-Mail Addresses**   When you create account names that will also be used for the users' e-mail addresses, be sure to consider the character limitations of your e-mail software. Some e-mail systems cannot use names that contain spaces or parentheses, even though Windows Server 2003 will accept them.

To form an account name, many organizations use some combination of the user's first or last name and one or more initials. For example, the user Mark Lee might have the account name mlee or markl. However, for an organization of any substantial size, using first names can be impractical because you can easily have two users called Mark and possibly even two Marks with surnames beginning with L.

Whatever form you choose for your account names, the most important thing is to create a set of rules for forming the names and then to stick to it. Assigning account names inconsistently or using obscure nicknames and user preferences only leads to confusion when other administrators have to determine the account name for a particular user. Your rules should specify a standard combination of first or last names and initials, as well as a standardized method for dealing with users for whom the rules produce identical account names. An administrator should be able to hear a user's name for the first time and guess the user's account name with a reasonable degree of certainty.

Choosing Passwords

Security is a pervasive influence on virtually all network administration tasks today, and creating user accounts is no exception. When you create a new account, you must specify a password for it, and what policies you use to control the account passwords should depend on the degree of security your organization needs.

By default, when you create a new domain user account in Windows Server 2003, you must specify a complex password at least seven characters long. These restrictions are imposed by group policy settings that the operating system configures in the default domain policy group policy object (GPO). Local user accounts are not subject to these restrictions. You can modify these requirements and other default password assignment rules by altering the settings of the following password policies using the Group Policy Object Editor console:

- **Enforce Password History**   Specifies the number of unique passwords that users have to supply before the operating system permits them to reuse an old password. The default value is 24.

- **Maximum Password Age**   Specifies how long a single password can be used before the operating system forces the user to change it. The default value is 42 days.

- **Minimum Password Age**   Specifies how long a single password must be used before the operating system permits the user to change it. The default value is one day.

- **Minimum Password Length**   Specifies the minimum number of characters the operating system permits in user-supplied passwords. The default value is seven.

- **Password Must Meet Complexity Requirements**   Specifies criteria for passwords, such as length of at least six characters; no duplication of all or part of the user's account name; and inclusion of characters from at least three of the following four categories: uppercase letters, lowercase letters, numbers, and symbols. By default, the Windows operating system enables this policy.

Practice altering password policies by doing Exercise 6-1, "Changing Password Policy Settings," now.

The default settings for a new user object also enable the User Must Change Password At Next Logon setting. This setting assumes that users will be responsible for supplying their own passwords and changing them at regular intervals. The administrator creating the account, therefore, only has to supply a temporary password for a user's first logon.

Whether you want users to supply their own passwords is another security decision you must make before you start creating accounts. Generally speaking, it is preferable to have users specify their passwords, both because it will be easier for them to remember passwords they created themselves and because changing all of the users' passwords every 42 days would be a severe burden on the network administrators. The default password policy settings force users to change their passwords and also prevent them from reusing the same passwords too often.

Depending on your network's security requirements, you might want to impose on your users other password policies that are not enforceable using software, such as the following:

- Do not share passwords with coworkers or anyone inside or outside the organization.

- Do not write down passwords and leave them where they can easily be found.

- Do not create passwords using commonly held information such as birth-days or names of spouses, children, or pets.

- Refer all telephone or e-mail inquiries regarding passwords to network administrators or security officers.

Designing an Active Directory Hierarchy

Because local user accounts are not intended for use on large networks, they are stored in a simple flat-file (nonhierarchical) database. The SAM is really little more than a list of user (and group) accounts with a few basic attributes for each account. Therefore, no design issues are associated with creating this type of account. Domain user accounts, however, are part of an Active Directory hierarchy, and the design of this hierarchy is a critical part of the network infrastructure planning process.

As you learned in Chapter 1, the basic structure of an Active Directory domain is tree-like and similar to the directory structure of a file system. The domain object is at the top of the tree (which is known, somewhat confusingly, as the root) and one or more levels of organizational unit (OU) objects are located beneath. The actual task of designing the hierarchy is best left to the network's architects, but the administrators responsible for creating user accounts must be familiar with the hierarchy and the basic paradigms used to construct it.

To create a domain user object, you must first decide what OU to put it in. This decision should be based on the functions of the OUs created in the hierarchy. An Active Directory tree design can be based on the political divisions of the organization, such as departments and workgroups, or it can be based on geographical locations, such as buildings, floors, wings, and offices, or a combination of these and other factors. The point of having a directory hierarchy is to simplify the process of locating objects in the tree and to facilitate the dissemination of attributes to large numbers of objects by assigning them to an OU and letting them flow downward through the tree.

Placing new user objects in their correct locations in the hierarchy enables them to receive the settings they need without individual configuration and prevents you from having to move them around later.

WORKING WITH LOCAL USER ACCOUNTS

Local accounts enable users to access the resources of the computer on which you create the accounts, either by logging on at the console or by connecting over the network. By default, Windows Server 2003 always creates the following three local user accounts:

- **Administrator**   This account is required for the first system logon, using a password supplied during the operating system installation. The Administrator user is a member of the Administrators group, which gives him or her complete access to all areas of the operating system. This access includes the ability to create new local user accounts, specify permissions and rights for local user accounts, and install new hardware and software.

The local Administrator account is always needed, even on an Active Directory network, because certain tasks require local Administrator access to the computer.

- **Guest**   This account is intended for use by temporary users who need only limited access to the system. The account is created during the operating system installation, but is left in a disabled state and with no password. You must first enable the account before anyone can use it to log on. The Guest account is a member of the Guests group and has limited access to the operating system. In most cases, it is recommended that you leave the Guest account disabled and create new, individual accounts for specific users rather than letting them all log on using the Guest account.

- **SUPPORT_*number***   This account was created for use by Microsoft technical support personnel when they connect to the system using the Remote Assistance feature. The account is disabled by default and must be enabled before a Microsoft technician can access the computer.

If the computer is connected to a domain, there is no need to create any additional local user accounts because users will log on using their domain accounts and be able to access system resources that way. However, if the computer is part of a workgroup, you can create new local user accounts using the Local Users And Groups snap-in. On non-domain controllers, this snap-in is incorporated into the Computer Management console (as shown in Figure 6-2), which you can access from the Administrative Tools program group on the Start menu.

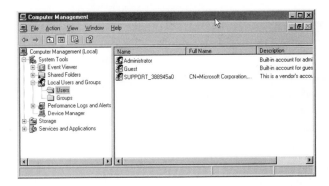

Figure 6-2   The Local Users And Groups snap-in

Creating a Local User Account

To create a local user account, you select the Users folder in the scope pane of the snap-in and, from the Action menu, select New User to display the New User dialog box (as shown in Figure 6-3). In this dialog box, you specify the following information:

- **User Name**   The account name that the user employs while logging on to the computer (required).

- **Full Name**   The user's full name (optional).

- **Description**   Text describing the user or the function of the user account (optional).

- **Password**   A password of up to 127 characters used to authenticate the account (optional).

- **Confirm Password**   Reenter the same password to ensure that you have typed it correctly. If the two passwords do not match, you are prompted to enter them again.

- **User Must Change Password At Next Logon**   Select this check box if you want the user to change the password after logging on for the first time. You cannot select this option if you have selected the Password Never Expires check box. Selecting this option automatically clears the User Cannot Change Password option.

- **User Cannot Change Password**   Select this check box if you have more than one person using the same domain user account or to maintain control over user account passwords. This option is commonly used to manage service account passwords. You cannot select this option if you have selected the User Must Change Password At Next Logon option.

- **Password Never Expires**   Select this check box if you never want the password to expire. You cannot select this option if you have selected the User Must Change Password At Next Logon option. This option is commonly used to manage service account passwords.

- **Account Is Disabled**   Select this check box to disable the user account, such as when you create an object for a newly hired employee who does not yet need access to the network.

Figure 6-3   The New User dialog box

Managing Local User Accounts

Local user accounts have a relatively small number of attributes. When you select an account in the Users folder of the Local Users And Groups snap-in and select Properties from the Action menu, the user's Properties dialog box appears (as shown in Figure 6-4). This dialog box enables you to modify the Properties you specified while creating the user account, except for the username and the password, which you can change by using the Rename and Set Password commands on the Action menu, respectively. In addition, the dialog box provides access to the other user account parameters found on the following tabs:

- General

- Member Of

- Profile

- Environment

- Sessions

- Remote Control

- Terminal Services Profile

- Dial-in

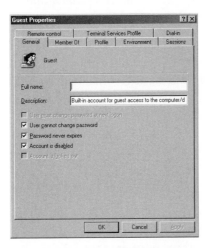

Figure 6-4   A local user's Properties dialog box

The settings on these tabs are identical to those found on the tabs of the same names in a domain user's Properties dialog box. For more information about the specific settings on each tab, see "Managing Domain User Accounts" later in this chapter.

WORKING WITH DOMAIN USER ACCOUNTS

Working with domain user accounts is similar to working with local user accounts, except that domain accounts are capable of containing a lot more information about the user. When you create an Active Directory domain by promoting the first domain controller, Windows Server 2003 creates the following user accounts by default:

- **Administrator**   The domain Administrator account is a member of the domain's Administrators group and performs basically the same function as the local Administrator account: it provides the account needed for the initial domain logon and provides complete access to all domain functions and features. It is critical to understand that the domain Administrator account is a completely separate entity from the local Administrator account. The two can have different passwords, permissions, and other capabilities. On a Windows Server 2003 computer that is a member of a domain (but not a domain controller), it is possible to log on using either the local or the domain Administrator account, depending on the setting in the Log On To drop-down list in the Log On To Windows dialog box.

- **Guest** As with the local Guest account, the domain Guest account is disabled by default and intended for users requiring temporary access to the domain.

> **NOTE** Exam Objectives   The objectives for the 70-290 exam specify that students should be able to "create and manage user accounts."

Windows Server 2003 also creates other built-in accounts by default when you install certain services on the computer. For example, promoting a server to a domain controller creates a hidden user object called *krbtgt* to function as the security principal for the Key Distribution Center service. When you install Microsoft Internet Information Services (IIS), two users are created, IUSR_*computername*, which anonymous users use to connect to the server, and IWAM_*computername*, which IIS uses to start out-of-process applications.

The built-in user objects in a domain are all located in a container object called *Users*. Although you can create new user objects in this or any container, or even directly in the domain itself, it is best to always create user objects in an OU so you can manage them later using group policies. You can only link a GPO to a domain, site, or OU object, and the Users container is none of these. Therefore, your Active Directory installation should have appropriate OUs in it, in accordance with your organization's Active Directory design, before you begin creating user objects.

> **NOTE** Container Objects   The *Users, Builtin, Computers,* and *ForeignSecurity-Principals* objects belong to a special object class called a *container*. In directory services parlance, the term *container* is mostly used generically, to refer to any objects that can have other objects subordinate to them. However, in the case of the four objects listed here, each is literally an object type called a *container*. You cannot apply GPOs to these four container objects, nor can you delete them or create new objects of the same type. You can, however, move the subordinate objects from those containers to OU objects of your own creation, which are more manageable.

On a Windows Server 2003 domain controller, you create domain user objects by using the Active Directory Users And Computers snap-in (as shown in Figure 6-5), which is accessible from the Administrative Tools program group on the Start Menu. To create user objects, you must be a member of the Enterprise Admins, Domain Admins, or Account Operators groups, or you must have been delegated the administrative permissions necessary to create user objects.

> **NOTE** Installing Consoles   Although the Active Directory management consoles appear in the Administrative Tools program group only on domain controllers, you can run them from Windows Server 2003 member servers and even Windows XP workstations. To install the Administrative Tools package on another computer, run the Adminpak.msi file from the i386 folder of the Windows Server 2003 installation CD.

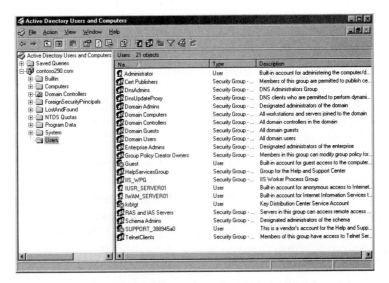

Figure 6-5   The Active Directory Users And Computers console

Creating a Domain User Account

To create a user object, select from the console's scope pane the container in which you want to create the object and, from the Action menu, point to New and select User to display the New Object – User wizard. Unlike the New User dialog box that you use to create local user objects, the New Object – User wizard has two pages of configuration parameters that are presented wizard-style.

The first page of the wizard (shown in Figure 6-6) contains the following parameters:

- **First Name**   The user's first name (optional).
- **Initials**   The user's middle initials (optional).
- **Last Name**   The user's last name (optional).

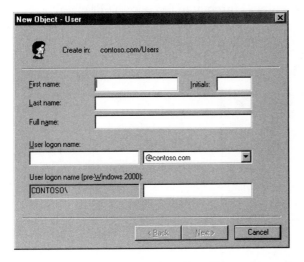

Figure 6-6   The first page of the New Object – User wizard

- **Full Name**   The user's full name (required). If you enter values for the first or last name, the full name field is populated automatically, but you can modify the suggested value. The value entered here generates several user object properties: the common name (CN), the distinguished name (DN), the name, and the displayName properties. Because the CN property must be unique within a container, the name entered here must be unique relative to all other objects in the OU (or other container) in which you create the user object.

- **User Logon Name**   The account name that the user will use to log on (required). This value is used to form the user principal name (UPN), which consists of a logon name and a UPN suffix that is, by default, the Domain Name System (DNS) name of the domain in which you are creating the object. The entire UPN, in the format *logon-name@UPN-suffix*, must be unique within the Active Directory forest. A sample UPN would be *someone@contoso.com*. The UPN can be used to log on to any computer in the domain running Windows Server 2003, Windows XP, or Windows 2000.

- **User Logon Name (Pre–Windows 2000)**   The account name that the user will use when logging on to down-level clients (required). Down-level clients are computers running Windows 95, Windows 98, Windows Millennium Edition (Windows Me), or Microsoft Windows NT. The wizard automatically populates this field with up to 20 characters from the User Logon Name value you supplied. This field must be unique within the domain.

Once you have entered the values in the first page of the New Object – User wizard, click Next. The second page of the wizard, shown in Figure 6-7, contains the following parameters:

- **Password**   A password of up to 127 characters used to access the account. The value you enter for the password must conform in length and complexity to the password policy settings currently in force in the domain.

- **Confirm Password**   Reenter the same password to ensure that you have typed it correctly. If the two passwords do not match, you are prompted to enter them again.

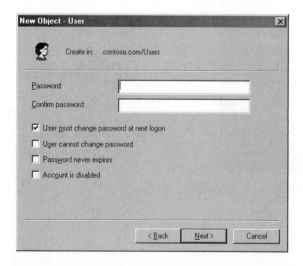

Figure 6-7   The second page of the New Object – User wizard

- **User Must Change Password At Next Logon** Select this check box if you want the user to change the password after logging on for the first time. You cannot select this option if you have selected the Password Never Expires check box. Selecting this option automatically clears the User Cannot Change Password option.

- **User Cannot Change Password** Select this check box if you have more than one person using the same domain user account or to maintain control over user account passwords. This option is commonly used to manage service account passwords. You cannot select this option if you have selected the User Must Change Password At Next Logon check box.

- **Password Never Expires** Select this check box if you never want the password to expire. This option automatically clears the User Must Change Password At Next Logon check box. This option is commonly used to manage service account passwords.

- **Account Is Disabled** Select this check box to disable the user account, such as when you create a template account or an object for a newly hired employee who does not yet need access to the network.

Some of these account options have the potential to contradict group policy settings that the user object will inherit from the domain or other container objects. For example, the default domain policy GPO specifies that passwords for all user accounts in the domain must be changed every 42 days. However, if you enable the Password Never Expires option in a user object, it overrides the group policy setting and the user will not be prompted to change the password.

Once you have entered the values in the second page of the New Object – User wizard, click Next to display a final summary page. Clicking Finish closes the wizard and creates the new user object in the selected container.

Practice creating domain user accounts by doing Exercise 6-2, "Creating a Domain User Object," now.

Managing Domain User Accounts

Once you have created a user object, you can use the Active Directory Users And Computers console to manage its properties. By selecting a user object and clicking the Action menu, you can perform a variety of tasks, such as the following:

- **Add To A Group** Makes the user object a member of an existing group.

- **Disable Account** Causes the account to be rendered inoperable, preventing users from logging on with the account. To reenable the account, you must open the user object's Properties dialog box, select the Account tab, and clear the Account Is Disabled check box in the Account Options list.

- **Reset Password** Enables an administrator to specify a new password for the account without knowing the old password.

- **Open Home Page** Opens a Microsoft Internet Explorer window and connects to the Uniform Resource Locator (URL) specified in the Web Page text box on the General tab in the user object's Properties dialog box.

- **Send Mail**   Using the computer's default e-mail client application, opens a new mail message with the address specified in the E-mail text box on the General tab in the user object's Properties dialog box.

- **Delete**   Permanently deletes the user object from Active Directory.

- **Rename**   Modifies the value of the user object's Full Name field and opens a Rename User dialog box, in which you can also modify the First Name, Last Name, Display Name, User Logon Name, and User Logon Name (Pre–Windows 2000) text box values.

> **NOTE   Exam Objectives**   The objectives for the 70-290 exam specify that students should be able to "create and modify user accounts by using the Active Directory Users And Computers MMC snap-in."

When you create a new domain user account, you specify values for only the most basic user object properties. By far, the most powerful management tool for a user object is its Properties dialog box, which you open by selecting the user object and, from the Action menu, selecting Properties. By default this dialog box has 13 tabs, which contain dozens of user object properties, which you can use to control the account's capabilities and populate with information about the user. These tabs can be divided into the categories shown in Table 6-2.

> **NOTE   Active Directory Schema and Object Properties**   In some cases, you might notice that the user objects' Properties dialog boxes on a particular network have more than 13 tabs or have additional fields on some of the default tabs. This is because the Active Directory schema, specifying which properties each object type in the directory service has, is extensible. Administrators can extend the schema manually by adding properties to an object type (although Microsoft does not recommend this), or the schema can be automatically extended by the installation of software products. For example, installing Microsoft Exchange extends the schema to create Exchange General, Exchange Features, and E-mail Addresses tabs in each user's Properties dialog box.

Table 6-2   Categories of User Properties Dialog Box Tabs

Category	Dialog Box Tabs
Personal information	■ General
	■ Address
	■ Telephones
	■ Organization
Account properties	■ Account
User configuration management	■ Profile
Group membership	■ Member Of
Terminal Services	■ Terminal Services Profile
	■ Environment
	■ Remote Control
	■ Sessions
Remote Access	■ Dial-in
Applications	■ COM+

The settings on each tab are discussed in the following sections.

The General Tab

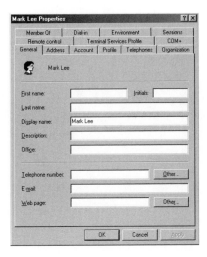

The General tab contains basic information about the user, such as the first and last names you specified when creating the object. There are also fields in which you can specify a display name, office location, and a text description for the user, plus the user's telephone numbers, Web page addresses, and e-mail address.

Many of the fields in the General, Address, Telephones, and Organization tabs are purely informational in nature. The use of these fields is optional, and their values are not directly related to the operation of the user object or Active Directory services; they provide only background information about the user. Providing values for these fields enables administrators to locate domain user accounts by searching the directory using whatever information they have about the user they need to find. Other people on the network can also look up a specific user to find contact information for them or other data.

The Address Tab

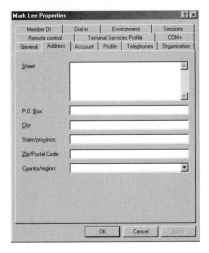

The Address tab contains informational fields that enable administrators to enter the user's mailing address information into Active Directory.

The Telephones Tab

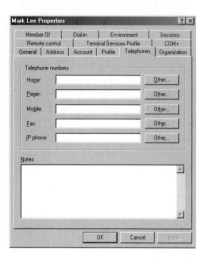

The Telephones tab contains informational fields in which administrators can record the user's various telephone numbers. Although fields such as these are purely informational in the default Active Directory configuration, this is not to say that applications cannot make use of them. For example, it would be possible to create a telephone dialer application that enabled you to search for another user's account in Active Directory and automatically dial a telephone number specified on this tab in that user's object.

The Organization Tab

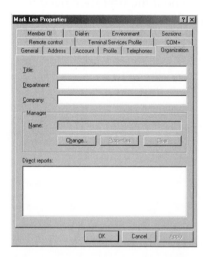

The Organization tab contains informational fields in which administrators can specify information about the user's place in the organization, including a field in which you select the account of the user's manager from the Active Directory.

The Account Tab

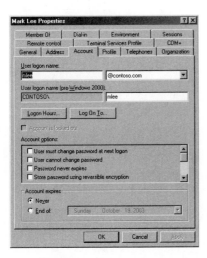

The Account tab contains the User Logon Name, UPN Suffix, and User Logon Name (Pre–Windows 2000) fields, with the values you specified when creating the user object, along with the four check boxes from the Create Object – User wizard. The tab also includes a number of other account options, including the following:

■ **Logon Hours**   Displays the Logon Hours dialog box, in which administrators can specify which times of day and which days of the week the user is permitted to log on to the domain. By default, this feature only prevents the user from logging on. If the user is already logged on when the allowed logon time ends, service is not interrupted. However, a security option is available in group policy objects called Network Security: Force Logoff When Logon Hours Expire, which enables an administrator to automatically disconnect the user. Logon hours restrictions apply only to domain logons, not local logons.

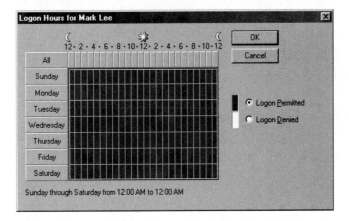

■ **Log On To**   Displays the Logon Workstations dialog box, in which administrators can specify the names of specific computers on the network that can use this user object to log on. This feature is called Computer Restrictions in other parts of the user interface. You must have NetBIOS over TCP/IP enabled on your network to use this feature because it restricts logons based on NetBIOS computer names.

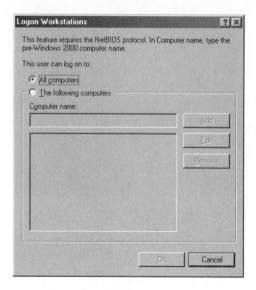

- **Account Is Locked Out**   Disabled by default, this check box is activated and selected when the user account is locked by too many failed logon attempts. You can configure the object's account lockout behavior by defining values for the Account Lockout Duration, Account Lockout Threshold, and Reset Account Lockout Counter After group policies. For example, an Account Lockout Threshold value of 3 causes the account to be locked after three failed logon attempts. When an account is locked out, an administrator can reopen it by clearing this check box.

- **Store Password Using Reversible Encryption**   Causes Active Directory to store the object's password using a reversible encryption algorithm, rather than the stronger, non-reversible algorithm it usually uses. This option is designed to support applications that require a reversible password, such as the original Challenge Handshake Authentication Protocol (CHAP). In all other instances, the option should be left disabled. It is also possible to enable or disable this same option using group policies. When this check box is selected, the setting overrides a conflicting group policy value.

- **Account Is Disabled**   Enables administrators to disable and reenable the user account.

- **Smart Card Is Required For Interactive Logon**   Causes the user object to require a smart card to log on. A smart card is a credit card-sized hardware device that contains identification information for the user, typically in the form of a digital certificate and private encryption key. For a user to log on with a smart card, the computer must be equipped with card reader hardware and the appropriate software, and the user must have the correct personal identification number (PIN) for the card. This option is used only for accounts requiring exceptional security. Because the use of a smart card eliminates the need for a password, selecting this check box changes the account password to a complex, random value and enables the Password Never Expires option.

- **Account Is Trusted For Delegation**   This option enables a service running under a user account (called a *service account*) to impersonate a client to access computer resources on behalf of other user accounts on the network. This option is rarely, if ever, selected in user objects representing actual users.

- **Account Is Sensitive And Cannot Be Delegated**   Delegation enables administrators to grant others control over a particular user account, typically one intended for temporary use, such as the Guest account. Selecting this option prevents the account from being delegated by another account.

- **Use DES Encryption Types For This Account**   Causes Active Directory to use Data Encryption Standard (DES) encryption algorithms for this user object.

- **Do Not Require Kerberos Preauthentication**   Causes Active Directory to omit the Kerberos preauthentication procedure when authenticating this user. This option is for accounts using an alternate implementation of the Kerberos authentication protocol; this alternate implementation does not support preauthentication. Omitting preauthentication reduces the security provided by the protocol, so this option should not be enabled unless there is specific reason for it.

- **Account Expires**   Enables administrators to specify a date on which the user account will be automatically disabled, using the following interface:

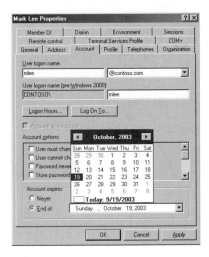

The Profile Tab

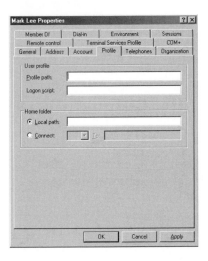

The Profile tab contains fields in which you can specify the location of the user's profile, home folder, and a logon script that should execute whenever the user logs on.

> **MORE INFO**   For more information about user profiles, see "Managing User Profiles" later in this chapter.

The Member Of Tab

The Member Of tab lists the groups of which the user is a member and enables administrators to modify the user's group memberships. By default, new users are made members of the Domain Users group.

> **NOTE**   For more information about Active Directory groups, see Chapter 7, "Working With Groups."

The Terminal Services Profile Tab

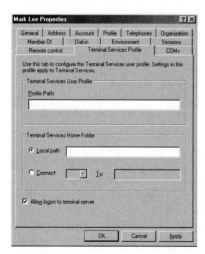

The Terminal Services Profile tab enables administrators to enable the user to connect to terminal servers and also to specify the locations of the user profile and home folder that apply when the user is connected to a terminal server.

The Environment Tab

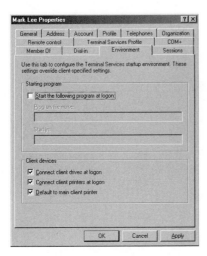

The Environment tab enables administrators to specify an application that should run as soon as the user connects to a terminal server, to specify whether the user should connect to the mapped client drives and printers immediately at logon, and to specify whether to automatically print to the client's default printer.

The Remote Control Tab

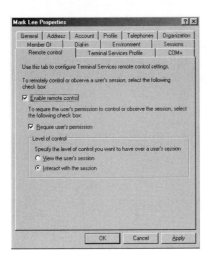

The Remote Control tab contains settings that enable you to configure the Terminal Services remote control settings for the user object. These options specify whether the user's session can be accessed using the remote control feature of Terminal Services, whether the user's permission is required for this access, and whether the auditor can merely observe the user's session or actually take part in it. These options can also be configured using the Terminal Services Configuration console, or with group policies; in the event of a conflict, the group policy settings take precedence.

The Sessions Tab

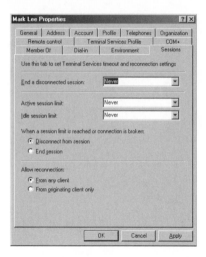

The Sessions tab enables an administrator to configure the user's Terminal Services disconnection behavior, using the following controls:

- **End A Disconnected Session**   Specifies the amount of time that the user's Terminal Services session remains open on the server after the user is disconnected.

- **Active Session Limit**   Specifies the maximum duration for the user's Terminal Services sessions. When a session reaches the limit, it is disconnected.

- **Idle Session Limit**   Specifies the maximum amount of idle time permitted during a Terminal Services session before the server disconnects.

- **When A Session Limit Is Reached Or Connection Is Broken**   Specifies whether a terminal server should disconnect or end the session when a session limit is reached or the connection broken. The user can reestablish a disconnected session but cannot reconnect to the session if the server has ended it.

- **Allow Reconnection**   Specifies whether the user should be permitted to reconnect to a terminal server from any client or from the client where the session originated only.

The Dial-in Tab

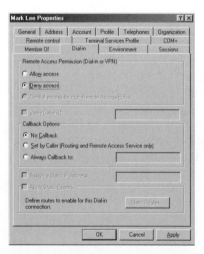

The Dial-in tab contains controls that enable administrators to specify the user's remote access capabilities. These controls are as follows:

- **Remote Access Permission (Dial-In Or VPN)**   Specifies whether remote access should be explicitly allowed, explicitly denied, or determined by remote access policy settings. If access is explicitly allowed, remote access policy conditions, user account properties, or profile properties can still cause the connection attempt to be denied.

- **Verify Caller ID**   Causes the remote access server to verify the number from which the user is connecting using caller ID. If the user's number cannot be verified or does not match the specified telephone number, the connection attempt is denied.

- **Callback Options**   Enables an administrator to specify whether the user should employ the callback feature when connecting to a remote access server. If this feature is enabled, the server disconnects during the connection establishment process and calls the user back at a telephone number that is either specified by the user or configured by the network administrator on this tab. The callback feature can be an economy measure, placing the bulk of the connection charges on the company lines, or a security measure, in which only callers at specific telephone numbers are permitted remote access to the network.

- **Assign A Static IP Address**   Enables an administrator to specify the IP address that the remote access server should always assign to this user.

- **Apply Static Routes**   Enables administrators to specify static routes that are to be added to the remote router's routing table when a demand-dial connection is established.

The COM+ Tab

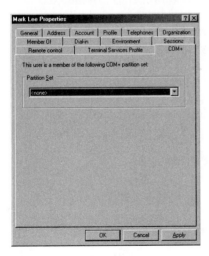

The COM+ tab contains a single control that enables administrators to assign a specific COM+ partition set to the user. A COM+ partition set is a collection of COM+ partitions, which is where COM+ applications are stored. Selecting a COM+ partition set on this tab enables the user to access the applications in the various COM+ partitions that comprise the set.

Managing Multiple Users

When you manage domain user accounts, there will likely be times when you have to make the same changes to multiple user objects and modifying each one individually would be a tedious chore. In these instances, it is possible to modify the properties of multiple user accounts simultaneously, using the Active Directory Users And Computers console. You simply select several user objects by holding down the Ctrl key as you click each user in the details pane, and then select Properties from the Action menu. A Properties On Multiple Objects dialog box then appears, as shown in Figure 6-8.

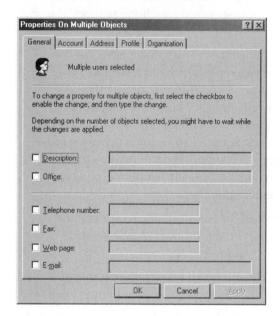

Figure 6-8   The Properties On Multiple Objects dialog box

> **NOTE**   *Modifying Object Classes   When you select multiple objects to modify, you get the best results when the objects are all of the same class. For example, you can select multiple user objects and modify a variety of properties, but if you select a user object and a computer object, the only property you can modify is Description.*

The Properties On Multiple Objects dialog box is slightly different from the standard user object Properties dialog box. The former dialog box contains only a limited subset of the object's properties—the ones that are likely to apply to multiple objects. The tabs in the dialog box and the properties on each tab are summarized in Table 6-3.

Table 6-3   Properties Available for Multiple User Object Modification

Tab	Properties
General	■ Description
	■ Office
	■ Telephone Number
	■ Fax
	■ Web Page
	■ E-mail
Account	■ UPN Suffix
	■ Logon Hours
	■ Computer Restrictions
	■ Account Options
	■ Account Expires

(continued)

Table 6-3 **Properties Available for Multiple User Object Modification**

Tab	Properties
Address	■ Street
	■ P.O. Box
	■ City
	■ State/Province
	■ Zip/Postal Code
	■ Country/Region
Profile	■ Profile Path
	■ Logon Script
	■ Home Folder
Organization	■ Title
	■ Department
	■ Company
	■ Manager

Moving User Objects

Although it is a good idea to have the organization's Active Directory hierarchy design when you create your user objects, so that you can create them in the correct containers, it is still possible to move them after creation. This capability also enables you to accommodate personnel transfers and business reorganizations.

To move a user object (or any object), you select it and, from the Action menu, select Move to display the Move dialog box (shown in Figure 6-9). Then you select the desired destination container and click OK. You can also move objects by dragging and dropping them.

Figure 6-9 The Move dialog box

To practice moving objects, do Exercise 6-3, "Moving a User Object," now.

NOTE **Deleting Objects** When you move objects around in the Active Directory hierarchy, be careful not to delete them accidentally. The SID associated with a user object is a unique value that is assigned when the object is created. When you delete an object accidentally and then re-create it with the exact same name and property settings, the SID is still different. This is not a big issue for newly created objects, but if you delete an older object, you must then reconfigure all of the user's permissions because these are referenced using the object's SID.

CREATING MULTIPLE USER OBJECTS

At times, network administrators are required to create multiple user objects quickly, to accommodate the arrival of a group of new hires or a new class of incoming students. For these times, there are methods that you can use to facilitate or automate the user object creation process so that you do not have to create each account individually. The Active Directory Users And Computers console is a tool that is designed primarily for individual object creation and management. However, Windows Server 2003 also includes other tools that can streamline the object creation process by using techniques such as importation and command-line scripting.

Using Object Templates

It is common for Active Directory objects of the same class to share similar properties. For example, all of the members of a particular department probably are members of the same groups, are allowed to log on to the network during the same hours, and have home folders and roaming profiles on the same server. In such cases, it can be helpful when creating a new user account to start out with an object that is prepopulated with common properties. You can accomplish this by creating a generic user object—called a *template*—and then copying that object to create new users.

To create a user object template, create a new user object, assign it an identifying name, such as UserTemplate, and configure the properties that are likely to be common to all of the new users you create, just as you would when configuring an object for an individual user. The properties that are copied to a new object are summarized in Table 6-4. After you have configured the properties, be sure to disable the template object so that no one can use it to access network resources.

Table 6-4   Properties Copied to New User Objects

Tab	Properties Copied
General	None
Address	All, except Street Address
Telephones	None
Organization	All, except Title
Account	All, except User Logon Name and User Logon Name (Pre–Windows 2000), which are specified during the copy process
Profile	All, including Profile Path and Local Path, which are modified to reflect the new user's logon name
Member Of	All
Terminal Services Profile	None
Environment	None
Remote Control	None
Sessions	None
Dial-in	None
COM+	None

> **NOTE** Creating Multiple Templates Depending on the size of your organization and the complexity of your user object configurations, you might want to create multiple templates at various locations in your Active Directory tree. For example, creating a separate user object template in each of your OUs would enable you to configure each one with property values specific to that OU.

Once the template is in place, you can use it to create a new user account by selecting it and, from the Action menu, selecting Copy. A Copy Object – User wizard appears that is nearly identical to the New Object – User wizard you used earlier in this chapter. The wizard walks you through the process of configuring the object properties that must have unique values, such as the user's first and last names, initials, logon names, password, and account options. When the wizard finishes, the new user object is created, with the template values for properties listed in the table.

> **EXAM TIP** Object Copying and Permissions A user that has been generated by copying a template has the same group memberships as the template, so the permissions and rights assigned to those groups apply to the new user as well. However, permissions or rights assigned explicitly to the template user object are not copied to new objects or adjusted, so the new user will not have those permissions or rights.

Importing User Objects Using CSV Directory Exchange

CSV Directory Exchange (Csvde.exe) is a command-line utility that imports objects to or exports them from Active Directory using comma-delimited text files. A comma-delimited text file (also known as a CSV, or comma-separated value, file), is a plain-text listing of database information with each record forming a separate line and commas separating the different fields in each record.

> **NOTE** Exam Objectives The objectives for the 70-290 exam specify that students should be able to "import user accounts."

Creating a CSV File

The most difficult part of using CSV Directory Exchange to create user objects is the format of the CSV file itself. The first line of a CSV file, called the header, must contain a list of the attributes that will be included in all of the subsequent lines. You list the attributes using the names assigned to them in Lightweight Directory Access Protocol (LDAP), which is the standard Active Directory communication protocol. A typical CSV header line might appear as follows:

```
DN,objectClass,sAMAccountName,sn,givenName,userPrincipalName
```

In this line, the field names stand for the following attributes:

■ *DN* The object's distinguished name (DN), which specifies not only the name of the object itself but also its place in the Active Directory tree hierarchy. A DN consists of the user's common name (CN) followed by the names of all the containers above the user object, all the way to the root of the tree.

■ *objectClass* Specifies the type of object.

- **sAMAccountName**   Specifies the object's pre–Windows 2000 logon name.

- **sn**   Specifies the user's surname.

- **givenName**   Specifies the user's first name.

- **userPrincipalName**   Specifies the user's full UPN, including the domain name.

Every subsequent line following this header must specify a value for each of the attributes listed in the header. An example of a record in the CSV file is as follows:

```
"CN=Scott Bishop,OU=Employees,DC=contoso,DC=com",
    user,sbishop,Bishop,Scott,scott.bishop@contoso.com
```

This file, when imported, creates a user object in the Employees OU called Scott Bishop. The logon names, first name, and last name are configured by the file. This is a simple example of a CSV file with only a few attributes. The header can be much longer and contain any of the attributes normally found in an object.

> **NOTE**   **Creating Blank Attributes**   When creating the records in a CSV file, you can leave the value for a particular attribute blank, but you must still account for it in the field layout. For example, to omit the user's first name from this sample record, you would use the following format:
>
> ```
> "CN=Scott Bishop,OU=Employees,DC=contoso,DC=com",
>     user,sbishop,Bishop,,scott.bishop@contoso.com
> ```
>
> The number of commas remains the same, so the givenName field is accounted for, but it contains no value.

The best way to create your own CSV file is to use an existing one as an example. You can use CSV Directory Exchange to export your entire Active Directory database to a CSV file by typing the following command in a command prompt window:

```
csvde -f outputFileName
```

You can then open the output file in any text editor, such as Notepad, and use it to determine the LDAP names for the attributes you want to use and the proper format for each record.

Importing a CSV File

Once you have created a properly formatted CSV file containing the information for multiple Active Directory objects, you can import them all into your directory at once by running the Csvde.exe program from the Windows command line with the name of the CSV file, using the following syntax:

```
csvde -i -f FileName -k
```

The functions of the command line switches are as follows:

- **-i**   Switches the program into import mode. If not specified, the default mode is export.

- **-f filename**   Specifies the name of the CSV file to be imported.

- **-k**   Causes the program to ignore errors, such as "object already exists," "constraint violation," and "attribute or value already exists," during the import operation and continue processing.

Creating User Objects with Dsadd.exe

Dsadd.exe is a Windows Server 2003 program that enables you to create new Active Directory objects, complete with attribute values, from the command prompt. When you have a large number of user objects to create, the advantage of using Dsadd.exe is that you can create a batch file containing multiple commands and create as many objects as you need at one time.

> **NOTE** **Exam Objectives** *The objectives for the 70-290 exam specify that students should be able to "create and modify user accounts by using automation."*

The basic syntax for creating user objects with Dsadd.exe is as follows:

```
dsadd user UserDN [parameters]
```

> **NOTE** **Creating Other Object Types** *You can use Dsadd.exe to create any type of Active Directory object by replacing the user parameter with the name of any object class the directory supports, and by supplying additional parameters appropriate to that object class.*

The *UserDN* parameter is one or more distinguished names for the new user object(s). The DN uses the same format as it does in CSV files, as discussed earlier in this chapter. If a DN includes a space, you must surround the entire DN with quotation marks. When using Dsadd.exe interactively from the command prompt, you can supply the *UserDN* parameter in any one of the following ways:

- By typing each DN on the command line, separated by spaces.
- By piping a list of DNs from another command, such as Dsquery.exe.
- By leaving the DN parameter empty, at which point you can type the DNs, one at a time, at a prompt presented by the program. Press Enter after each DN, and press Ctrl+Z and Enter after the last DN.

In addition to the *UserDN* parameter, you can include any of the following parameters on the Dsadd user command line to specify values for other object attributes:

- **-samid** *SAMName*
- **-upn** *UPN*
- **-fn** *FirstName*
- **-mi** *Initial*
- **-ln** *LastName*
- **-display** *DisplayName*
- **-empid** *EmployeeID*
- **-pwd** {*Password* | *}, where * will cause you to be prompted for a password
- **-desc** *Description*
- **-memberof** *GroupDN*
- **-office** *Office*

- **-tel** *PhoneNumber*
- **-email** *Email*
- **-hometel** *HomePhoneNumber*
- **-pager** *PagerNumber*
- **-mobile** *CellPhoneNumber*
- **-fax** *FaxNumber*
- **-iptel** *IPPhoneNumber*
- **-webpg** *WebPage*
- **-title** *Title*
- **-dept** *Department*
- **-company** *Company*
- **-mgr** *ManagerDN*
- **-hmdir** *HomeDirectory*
- **-hmdrv** *DriveLetter*
- **-profile** *ProfilePath*
- **-loscr** *ScriptPath*
- **-mustchpwd** {yes | no}
- **-canchpwd** {yes | no}
- **-reversiblepwd** {yes | no}
- **-pwdneverexpires** {yes | no}
- **-acctexpires** *NumberOfDays*
- **-disabled** {yes | no}

You can also add the *-s*, *-u*, and *-p* parameters to specify the domain controller against which Dsadd.exe will run and the username and password that will be used to execute the command.

- **{-s** *Server* | **-d** *Domain*}
- **-u** *UserName*
- **-p** {*Password* | *}

The special variable *$username$* (case-insensitive) can be used to supply the user's SAM account name in the value of the *-email*, *-hmdir*, *-profile*, and *-webpg* parameters. For example, if a SAM account name is Denise, the *-hmdir* parameter can be written in either of the following formats:

```
-hmdir\users\Denise\home
-hmdir\users\$username$\home
```

To create an object for the Scott Bishop user from the earlier example, you would use the following Dsadd.exe command line:

```
dsadd user "CN=Scott Bishop,OU=Employees,DC=contoso,DC=com" -samid sbishop
    -ln Bishop -fn Scott -upn scott.bishop@contoso.com
```

Modifying User Objects with Dsmod.exe

Dsmod.exe is another Windows Server 2003 command-line tool that you can use to modify existing Active Directory objects. The syntax and command-line switches for modifying user objects with Dsmod.exe are exactly the same as those for Dsadd.exe, as follows:

```
dsmod user UserDN [parameters]
```

The only exceptions are that you cannot use the *–samid* switch to modify an object's User Logon Name property, and you cannot use the *–memberof* parameter to change the user's group memberships. You can, however, modify group memberships by using the Dsmod group command.

MANAGING USER PROFILES

A *user profile* is a collection of folders and data that stores the user's current desktop environment, application settings, and personal data. A user profile also contains all of the user's Start menu items and mapped drives to network servers. User profiles maintain consistency by providing users with the same desktop environment that they had the last time they logged on to the computer.

> **NOTE Exam Objectives** *The objectives for the 70-290 exam specify that students should be able to "manage local, roaming, and mandatory user profiles."*

On computers running Windows Server 2003, user profiles automatically create and maintain the desktop settings for each user's work environment on the local computer. The system creates a new user profile for each user logging on to the computer for the first time.

User profiles provide several advantages to users:

- Multiple users can work on the same computer, with all users maintaining their own desktop settings each time they log on.

- When users log on to their workstations, they receive the same desktop settings that they had when they logged off.

- Customization of the desktop environment by one user does not affect another user's settings.

- User profiles can be stored on a server so that they can follow users to other computers on the network. Server-based profiles are called **roaming user profiles**.

- Applications that are certified for Windows 2000 and later operating systems store their settings in user profiles.

- As an administrative tool, user profiles provide the following options:

  - You can create a default user profile that is appropriate for the user's tasks.

  - You can set up a **mandatory user profile**, which is a profile that does not change, enforcing a particular system configuration for all users.

  - You can specify the default user settings to be included in all of the individual user profiles.

User Profile Contents

A user profile contains configuration preferences and options for a specific user, forming a snapshot of a user's desktop environment. Table 6-5 lists the settings contained in a user profile.

Table 6-5   **Settings Contained in a User Profile**

Parameters Saved	Source
All user-definable settings for Windows Explorer	Windows Explorer
User-stored documents	My Documents
User-stored image files	My Pictures
Shortcuts and cookies for favorite locations on the Internet	Favorites/Cookies
User-created mapped network drives	Mapped network drive
Links to other computers on the network	My Network Places
Items stored on the desktop and in the taskbar, and shortcut elements	Desktop contents
All user-definable screen colors and display text settings	Screen colors and fonts
Application data and user-defined configuration settings	Application data and registry
Network printer connections	Printer settings
All user-defined settings in Control Panel	Control Panel
Per-user program settings for applications designed to track program settings	Programs certified for use with Windows 2000 and later operating systems
Certificates	Certificate store

User Profile Directory Structure

Local user profiles are stored on the computer's system drive in the Documents And Settings folder. When a user logs on for the first time, Windows Server 2003 creates a subfolder in Documents And Settings, named with the user's logon name, and also a new user profile. Figure 6-10 shows the directory structure of a user profile.

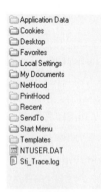

Figure 6-10   The user profile directory structure

The functions of the folders in a user profile are as follows:

- **Application Data**   A hidden folder that contains program-specific data, such as a custom dictionary. Application developers decide which data to store in this folder.

- **Cookies**   Contains Web site user information and preferences stored by Internet Explorer.

- **Desktop**   Contains desktop icons, including shortcuts to files and folders.

- **Favorites**   Contains shortcuts to favorite locations on the Internet.

- **Local Settings**   A hidden folder that contains the Application Data folder and History folder, as well as additional folders for the storage of temporary files.

- **My Documents**   Contains user-stored document files.

- **My Recent Documents**   Hidden folder that contains shortcuts to the most recently used documents and most recently accessed folders.

- **NetHood**   Hidden folder that contains shortcuts to My Network Places items.

- **PrintHood**   Hidden folder that contains shortcuts to printer folder items.

- **SendTo**   Hidden folder that contains shortcuts to document-handling utilities.

- **Start Menu**   Contains shortcuts to executables and other files that form the Start menu.

- **Templates**   Contains user template items.

In addition to these folders, a user profile also contains a copy of the Ntuser.dat file, which is the Windows Server 2003 registry file where user-specific settings are stored. Among other things, these settings include many of the options you can configure in Control Panel.

Using Local Profiles

The use of local user profiles on a computer running Windows Server 2003 is completely invisible to the average user. The operating system automatically creates the user profile for each user logging on for the first time. When that user logs on again, Windows Server 2003 loads the settings from the correct profile.

Users change their local user profiles without even knowing it, simply by changing their desktop settings, saving new favorites, or changing screen colors. When the user modifies the desktop environment while logged on, Windows Server 2003 incorporates the changes into the user profile stored on the computer the next time the user logs off. Thus, a user logging on to a computer running Windows Server 2003 always receives the desktop settings and connections as they were at the end of the previous session. When multiple users share the same computer, each user maintains and receives a separate profile.

Using Roaming Profiles

To support users who work at multiple computers, network administrators can set up roaming user profiles. A roaming user profile is simply a copy of a local user profile that is stored on a network share (to which the user has appropriate permissions) so that the user can access it from any computer on the network. No matter which computer a user logs on from, the user always receives the desktop settings and connections from the profile stored on the server, in contrast to a local user profile, which resides on only one client computer.

To enable a user to access a roaming user profile, rather than a local profile, you must open the user's Properties dialog box and specify the location of the roaming profile in the Profile Path text box on the Profile tab. Then, the next time the user logs on, Windows Server 2003 accesses the roaming user profile in the following manner:

1. During the user's first logon, the computer copies the entire contents of the roaming profile to the appropriate subfolder in the Documents And Settings folder on the local drive.

   Having the roaming user profile contents stored on the local drive enables the user to log on and access the profile, even if the server containing the roaming profile is not available.

2. The computer applies the roaming user profile settings to the computer.

3. As the user works, any changes made to the user profile are saved to the copy on the local drive.

4. When the user logs off, the computer replicates any changes that were made to the local copy of the user profile back to the server where the roaming profile is stored.

5. The next time the user logs on to the same computer, the system compares the contents of the locally-stored profile with the roaming profile stored on the server.

6. The computer copies only the roaming profile components that have changed to the copy on the local drive, which makes the logon process shorter and more efficient.

You should create roaming user profiles on a file server that you frequently back up so that you have copies of the most recent profiles for your users. To improve logon performance for a busy network, place the users' roaming profiles folder on a member server instead of a domain controller. Copying roaming user profiles between the server and client computers can consume a lot of system resources, such as network bandwidth and processor cycles. If the profiles are on a domain controller, the domain user authentication processes can be delayed.

> **NOTE Shared Profile Cautions** When you create a single roaming profile for multiple clients, be sure to consider the potential ramifications of having different hardware configurations on systems using the same profile. For example, if desktop shortcuts are arranged assuming a 1024x768 screen resolution and the user logs on to a system with a display adapter capable of only 800x600 resolution, some shortcuts might not be visible. Profiles are also not fully cross-platform. A profile designed for Windows 98 will not function properly on a Windows Server 2003 system. You will even encounter inconsistencies when roaming between Windows Server 2003 systems and computers running Windows XP or Windows 2000.

Using Mandatory Profiles

A mandatory user profile is a read-only roaming user profile. Users receive desktop settings as they would with any roaming profile, and they can modify the desktop settings of the computer while they are logged on, but none of these changes is saved when they log off. The next time the user logs on, the profile is the same as that of the previous logon. Windows Server 2003 downloads the mandatory profile settings to the local computer each time the user logs on. You can assign one mandatory profile to multiple users who require the same desktop settings, such as a group of users who all do the same job. Because the profile never changes, you do not have to worry about one user making changes that affect all of the other users. Also, a mandatory profile makes it possible to modify the desktop environment for multiple users by changing only one profile.

To create a mandatory user profile, you rename the Ntuser.dat file in the folder containing the roaming profile to Ntuser.man. The Ntuser.dat file is a hidden file that consists of the Windows Server 2003 system registry settings that apply to the individual user account and contains the user environment settings, such as desktop appearance. Renaming this file with a .man extension makes it read-only, preventing the client computers from saving changes to the profile when a user logs off.

MONITORING AND TROUBLESHOOTING USER AUTHENTICATION

Once you have configured user objects and users are authenticating against those accounts, you expose yourself to two additional challenges: security vulnerabilities, which if unaddressed could compromise the integrity of your enterprise network, and social engineering challenges, as you work to make the network authentication process friendly and reliable for users. Unfortunately, these two dynamics are at odds with each other—the more secure a network is, the less user-friendly it becomes.

Implementing the Windows Server 2003 features that provide security for the user authentication process frequently results in users having trouble logging on, and part of the network administrator's job is to troubleshoot these problems as they occur. The following sections examine some of the most common causes of user authentication problems and the tools that you can use to detect and address them.

Using Password Policies

Earlier in this chapter, in "Choosing Passwords," you learned about the password policies that Windows Server 2003 provides, which enable you to specify the length, complexity, and age of the passwords supplied by users for their accounts. The basic goals of these policies are to compel users to specify effective passwords and to force them to change the passwords at regular intervals.

It is easy to use these password policies to enforce the use of extremely secure passwords, but requiring each user to supply a new 15-character complex password every week is likely to cause more problems than it solves. The network support staff will probably start receiving a rash of forgotten password calls, but even worse, users will be more likely to write down their passwords and store them in unsafe places. You must design a password policy that is sufficiently daunting to attackers while being sufficiently convenient for users, so that they do not forget their passwords or have to write them down.

> **NOTE   Specifying Password Lengths**   When you implement password policies, keep in mind that while Windows Server 2003, Windows XP Professional, and Windows 2000 support 127-character passwords, Windows 95, Windows 98, and Windows Me only support passwords up to 14 characters long.

The five password policies listed earlier in this chapter are available in Active Directory group policy objects, which you configure using the Group Policy Object Editor console, by browsing to the Computer Configuration\Windows Settings \Security Settings\Account Policies\Password Policy node. However, you can also define the same policies for local user accounts using the Local Security Policy console, which is available in the Administrative Tools program group on any Windows Server 2003 member server.

> **NOTE   Changing Password Policies**   Configuring password length and complexity requirements does not affect existing passwords. These changes affect only new accounts and passwords that change after the policy is applied.

Using Account Lockout Policies

Account lockout happens when, after several failed logon attempts by a single user, the system assumes that an attacker is attempting to compromise the account by discovering its password, and locks the account so no further logons can be attempted. Domain account lockout policies determine how many invalid logon attempts can be made in a given period of time before the account is locked out. These policies also determine whether an administrator must be contacted to unlock the account, or if it simply becomes unlocked after a specified period of time.

> **NOTE   Exam Objectives**   The objectives for the 70-290 exam specify that students should be able to "diagnose and resolve account lockouts."

The group policies you use to control account lockouts are as follows:

- **Account Lockout Threshold**   Specifies the number of invalid logon attempts that will trigger an account lockout. Possible values range from 0 to 999. A value that is too low (3, for example) might cause lockouts due to normal user error during logon. A value of 0 prevents accounts from ever being locked out.

- **Account Lockout Duration**   Determines the period of time that must pass after a lockout before Active Directory will automatically unlock a user's account. The policy is not set by default because it is useful only in conjunction with the Account Lockout Threshold policy. Possible values range from 0 to 99,999 minutes (about 10 weeks). A low setting (5 to 15 minutes) is sufficient to reduce attacks significantly without unreasonably affecting legitimate users who are mistakenly locked out. A value of 0 requires the user to contact an administrator to unlock the account manually.

■ **Reset Account Lockout Counter After** Specifies the period of time that must pass after an invalid logon attempt before the lockout counter resets to 0. Possible values range from 1 to 99,999 minutes and must be less than or equal to the value of the Account Lockout Duration.

As with password policies, you configure account policies in the Group Policy Object Editor console, in the Computer Configuration\Windows Settings\Security Settings\Account Policies\Account Lockout Policy node. Account lockout policies are also available in the Local Security Policy console.

When you implement an account lockout policy on your network, you are all but guaranteed to receive a certain number of technical support calls from users who have unknowingly locked themselves out from their accounts. These calls might be reported as something else, such as lost passwords or other malfunctions, but savvy help desk technicians should be conscious of the account lockout policies in place on the network and of the procedure for unlocking a locked account.

> **NOTE** *Exam Objectives* *The objectives for the 70-290 exam specify that students should be able to "troubleshoot user accounts" and "troubleshoot user authentication issues."*

Active Directory Clients

When you run a heterogeneous network, you must keep in mind that not all operating systems, and not even all Windows operating systems, support Active Directory right out of the box. Active Directory was first introduced in Windows 2000, and only the Windows 2000, Windows XP, and Windows Server 2003 operating systems include Active Directory client capabilities.

Computers running Windows 95, Windows 98, Windows Me, and Windows NT 4 can function as Active Directory clients, but first you must download the Active Directory client software from Microsoft's Web site and install it. This client enables those platforms to participate in many of the Active Directory features available to Windows Server 2003, Windows XP, and Windows 2000 systems, including the following:

■ **Site-awareness** A computer running the Active Directory Client will attempt to log on to the closest domain controller on the network rather than to the primary domain controller (PDC).

■ **Active Directory Service Interfaces (ADSI)** Enables the use of scripting to manage Active Directory.

■ **Distributed File System (Dfs)** Enables the client to access Dfs shared resources on servers running Windows Server 2003 and Windows 2000.

■ **NT LAN Manager (NTLM) version 2 authentication** The client uses the improved authentication features in NTLM version 2.

■ **Active Directory search capability**   The client can search for Active Directory objects using the Find or Search feature. Users with proper permissions can also use the Windows Address Book (WAB) property pages to modify the properties of objects.

The following types of functionality, supported on Windows 2000 Professional and Windows XP Professional, are *not* provided by the Active Directory client on Windows 95, Windows 98, and Windows NT 4:

■ Kerberos V5 authentication

■ Group Policy or Change And Configuration Management support

■ Service principal name (SPN) or mutual authentication

■ Internet Protocol Security (IPSec) or Layer 2 Tunneling Protocol (L2TP) support

In addition, you should be aware of the following issues in mixed environments:

■ Without the Active Directory client, users on systems running versions of Windows prior to Windows 2000 can change their passwords only if the system has access to the domain controller functioning as the primary domain controller (PDC) emulator. To determine which system is the PDC emulator in a domain, open Active Directory Users And Computers, select the domain node, select the Operations Masters command from the Action menu, and then select the PDC tab. If the PDC emulator is unavailable (that is, if it is offline or on the distant side of a downed network connection), the user cannot change her password.

■ As you learned earlier in this chapter, user objects maintain two user logon name properties. The Pre–Windows 2000 logon name, or SAM name, is equivalent to the username in Windows 95, Windows 98, or Windows NT 4. When users log on, they enter their username and must select the domain from the Log On To drop-down list. In other situations, the username can be entered in the format *DomainName\UserLogonName*. Users logging on using Windows 2000 or later platforms can log on in the same way, or they can log on using the more efficient UPN. The UPN takes the format *UserLogonName@UPN Suffix*, where the UPN suffix is, by default, the DNS domain name in which the user object resides. It is not necessary to select the domain from the Log On To box when using UPN logon. In fact, the box becomes disabled as soon as you type the @ symbol.

Auditing Authentication

If you are concerned that attacks might be taking place to discover user passwords, or if you want more information to troubleshoot authentication problems, you can configure an auditing policy that creates entries in the Security log that might prove illuminating. The following audit policies are located in the Computer Configuration \Windows Settings\Security Settings\Local Policies\Audit Policy node of both the Group Policy Object Editor console and the Local Security Policy console. You can configure auditing for successful or failed events.

- **Audit Account Logon Events**   Audits each successful or failed user logon event. For domain controllers, this policy is defined in the Default Domain Controllers Policy GPO. Enabling the policy creates a Security log entry on a domain controller each time a user logs on interactively or over the network using a domain account. To evaluate fully the results of the auditing, you must examine the Security logs on all domain controllers because user authentication is distributed among the domain controllers in a site or domain.

- **Audit Account Management**   Configures auditing of administrative activities, including the creation, deletion, or modification of user, group, or computer accounts, as well as password resets.

- **Audit Logon Events**   Logon events include logon and logoff, interactively or through network connection. If you have enabled the Audit Account Logon Events policy for successes on a domain controller, workstation logons will not generate logon audits. Only interactive and network logons to the domain controller itself generate logon events. Account logon events are generated on the local computer for local accounts and on the domain controller for network accounts. Logon events are generated wherever the logon occurs.

  NOTE Exam Objectives   The objectives for the 70-290 exam specify that a student should be able to "diagnose and resolve issues related to user account properties."

Once you have configured the auditing policies, the Security logs will begin to fill with event messages. You can view these messages using the Event Viewer console.

  MORE INFO   For more information on using the Event Viewer console, see Chapter 3, "Monitoring Microsoft Windows Server 2003."

SUMMARY

- Computers running Windows Server 2003 can have local user accounts and domain user accounts. Local user accounts are stored on the local system and can provide users with access only to local resources. Domain user accounts are stored on Active Directory domain controllers and can provide users with access to resources all over the network.

- To create domain user accounts, you must be a member of the Enterprise Admins, Domain Admins, or Account Operators groups, or you must have been delegated administrative permissions to create user objects.

- User objects include the properties typically associated with a user "account," including logon names, password, and the unique SID for the user. They also include a number of properties related to the individuals they represent, including personal information, group membership, and administrative settings. Windows Server 2003 enables you to change some of these properties for multiple user objects simultaneously.

- A user object template is an object that is copied to produce new users. If the template is not a "real" user, it should be disabled. Only a subset of user properties is copied from templates.

- CSV Directory Exchange enables you to import directory objects from a comma-delimited text file.

- Windows Server 2003 includes command-line tools that you can use to create and manage Active Directory objects, including Dsadd.exe and Dsmod.exe

- A user profile is a collection of folders and files that make up the desktop environment for a specific user. User profiles include the user's personal documents, desktop icons, Start menu shortcuts, and Control Panel settings, such as those that control the screen colors.

- Windows Server 2003 generates an individual user profile for each person who logs on to the system. Profiles are stored, by default, on the local system in *Systemdrive*\Documents and Settings*Username*.

- A local user profile is one that is stored on the local drive, whereas a roaming user profile is one that is stored on a network server. Roaming profiles provide users with the same profile from any computer on the network.

- A mandatory user profile is one that never changes, providing the same desktop configuration each time the user logs on.

- Auditing for authentication generates events in each domain controller's security logs.

EXERCISES

Exercise 6-1: Changing Password Policy Settings

In this exercise, you modify the default password policy settings on your computer.

1. Log on to a Windows Server 2003 domain controller as Administrator.

2. Click Start, point to Administrative Tools, and click Active Directory Users And Computers. The Active Directory Users And Computers console appears.

3. Select the domain object and, from the Action menu, select Properties. The domain's Properties dialog box appears.

4. In the Group Policy tab, select Default Domain Policy and click Edit. The Group Policy Object Editor console appears.

5. Under Computer Configuration, expand the Windows Settings, Security Settings, and Account Policies nodes. Then select the Password Policy node.

6. Double-click the Minimum Password Length policy. The Minimum Password Length Properties dialog box appears.

7. Change the minimum password length setting to 8 characters, and then click OK.

8. Double-click the Maximum Password Age policy. The Maximum Password Age Properties dialog box appears.

9. Change the maximum password age setting to 7 days, and then click OK.

10. Close the Group Policy Object Editor console.

11. Click OK to close the domain's Properties dialog box.

12. Close the Active Directory Users And Computers console.

Exercise 6-2: Creating a Domain User Object

In this exercise, you create a new user object in an Active Directory container.

1. Log on to a Windows Server 2003 domain controller as Administrator.

2. Click Start, point to Administrative Tools, and click Active Directory Users And Computers. The Active Directory Users And Computers console appears.

3. Expand the domain object in the scope pane and select the Users container. On the Action menu, point to New and click User. The New Object – User wizard appears.

4. In the Full Name text box, type **Mark Lee**.

5. In the User Logon Name text box, type **mlee**, and then click Next.

6. In the Password and Confirm Password text boxes, type **rabbit!runs4all**, and then click Next.

7. Click Finish to create the new object.

8. Close the Active Directory Users And Computers console.

Exercise 6-3: Moving a User Object

In this exercise, you move a user object to a different container.

1. Log on to a Windows Server 2003 domain controller as Administrator.

2. Click Start, point to Administrative Tools, and click Active Directory Users And Computers. The Active Directory Users And Computers console appears.

3. Expand the domain object in the scope pane and select the Users container. In the details pane, select the Guest user object. On the Action menu, select Move. The Move dialog box appears.

4. Select the Computers container, and then click OK. The Guest object is moved to the Computers container.

5. Select the Computers container in the scope pane.

6. In the details pane, click the Guest user object and drag it to the Users container in the scope pane. The Guest object is moved back to the Users container.

REVIEW QUESTIONS

1. You are using the Active Directory Users And Computers console to configure user objects in your domain, and you are able to change the address and telephone number properties of the user object representing yourself. However, the New User command is unavailable to you. What is the most likely explanation?

2. Which of the following properties can be configured simultaneously on more than one user object?

   a. Password Never Expires

   b. Direct Reports

   c. User Must Change Password At Next Logon

   d. Last Name

   e. Logon Hours

   f. Computer Restrictions (Logon Workstations)

   g. User Logon Name

   h. Title

3. Of the three methods for creating multiple user objects discussed in this chapter, which method would be most efficient for generating 100 new user objects, all with identical Profile Path, Home Folder, Title, Web Page, Company, Department, and Manager settings?

4. What variable can be used with the Dsadd.exe and Dsmod.exe program commands to create user-specific home folders and profile folders?

   a. *%Username%*

   b. *$Username$*

   c. *CN=Username*

   d. *<Username>*

5. How do you make a roaming profile mandatory?

   a. Configure the permissions on the folder's Security property sheet to deny write permission.

   b. Configure the permissions on the folders Sharing property sheet to allow only read permission.

   c. Modify the attributes of the profile folder to specify the Read Only attribute.

   d. Rename Ntuser.dat to Ntuser.man.

6. What is the difference between a local user profile and a roaming user profile?

7. What do you do to ensure that a user on a computer running Windows Server 2003 has a roaming user profile?

8. You have enabled the Password Must Meet Complexity Requirements in your domain. Describe the requirements for passwords and when those requirements will take effect.

CASE SCENARIOS

Scenario 6-1: Configuring User Object Properties

You are creating a number of user objects for a team of your organization's temporary workers. They will work daily from 9 A.M. to 5 P.M. on a contract that is scheduled to begin in one month and end two months later. They will not work outside of that schedule. Which of the following properties should you configure initially to ensure maximum security for the objects?

   a. Password

   b. Logon Hours

   c. Account Expires

   d. Store Password Using Reversible Encryption

    e. Account Is Trusted For Delegation

    f. User Must Change Password At Next Logon

    g. Account Is Disabled

    h. Password Never Expires

Scenario 6-2: Managing Account Lockouts

A user has forgotten his or her password and attempts to log on several times with an incorrect password. Eventually, the user receives a logon message indicating that the account is either disabled or locked out. The message suggests that the user contact an administrator. What must the administrator do?

    a. Delete the user object and recreate it.

    b. Rename the user object.

    c. Enable the user object.

    d. Unlock the user object.

    e. Reset the password for the user object.

CHAPTER 7
WORKING WITH GROUPS

In Chapter 6, you learned how user objects provide network users with access to resources on an Active Directory network. Another important tool for administrators is the group object. Using groups, administrators can simplify the process of assigning access permissions to users. In this chapter, you learn about the various types of groups that Active Directory supports, how to create them, and how to use them effectively.

Upon completion of this chapter, you will be able to:

- Understand the functions of groups and how to use them

- Understand the difference between local groups and domain groups

- Identify the two group types and three group scopes and their proper use

- List the predefined and built-in groups included in Microsoft Windows Server 2003

- Understand the difference between groups and special identities

- Create, manage, and delete groups

UNDERSTANDING GROUPS

For users to be able to access resources on an Active Directory network, they must have the appropriate permissions. Shared folders and drives, printers, and virtually all other resources on a network have an *access control list (ACL)*. An ACL is a list of objects that are permitted to access the resource, along with the degree of access that each object is permitted. In Windows Server 2003, ACLs are displayed in the Security tab of most any Properties dialog box, as shown in Figure 7-1. The objects in an ACL are referred to as *security principals*. You can use user objects as security principals to grant the user access to all of the resources they need, because a user object establishes the identity of the user through the authentication process.

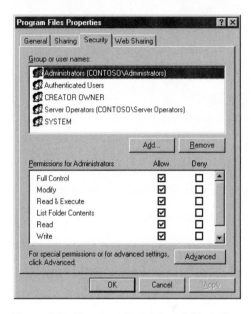

Figure 7-1   The Security tab in a folder's Properties dialog box

Theoretically, administrators can create all permission assignments by adding user objects to ACLs, but on all but the smallest of networks, this process is incredibly time- and labor-intensive. Imagine hiring a group of 250 new employees and, after creating user objects for them, having to grant each one access to a dozen or more resources scattered around the network. Even worse, suppose a server fails and you have to quickly install a substitute server and then change the permissions for 250 users so they can access the new server.

To prevent nightmares like these, network administrators use groups. A group is simply a list of users that functions as a security principal. In Active Directory, group objects can contain user objects, computers, contacts, and, under certain conditions, even other groups. When you use a group object as a security principal by adding it to an ACL, all of the group's members receive the permissions that you assigned to the group (as shown in Figure 7-2). If you add new members to the group later, they also receive the permissions. If you remove members, their permissions are removed.

In the examples cited earlier, you can create a group object and assign it all of the permissions that new hires need. When a new employee arrives, all you have to do is create a new user object and add it to the group. To simplify the process of deploying a substitute server, you create a group containing all of the users of the original server. If the server fails and you have to switch to a new one, all you do is grant the group object permission to access the new server, and all of the users are instantly switched over. On a network with a well-designed system of groups, network administrators rarely, if ever, have to assign permissions to individual users.

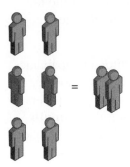

Figure 7-2   As a security principal, one group is equivalent to multiple users.

Groups also make it possible to assign user rights to multiple users at once. In Windows Server 2003, rights are distinctly different from permissions. A *user right* grants a user or group the ability to perform a particular system task, such as access the computer from the network, change the system time, or take ownership of files and other objects. In addition, you can also use groups to create e-mail distribution lists.

Using Groups and Group Policies

In Chapter 6, you learned that the structure of the Active Directory hierarchy is a critical part of the domain user account creation process because rights and permissions granted to a container object are inherited by the objects they contain, including user objects. Group inheritance works in much the same way, with the members receiving the settings assigned to the group. The main difference between a group and a container is that the group is not restricted by the structure of the Active Directory tree. You can create groups with members anywhere in the domain, and even in other domains, and grant them all privileges in one quick step.

Group policies, despite their name, are as closely associated with containers as they are with groups. Group policy objects (GPOs) can be assigned only to Active Directory domain, site, and organizational unit (OU) objects, and their settings are passed down through the Active Directory tree. You cannot assign a group policy object to a group, although in many cases you can configure particular group policy settings to configure an operating system feature on all the members of the group.

For example, you can create an OU object in your Active Directory tree containing all the workstation computer objects in your domain and assign a GPO to that OU. The computers in the OU will all inherit the group policy settings from that GPO, and one of those policy settings might enable the Manage Auditing And Security Log user right, granting that right to a group object containing the users comprising the IT technical support staff. In this case, the computers in the OU receive policy settings from a GPO, and those same group policies grant rights to specific group objects.

Understanding Domain Functional Levels

One of the more widely misunderstood Active Directory concepts is that of the functional level. Administrators are sometimes daunted by the prospect of changing the functional level of a domain or forest because it is one of the few decisions in Windows Server 2003 that is irrevocable. Once you change the functional level, you cannot change it back.

Simply put, the different versions of Windows have slightly different capabilities built into their Active Directory implementations. Each successive version has some new features that are not usable when some of the domain controllers in a domain are running older versions of Windows. Changing the **domain functional level** informs the operating system that all of the domain controllers are compatible and that it is safe to activate the version-specific features.

In Windows Server 2003, four domain functional levels are available: Windows 2000 mixed, Windows 2000 native, Windows Server 2003 interim, and Windows Server 2003. These functional levels support domain controllers running various combinations of operating systems, and they provide various additional features, several of which apply to the functionality of group objects in the domain. The characteristics of the domain functional levels are as follows:

> **NOTE** Domain Functional Levels and Member Servers Raising the domain functional level does not prevent computers running older versions of Windows from joining the domain. The functional level refers only to the Windows version on the domain controllers. A domain running at the Windows Server 2003 functional level can still support member servers and workstations running Windows 2000, Windows NT, Windows XP, Windows Me, Windows 98, and Windows 95, as long as they have the correct Active Directory client software installed.

- **Windows 2000 mixed** The default functional level of a Windows Server 2003 domain controller.
  - ❑ Supports domain controllers running Windows Server 2003, Windows 2000, and Windows NT 4.
  - ❑ Supports universal **distribution groups** but not universal **security groups**.
  - ❑ Global groups cannot have other groups as members (group nesting).
  - ❑ No group conversion allowed.
- **Windows 2000 native** Supports domain controllers running Windows Server 2003 and Windows 2000.
  - ❑ Supports universal security and distribution groups.
  - ❑ Allows groups to be members of other groups.
  - ❑ Allows conversions between security groups and distribution groups.
  - ❑ Allows migration of security principals from one domain to another (security identifier [SID] history).

- **Windows Server 2003 interim** Supports domain controllers running Windows Server 2003 and Windows NT 4. This functional level is used only when upgrading domain controllers in Windows NT 4 domains to Windows Server 2003 domain controllers.

  ❑ Provides no additional features.

- **Windows Server 2003** Supports domain controllers running Windows Server 2003 only.

  ❑ Supports universal security and distribution groups.

  ❑ Allows groups to be members of other groups (group nesting).

  ❑ Allows conversions between security groups and distribution groups.

  ❑ Allows migration of security principals from one domain to another (SID history).

> **NOTE** **Domain Functional-Level Features** *The previous lists contain only the Active Directory features of the functional levels that pertain to group objects and their operations. Raising the domain functional level also activates other features, such as the ability to rename domains. Additional Active Directory features are activated when you raise the* **forest functional level** *on your network, when all the domain controllers in the entire forest are running Windows Server 2003. None of these features affects the use of group objects, however.*

To manage the functional level in Windows Server 2003, you use the Active Directory Domains And Trusts console, which is accessible from the Administrative Tools program group. To view the current functional levels of your domain and forest, select the domain object in the scope pane and, from the Action menu, select Properties. The Properties dialog box for the domain displays the current functional levels on the General tab, as shown in Figure 7-3.

Figure 7-3   A domain's Properties dialog box

To change the functional level, select the domain object and, from the Action menu, select Raise Domain Functional Level to display the dialog box shown in Figure 7-4. In the Select An Available Domain Functional Level drop-down list, choose the functional level you want to use and click Raise. As stated earlier, you cannot lower the functional level after you raise it, except by reinstalling Active Directory on all of your domain controllers, so the program cautions you to be sure before committing yourself. Once the functional level is raised on that one domain controller, the change is replicated to all of the other domain controllers in the domain.

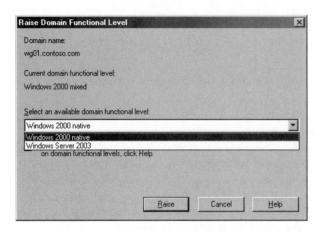

Figure 7-4   The Raise Domain Functional Level dialog box

NOTE   Raising the Forest Functional Level   To raise the forest functional level, select the Active Directory Domains and Trusts object in the scope pane and, from the Action menu, select Raise Forest Functional Level.

USING LOCAL GROUPS

In Chapter 6, you learned that Windows Server 2003 supports both local user accounts and domain user accounts. The same is true for groups. Windows Server 2003 supports **local groups** and domain groups.

A *local group* is a collection of local user accounts on a particular computer. Local groups perform the same basic function as all groups: they enable you to assign permissions to multiple users in one step. You create local groups using the Local Users And Groups snap-in, which is integrated into the Computer Management console (which is accessible from the Administrative Tools program group), as shown in Figure 7-5. When you create a local group, the system stores it in the local Security Accounts Manager (SAM) database.

Local groups are subject to restrictions, just as local users are. The local group restrictions are as follows:

- You can use local groups only on the computer where you create them.

- Only local users from the same computer can be members of local groups.

- When the computer is a member of a domain, local group members can include users and **global groups** from the domain or any trusted domain.

- Local groups cannot have other local groups as members.

- Local group permissions provide access only to resources on the computer where you created the local group.

- You cannot create local groups on a Windows Server 2003 computer that is functioning as a domain controller.

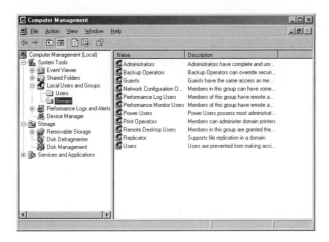

Figure 7-5 The Local Users And Groups snap-in

USING ACTIVE DIRECTORY GROUPS

Active Directory groups are characterized by their type and their scope. There are two types of Active Directory groups, each with three distinct scopes. Understanding the constructions of these groups within the correct scope ensures the best use of administrative resources when you create, assign, and manage access to resources. The possibilities of group construction also depend on the functional level of the domain in which the groups are created. Windows Server 2003 comes with a large number of groups created, and you can create as many additional groups as you need.

Active Directory groups, no matter what their type or scope, take the form of objects in the Active Directory database, just as user accounts and containers are objects. Compared to user objects, group objects are quite simple. Instead of the dozens of attributes you find in a user object, a group object consists of only a few attributes, the most important of which is its member list. As the name implies, the member list is simply a list of objects, such as users, other groups, computers, and contacts, that are members of the group. All permissions and rights assigned to the group are inherited by every object in the member list.

You create and manage all Active Directory groups using the Active Directory Users And Computers console, which is accessible from the Administrative Tools program group in Windows Server 2003, as shown in Figure 7-6. As with any Active Directory object, to create and manage groups you must have the appropriate permissions for the containers where the groups are located.

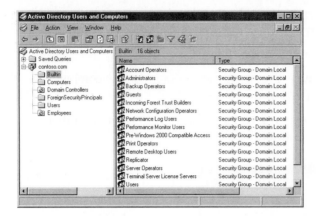

Figure 7-6   The Active Directory Users And Computers console

Active Directory Group Types

There are two types of Active Directory group objects: security groups and distribution groups.

Security Groups

Security groups are the ones you use to assign access permissions for network resources. When someone speaks of a group in relation to Windows Server 2003 or Active Directory, they are usually speaking of a security group. Programs that are designed to work with Active Directory can also use security groups for nonsecurity-related purposes, such as retrieving user information for use in a Web application.

> **NOTE**   **Windows Server 2003 Uses Only Security Groups**   Security groups can be used as distribution groups, but distribution groups cannot be used as security groups. Windows Server 2003 itself can only make use of security groups, but because security groups have all the capabilities of distribution groups, this is not a shortcoming.

Distribution Groups

Distribution groups are intended for use by applications as lists for nonsecurity-related functions. You use distribution groups when the only function of the group is not security-related, such as sending e-mail messages to a group of users at the same time. You cannot use distribution groups to assign rights and permissions. Only applications that are designed to work with Active Directory can use distribution groups. For example, Microsoft Exchange uses distribution groups as mailing lists for sending e-mail messages.

Active Directory Group Scopes

Group scopes define how permissions are assigned to the group members. All Active Directory groups, both security and distribution groups, can be classified into one of three scopes: domain local, global, and universal.

Domain Local Groups

Domain local groups are most often used to assign access permissions to resources, either directly or by adding a global group to a domain local group. Domain local groups have the following characteristics:

- Domain local groups are available in all functional levels: Windows 2000 mixed, Windows 2000 native, Windows Server 2003 interim, and Windows Server 2003.

- You can use a domain local group to grant access permissions to resources only in the same domain where you create the domain local group.

- When you use the Windows 2000 mixed or Windows 2003 interim functional level, domain local group members can include user and computer accounts and global groups from any domain in the forest. No other group nesting is permitted.

- When you use the Windows 2000 native or Windows Server 2003 functional level, domain local group members can include user and computer accounts, global and **universal groups** from any domain in the forest, and other domain local groups from the same domain. Domain local groups can be converted to the universal scope as long as they do not have other domain local groups as members.

> **NOTE** **Local Groups and Domain Local Groups** Because Active Directory groups with a domain local scope are sometimes referred to as local groups, be sure to distinguish between a local group on a particular computer (sometimes called a machine local group) and an Active Directory group with a domain local scope.

Domain local groups are most commonly used to control access to resources within a single domain. For example, you might create a domain local group with permissions that grant members access to a particular printer. Then you can add users in the domain directly to the domain local group, or you can create a global group containing users that need printer access and make the global group a member of the domain local group.

Global Groups

Global groups are used primarily to provide categorized membership in domain local groups for individual security principals or for direct permission assignment (particularly in the case of a network using the Windows 2000 mixed or Windows Server 2003 interim domain functional level). Often, global groups are used to collect users or computers in the same domain that share the same job, role, or function or that have similar network access requirements. Global groups have the following characteristics:

- Global groups are available in all functional levels: Windows 2000 mixed, Windows 2000 native, Windows Server 2003 interim, and Windows Server 2003.

- Global groups can only include members from within their domain.

- When you use the Windows 2000 native or Windows Server 2003 functional level, global group members can include user and computer accounts as well as other global groups from the same domain.

- Global groups can be converted to universal groups as long as the group is not a member of any other global group.

- When you use the Windows 2000 mixed functional level, global group members can include user and computer accounts from the same domain only.

- Global groups can be members of machine local or domain local groups.

- Global groups can be granted access permissions for resources in any domain in the forest, and in trusted domains in other forests.

Global groups are most commonly used to manage permissions for directory objects, such as user and computer accounts, that require frequent maintenance. On a network consisting of multiple domains, the main advantage of using global groups for this purpose rather than universal groups is that global groups are not replicated outside of their domain. This minimizes the amount of replication traffic to the *global catalog*, which is a directory of resources for the entire forest. Global groups are preferable to domain local groups when you assign permissions for any objects replicated to the global catalog.

Universal Groups

Universal groups are used primarily to grant access to related resources in multiple domains. Universal groups have the following characteristics:

- Universal groups are available only in the Windows 2000 native and Windows Server 2003 functional levels.

- Universal group members can include user and computer accounts, global groups, and other universal groups from any domain in the forest. Universal groups can be converted to domain local groups or to global groups as long as they do not have other universal groups as members.

- When you use the Windows 2000 mixed functional level, you cannot create universal groups.

- Universal groups can be granted access permissions for resources in any domain in the forest and in domains in other trusted forests.

The primary function of universal groups is to consolidate groups that span multiple domains. Universal groups are generally not needed on single-domain networks. To use universal groups effectively, the best practice is to create a global group in each domain, with user or computer accounts as members, and then make the global groups members of a universal group. This enables you to create a single universal group that is usable throughout the enterprise, but with a membership that does not change frequently.

This method is preferable to adding users and computers to the universal group directly because every change to the universal group's membership causes the entire membership to be replicated to the global catalog, throughout the forest. Managing the users and computers in the global groups does not affect the universal group's membership and therefore generates no additional replication traffic.

Universal groups are also useful when you want to grant users access to resources that are located in more than one domain. Unlike domain local groups, you can assign permissions to universal groups for resources in any domain on your network. For example, if executives need access to printers throughout your network, you can create a universal group for this purpose and assign it permissions enabling its members to use all of the printers in all of your domains.

Nesting Groups

As you learned in the previous sections, the ability to make groups members of other groups is one of the most powerful features of Active Directory's group object implementation. This practice is called *group nesting*. Nesting groups enables you to manage resource permissions efficiently for an entire enterprise without generating inordinate amounts of replication traffic. As mentioned earlier, your domain must be using the Windows 2000 native or Windows Server 2003 functional level to take full advantage of Active Directory's group nesting capabilities, and even then, there are restrictions on the nesting of the various group scopes. These nesting restrictions, along with all membership restrictions for the three group scopes, are summarized in Table 7-1.

Table 7-1   Group Scope Membership Rules

Group Scope	Members Allowed in Windows 2000 Mixed or Windows Server 2003 Interim Functional Level	Members Allowed in Windows 2000 Native or Windows Server 2003 Functional Level
Domain Local	User and computer accounts and global groups from any domain	User and computer accounts, universal groups, and global groups from any domain; other domain local groups from the same domain
Global	User and computer accounts from the same domain	User and computer accounts and other global groups from the same domain
Universal	Not available	User and computer accounts, other universal groups, and global groups from any domain

The membership rules in this table are an essential element of proper group management. If you encounter a situation where you cannot add a particular member to a group or use a group to provide access to a particular resource, the troubleshooting process should begin with an examination of the group's scope and the domain's functional level, to determine if you are actually supposed to be able to perform the task you are attempting.

Although group nesting is a valuable tool, administrators should be careful not to get carried away with its capabilities. While it is possible to nest groups many layers deep, this practice can make it difficult to keep track of the group memberships and how permissions are being disseminated throughout the network. As a general rule, a single level of nesting is sufficient for most environments and is easier to maintain.

Converting Groups

When you create a group, you must specify its type and its scope. However, in a domain using the Windows 2000 native or Windows Server 2003 functional level, you can convert groups to different scopes at any time, subject to certain membership restrictions. Table 7-2 summarizes the group scope conversions that are allowable and the conditions under which you can perform the conversion.

Table 7-2   **Active Directory Group Scope Conversion Restrictions**

	To Domain Local	To Global	To Universal
From Domain Local	Not applicable	Not permitted	Permitted only when the domain local group does not have other domain local groups as members
From Global	Not permitted	Not applicable	Permitted only when the global group is not a member of another global group
From Universal	No restrictions	Permitted only when the universal group does not have other universal groups as members	Not applicable

Planning Global and Domain Local Groups

It is a good idea to have a group strategy in place before you begin to create Active Directory groups. Creating groups of the wrong type or with the wrong scope can result in a failure of the groups to perform as expected. For most network installations, the most common method of deploying groups is to use global and domain local groups in the following manner:

- **Create domain local groups for resources to be shared**   Identify the resources, such as shared folders or printers, to which users need access, and then create one or more domain local groups for those resources. For example, if you have a number of color printers in your company, create a domain local group called Color Printers.

- **Assign resource permissions to the domain local group**   Assign the permissions needed for access to the resources to the appropriate domain local group. For example, you should assign the permissions needed to use the color printers to the Color Printers group.

- **Create global groups for users with common job responsibilities**   Identify users with common job responsibilities and add their user objects to a global group. For example, in an accounting department, add the user objects for all of the accountants to a global group called Accounting.

- **Add global groups that need access to resources to the appropriate domain local group**   Identify all global groups that require access to a particular resource, and make the global groups members of the appropriate domain local group. For example, to provide the accountants with access to the color printers, add the Accounting global group to the Color Printers domain local group. Users in the Accounting group then receive the permissions granted to the Color Printers group.

Once you have created your groups in this manner, you modify the domain local group permissions when resource requirements change and modify the global group memberships when there are personnel changes.

It might seem as though using both domain local groups and global groups is unnecessary. After all, it would be possible just to create a single domain local or global group, grant it the permissions needed to access resources, and add the user objects of the people needing those resources as members. However, there are distinct drawbacks to this strategy, whether you use domain local groups or global groups.

- **Placing user objects in domain local groups and assigning permissions to the domain local groups**   This strategy does not enable you to assign permissions for resources outside of the domain, which reduces the flexibility of your group strategy when your network grows.

- **Placing user accounts in global groups and assigning permissions to the global groups**   This strategy can complicate administration when you are using multiple domains. If global groups from multiple domains require the same permissions, you have to assign permissions for each global group.

WINDOWS SERVER 2003 DEFAULT GROUPS

Windows Server 2003 automatically creates a large number of groups in which it places its built-in user accounts. You can use these groups as they are, modify them as needed (in some cases), or create new groups of your own. There are four default group types in Windows Server 2003: built-in local groups, which exist only on computers that are not domain controllers, and three types of default groups in Active Directory—predefined groups, built-in groups, and special identities. These default groups are discussed in the following sections.

Built-In Local Groups

Windows Server 2003 standalone servers and member servers all have built-in local groups. Domain controllers do not have local groups (or local users) because their SAM is converted for Active Directory use. *Built-in local groups* give users the rights to perform system tasks on a single computer, such as backing up and restoring files, changing the system time, and administering system resources. The built-in local groups are located in the Groups folder in the Local Users And Groups snap-in.

The Windows Server 2003 built-in local groups and their capabilities are as follows. Except where noted, no initial members exist in these groups.

- **Administrators**   Members have complete and unrestricted access to the computer and the domain, enabling them to perform all administrative tasks. By default, the computer's built-in Administrator local user account is a member. When the computer joins a domain, Windows Server 2003 adds the Domain Admins predefined global group to the local Administrators group.

- **Backup Operators**   Members have user rights that enable them to override security restrictions for the sole purpose of backing up and restoring files.

- **Guests**   Members can perform only tasks for which you have specifically granted rights and can access only resources for which you have assigned permissions; members cannot make permanent changes to their desktop environment. By default, the computer's built-in Guest local user account is a member. When the computer joins a domain, Windows Server 2003 adds the Domain Guests predefined global group to the local Guests group.

- **Network Configuration Operators**   Members of this group have limited administrative privileges enabling them to make changes to TCP/IP settings, and to renew and release IP addresses.

- **Performance Log Users**   Members of this group are granted privileges enabling them to manage performance counters, logs, and alerts on the computer, both locally and from remote locations.

- **Performance Monitor Users**   Members of this group are granted privileges enabling them to monitor performance counters on the computer, both locally and from remote locations.

- **Power Users**   Members can create local user and group accounts on the computer and modify the users and groups they have created. They can also add or remove users from the Power Users, Users, and Guests local groups, create share resources, and administer the shared resources they have created. Power Users cannot take ownership of files, back up or restore folders, load or unload device drivers, or manage security logs.

- **Print Operators**   Members can manage printers and print queues on the computer.

- **Remote Desktop Users**   Members can log on to the computer remotely using Terminal Services.

- **Replicator**   This group is intended to support directory replication functions. The only member should be a domain user account used to log on to the Replicator services of the domain controller. Do not add the accounts of actual users to this group.

- **Users**   Members can perform tasks such as running applications, using local and network printers, and locking the server. Users cannot share directories or create local printers. All new local user accounts created on the computer are automatically added to the local Users group. When the computer joins a domain, Windows Server 2003 adds the Domain Users, Authenticated Users, and Interactive groups to the local Users group. As a result, all domain user accounts become members of this group as well.

In most cases, the privileges possessed by these local groups are granted by the assignment of user rights to the group. Table 7-3 lists the user rights assigned to the built-in local groups. (Groups not listed have no default user rights assigned to them.)

Table 7-3   **Default User Rights Assigned to Built-In Local Groups**

Local Group	Default User Rights
Administrators	■ Access This Computer From The Network
	■ Adjust Memory Quotas For A Process
	■ Allow Log On Locally
	■ Allow Log On Through Terminal Services
	■ Back Up Files And Directories
	■ Bypass Traverse Checking
	■ Change The System Time
	■ Create A Pagefile
	■ Debug Programs
	■ Force Shutdown From A Remote System
	■ Increase Scheduling Priority
	■ Load And Unload Device Drivers
	■ Manage Auditing And Security Log
	■ Modify Firmware Environment Variables
	■ Perform Volume Maintenance Tasks
	■ Profile Single Process
	■ Profile System Performance
	■ Remove Computer From Docking Station
	■ Restore Files And Directories
	■ Shut Down The System
	■ Take Ownership Of Files Or Other Objects
Backup Operators	■ Access This Computer From The Network
	■ Allow Log On Locally
	■ Back Up Files And Directories
	■ Bypass Traverse Checking
	■ Restore Files And Directories
	■ Shut Down The System
Power Users	■ Access This Computer From The Network
	■ Allow Log On Locally
	■ Bypass Traverse Checking
	■ Change The System Time
	■ Profile Single Process
	■ Remove Computer From Docking Station
	■ Shut Down The System
Remote Desktop Users	■ Allow Log On Through Terminal Services
Users	■ Access This Computer From The Network
	■ Allow Log On Locally
	■ Bypass Traverse Checking

Predefined Active Directory Groups

All Active Directory domains have a collection of *predefined groups*. These are security groups, most with a global scope, that are intended to group together common types of domain user accounts. By default, Windows Server 2003 automatically adds members to some predefined global groups. You can add user objects to these predefined groups to provide additional users with the privileges and permissions assigned to the group.

When you create an Active Directory domain, Windows Server 2003 creates the predefined global groups in the domain's Users container, as shown in the Active Directory Users and Computers console in Figure 7-7. By default, these predefined groups do not have any inherent rights or permissions. You can assign rights or permissions to them by adding the predefined global groups to domain local groups or by explicitly assigning rights or permissions to the predefined global groups.

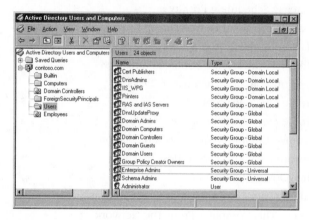

Figure 7-7   The Users folder of an Active Directory domain containing predefined global groups

The predefined global groups that Windows 2000 creates and their members include the following:

- **CertPublishers**   Members are granted permission to publish certificates for users and computers. Unlike most of the other predefined groups, this is a domain local group.

- **Domain Admins**   Members have full administrative control over the domain. The domain Administrator user is a member of this group by default. When a computer joins the domain or is promoted to a domain controller, the Domain Admins group is made a member of the computer's local Administrators group. This enables domain administrators to have full access to all of the computers in the domain.

- **Domain Computers**   This group has as its members all computers in the domain (except domain controllers). By default, all new computer objects created in the domain (except those of domain controllers) become members of this group.

- **Domain Controllers** This group has as its members the computer objects for all domain controllers in the domain. By default, the computer objects for all domain controllers added to the domain become members of this group.

- **Domain Guests** By default, the domain Guest object is a member of this group, and Windows Server 2003 automatically adds the Domain Guests global group to the Guests built-in domain local group.

- **Domain Users** This group is intended to represent all users in the domain. Windows Server 2003 automatically adds all domain User objects to this group and also adds the Domain Users global group to the Users built-in domain local group.

- **Enterprise Admins** The Enterprise Admins group appears only in the forest root domain (the first domain created in the forest); its members have full administrative control over all domains in the forest. By default, the Enterprise Admins group is a member of the Administrators domain local group and the domain Administrator user object is a member of Enterprise Admins.

- **Group Policy Creator Owners** Members are permitted to modify group policy settings in the domain. By default, the domain Administrator account is a member of this group.

- **RAS and IAS Servers** Servers that are members of this group are permitted to access the remote access properties of users.

- **Schema Admins** The Schema Admins group appears only in the forest root domain, and its members are permitted to modify the Active Directory schema. By default, the domain Administrator account is a member of this group.

> **NOTE** **Enterprise Admins and Schema Admins** The scopes of the Enterprise Admins and Schema Admins predefined groups are dependent on the functional level of their domain. In a domain running at the Windows 2000 mixed or Windows Server 2003 interim functional level, these are global groups. In a domain running the Windows 2000 native or Windows Server 2003 functional level, Enterprise Admins and Schema Admins are universal groups.

In addition to the groups listed here, other predefined groups are created when you install specific Windows Server 2003 software components on a computer, such as DnsAdmins and DnsUpdateProxy (which are created when the DNS Server service is installed), and IIS_WPG (which is created when Microsoft Internet Information Services [IIS] is installed).

As with the built-in local groups, some of the predefined Active Directory groups have privileges granted to them through the assignment of user rights. In this case, however, this is true only for the Domain Admins and Enterprise Admins groups. The user rights assigned to these groups by default are listed in Table 7-4.

Table 7-4   **Default User Rights Assigned to Predefined Active Directory Groups**

Local Group	Default User Rights
Domain Admins and Enterprise Admins	■ Access This Computer From The Network ■ Adjust Memory Quotas For A Process ■ Back Up Files And Directories ■ Bypass Traverse Checking ■ Change The System Time ■ Create A Pagefile ■ Debug Programs ■ Enable Computer And User Accounts To Be Trusted For Delegation ■ Force Shutdown From A Remote System ■ Increase Scheduling Priority ■ Load And Unload Device Drivers ■ Allow Log On Locally ■ Manage Auditing And Security Log ■ Modify Firmware Environment Values ■ Profile Single Process ■ Profile System Performance ■ Remove Computer From Docking Station ■ Restore Files And Directories ■ Shut Down The System ■ Take Ownership Of Files Or Other Objects

Built-In Active Directory Groups

Every Active Directory domain has a Builtin container in which the system creates another series of security groups, all of which have a domain local scope. These groups provide users with user rights and permissions to perform tasks on domain controllers and in the Active Directory tree. Built-in domain local groups provide these predefined rights and permissions to user accounts when you add user objects or global groups as members.

The built-in domain local groups and the capabilities granted to their members are as follows:

- **Account Operators**   Members can create, delete, and modify user, computer, and group objects in the Users and Computers containers and in all OUs except Domain Controllers. Members do not have permission to modify the Administrators or Domain Admins groups, nor can they modify the accounts for members of those groups. Members of this group can log on locally to domain controllers in the domain and shut them down.

- **Administrators**   Members have full administrative access to all domain controllers and to the domain itself. By default, the Domain Admins and Enterprise Admins groups and the domain Administrator are members of this group.

- **Backup Operators**   Members have user rights enabling them to back up and restore files on all domain controllers in the domain, even when they do not have individual permissions for the files. Members can also log on to domain controllers and shut them down.

- **Guests**   Members have no default user rights. By default, the Domain Guests global group and the domain Guest user object are members of this group.

- **Incoming Forest Trust Builders**   Members can create one-way, incoming forest trusts to the forest root domain.

- **Network Configuration Operators**   Members can modify TCP/IP settings and renew and release TCP/IP addresses on domain controllers in the domain.

- **Performance Log Users**   Members of this group are granted privileges enabling them to manage performance counters, logs, and alerts on domain controllers in the domain, both locally and from remote locations.

- **Performance Monitor Users**   Members of this group are granted privileges enabling them to monitor performance counters on domain controllers in the domain, both locally and from remote locations.

- **Pre-Windows 2000 Compatible Access**   Members of this group have read access for all user and group objects in the domain. This group is provided for backward compatibility for computers running Windows NT 4 and earlier. When you select the Permissions Compatible With Pre-Windows 2000 Server Operating Systems option in the Active Directory Installation Wizard, the Everyone special identity is made a member of this group.

- **Print Operators**   Members can manage, create, share, and delete printers connected to domain controllers in the domain and also manage Active Directory printer objects. Members can also log on locally to domain controllers in the domain and shut them down.

- **Remote Desktop Users**   Members can remotely log on to domain controllers in the domain using Terminal Services.

- **Replicator**   This group is intended to support directory replication functions. The only member should be a domain user account used to log on to the Replicator services of the domain controller. Do not add the accounts of actual users to this group.

- **Server Operators**   On domain controllers, members of this group can log on, create and delete shared resources, start and stop some services, back up and restore files, format the hard disk, and shut down the computer.

- **Terminal Server License Servers**   Members of this group have access to Terminal Server License Servers, which are used to supply licenses to Terminal Services clients on the network.

■ **Users** Members of this group can perform most common tasks, such as running applications, using local and network printers, and locking the server. By default, the Domain Users group and the Authenticated Users and Interactive special identities are members of this group. Therefore, any user account created in the domain becomes a member of this group.

■ **Windows Authorization Access Group** Members have access to the computed *tokenGroupsGlobalAndUniversal* attribute on domain User objects.

> **NOTE** Built-In Local Groups and Domain Local Groups Several of the built-in domain local groups, such as Backup Operators, Network Configuration Operators, and Remote Desktop Users, are virtual duplicates of the built-in local groups with the same names on Windows Server 2003 standalone and member servers. These groups are intended to perform the same functions as their local group counterparts for domain controllers, which do not have local groups of their own.

The default user rights that grant the built-in domain local groups their privileges are listed in Table 7-5.

Table 7-5 Default User Rights Assigned to Built-In Active Directory Groups

Local Group	Default User Rights
Account Operators	■ Allow Log On Locally ■ Shut Down The System
Administrators, domain local	■ Access This Computer From The Network ■ Adjust Memory Quotas For A Process ■ Back Up Files And Directories ■ Bypass Traverse Checking ■ Change The System Time ■ Create A Pagefile ■ Debug Programs ■ Enable Computer And User Accounts To Be Trusted For Delegation ■ Force Shutdown From A Remote System ■ Increase Scheduling Priority ■ Load And Unload Device Drivers ■ Allow Log On Locally ■ Manage Auditing And Security Log ■ Modify Firmware Environment Values ■ Profile Single Process ■ Profile System Performance ■ Remove Computer From Docking Station ■ Restore Files And Directories ■ Shut Down The System ■ Take Ownership Of Files Or Other Objects
Backup Operators, domain local	■ Back Up Files And Directories ■ Allow Log On Locally ■ Restore Files And Directories ■ Shut Down The System

(continued)

Table 7-5   **Default User Rights Assigned to Built-In Active Directory Groups**

Local Group	Default User Rights
Pre–Windows 2000 Compatible Access	■ Access This Computer From The Network ■ Bypass Traverse Checking
Print Operators	■ Allow Log On Locally ■ Shut Down The System
Server Operators	■ Back Up Files And Directories ■ Change The System Time ■ Force Shutdown From A Remote System ■ Allow Log On Locally ■ Restore Files And Directories ■ Shut Down The System

Special Identities

Special identities exist on all computers running Windows Server 2003. These are not really groups because you cannot create them, delete them, or directly modify their memberships. Special identities do not appear in the Local Users And Groups snap-in or the Active Directory Users and Computers console, but you can use them like groups, by adding them to the ACLs of system and network resources, as shown in Figure 7-8.

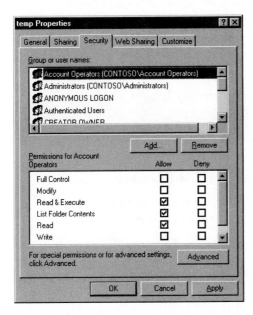

Figure 7-8   Special identities in an ACL

Special identities are essentially placeholders for one or more users. When you add a special identity to an ACL, the system substitutes the users that conform to the identity at the moment the ACL is processed. Special identities represent different users at different times, depending on how users access a computer or resource. For example, the Authenticated Users special identity includes all users that are currently logged on, having successfully been authenticated by a computer or domain controller. At any given moment, the list of users represented by the Authenticated Users special identity can change, as users log on and log off.

The exact list of users substituted for the Authenticated Users placeholder is determined at the time a resource is accessed and its ACL processed, not at the time the special identity is added to the ACL.

The special identities included in Windows Server 2003 are as follows:

- **Anonymous Logon**   Includes all users who have connected to the computer without authenticating.

- **Authenticated Users**   Includes all users with a valid local or domain user account whose identities have been authenticated. The Authenticated Users special identity does not include the Guest user even if the Guest account has a password.

- **Batch**   Includes all users who are currently logged on through a batch facility such as a task scheduler job.

- **Creator Owner**   Includes the account for the user who created or took ownership of a resource.

- **Creator Group**   Includes the primary group of the user who created or took ownership of the resource.

- **Dialup**   Includes all users who are currently logged on through a dial-up connection.

- **Everyone**   On computers running Windows Server 2003, Everyone includes the Authenticated Users special identity plus the Guest user account. On computers running earlier versions of Windows, Everyone includes Authenticated Users, the Guest account, and the Anonymous Logon special identity.

- **Interactive**   Includes all users who are currently logged on locally or through a Remote Desktop connection.

- **Network**   Includes all users who are currently logged on through a network connection.

- **Service**   Includes all security principals that have logged on as a service.

- **Terminal Server Users**   Includes all users who are currently logged on to a Terminal Services server that is in Terminal Services version 4 application compatibility mode.

CREATING AND MANAGING GROUP OBJECTS

Once you have determined how you intend to use groups on your network and have studied the guidelines and restrictions for the various group types and scopes, you are ready to begin actually creating the groups you need. Fortunately, the process of creating groups is far easier than learning about them and their capabilities. The following sections describe some of the most common group administration activities that system and network administrators have to perform on a regular basis.

> **NOTE**   **Exam Objectives**   *The objectives for exam 70-290 require that students be able to "create and manage groups."*

▶ Creating Local Groups

To create local groups in Windows Server 2003, you must be working on a computer that is a standalone or member server because domain controllers do not have local groups. You must also be logged on with a user account that is a member of the Administrators or Power Users local group (or the Domain Admins group in a domain, which is itself a member of the local Administrators group).

To create a local group, use the following procedure:

1. Log on to the computer as Administrator (or use another account with the appropriate privileges).

2. Click Start, point to Administrative Tools, and select Computer Management. The Computer Management console appears.

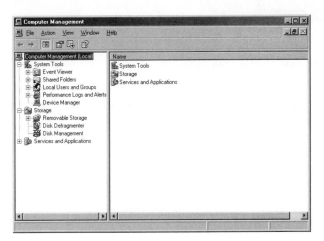

3. Expand the Local Users And Groups node in the scope pane, and then select the Groups folder.

   In the Local Users And Groups snap-in, users and groups have their own separate folders; they are not mixed together in containers as in Active Directory.

4. From the Action menu, select New Group. The New Group dialog box appears.

5. In the Group Name text box, type a name for the group you are creating.

6. Click Add. The Select Users dialog box appears.

7. Type the name of a local user or special identity in the Enter The Object Names To Select text box, and then click OK. The user or identity is added to the Members list.

You can also click Advanced to search for local users and special identities.

8. Click Create.

The snap-in creates the new group in the Groups folder, and it clears the New Group dialog box so that you can create another group.

9. Click Close.

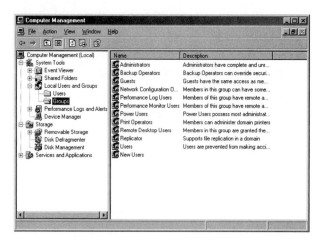

After creating a local group, you can select it and, from the Action menu, select Properties to open the group's Properties dialog box, as shown in Figure 7-9. Here you can add members to or remove them from the group at any time.

Figure 7-9 A local group's Properties dialog box

You can also manage local group memberships from the Properties dialog boxes of user accounts, as shown in Figure 7-10. Every local user's Properties dialog box contains a Member Of tab that you can use to add the local groups of which you want the user to be a member.

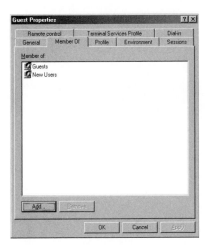

Figure 7-10 The Member Of tab in a local user's Properties dialog box

Working with Active Directory Groups

Although Active Directory groups are more complicated than local groups, because of the various types and scopes available, the procedures for creating and managing them are still rather simple. In the following sections, you learn how to use the Active Directory Users and Computers console to create new groups, manage their memberships, and modify their properties.

NOTE **Exam Objectives** The objectives for exam 70-290 require that students be able to "create and modify groups by using the Active Directory Users and Computers Microsoft Management Console (MMC) snap-in."

Creating Security Groups

Unlike the Local Users And Groups console, which forces you to create your groups in a specific folder, the Active Directory Users and Groups console lets you create group objects anywhere you want. You can create your groups in the Users container with the predefined global groups, in the Builtin container with the built-in domain local groups, in any OU object of your own creation, and even directly beneath the domain object. As with the creation of any Active Directory object, the location you select for the object should be based on the design of your directory tree.

If you plan on using groups to disseminate user rights to your users, you will probably want to create appropriate OU objects in which to put the groups. As you learned in Chapter 6, the Users and Builtin containers are not OUs and you cannot assign group policy objects to them. To assign user rights to a group in one of these containers, you must use a GPO applied to the domain or site object, and the policies will be inherited by all of the objects in the domain or site.

To create a group object, you select a container object in the scope pane of the Active Directory Users and Computers console and, from the Action menu, point to New and select Group. The New Object – Group dialog box appears, shown in Figure 7-11.

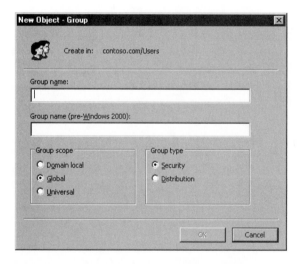

Figure 7-11 The New Object – Group dialog box

In this dialog box, you specify the following information:

■ **Group Name** The name you want to assign to the group object. The name you select can be up to 64 characters long and must be unique in the domain.

- **Group Name (Pre–Windows 2000)**   As you type the Group Name value, the object's pre–Windows 2000–compatible name appears in this text box.

- **Group Scope**   Select the option corresponding to the scope you want to use for the group: domain local, global, or universal. The scopes available to you depend on your domain's functional level, as described earlier in this chapter. The Active Directory Users And Computer console does not allow you to create groups that are not allowed in your current functional level.

- **Group Type**   Select the option corresponding to the type of group you want to create: security or distribution. In the vast majority of cases, you will want to create a security group.

Practice creating groups by doing Exercise 7-1, "Creating a Security Group," now.

Once you click the OK button, the console creates your new group object in the container you selected.

Managing Group Membership

Unlike the Local Users And Groups snap-in, which enables you to specify a group's members as you create it, in Active Directory Users and Computers, you must create the group object first, and then add members to it. To add members to a group, you select it in the console and, from the Action menu, select Properties to open the group's Properties dialog box, as shown in Figure 7-12.

> **NOTE   Exam Objectives**   *The objectives for exam 70-290 require that students be able to "manage group membership."*

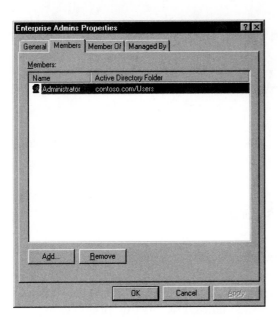

Figure 7-12   A group object's Properties dialog box

Every group object's Properties dialog box has a Members tab and a Member Of tab, which you can use to add members to the group or make the group a member of another group, respectively. To add members to the group, select the Members tab and then click Add. This produces a standard Select Users, Contacts, Computers, Or Groups dialog box, as shown in Figure 7-13.

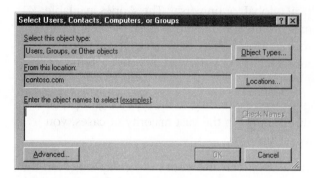

Figure 7-13   The Select Users, Contacts, Computers, Or Groups dialog box

In this dialog box, you can type the name of the object you want to add as a member of the group, or you can click Advanced to display the dialog box shown in Figure 7-14, in which you can search for the objects you want to add.

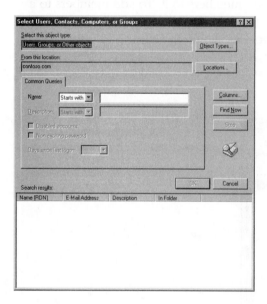

Figure 7-14   The advanced version of the Select Users, Contacts, Computers, Or Groups dialog box

Once you enter or find the object you want to add, clicking OK in the Select Users, Contacts, Computers, Or Groups dialog box adds the object to the group's Members list. Once you have added all the member objects you need, click OK to close the Properties dialog box. At this point, you should be able to open the Properties dialog box for the object you just added to the group and see the group object in its Member Of tab, as shown in Figure 7-15.

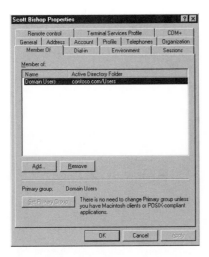

Figure 7-15   The Member Of tab in a user object's dialog box

Practice managing group members hips by doing Exercise 7-2, "Adding Members to a Group," now.

Nesting Groups

As you learned earlier in this chapter, the ability to nest group objects depends on your domain's functional level and on the types and scopes of the groups you are using. Review Table 7-1 if you are not sure whether your domain functional level supports the group nesting you want to perform.

You cannot nest groups in Active Directory Users and Computers by creating a new group inside an existing group. Instead, you must create both groups separately, using the process you learned earlier, and then add one group to the other as a member. Active Directory Users and Computers will not enable you to create a nesting arrangement that your domain does not support.

Practice nesting groups by doing Exercise 7-3, "Nesting Groups," now.

Changing Group Types and Scopes

As group functions change, you might need to change a group object from one type to another. For example, you might have created a distribution group that contains 100 members from multiple departments working on the same project for the purpose of sending e-mail messages. As the project progresses, members might need to access a common database. By converting the distribution group to a security group and assigning permissions to the group, you can provide the project members with access to the common database without having to create a new group and add 100 members to it all over again. You can change the group type only when the domain is using the Windows 2000 native or Windows Server 2003 functional level.

> **NOTE   Exam Objectives**   The objectives for exam 70-290 require that students be able to "identify and modify the scope of a group."

To change the type of a group, open the group's Properties dialog box in the Active Directory Users and Computers console, as shown in Figure 7-16. On the General tab, you see the Group Type options. Click the unselected option and then click OK.

The process for changing the group's scope is exactly the same, except that you select one of the Group Scope options on the General tab. The console only enables you to perform permissible scope changes. In this figure, for example, you see that the Domain Local option is disabled because you cannot change a global group to a domain local group. Consult Table 7-2 for information on the scope changes that are permitted.

Figure 7-16   The General tab in a group object's Properties dialog box

Deleting a Group

As with user objects, each group object that you create in Active Directory has a unique, nonreusable SID. Windows Server 2003 uses the SID to identify the group and the permissions assigned to it. When you delete a group, Windows Server 2003 does not use the same SID for that group again, even if you create a new group with the same name as the one you deleted. Therefore, you cannot restore the access permissions you assigned to resources by re-creating a deleted group object. You must add the newly re-created group as a security principal in the resource's ACL all over again.

When you delete a group, you delete only the group object and the permissions and rights specifying that group as the security principal. Deleting a group does not delete the objects that are members of the group.

> **NOTE** *Group Deletion Failures*   *You cannot delete a group if one of the group's members has the group set as its primary group. Apart from inhibiting group deletions, primary groups are relevant only on Macintosh clients and in POSIX-compliant applications. To change a user's primary group, open the user object's Properties dialog box, and, in the Member Of tab, select a different group and then click Set Primary Group.*

To delete a group, you select it in the Active Directory Users And Computers console and, from the Action menu, select Delete. An Active Directory message box appears, prompting you to confirm your decision. Clicking Yes causes the group to be deleted.

AUTOMATING GROUP MANAGEMENT

Although the Active Directory Users and Computers console is a convenient tool for creating and managing groups individually, it is not the most efficient method for creating large numbers of security principals. The Active Directory command-line tools included with Windows Server 2003 enable you to create and manage groups in large numbers using batch files or other types of scripts, just as you learned to do with users in Chapter 6. Some of these tools are discussed in the following sections.

> **NOTE** **Exam Objectives** *The objectives for exam 70-290 require that students be able to "create and modify groups by using automation."*

Creating Group Objects Using Dsadd.exe

You used the Dsadd.exe tool in Chapter 6 to create new user objects; you can use the same program to create group objects as well.

The basic syntax for creating group objects using Dsadd.exe is as follows:

```
dsadd group GroupDN [parameters]
```

The *GroupDN* parameter is a distinguished name (DN) for the new group object you want to create. The DNs use the same format as those in CSV files, as discussed in "Importing User Objects Using CSV Directory Exchange" in Chapter 6. If the DN includes a space, you must surround the entire DN with quotation marks. When you use Dsadd.exe interactively from the command prompt, you can supply the *GroupDN* parameter in any one of the following ways:

- By typing DNs on the command line, separated by spaces.

- By piping a list of DNs from another command, such as Dsquery.exe.

- By leaving the DN parameter empty, at which point you can type the DNs, one at a time, at a prompt presented by the program. Press Enter after each DN, and press Ctrl+Z and Enter after the last DN.

By default, Dsadd.exe creates global security groups, but you can use command-line parameters to create groups with other types and scopes, as well as to specify members and memberships for the groups and other group object properties. The most commonly used command-line parameters are as follows:

- **-secgrp {*yes* | *no*}** Specifies whether the program should create a security group (*yes*) or a distribution group (*no*). The default value is *yes*.

- **-scope {*l* | *g* | *u*}** Specifies whether the program should create a domain local (*l*), global (*g*), or universal (*u*) group. The default value is *g*.

- **-samid *SAMName*** Specifies the SAM name for the group object, to be used by pre–Windows 2000 systems.

- **-desc *description*** Specifies a description for the group object.

- **-memberof *GroupDN*** Specifies the DNs of one or more groups of which the new group should be made a member.

- **-members *GroupDN*** Specifies the DNs of one or more objects that should be made members of the new group.

You can also add the *-s*, *-u*, and *-p* parameters to specify the domain controller against which Dsadd.exe will run, and the username and password that will be used to execute the command:

- **{-s *Server* | -d *Domain*}**
- **-u *UserName***
- **-p {*Password* | *}**

> **NOTE** Specifying Passwords Using Dsadd.exe   Including an asterisk with the -p switch instead of a password causes the program to prompt you for a password before it executes the command.

For example, to create a new group called Sales in the Users container and make the Administrator user a member, you would use the following command:

```
dsadd group "CN=Sales,CN=Users,DC=contoso,DC=com" -members
  "CN=Administrator,CN=Users,DC=contoso,DC=com"
```

Managing Group Objects Using Dsmod.exe

Dsmod.exe enables you to modify the properties of existing group objects from the Windows Server 2003 command prompt. Using this program, you can perform tasks such as adding members to a group, removing them from a group, and changing a group's type and scope. The basic syntax for Dsmod.exe is as follows:

```
dsmod group GroupDN [parameters]
```

The most commonly used command-line parameters are as follows:

- **-secgrp {*yes* | *no*}**   Sets the group type to security group (*yes*) or distribution group (*no*).
- **-scope {*l* | *g* | *u*}**   Sets the group scope to domain local (*l*), global (*g*), or universal (*u*).
- **-addmbr *members***   Adds members to the group. Replace *members* with the DNs of one or more objects.
- **-rmmbr *members***   Removes members from the group. Replace *members* with the DNs of one or more objects.
- **-chmbr *members***   Replaces the complete list of group members. Replace *members* with the DNs of one or more objects.

For example, to add the Administrator user to the Guests group, you would use the following command:

```
dsmod group "CN=Guests,CN=Builtin,DC=contoso,DC=com" -addmbr
  "CN=Administrator,CN=Users,DC=contoso,DC=com"
```

Finding Objects Using Dsget.exe

Once an Active Directory installation begins to grow, it can quickly get to a size where working with individual objects using consoles like Active Directory Users and Computers is time consuming and difficult. When this happens, many administrators turn to the Active Directory command-line tools. One such tool, the

Dsget.exe program, enables you to locate and display information about any object in the Active Directory database.

Dsget.exe uses a syntax similar to that of Dsadd.exe and Dsmod.exe, in which you specify an object class, the DN of one or more objects, and parameters indicating the information you want to display, as follows:

```
dsget objectclass ObjectDN [parameters]
```

The values for the *objectclass* variable include the following:

- computer
- contact
- subnet
- group
- ou
- server
- site
- user
- quota
- partition

Each of these object classes has a set of parameters particular to that class, which enables you to display the values of the properties for that type of object. For the *dsget user* command, some of the available parameters are as follows:

- **–dn**   Shows the DN of the user
- **–samid**   Shows the SAM account name of the user
- **–sid**   Shows the user's security ID
- **–upn**   Shows the principal name of the user
- **–fn**   Shows the first name of the user
- **–ln**   Shows the last name of the user
- **–display**   Shows the display name of the user
- **–tel**   Shows the telephone number of the user
- **–email**   Shows the e-mail address of the user
- **–memberof**   Displays the immediate groups of which the user is a member
- **–expand**   Displays a recursively expanded list of groups of which the user is a member

For example, to display a list of the groups of which a user is a member, use the following command:

```
dsget user "CN=Administrator,CN=Users,DC=contoso,DC=com" -memberof
```

> **NOTE   Exam Objectives**   The objectives for exam 70-290 require that students be able to "find domain groups in which a user is a member."

SUMMARY

- A group is an object that consists of a list of users. You can assign security permissions to a group by adding it to an ACL, just as with any other security principal, such as a user or computer. All permissions assigned to the group are inherited by its members.

- Windows Server 2003 supports local groups and Active Directory domain groups in the same way that it supports local and domain users.

- An Active directory domain's functional level determines which group types and scopes you can use, what groups can be nested, and what group conversions you can perform.

- In Active Directory, there are two types of groups: security and distribution; there are also three group scopes: domain local, global, and universal.

- Security groups can be assigned permissions, while distribution groups are used for query containers, such as e-mail distribution groups, and cannot be assigned permissions to a resource.

- Domain local groups are for assigning permissions to resources. Global groups are for gathering together users with similar resource requirements. Universal groups are used primarily to grant access to related resources in multiple domains.

- To create and manage local groups, you use the Local Users And Groups snap-in. To create and manage Active Directory groups, you use the Active Directory Users And Computers console.

- You can create domain groups in any container or OU in the Active Directory tree.

- Group nesting means making one group a member of another group.

- You can create and modify groups from the command line using tools such as Dsadd.exe, Dsmod.exe, and Dsget.exe.

EXERCISES

Exercise 7-1: Creating a Security Group

In this exercise, you create a new Active Directory group in your domain.

1. Log on to a Windows Server 2003 domain controller as Administrator.

2. Click Start, point to Administrative Tools, and click Active Directory Users And Computers. The Active Directory Users And Computers console appears.

3. Select the Users container in the scope pane, and, on the Action menu, point to New and click Group. The New Object – Group dialog box appears.

4. In the Group Name textbox, type **Accountants**.

5. In the Group Scope box, select the Global option, and then click OK.

6. Create a second security group object using the Global scope with the name Development.

Exercise 7-2: Adding Members to a Group

In this exercise, you add user objects to a group as members.

1. Log on to a Windows Server 2003 domain controller as Administrator.

2. Click Start, point to Administrative Tools, and click Active Directory Users And Computers. The Active Directory Users And Computers console appears.

3. Select the Users container in the scope pane.

4. In the details pane, select the Domain Users group and, from the Action menu, select Properties. The Domain Users Properties dialog box appears.

5. Select the Members tab and then click Add. The Select Users, Computers, Contacts, Or Groups dialog box appears.

6. In the Enter The Object Names To Select box, type **Guest**, and then click OK. The Guest user object is added to the Members list.

7. Click OK to close the Domain Users Properties dialog box.

Exercise 7-3: Nesting Groups

1. In this exercise, you create nested groups by adding one group to another as a member. Log on to a Windows Server 2003 domain controller as Administrator.

2. Click Start, point to Administrative Tools, and click Active Directory Users And Computers. The Active Directory Users And Computers console appears.

3. Select the Users container in the scope pane, and, on the Action menu, point to New and click Group. The New Object – Group dialog box appears.

4. In the Group Name textbox, type **Printers**.

5. In the Group Scope box, select the Domain Local option, and then click OK.

   At this point, you would grant the Printers group the permissions needed to access the printers on the network.

6. Create a second security group object using the Global scope with the name Sales.

7. Select the Printers group object you created, and, from the Action menu, select Properties. The Printers Properties dialog box appears.

8. Select the Members tab, and then click Add. The Select Users, Computers, Contacts, Or Groups dialog box appears.

9. In the Enter The Object Names To Select box, type **Sales**, and then click OK. The Sales group object is added to the Members list.

10. Click OK to close the Domain Users Properties dialog box.

    At this point, the Sales group would inherit all the permissions granted to the Printers group and pass them on to its members.

REVIEW QUESTIONS

1. What type of domain group is most like the local group on a member server? How are they alike?

2. In a domain running in Windows Server 2003 domain functional level, what security principals can be a member of a global group? (Choose all correct answers.)

   a. Users

   b. Computers

   c. Universal groups

   d. Global groups

3. In the properties of a group, which tab do you access to add users to the group?

4. You want to nest the IT Administrators group responsible for the Sales group inside the Sales group so that its members will have access to the same resources (set by permissions in an ACL) as the Sales group. From the Properties page of the IT Administrators group, what tab do you access to make this setting?

5. If your environment consists of two domains, one Windows Server 2003 and one Windows NT 4, what group scopes can you use for assigning permissions on any resource on any domain member computer?

6. Which of the following group scope modifications are not permitted? (Choose all correct answers.)

   a. Global to universal

   b. Domain local to universal

   c. Universal to global

   d. Domain local to local

   e. Global to domain local

7. What tool do you use to create local groups on a Windows 2000 computer that is not a domain controller?

8. You are attempting to delete a global security group in the Active Directory Users And Computers console, and the console will not let you complete the task. Which of the following could be causes of the failure? (Choose all correct answers.)

   a. There are still members in the group.

   b. One of the group's members has the group set as its primary group.

   c. You do not have the proper permissions for the container in which the group is located.

   d. You cannot delete global groups from the Active Directory Users And Computers console.

9. Why shouldn't you use local groups on a computer after it becomes a member of a domain?

CASE SCENARIOS

Scenario 7-1: Using Group Scopes

You are the administrator of a Windows Server 2003 domain that is currently running at the Windows 2000 mixed domain functional level. Your Windows 2003 domain, contoso.com, has an external trust established with a Windows NT 4 domain, contoso_north, which makes contoso_north a trusted domain. You are planning the use of groups in your domain and need to determine what group scopes can be used in any domain in your forest. What group scope can be used in this context as a security principal?

- **a.** Domain local

- **b.** Global

- **c.** Universal

- **d.** Domain local with a nested global group

Scenario 7-2: Creating Groups Using Dsadd.exe

You are a network administrator who is building an Active Directory on a new network for a company called Fabrikam, Inc., and you have to create user objects for the 75 users in the Inside Sales department. You have already created the fabrikam.com domain and an OU called Inside Sales for this purpose. The human resources department has provided you with a list of the users' names and has instructed you to create the account names by using the first initial and the last name. Each user object must also have the value *Inside Sales* in the *Department* property and *Fabrikam, Inc.* in the *Company* property. Using the first name in the list, Mark Lee, as an example, which of the following command-line formats would enable you to create the 75 user objects, with the required property values?

- **a.** `dsadd "Mark Lee" -company "Fabrikam, Inc." -dept "Inside Sales"`

- **b.** `dsadd user CN=Mark Lee,CN=Inside Sales,DC=fabrikam,DC=com -company`
  `    Fabrikam, Inc. -dept Inside Sales`

- **c.** `dsadd -company "Fabrikam, Inc." -dept "Inside Sales"`
  `    "CN=Mark Lee,CN=Inside Sales,DC=fabrikam,DC=com"`

- **d.** `dsadd user "CN=Mark Lee,CN=Inside Sales,DC=fabrikam,DC=com" -company`
  `    "Fabrikam, Inc." -dept "Inside Sales"`

CHAPTER 8
WORKING WITH COMPUTER ACCOUNTS

In the previous two chapters, you learned a lot about Microsoft Active Directory objects such as users, groups, and organizational units (OUs), which are logical constructs that enable people to access computer network resources. However, there are also Active Directory objects that represent concrete, physical resources, and one of the most important of these is the **computer object**. Without computer objects, users might have permission to access resources, but they have no physical mechanism to provide that access. In this chapter, you learn how to create and manage computer objects on an Active Directory network.

Upon completion of this chapter, you will be able to:

- Describe the process of adding a computer to an Active Directory domain

- Create and manage computer objects

- Troubleshoot computer accounts

UNDERSTANDING COMPUTER OBJECTS

In the default configuration of Windows Server 2003 and all other Windows operating systems, the computer belongs to a workgroup. As you learned in Chapter 6, workgroup computers authenticate users with accounts stored on the local system. If a user wants to access a resource on a workgroup computer, the person must have a user account on that computer, as shown in Figure 8-1. Even though you can connect to a workgroup computer over a network, each system is responsible for its own security and access control. Therefore, on a workgroup, there is never any question about what computer you are using because you must be authenticated using an account on that same computer.

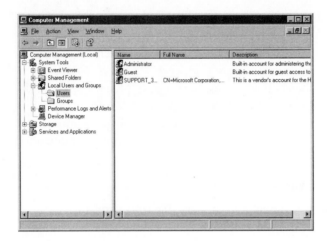

Figure 8-1   Workgroup user account storage

Most Windows networks with more than a handful of computers, however, do not use the workgroup model—they use domains, which are implemented in Windows Server 2003 by the Active Directory directory service. In Active Directory, users have accounts in a domain rather than on individual computers. Administrators can use one domain account to grant a user access to resources on computers all over the network. Because domain user accounts are stored in a centralized directory on servers called domain controllers, a user can log on to the domain from any computer on the network and be authenticated by a domain controller.

Because a Windows domain network uses a centralized directory, there has to be some means of tracking the actual computers that are part of the domain. To do this, Active Directory uses computer accounts, which take the form of computer objects in the Active Directory tree (as shown in Figure 8-2). You might have a valid Active Directory user account and a password, but if your computer is not represented by a computer object, you cannot log on to the domain.

Computer objects are stored in the Active Directory hierarchy just as user and group objects are, and they possess many of the same capabilities, such as the following:

■   They consist of properties that specify the computer's name, where it is located, and who is permitted to manage it.

■   They inherit group policy settings from container objects such as domains, sites, and OUs.

- They can be members of security and distribution groups and inherit permissions from group objects.

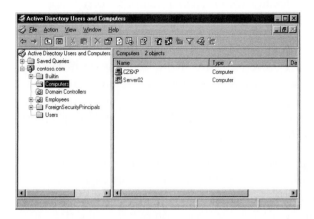

Figure 8-2   Active Directory domain computer account storage

When a user attempts to log on to an Active Directory domain, the client computer establishes a connection to a domain controller to authenticate the user's identity. But before the user authentication occurs, the two computers perform a preliminary authentication using their respective computer objects to ensure that both systems are part of the domain. The NetLogon service running on the client computer connects to the same service on the domain controller, and then each one verifies that the other system has a valid computer account. When this validation is completed, the two systems establish a secure communications channel between them, which they can then use to begin the user authentication process.

The computer account validation between the client and the domain controller is a genuine authentication process using account names and passwords, just as when a user authenticates to the domain. The difference is that the passwords used by the computer accounts are generated automatically and kept hidden. Administrators can reset a computer account, but they do not have to supply passwords for them.

> **NOTE** **Windows Operating Systems and Computer Objects**   Computers running Windows NT–based operating systems, such as Windows Server 2003, Windows XP, Windows 2000, and Windows NT, have native domain support and are always represented by computer objects in Active Directory. The MS-DOS–based Windows operating systems, including Windows Millennium Edition (Me), Windows 98, and Windows 95, can participate in a domain through the installation of an Active Directory client, but they use a domain name specified during the client installation and do not have computer objects in the domain.

ADDING COMPUTERS TO A DOMAIN

What all this means for Windows network administrators is that, in addition to creating user and group accounts in the domain, they also have to make sure that the network computers are part of the domain. Adding a computer to an Active Directory domain consists of two steps:

- **Creating a computer account**   You create a computer account by creating a new computer object in Active Directory and assigning it the name of an actual computer on the network.

■ **Joining the computer to the domain**   When you join a computer to the domain, the system contacts a domain controller, establishes a trust relationship with the domain, locates (or creates) a computer object corresponding to the computer's name, alters its security identifier (SID) to match that of the computer object, and modifies its group memberships.

How these steps are performed, and who performs them, depends on how the computers are deployed on a network. There are many ways to create new computer objects, and how administrators choose to do this depends on several factors, including the number of objects they need to create, where they will be when creating the objects, and what tools they prefer to use.

Generally speaking, you create computer objects when you deploy new computers in the domain. Once a computer is represented by an object and joined to the domain, any user in the domain can log on from that computer. For example, you do not have to create new computer objects or rejoin computers to the domain when employees leave the company and new hires start using their computers. However, if you reinstall the operating system on a computer, you must create a new computer object for it (or reset the existing one) because the computer will have a different SID after the reinstallation.

The joining of a new computer to a domain must always be performed at the computer itself, either by an administrator or by the end user. However, the creation of the computer object can occur either before or during the joining process. Administrators are often responsible for creating the computer objects, but it is also possible for end users to create the objects themselves under certain conditions.

> **NOTE** **Exam Objectives**   The objectives for exam 70-290 require students to be able to "create and manage computer accounts in an Active Directory environment."

Creating Computer Objects

The creation of a computer object must always occur before the corresponding computer can actually join the domain, although it sometimes does not appear that way. There are two basic strategies for creating Active Directory computer objects:

■ Create the computer objects in advance using an Active Directory tool so the computers can locate the existing objects when they join the domain.

■ Begin the joining process first, and allow the computer to create its own computer object.

In each case, the computer object exists before the joining takes place. In the second strategy, the joining process appears to begin first, but the computer creates the object before the actual joining process begins.

When you have a number of computers to deploy, particularly in different locations, most administrators prefer to create the computer objects in advance. For large numbers of computers, it is even possible to automate the computer object creation process by using command-line tools and batch files. The following sections examine the tools you can use for computer object creation.

Creating Computer Objects Using Active Directory Users And Computers

As with the user and group objects you studied in the previous chapters, the primary Windows Server 2003 utility for creating computer objects is the Active Directory Users And Computers console, as shown in Figure 8-3.

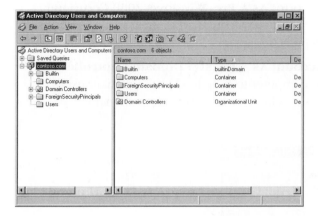

Figure 8-3   The Active Directory Users And Computers console

To create computer objects in an Active Directory domain using the Active Directory Users And Computers console or any other utility, you must have the appropriate permissions for the container in which the objects will be located. By default, the Administrators group has permission to create objects anywhere in the domain, and the Account Operators group has the Create Computer Objects and Delete Computer Objects special permissions needed to create computer objects in and delete them from the Computers container, as well as from any new OUs you create. The Domain Admins and Enterprise Admins groups are members of the Administrators group, so members of those groups can also create computer objects anywhere. An administrator can also explicitly delegate control of containers to particular users or groups, enabling them to create computer objects in those containers.

> **MORE INFO**   Ordinary users are also permitted to create a limited number of computer objects. For more information, see "Joining Computers to a Domain" later in this chapter.

The process of creating a computer object in Active Directory Users And Computers is similar to that of creating a user or group object. You select the container in which you want to place the object and, from the Action menu, point to New and select Computer. The New Object – Computer wizard appears, as shown in Figure 8-4.

In the first page of this wizard, you can configure the following properties of the computer object:

- **Computer Name**   Specifies a name up to 63 characters long, to be assigned to the computer object. This name must match the name of the computer joined with the object.

- **Computer Name (Pre–Windows 2000)**   When you enter the Computer Name, the first 15 characters appear in this field. This is the computer name that pre–Windows 2000 computers on the network will use.

- **User Or Group**   Specifies the user or group that is permitted to join the computer to the domain. The default value is the Domain Admins group. To change the default, click Change to open a standard Select User Or Group dialog box.

- **Assign This Computer Account As A Pre–Windows 2000 Computer** Select this check box if the computer to be joined to the domain using this object is running Windows NT 4.0.

- **Assign This Computer Account As A Backup Domain Controller** Select this check box if the computer to be joined to the domain using this object is functioning as a Windows NT 4.0 backup domain controller (BDC).

Figure 8-4   The New Object – Computer wizard

After completing this page, click Next to display the Managed page, shown in Figure 8-5. On this page, you can specify whether the computer to be joined to this object is a managed computer that you will install using Remote Installation Services (RIS). If you select this check box, you must supply a globally unique identifier (GUID) or a universally unique identifier (UUID) for the computer.

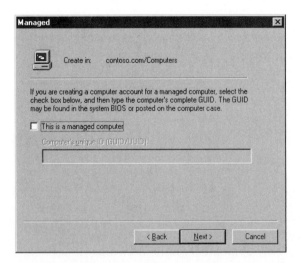

Figure 8-5   The Managed page of the New Object – Computer wizard

Clicking Next displays a summary page, and clicking Finish creates the computer object in the container you selected.

Practice creating computer objects by doing Exercise 8-1, "Creating a Computer Object Using Active Directory Users and Computers," now.

Creating Computer Objects Using Dsadd.exe

As with users and groups, the Active Directory Users And Computers console is good for creating and managing single objects, but many administrators turn to the Active Directory command-line tools included with Windows Server 2003 when they have to create multiple objects.

The Dsadd.exe utility enables you to create computer objects from the command line, just as you created user and group objects in the previous chapters. You can create a batch file of Dsadd.exe commands to generate multiple objects in one process. The basic syntax for creating a computer object with Dsadd.exe is as follows:

```
dsadd computer ComputerDN [parameters]
```

The *ComputerDN* parameter is a distinguished name for the new group object you want to create. The DNs use the same format as those in comma-separated value (CSV) files, as discussed in Chapter 6. If the DN includes a space, you must surround the entire DN with quotation marks. When using Dsadd.exe interactively from the command prompt, you can supply the *ComputerDN* parameter in any one of the following ways:

- By typing DNs on the command line, separated by spaces.

- By piping a list of DNs from another command, such as Dsquery.exe.

- By leaving the DN parameter empty, at which point you can type the DNs, one at a time, at a prompt presented by the program. Press Enter after each DN, and press Ctrl+Z and Enter after the last DN.

You can also add any of the following parameters to the Dsadd.exe command line, to define values for certain computer object properties:

- **-samid *SAMName***   Specifies the Security Accounts Manager (SAM) name for the computer object, to be used by pre–Windows 2000 systems

- **-desc *description***   Specifies a description for the computer object

- **-loc *location***   Specifies the location of the computer associated with the computer object

- **-memberof *GroupDN***   Specifies the DNs of one or more groups of which the new computer should be made a member

You can also add the *-s*, *-u*, and *-p* parameters to specify the domain controller against which Dsadd.exe will run, and the username and password that will be used to execute the command, as shown here:

- **{-s *Server* | -d *Domain*}**

- **-u *UserName***

- **-p {*Password* | *}**   , where * causes you to be prompted for a password

For example, to create a new computer object called webserver1 in the Computers container, you would use the following command:

```
dsadd computer "CN=webserver1,CN=Computers,DC=contoso,DC=com"
```

Practice creating computer objects from the command line by doing Exercise 8-2, "Creating a Computer Object Using Dsadd.exe," now.

Creating Computer Objects Using Netdom.exe

Netdom.exe is another command-line tool that you can use to create computer objects as well as perform many other domain account and security tasks. The advantage of using Netdom.exe instead of Dsadd.exe is that you do not have to specify the name of the computer object you want to create as a DN. A simple command such as the following creates a computer object in the default Computers container:

```
netdom add webserver1
```

> **NOTE   Obtaining Netdom.exe**   Netdom.exe is included with Windows Server 2003, but it is not installed with the operating system. You can install Netdom.exe with the Windows Support Tools, by running Suptools.msi from the Support\Tools folder on the Windows Server 2003 installation CD.

The full syntax of Netdom.exe, when you use the add subcommand, is as follows:

```
netdom add computername [/Domain:DomainName] [/UserD:User/PasswordD:UserPassword]
    [/OU:OUDN]
```

The functions of the command-line parameters are as follows:

■ ***computername***   Specifies the common name for the computer object to be created.

■ **/Domain:*DomainName***   Specifies the name of the domain in which to create the computer object. When this is omitted, the program creates the object in the domain in which the current user is logged on.

■ **/UserD:*User***   Specifies the name of the user account that the program should use to create the computer object. When this is omitted, the program uses the account of the currently logged-on user.

■ **/PasswordD:*UserPassword***   Specifies the password associated with the user account indicated by the */UserD* parameter. This parameter must be included when the command line includes the */UserD* parameter. The wildcard character (*) can be used to cause a prompt for the password.

■ **/OU:*OUDN***   Specifies the DN of the OU in which the computer object should be created. When this is omitted, the program creates the object in the Computers container.

Joining Computers to a Domain

The process of actually joining a computer to a domain must occur at the computer itself and be performed by a member of the computer's local Administrators group. After logging on, you join a computer running Windows Server 2003 to a domain from the Computer Name tab in the System Properties dialog box (which is accessible from the System icon in Control Panel), as shown in Figure 8-6.

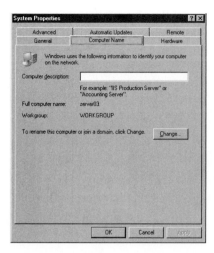

Figure 8-6   The Computer Name tab in the System Properties dialog box

On a computer that is not joined to a domain, the Computer Name tab displays the name assigned to the computer during the operating system installation and the name of the workgroup to which the system currently belongs (which is WORKGROUP by default). To join the computer to the domain, click Change to display the Computer Name Changes dialog box (shown in Figure 8-7).

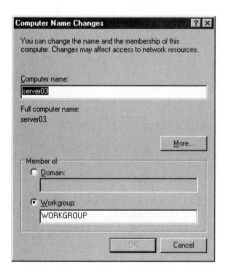

Figure 8-7   The Computer Name Changes dialog box

In this dialog box, the Computer Name text box enables you to change the name assigned to the computer during installation. Depending on whether you have already created a computer object, observe the following precautions:

- If you want to join a domain in which you have already created a computer object for the system in Active Directory, the name entered in this text box must match the name of the object exactly.

- If you intend to create a computer object during the joining process, the name in this text box must not already exist in the domain.

Next, select the Domain option and enter the name of the domain the computer will join, and then click OK. When the computer establishes contact with a domain controller for the domain, a second Computer Name Changes dialog box appears, as shown in Figure 8-8, prompting you for the username and password of a domain user account with permission to join the computer to the domain.

Figure 8-8   The Computer Name Changes authentication dialog box

NOTE   Domain Controller Communications   If you see a message box informing you that the computer was unable to locate a domain controller for the domain you specified, the problem is most likely due to a network configuration error. Most likely, the Preferred DNS Server address in the computer's TCP/IP configuration is incorrect. Windows Server 2003 relies on the Domain Name System (DNS) to locate domain controllers, and if the computer does not have access to a DNS server that is hosting the domain, communication with the domain controller is not possible.

Once you have authenticated with the domain controller, the computer is welcomed to the domain and you are instructed to restart the computer.

Joining a Domain Using Netdom.exe

You can also use the Netdom.exe command-line utility to join a computer to a domain. The syntax for the command is as follows:

```
netdom join computername /Domain:DomainName [/UserD:User /PasswordD:UserPassword]
    [/UserO:User /PasswordO:UserPassword] [/OU:OUDN] [REBoot:seconds]
```

The functions of the command-line parameters are as follows:

- ***computername***   Specifies the name of the computer to be joined.

- **/Domain:*DomainName***   Specifies the name of the domain the computer will join.

- **/UserD:*User***   Specifies the name of the domain user account that the program should use to join the computer to the domain.

- **/PasswordD:*UserPassword***   Specifies the password associated with the domain user account indicated by the */UserD* parameter.

- **/UserO:*User***   Specifies the name of the local user account that the program should use to access the computer.

- **/PasswordO:*UserPassword*** Specifies the password associated with the local user account indicated by the */UserO* parameter.

- **/OU:*OUDN*** Specifies the DN of the OU in which the program should create a computer object. When this is omitted, the program creates the object in the Computers container.

- **/REBoot:*seconds*** Specifies that the computer should automatically shut down and reboot after it is joined to the domain. You can also specify the number of seconds that should elapse before the restart. The default value is 20 seconds.

Creating Computer Objects While Joining to a Domain

You can join a computer to a domain whether or not you have already created a computer object for it. Once the computer authenticates to the domain controller, the domain controller scans the Active Directory database for a computer object with the same name as the computer. If it does not find a matching object, the domain controller creates one in the Computers container, using the name supplied.

For the computer object to be created automatically in this manner, one would expect that the user account you specify when connecting to the domain controller must have object creation privileges for the Computers container, such as membership in the Administrators group. However, this is not always the case. Domain users can also create computer objects themselves through an interesting, indirect process. The Default Domain Controllers Policy group policy object (GPO) grants a user right called Add Workstations To Domain to the Authenticated Users special identity, as shown in Figure 8-9. This means that any user who is successfully authenticated to Active Directory is permitted to join up to 10 workstations to the domain and create 10 associated computer objects, even if they do not possess explicit object creation permissions.

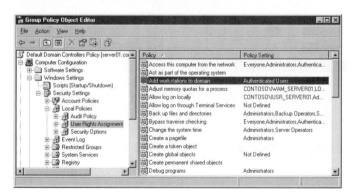

Figure 8-9 The Default Domain Controllers Policy user rights assignments

The important thing to remember about the Add Workstations To Domain user right, however, is that *workstations* is the operative word. Authenticated users can add up to 10 workstations to the domain, but not servers. This means that the computers must be running Windows XP Professional, Windows 2000 Professional, or one of the down-level Active Directory clients. Authenticated users cannot join computers running Windows Server 2003 or Windows 2000 Server to the domain.

Joining a Domain During Operating System Installation

Although you can join an existing Windows Server 2003 computer to a domain at any time, you can also perform the join during the operating system installation. When the Windows Setup wizard displays the Workgroup Or Computer Domain page, as shown in Figure 8-10, you can specify the name of the domain the computer is to join. You are prompted for a domain user account and password to authenticate to the domain controller, and the joining process proceeds as described earlier.

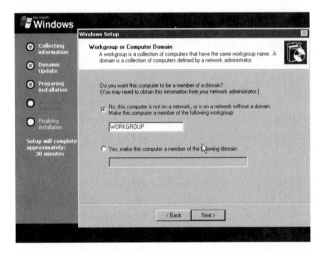

Figure 8-10   The Workgroup Or Computer Domain page of the Windows Setup wizard

Locating Computer Objects

By default, every new Active Directory domain has two containers, which are called Computers and Domain Controllers, as shown in Figure 8-11. When you create the domain by promoting your first domain controller, the Active Directory Installation wizard creates these two containers and then creates a computer object for the new domain controller in the Domain Controllers container.

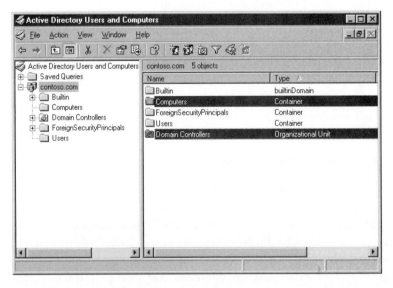

Figure 8-11   The Computers and Domain Controllers containers in an Active Directory domain

Locating Domain Controller Computer Objects

The Domain Controllers container is an OU object. You never have to create computer objects for domain controllers because the Active Directory Installation wizard creates them for you and puts them in the Domain Controllers OU. This container must be an OU because there is a GPO applied to it called the Default Domain Controllers Policy GPO. This GPO contains group policy settings that are essential for the security of the domain controllers. In most Active Directory installations, the computer objects for domain controllers can remain where they are. If you move them, be sure to apply the Default Domain Controllers Policy GPO to the OU at their new location, or create an equivalent GPO containing settings specific to the domain controller role.

Locating Other Computer Objects

The Computers container is the default location for all other computer objects that are created by automatic means, such as when a computer joins a domain and there is no computer object there for it already. Using the Active Directory Users And Computers console, you can manually create computer objects in any container, manage them, and move them around at will.

Oddly enough, the Computers container is not an OU; it is one of those strange objects whose object class literally is a container, like the Users, Builtin, and Foreign-SecurityPrincipals containers. As you learned in Chapter 6, you cannot create or delete these containers, and you cannot apply GPOs to them, which makes it impossible to deploy group policy settings to the computer objects stored there in one step. For this reason, it is usually a good idea to create at least one OU and move the computer objects from the Computers container there.

Many Active Directory networks create multiple OUs for computer objects, either to implement an organizational or geographical hierarchy in the Active Directory tree or to create separate containers for the different roles performed by the computers. For example, you might create an OU for your workstation computers and a series of OUs for the roles performed by your member servers. This would enable you to deploy a GPO containing different policy settings for each OU, thereby creating a different system configuration for each computer role.

Redirecting Computer Objects

Although you can create computer objects in the Computers container and manually move them to any location you want, it is also possible to configure Windows Server 2003 to place its automatically created computer objects in another container. This is generally preferable because it enables you to place the new computer objects into the proper OU before the computer actually joins the domain. This ensures that the computer is governed by the policies applied to the OU immediately upon joining the domain.

To redirect new computer objects, your domain must be using the Windows Server 2003 domain functional level. Open a Command Prompt window and, from the command line, run a utility called Redircmp.exe, which is supplied with Windows Server 2003, specifying the distinguished name (DN) of the OU or other container you want to be the location of your new computer objects, as in the following example:

```
redircmp ou=workstations,DC=contoso,dc=com
```

MORE INFO   For more information on domain functional levels and how they affect the creation and management of Active Directory objects, see "Understanding Domain Functional Levels" in Chapter 7.

MANAGING COMPUTER OBJECTS

Once you have created objects for your computers and joined them to the domain, you can manage the objects and the computers from the Active Directory Users and Computers console. Some of the management functions you can perform are described in the following sections.

Modifying Computer Object Properties

As with all other objects in Active Directory, computer objects consist of properties, which contain various pieces of information about the system the object represents. To modify the properties of a computer object, you select it in the Active Directory Users and Computers console and, from the Action menu, select Properties to display the object's Properties dialog box, as shown in Figure 8-12.

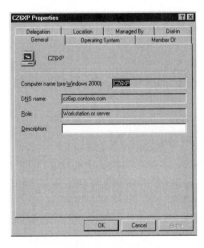

Figure 8-12   A computer object's Properties dialog box

The dialog box has seven tabs:

- **General**   On this tab, you can enter descriptive text for the computer represented by the object. The other text boxes (Computer Name [Pre–Windows 2000], DNS Name, and Role) contain information that is automatically supplied when the computer joins the domain.

- **Operating System**   Contains the name, version, and service pack level of the operating system running on the computer represented by the object. This information is supplied automatically when the computer joins the domain. There are no user-definable properties on this tab.

- **Member Of**   Enables you to specify the groups of which the computer object is a member. By default, all new computer objects that are not domain controllers are added to the Domain Computers global group.

- **Delegation** Enables you to grant services running under the computer account permission to send service requests to other network computers on behalf of a user. You can permit the object to request any service or create a list of specific services that it can request, using another account's credentials.

- **Location** Contains a text box that you can use to specify the location of the computer represented by this object.

- **Managed By** Enables you to specify a user object that is responsible for the management of the computer represented by the object. When you do this, pertinent informational properties from the selected user object appear on this tab, as shown in Figure 8-13. This information is retrieved dynamically from the user object; only the name of the user is stored as part of the computer object.

- **Dial-In** Enables you to specify values for properties controlling remote dial-in access to the computer represented by the object, such as whether access should be permitted or denied and whether features such as caller ID and callback should be used.

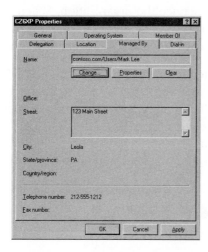

Figure 8-13 The Managed By tab in a computer object's Properties dialog box

Deleting, Disabling, and Resetting Computer Objects

Under normal usage conditions, computer objects require no maintenance and no attention from administrators. However, in some situations administrators might have to manipulate computer objects, such as to prevent them from being abused, or to accommodate changes in the physical computer itself.

Deleting Computer Objects

Deleting a computer object in the Active Directory Users and Computers console is simply a matter of selecting the object and, from the Action menu, selecting Delete. After you confirm your action, the object is permanently deleted. However, before you begin deleting computer objects, be sure you fully understand the ramifications of your actions.

As with user and group objects, computer objects have a unique SID value that is lost when the object is deleted. Creating a new object with the same name and property value will not re-create the same SID, and any permissions and group memberships granted to the original, deleted computer object will be irretrievably lost. You should therefore not delete computer objects (or any objects, for that matter) unless you are absolutely sure you will not need them again. You can prevent an object from being used by disabling it instead.

> **TIP   Disjoining Computers**   When a computer is removed from a domain, by being joined to a workgroup or to a different domain, the system attempts to delete its computer object. If the computer cannot delete the object because of networking problems, insufficient permissions, or any other reason, the account remains in Active Directory. It might appear, immediately or eventually, as disabled. If the object is no longer needed in that domain, it must be deleted manually.

Disabling Computer Objects

If you plan to have a computer offline for an extended period of time, the best practice is not to delete it, but to disable it. One of the most basic security principles is to keep identity stores as small as possible, allowing authentication only of the minimum number of accounts needed to service the organization. When you disable a computer object, its SID and all of its property values remain intact, so that when you enable it again, the object is ready for use with no modification.

To disable a computer object in the Active Directory Users And Computers console, select it and, from the Action menu, select Disable Account. A red X appears in the object's icon to indicate that it is disabled, as shown in Figure 8-14. While the object is disabled, the computer cannot establish a secure channel with the domain. Users who have not previously logged on to the computer, and who therefore do not have cached credentials on the computer, cannot log on until you reestablish the secure channel by enabling the account.

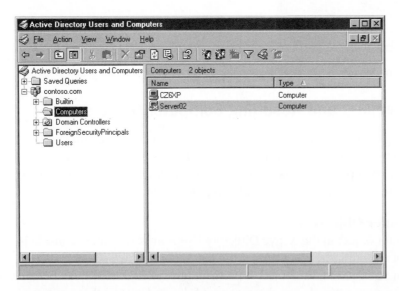

Figure 8-14   A disabled computer account

To reenable the object, use the same procedure, selecting Enable Account from the Action menu.

Practice managing computer objects by doing Exercise 8-3, "Disabling and Enabling a Computer Object," now.

Resetting a Computer Object

Sometimes an administrator might want to replace a computer on the network, to upgrade hardware or for other reasons, but still continue to use the original computer object, along with its group memberships and permission assignments. Once a computer is joined to a domain and associated with a particular computer object, you cannot join a different computer to that same object, nor can you disjoin the computer from the domain and rejoin another computer with the same name without re-creating the object and losing the object's SID, as well as its associated group memberships and permissions.

However, you can reuse the same computer object for two different computers by resetting the object. Resetting a computer object resets its password but maintains all of its properties. With a reset password, the object is rendered available for use again. Any appropriately named computer can join the domain using that object. To reset a computer object using the Active Directory Users And Computers console, select the object and, from the Action menu, select Reset Account. After confirming your action, a message box appears stating that the account was successfully reset. You can also reset computer accounts from the command line using the Netdom.exe utility.

> **NOTE** **Exam Objectives** *The objectives for exam 70-290 require students to be able to "reset computer accounts."*

Managing Remote Computers

In addition to manipulating computer objects, the Active Directory Users And Computers console also enables you to access the computer itself. When you select a computer object and, from the Action menu, select manage, a new Computer Management console opens, with the focus on the selected Computer. You can then perform any of the standard functions provided by that console on the selected computer (permissions permitting).

Managing Computer Objects from the Command Line

All of the computer object management tasks you learned about in the previous sections are also possible using the command-line tools included with Windows Server 2003. The following sections examine the use of these tools.

Managing Computer Object Properties with Dsmod.exe

The Dsmod.exe tool can modify the properties of computer objects, just as it can for user and group objects. In addition, you can use Dsmod.exe to disable, enable, and reset computer objects (but not delete them). The syntax for computer object modifications with the tool is as follows:

```
dsmod computer ComputerDN [parameters]
```

The functions of the command-line parameters are as follows:

- ***ComputerDN*** Specifies the DN of the computer object to be modified.

- **-desc** *Description* Specifies a value for the computer object's *Description* property.

- **-loc *Location*** Specifies a value for the computer object's *Location* property.

- **-disabled [yes | no]** Disables or enables the specified computer object.

- **-reset** Resets the password of the specified computer object.

- **-s *Server*** Specifies the name of the domain controller that the program will use to access the computer object. When this is omitted, the program defaults to a domain controller in the domain to which the user is currently logged on.

- **-d *Domain*** Specifies the name of the domain in which the computer object is located. When this is omitted, the program defaults to the domain to which the user is currently logged on.

- **-u *UserName*** Specifies the name of the user account the program will use to access the domain. When this is omitted, the program defaults to the user account with which the system is currently logged on to the domain.

- **-p [*Password* | *]** Specifies the password associated with the user account identified in the *-u* parameter. Including an asterisk (*) causes the program to stop and prompt the user for a password.

To disable a computer account, use a command like the following:

```
dsmod computer CN=webserver1,CN=Computers,DC=contoso,DC=com -disabled yes
```

To reset a computer account, use a command like the following:

```
dsmod computer CN=webserver1,CN=Computers,DC=contoso,DC=com -reset
```

Deleting Computer Object Properties with Dsrm.exe

Dsmod.exe can modify computer objects but not delete them. To delete computer objects, you must use the Dsrm.exe utility. You specify the DN of the object you want to delete on the Dsrm.exe command line, using the following syntax:

```
Dsrm ObjectDN
```

Once you confirm your request, the program deletes the object. An example of a Dsrm.exe command follows:

```
dsrm CN=webserver1,CN=Computers,DC=contoso,DC=com
```

TROUBLESHOOTING COMPUTER ACCOUNTS

Active Directory treats computer objects as security principals. This means that a computer, just like a user, has properties, such as a name, a password, and an SID, that enable it to be added to the access control lists (ACLs) of other objects. Computer accounts, and the secure relationships between computers and their domain, are generally robust. However, like user accounts, computer accounts sometimes require maintenance and troubleshooting. In the rare circumstance that an account or secure channel breaks down, the symptoms of failure are generally obvious.

The most common signs of computer account problems are as follows:

- Messages at logon that indicate that a domain controller cannot be contacted, that the computer account might be missing, or that the trust (another way of referring to the secure channel) between the computer and the domain has been lost. A sample of such an error message, from a Windows XP client, is shown in Figure 8-15.

- Error messages or entries in an event log that indicate similar problems or suggest that passwords, trusts, secure channels, or relationships with the domain or a domain controller have failed.

- A computer account is missing in Active Directory.

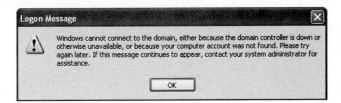

Figure 8-15   A Windows XP logon message indicating a possible computer account problem

NOTE Exam Objectives   The objectives for exam 70-290 require students to be able to "troubleshoot computer accounts" and "diagnose and resolve issues related to computer accounts by using the Active Directory Users and Computers MMC snap-in."

If one of these situations occurs, you must troubleshoot the computer account. You learned earlier how to delete, disable, and reset a computer account and how to join a computer to the domain. The rules that govern the troubleshooting of a computer account when one of these events occurs are as follows:

1. If the computer account exists in Active Directory, you must reset it.

2. If the computer account is missing from Active Directory, you must create a computer account.

3. If the computer still belongs to the domain, you must remove it from the domain by changing its membership to a workgroup. The name of the workgroup is irrelevant.

4. Rejoin the computer to the domain. Alternatively, join another computer to the domain, but the new computer must have the same name as the computer account.

To troubleshoot any computer account problem, apply all four of these rules. They can be carried out in any order, except that rule 4, rejoining the computer to the domain, must always be the final step. The following two scenarios illustrate the use of these rules:

- A user complains that when she attempts to log on, the system presents error messages indicating that the computer account might be missing. Applying rule 1, you open Active Directory Users And Computers and find that there is a computer account for the system in the domain. You reset the object. Rule 2 does not apply—the object does exist. Then, using rule 3, you remove the system from the domain and, following rule 4, rejoin it to the domain.

- A computer account is reset by accident, so rule 1 has already been completed. Although the reset is accidental, you must continue to recover by applying the remaining three rules. Rule 2 does not apply because the computer object exists in the domain. Follow rules 3 and 4, removing the computer from the domain and then rejoining it.

SUMMARY

- For users to log on to an Active Directory domain, they must have not only user objects, but also objects representing their computers. A computer object represents a specific system on the network and contains properties with information about the system.

- Computer objects can function as security principles. You can add them to groups and grant them permissions.

- To add a computer to a domain, you must create a computer object for it in Active Directory and then join the physical computer to the domain. The computer object can be created ahead of time, or it can be created as part of the join process.

- You must be logged on as a member of the local Administrators group to change the domain membership of a computer.

- To create computer objects, you can use the Active Directory Users And Computers console, the Dsadd.exe utility, or the Netdom.exe utility. The Administrators and Account Operators groups have sufficient permissions to create new computer objects, and you can also delegate the appropriate permissions to other users or groups.

- Computer objects for non–domain controllers are placed in the Computers container by default. You cannot apply group policies to this container, so it is usually preferable to locate the computer objects in an OU instead.

- To join a computer to a domain, you use the Computer Name tab in the System Properties dialog box or the Netdom.exe utility. If a computer object for the computer does not exist when you attempt to join it to the domain, the system creates the object (assuming you have the necessary permissions).

- Using the Active Directory Users and Computers console and the Dsmod.exe and Dsrm.exe utilities, you can manage the properties of computer objects, as well as delete, disable, and reset them.

- Computer objects have an SID that Active Directory uses to reference the computer in its group memberships and other permissions. Accidentally deleting a computer object causes its SID to be irretrievably lost, forcing you to create the permission. Be careful about deleting computer objects; disabling them instead makes it possible to enable the objects again, with no loss of information.

- The typical steps for troubleshooting a computer object problem include creating or resetting the object, removing the computer from the domain, and rejoining it to the domain.

EXERCISES

Exercise 8-1: Creating a Computer Object Using Active Directory Users And Computers

In this exercise, you create a new computer object using the Active Directory Users and Computers console.

1. Log on to a Windows Server 2003 domain controller as Administrator.

2. Click Start, point to Administrative tools, and select Active Directory Users And Computers. The Active Directory Users And Computers console appears.

3. In the scope pane, select the Computers container and, on the Action menu, point to New and select Computer. The New Object – Computer wizard appears.

4. In the Computer Name text box, type **Computer1**, and then click Next.

5. Click Next again, and then click Finish. The Computer1 computer object appears in the Computers container.

Exercise 8-2: Creating a Computer Object Using Dsadd.exe

In this exercise, you create a new computer object using the Dsadd.exe utility.

1. Log on to a Windows Server 2003 domain controller as Administrator.

2. Click Start and select Command Prompt. A command prompt appears.

3. At the command prompt, type the following command (where *xx* is your student number) and press Enter:

```
dsadd computer "CN=Computer2,CN=Computers,DC=contosoxx,DC=com" -desc
    "Mark Lee's Workstation"
```

4. Click Start, point to Administrative tools, and select Active Directory Users And Computers. The Active Directory Users And Computers console appears.

5. In the scope pane, select the Computers container. Confirm that the Computer2 computer object appears in the container and that the description "Mark Lee's Workstation" appears in the object's Properties dialog box on the General tab.

Exercise 8-3: Disabling and Enabling a Computer Object

In this exercise, you disable and reenable a computer object using the Active Directory Users And Computers console.

1. Log on to a Windows Server 2003 domain controller as Administrator.

2. Click Start, point to Administrative tools, and select Active Directory Users And Computers. The Active Directory Users and Computers console appears.

3. In the scope pane, select the Computers container. Then select the Computer1 computer object you created in Exercise 8-1 and, on the Action menu, select Disable Account. An Active Directory message box appears, prompting you to confirm your command to disable the object.

4. Click Yes. Another Active Directory message box appears, confirming that the Computer1 object has been disabled.

5. Click Yes. The Computer1 icon in the console appears with a red X.

6. Select the same Computer1 computer object and, on the Action menu, select Enable Account. An Active Directory message box appears, informing you that the object has been enabled.

7. Click Yes. The Computer1 icon appears without the red X.

REVIEW QUESTIONS

1. What are the minimum group memberships necessary to create a Windows Server 2003 computer account in an OU in a domain? Consider all steps of the process, and assume that the computer object for the system does not yet exist in Active Directory. (Choose all correct answers.)

    a. Domain Admins

    b. Enterprise Admins

    c. Administrators on a domain controller

    d. Account Operators on a domain controller

    e. Server Operators on a domain controller

    f. Account Operators on the computer

    g. Server Operators on the computer

    h. Administrators on the computer

2. Which of the following command-line tools can create a computer object in Active Directory?

    a. Dsmod.exe

    b. Dsrm.exe

    c. Netdom.exe

    d. Dsadd.exe

    e. Net.exe

3. Which of the following Windows platforms are capable of joining to a computer object in an Active Directory domain?

    a. Windows 95

    b. Windows NT 4

    c. Windows 98

    d. Windows 2000

    e. Windows Me

    f. Windows XP

    g. Windows Server 2003

4. When you open the Properties dialog box for a computer object in the Active Directory Users And Computers console, you discover that no properties are displayed in the Operating System tab. What causes these properties to be absent?

5. After a period of expansion, your company created a second domain. Last weekend, a number of machines that had been in your domain were moved to the new domain. When you open Active Directory Users And Computers, the objects for those machines are still in your domain and are displayed with a red X icon. What is the most appropriate course of action?

    a. Enable the objects

    b. Disable the objects

    c. Reset the objects

    d. Delete the objects

6. A user reports that during a logon attempt, he received a message stating that the computer cannot contact the domain because the domain controller is down or the computer account might be missing. You open Active Directory Users And Computers and discover that the account for that computer is missing. What steps should you take?

7. A user reports that during a logon attempt, he received a message stating that the computer cannot contact the domain because the domain controller is down or the computer account might be missing. You open Active Directory Users And Computers and see that the computer's account appears normal. What steps should you take?

CASE SCENARIOS

Scenario 8-1: Resetting a Computer Object

In your Windows Server 2003 domain contoso.com, you have a computer object for a member server called Pserver01 in an OU called Pservers. This object represents a print server that has been offline for a lengthy period and is not communicating with other computers in the domain to accept print jobs. You have determined that the password on this computer's account within the domain needs to be reset. Which command can you issue to correctly reset the computer account?

    a. dsmod CN=pserver01,CN=PSERVERS,DC=contoso,DC=com –reset

    b. dsmod computer pserver01.contoso.com –reset

    c. dsmod contoso\pserver01 –reset

    d. dsmod computer CN=pserver01,CN=PSERVERS,DC=contoso,DC=com –reset

Scenario 8-2: Computer Object Troubleshooting

After a consultant performs maintenance on the computers in the east branch office over the weekend, users complain of trouble logging on. You examine the event log on one of the branch office computers and discover the following entry:

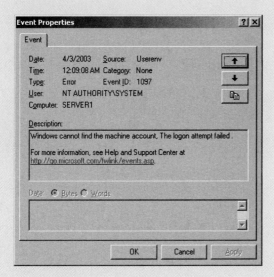

There seems to be a problem with the computer account. Specify which of the following steps you should perform to correct the problem, in the correct order.

   a. Delete the computer accounts.

   b. Reset the user accounts.

   c. Join the computers to a workgroup.

   d. Disable the computer accounts.

   e. Reset the computer accounts.

   f. Enable the computer accounts.

   g. Create new computer accounts.

   h. Join the computers to the domain.

PART 3
MANAGING AND MAINTAINING SHARED RESOURCES

CHAPTER 9
SHARING FILE SYSTEM RESOURCES

One of the primary reasons for the existence of data networks is the ability to share files among users working on different computers. On a small network, file sharing is often an informal process performed by trusted end users with little thought given to security. On a large network, however, and particularly in organizations dealing with sensitive data, it is the job of the network administrator to ensure that the appropriate files are shared, that they are protected from accidental or deliberate damage, and that they are accessible only by the people who should be authorized to work with them. In this chapter, we review the concepts and skills required to share data files with network users effectively and securely.

Upon completion of this chapter, you will be able to:

- Create and manage file system shares and work with **share permissions**

- Use NTFS file system permissions to control access to files

- Manage file sharing using Microsoft Internet Information Services (IIS)

UNDERSTANDING PERMISSIONS

One of the most fundamental concepts of Microsoft Windows Server 2003 system administration is that of permissions. As the name implies, a permission is a privilege granted to a particular entity, such as a user, group, or computer, enabling that entity to perform a particular action or access a particular resource. Windows Server 2003 and all of the other Windows operating systems use permissions in a variety of ways to control access to various elements of the operating system.

Windows Server 2003 has many types of permissions, the most prominent of which are as follows. Each of these permission types is completely separate from the others, although some can be applied to the same system elements.

- **File system permissions**   Controls access to files and folders on NTFS drives. All users require permissions to access NTFS files and folders, whether they are working on the network or on the computer where the data is stored.

- **Share permissions**   Controls access to file system and printer shares. Users must have permissions to access shared resources over the network.

- **Active Directory permissions**   Controls access to Microsoft Active Directory objects. Users must have some access to Active Directory objects to log on to the network to access network resources. Administrators need greater access to maintain the object properties and the Active Directory tree structure.

- **Registry permissions**   Controls access to registry keys. To modify registry keys, administrators must have the appropriate permissions.

Some of these systems require more maintenance than others. A typical network administrator might work with file system permissions every day but never have to manually modify registry permissions. In Chapters 6, 7, and 8, you learned something about the Active Directory permissions that administrators need to create and manage objects, such as users, groups, and computers. In many cases, Active Directory permissions are delegated to specific groups of administrators once and need not be adjusted again unless a dramatic reorganization tales place.

Access Control Lists

The functionality of these permission systems is based on the concept of the **access control list** (**ACL**). Most Windows elements, including files, shares, Active Directory objects, and registry keys, have an ACL. An ACL is simply a list of permissions specifying who has access to that particular element and what degree of access they have. The ACL for a particular element consists of **access control entries** (**ACEs**). An ACE specifies the name of a *security principal* (that is, the user, group, or computer being granted permissions) and the specific permissions granted to that security principal.

NOTE   Where Is the ACL?   It is critical for the system administrator to understand that the ACL is always stored with the element being controlled, not with the security principal being granted access to the element. For example, a particular folder on an NTFS drive has an ACL containing a list of users or groups that have permission to access that folder. If you look at a particular user or group object, you will not find a list of the folders to which that user or group has access. This is a particularly important point when you move elements to different locations or back them up to another storage medium. Moving files from an NTFS drive to a FAT drive, for example, causes the permissions to be lost because the FAT file system cannot store the ACLs.

Working with ACLs is relatively simple because all of the permissions systems in Windows Server 2003 use a similar interface. Virtually all system elements protected by permissions have a Properties dialog box that contains a Security tab, like the one shown in Figure 9-1. The upper list box in the tab displays a list of ACEs (that is, security principals), and the lower list box specifies the permissions allocated to the ACE selected in the upper list box. You can add and remove ACEs as needed and specify the permissions granted or denied to each one.

Figure 9-1   The Security tab in a Properties dialog box

Permissions

The permissions specified in the ACEs are designed to provide granular access control over the elements to which they are applied. When you grant a user permission to access a folder, for example, the access is not simply a yes-or-no proposition. You have a great many options as to how much access the user receives. Each of the permissions systems listed earlier has its own list of individual permissions that are specific to the types of resources they control. When you create an ACE, you select a security principal, and then you select the individual permissions that you want to grant that security principal.

For example, NTFS permissions enable you to specify that a particular user be able to read the files in a folder but not modify them, or you can provide the user with however much additional access he needs. Depending on the resource you are working with, you might have dozens of permissions available, which you can combine in any way you wish.

In many cases, the sheer number of permissions involved can make the ACL administration process rather complicated. To simplify matters, Windows Server 2003 uses two levels of permissions, standard permissions and special permissions. **Standard permissions** are the permissions you see on the Security tab of a Properties dialog box. These are the permissions you will probably work with every day because they provide basic control over various aspects of the element being protected.

However, standard permissions are actually combinations of even more detailed permissions called **special permissions**. (You learn more about how to use special permissions for the NTFS file system later in this chapter.) To access special permissions, you click the Advanced button on the Security tab to display an Advanced Security Settings dialog box, as shown in Figure 9-2.

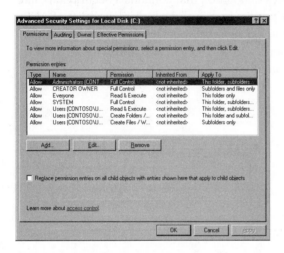

Figure 9-2   An Advanced Security Settings dialog box

In this dialog box, you can control access to a resource with much greater specificity, by selecting from a complete list of special permissions in a Permission Entry dialog box, as shown in Figure 9-3. This is often not necessary on a typical network, but some of the default permission settings created by Windows Server 2003 during the operating system installation rely on individual special permission assignments.

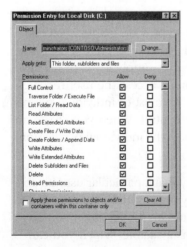

Figure 9-3   A Permission Entry dialog box

NOTE   You work with all the Windows Server 2003 permissions systems in much the same way, except that the standard and special permissions can be different, depending on the resource being protected.

Inheritance

One of the key features of the permissions systems in Windows Server 2003 is that, by default, subordinate objects inherit the permissions possessed by their parent objects. Permissions always flow downstream through a file system hierarchy, Active Directory hierarchy, or registry structure. When you grant a security principal permission to access an NTFS folder or share, an Active Directory object, or a registry key, that principal also receives the same permission to access the subfolders beneath the specified NTFS folder or share, the objects beneath the specified Active Directory object, or the keys subordinate to the specified key, respectively.

For example, granting a user permissions for the root of an NTFS drive means that the user receives the same permissions for all of the files and subfolders on that entire drive. In most cases, this permission inheritance is beneficial because it prevents administrators from having to create separate permissions for every subfolder, subordinate object, or subkey. In fact, for most administrators, it is second nature to take this inheritance into account when designing their directory structures, share strategies, and Active Directory trees.

However, sometimes inheritance is not desirable, and in these cases, there are two ways to counteract the default behavior of permissions:

- **Turn off inheritance**   When you are working with special permissions, you can control whether the permissions you assign to a particular element are inherited by some or all of its subelements.

- **Deny permissions**   All of the permissions systems enable you to explicitly deny a security principal specific permissions, counteracting the effect of any permissions the principal might have inherited from parent elements.

Effective Permissions

Because the security principals used to assign permissions can be users, groups, or computers, it is possible for a single principal to receive permissions from multiple sources, and in some cases those permissions can conflict. For this reason, there are rules that specify how the permissions from various sources interact. All of the permissions that the security principal receives individually, by inheritance, and through group memberships, are subject to these rules and are combined to create the user's **effective permissions**.

The rules forming a security principal's effective permissions are as follows:

- **Allowed permissions are cumulative.**   All of the allowed permissions granted to a security principal, no matter what their source, are combined to form the principal's effective permissions. For example, a specific user might be explicitly granted permissions providing full access to a particular folder on an NTFS drive. At the same time, the user might be a member of a group that also has permissions for that folder, but the group has read-only access to the folder. In addition, the user inherits read and write permissions from the folder's parent folder. In this case, all of the user's permissions, whether explicit or inherited from any source, are combined.

- **Denied permissions override allowed permissions.**   Explicitly denying permissions to a security principal overrides the allowed permissions the principal receives from any other source. For example, if a user receives full access permissions to a folder by inheritance and also receives full access from a group membership, permissions you create that explicitly deny the user all access to that folder override all of the permissions inherited from parents and groups. Therefore, in this case, the user's effective permissions provide no access at all to the folder.

- **Explicit permissions take precedence over inherited permissions.** When a security principal inherits permissions from a parent or a group, you can override those permissions by explicitly assigning different permissions to the principal itself. The inherited permissions form a rule, and the explicit permissions are an exception to that rule. Therefore, explicitly allowed permissions override inherited denied permissions.

SHARING FOLDERS

When you sit down at a computer running Windows Server 2003, you can access the files and folders on its drives from the system console, assuming that you have the appropriate credentials. You can also allow users elsewhere on the network access to the computer's files and folders, but to do so, you must first create a share specifying what files the users can access.

> **MORE INFO**   You can actually create two types of shares on computers running Windows: file system shares and printer shares. This chapter deals exclusively with file system shares. To learn about creating printer shares, see Chapter 10.

The ability to create shares in Windows Server 2003 is based on two services that run on every Windows computer: the Workstation service and the Server service. These two services are implemented by the Client For Microsoft Networks module and the File And Printer Sharing For Microsoft Networks module, respectively, both of which appear in the Local Area Connection Properties dialog box for every network interface adapter installed on the computer, as shown in Figure 9-4. The Server service is responsible for making shared system resources available on the network, and the Workstation service enables other computers to access those shared resources.

> **NOTE**   **Workstations and Servers**   Despite the names of its various versions and editions, Windows is a peer-to-peer operating system, meaning that every computer is capable of functioning both as a client and as a server simultaneously. Even computers that are not running an operating system with *Server* in its name can still run the Server service.

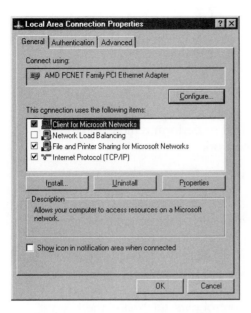

Figure 9-4 A Local Area Connection Properties dialog box

Administrative Shares

Windows Server 2003 has some file system shares even before you create any of your own. By default, the Windows Server 2003 installation program creates the following administrative file system shares (as shown in Figure 9-5):

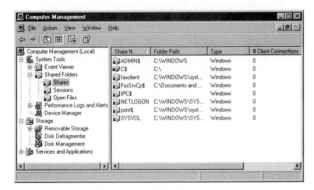

Figure 9-5 Administrative shares in the Shared Folders snap-in

- **Drive shares** Every volume on the computer's hard drives has a default administrative share at its root, which is named using its drive letter in uppercase, plus a dollar sign (as in C$). The inclusion of the dollar sign causes these shares to be hidden from view in My Network Places, although it is still possible to access them directly by using the Shared Folders snap-in for Microsoft Management Console (MMC), by creating a network place shortcut or by using Windows Explorer. The default share permissions for these administrative shares grant full control to the Administrators group; these permissions cannot be changed, nor can you delete the shares.

- **Admin$** The system root folder, C:\Windows by default, is automatically shared with the name Admin$. This, too, is a hidden share, and it enables members of the Administrators group to exercise full control over the system root without having to know exactly where it is located.

- **IPC$** A share that provides remote access to the computer's named pipes, which are portions of memory used to pass information from one process to another. This share is required to perform remote administration tasks on the computer over the network.

In addition, Windows Server 2003 creates other administrative shares when you install specific operating system elements:

- **Print$** When you install the first shared printer on the computer, Windows Server 2003 creates a hidden share out of the *systemroot*\System32\Spool \Drivers folder with the name Print$. This share is designed to provide other systems on the network with access to the drivers for the printers installed on the computer. The Administrators, Print Operators, and Server Operators groups all have full control over this share; the Everyone special identity group has only the Read permission.

- **faxclient** When you install Fax Services on the computer, Windows Server 2003 creates a share of the C:\WINDOWS\system32\clients\faxclient folder with the name faxclient. This share provides network users with access to the fax client software on the server. The Everyone special identity has the Read permission for this share.

- **FxsSrvCp$** When you install Fax Services on the computer, Windows Server 2003 creates a hidden share of the C:\Documents and Settings \All Users\Application Data\Microsoft\Windows NT\MSFax\Common Coverpages folder with the name FxsSrvCp$. This share enables fax clients to access cover pages stored on the server. The Administrators group has full control of the share, while the Everyone special identity has only Read permission.

- **SYSVOL** When you promote a Windows Server 2003 computer to a domain controller, the system shares the *systemroot*\SYSVOL\sysvol folder, giving it the name SYSVOL. The SYSVOL share is used by domain controllers to store group policy objects (GPOs) and scripts that are replicated to other computers in the domain. The Administrators and Authenticated Users groups have full control of the share, while the Everyone special identity has only the Read permission.

- **NETLOGON** When you promote a Windows Server 2003 computer to a domain controller, the system shares the *systemroot*\SYSVOL\sysvol\ *domainname*\SCRIPTS folder, giving it the name NETLOGON. NETLOGON is a share, created for backward compatibility purposes, that provides the same basic function as SYSVOL for Windows NT 4 domain controllers. The Administrators group has full control of the share, while the Everyone special identity has only the Read permission.

NOTE Hiding Shares   The hidden nature of the administrative shares is not limited to these particular shares. You can hide any share by using a dollar sign as the last character of the share name. This practice does not prevent anyone from accessing the shares; it only prevents them from browsing to the shares in Windows Explorer.

Preparing to Create File System Shares

To create a file system share, you must have the following privileges:

- **On a domain controller**   On a computer functioning as a domain controller, you must be logged on as a member of the Administrators or Server Operators group to create file system shares. Because the Enterprise Admins and Domain Admins groups are members of the Administrators group, these groups can also create file system shares.

- **On a domain member server or workstation**   On a member server or a domain workstation, you must be logged on as a member of the Administrators, Server Operators, or Power Users group to create file system shares.

- **On a workgroup or standalone computer**   On a computer that is not a member of a domain, you must be logged on as a member of the Administrators or Power Users group to create file system shares.

- **On an NTFS drive**   If the folder you plan to share is on an NTFS drive, you must be logged on as a user with at least the NTFS Read permission for the folder.

As with many tasks in Windows Server 2003, you can create file system shares in several ways. The following sections examine some of the tools that you can use to create and manage shares.

NOTE Exam Objectives   The objectives for exam 70-290 require students to be able to "configure access to shared folders."

Creating a File System Share Using Windows Explorer

The most common method of creating a file system share is to use Windows Explorer to select a folder and then enable sharing for that folder. You can share any folder on any drive in the computer, creating as many shares as you need. When network users browse the shares on the computer, the shares appear as isolated folders with no context. Unless you tell users somehow, they have no way of knowing which drives the shares are on or where the folders are that you have shared.

To share a folder in Windows Explorer, you right-click it and select Sharing And Security to display the dialog box shown in Figure 9-6. You can also access this dialog box by selecting a folder and, from the File menu, selecting Properties, and then selecting the Sharing tab.

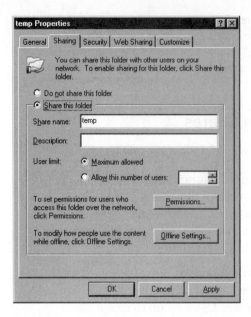

Figure 9-6   The Sharing tab of a folder's Properties dialog box

When you select the Share This Folder option, you activate the other controls in the Sharing tab, enabling you to configure the following parameters:

- **Share Name**   Specifies the name by which the share will be visible on the network. By default, the name of the folder appears in the text box, but you can supply any name up to 80 characters. This field is required.

- **Description**   Enables you to specify a description of the share's purpose, its contents, or any other information. This field is optional.

- **User Limit**   Enables you to specify how many users are permitted to access the shared folder at one time. You can use this feature to prevent system resources from being monopolized by too many clients accessing the share simultaneously.

- **Permissions**   Enables you to specify who has access to the share and to what degree. For more information, see "Managing Share Permissions" later in this chapter.

- **Offline Settings**   Enables you to specify whether network users are permitted to cache the shared folder contents on their computers. For more information, see "Controlling Offline Storage" later in this chapter.

Once you have configured the properties in the Sharing tab, clicking OK creates the share. You can tell that the share has been created in several ways, including the following:

- In Windows Explorer, under My Computer, the icon for the folder has an open hand affixed to it, metaphorically sharing its contents with the network.

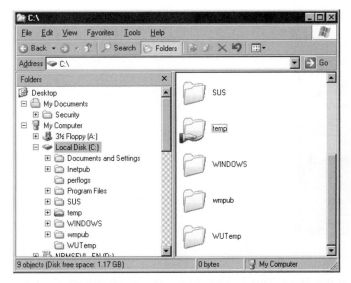

- In Windows Explorer, under My Network Places, the new share appears beneath the icon for the computer on which you created it.

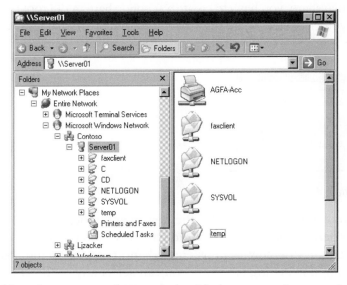

Practice creating shares with Windows Explorer by doing Exercise 9-1, "Creating a Share Using Windows Explorer," now.

At this point, users on the network with the appropriate permissions can access the share and the files and folders inside.

Sharing a Volume Using Windows Explorer

You can create a file system share out of an entire volume using Windows Explorer, but the procedure is slightly different, to account for the existence of the administrative share already present on every volume. When you select a volume root in Windows Explorer and access its Sharing tab, you see the interface shown in Figure 9-7.

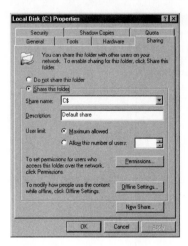

Figure 9-7   A shared volume root

Here you can see that the Share This Folder option is already selected, and the name of the administrative share appears in the Share Name text box. If you want to grant network users access to the entire volume without compromising the security of the administrative share, you have to create a second share in the root of the volume. To do this, you click New Share to display the New Share dialog box, as shown in Figure 9-8.

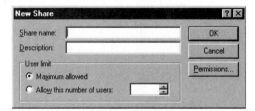

Figure 9-8   The New Share dialog box

In this dialog box, you specify the name for the new share, a description, a user limit, and share permissions, just as you did earlier when creating a folder share. When you click OK, the new share is created and is added to the Share Name drop-down list in the Sharing tab. Now you can select any of the volume root shares for management from the drop-down list. Whichever share you choose, this is the one controlled by the User Limit, Permissions, and Offline Settings controls.

Creating a File System Share Using the Shared Folders Snap-In

Using Windows Explorer is usually the most convenient way to create file system shares, but it does have one distinct drawback: you can create shares only on the computer where you are working. You cannot select a folder on another computer and share it. Windows Server 2003 includes a tool that provides this capability, however—an MMC snap-in called Shared Folders.

The Shared Folders snap-in is integrated into the Windows Server 2003 Computer Management console, as shown in Figure 9-9. As always, you can also create a custom MMC console containing Shared Folders and any other snap-ins you wish. Clicking the snap-in's Shares subfolder displays a list of the currently existing shares on the local computer, including the hidden shares that are not visible in Windows Explorer.

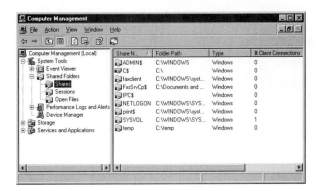

Figure 9-9 The Shared Folders snap-in

NOTE Managing Remote Shares To manage another computer on the network, select the Computer Management (Local) icon at the root of the scope pane and, on the Action menu, select Connect To Another Computer. Then enter or browse to the name of the computer you want to manage, and click OK. You can then create and manage shares on the other computer, just as you would on the local system.

To create a new share, select the Shares subfolder and, on the Action menu, select New Share to launch the Share A Folder Wizard. This wizard contains three pages:

■ **Folder Path** Specify the path to the folder you want to share, using drive letter notation.

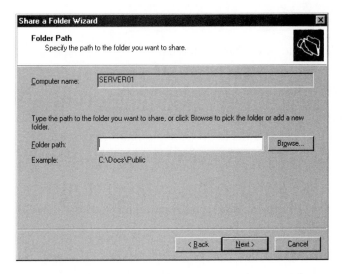

■ **Name, Description, And Settings** Specify a name and description for the share. You can also click Change to configure the offline settings for the share.

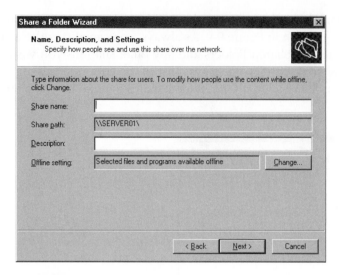

- **Permissions**   Select the permissions that you want to assign to the share.

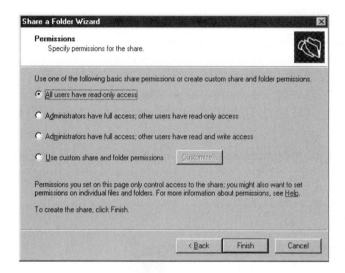

Completing the wizard adds the new share to the list.

Creating a File System Share Using Net.exe

In Windows Server 2003, it is also possible to create a share from the command line, using the Net.exe program with the *share* subcommand. The syntax is as follows:

```
net share sharename=drive:\path [parameters]
```

The additional parameters you can include on the command line are as follows:

- **/grant:*principal*,[read | change | full]**   Assigns the specified security principal the Read, Change, or Full Control permission for the share

- **/users:*number***   Specifies the maximum number of users that are permitted to access the share

- **/unlimited**   Specifies that an unlimited number of users are permitted to access the share

- **/cache:[manual|documents|programs|none]**   Configures offline settings for the share

The following example creates a share called Documents out of the C:\Docs folder and assigns the users group the Read permission:

```
net share documents=c:\docs /grant:users,read
```

MANAGING SHARED FOLDERS

Once you have created file system shares, you can manage them at any time using Windows Explorer by accessing the same Sharing tab of the folder's Properties dialog box that you used to create the share. You can also select the share in the Shared Folders snap-in and, on the Action menu, select Properties to display the dialog box shown in Figure 9-10.

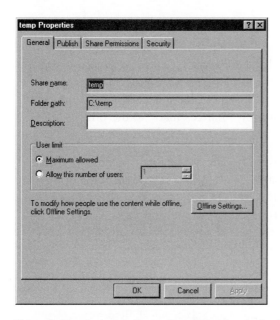

Figure 9-10   A share's Properties dialog box in the Shared Folders snap-in

In addition to modifying the share properties you set during the share's creation, such as its user limit and description, you can also configure the features described in the following sections.

Controlling Offline Storage

Security is often a critical aspect of file system sharing. You want the files stored on the shares to be made available to the right users, and only those users. Administrators can use permissions to control who accesses the shares, but they do not have as much control over what happens to the files after the network users access them. One way of exercising control of file system shares after they are accessed is to limit the Offline Files capabilities of the users who access the shares.

When you click Offline Settings in a share's Properties dialog box, you see the dialog box shown in Figure 9-11. Here you can specify whether the client computers accessing the share are permitted to cache its contents using the Windows Offline Files feature.

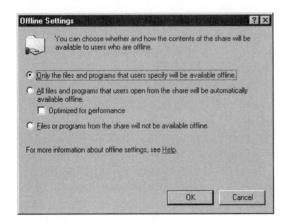

Figure 9-11   The Offline Settings dialog box

Offline Files is a mechanism in Windows Server 2003, Microsoft Windows XP, and Microsoft Windows 2000 that maintains local copies of files that users access over the network. If the client computer's connection to the server is lost or interrupted, the user can continue working with the cached copy of the files. When the connection is restored, the client computer replicates any changes made to the offline copies of the files back to their original locations on the share.

The problem with Offline Files with respect to security is that the file copies stored on client computers do not have the same permission protection as the copies on the source share. Sensitive files that are carefully protected on the share might be stored on client computers all over the network, with no protection at all. The options in the Offline Settings dialog box enable administrators to specify whether clients can cache the files in a share using Offline Files. The options are described below.

> **NOTE   Using Net.exe**   *You can also configure the offline settings from the command line, using the Net.exe program with the share subcommand. The command-line parameters corresponding to the options in the Offline Settings dialog box are listed in the following descriptions.*

- **Only The Files And Programs That Users Specify Will Be Available Offline**   Enables users to select which documents and executables to store offline on their client computers. The corresponding command-line parameter for Net.exe is */cache:manual*.

- **All Files And Programs That Users Open From The Share Will Be Automatically Available Offline**   Automatically stores all shared documents offline on client computers. Selecting the Optimized For Performance check box automatically caches all programs for local execution on the client computer. The corresponding command-line parameters for Net.exe are */cache:documents* and */cache:programs*.

■ **Files And Programs From The Share Will Not Be Available Offline**
Prevents all documents and executables from being stored offline on
client computers. The corresponding command-line parameter for
Net.exe is */cache:none.*

Publishing File System Shares in Active Directory

When you click the Publish tab of a share's Properties dialog box in the Shared
Folders snap-in, you see the controls shown in Figure 9-12, which you can use to
publish the folder in Active Directory. Publishing shared folders in Active Directory
does not actually store the shared files in the Active Directory database, but it does
create a shared folder object that points to the location of the share. Once a shared
folder is published, users can search for it in Active Directory, using the same tools
they would use to locate users and other resources.

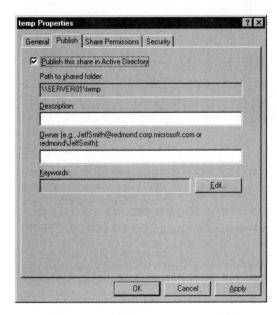

Figure 9-12   The Publish tab of a shared folder's Properties dialog box

To publish a shared folder in Active Directory, you must select the Publish This
Share In Active Directory check box and supply the name of the share's owner.
You can also supply keywords describing the contents of the share, to facilitate
searches for the information it contains.

Managing Share Permissions

As mentioned earlier in this chapter, shares have their own system of permissions,
which you can use to control who is allowed to access them. To specify permissions for a shared folder, you use one of the following interfaces:

■ In Windows Explorer, open the folder's Properties dialog box and, in the
Sharing tab, click Permissions.

■ In the Shared Folders snap-in, open the share's Properties dialog box and
select the Share Permissions tab.

NOTE   **Exam Objectives**   *The objectives for exam 70-290 require students to be able to "manage shared folder permissions."*

Whichever method you use, you see an interface like that shown in Figure 9-13.

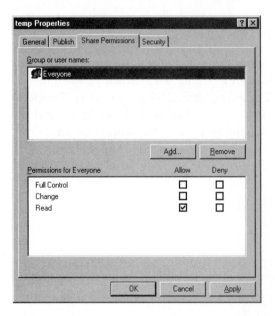

Figure 9-13   The Share Permissions tab in a shared folder's Properties dialog box

The permissions system for shares is the simplest one in Windows Server 2003. In this case, there is no distinction between standard permissions and special permissions; there are only the following three simple permissions:

■ **Read**   Users can display folder names, file names, file data, and attributes. Users can also execute program files and access other folders within the shared folder.

■ **Change**   Users can create folders, add files to folders, change data in files, append data to files, change file attributes, delete folders and files, and perform actions permitted by the Read permission.

■ **Full Control**   Users can change file permissions, take ownership of files, and perform all tasks allowed by the Change permission.

To set permissions, you click Add, select a security principal (such as a user, group, or computer), and specify the permissions you want to allow or deny that principal. You can select a principal already present in the Group Or User Names list to modify its permissions as needed.

Using Share Permissions

Share permissions are a form of access control that provides only limited protection to shared files. Some of the limitations of share permissions are as follows:

■ **Limited scope**   Share permissions apply only to files and folders accessed over the network. Share permissions do not prevent users from accessing the shared files while working at the system console or when accessing the computer by other network means, such as Web, FTP, Telnet, and Terminal Server applications.

- **Lack of flexibility**   Share permissions are not granular; they provide a single template containing only three possible permissions, which apply to every file and folder beneath the shared folder. You cannot modify permissions for particular folders or files beneath the shared folder.

- **No replication**   Share permissions are not replicated by the File Replication service (FRS).

- **No resiliency**   Share permissions are not included in a backup or restore of a data volume.

- **Fragility**   Share permissions are lost if you move or rename the folder that is shared.

- **No auditing**   You cannot configure auditing based on share permissions.

The only real advantages of using share permissions are the simplicity of the system and the fact that share permissions are available on any file system supported by Windows Server 2003. On a drive using the FAT file system, for example, share permissions are the only way to control access to the drive.

On a small network with few security requirements, share permissions might be an acceptable solution, but in most cases, network administrators prefer to use the more flexible and robust permissions provided by the NTFS file system. If you choose to do this, however, you must be conscious of the following facts:

- The share permissions system is still in place, whether you use NTFS permissions or not.

- The share permissions system is completely separate from the NTFS permissions system.

- Both share permissions and NTFS permissions can apply to the same elements.

Therefore, the best practice when you use NTFS permissions for access control is to grant all users (in the form of the Everyone special identity) the Full Control share permission for all shared folders. This prevents conflicts and confusion between the two permission systems. In other words, you should use either share permissions or NTFS permissions to protect your files, but not both.

If you do not do this, the effective permissions realized by your network users are a combination of the most restrictive settings imposed by both permission systems. For example, if your share permissions grant the Read permission to the Users group, you can give the same group the Full Control NTFS permission, but the users will still be subject to the limitations imposed by the share permissions. This factor, combined with the previously described complications provided by inheritance, group memberships, and denied permissions, can result in a nightmarish web of conflicting influences that is incredibly difficult to understand and maintain.

NOTE   **Exam Objectives**   The objectives for exam 70-290 require students to be able to "troubleshoot access to files and shared folders."

One of the most common causes of problems with accessing file system shares is a conflict between share permissions and NTFS permissions. When you troubleshoot problems like these, be sure to check both permission systems to make sure that users have appropriate access to the files they need.

> **MORE INFO**   The advantages and capabilities of the NTFS permissions system are described later in this chapter.

Share Permission Defaults

In all Windows operating systems up to and including Windows 2000, the default share permissions for a new file system share grant Full Control permission to the Everyone special identity. This leaves the share wide open from a security standpoint, which is a convenience to administrators who plan to use NTFS permissions, but a hindrance to those who want to provide some protection with share permissions. Beginning with the Windows XP release, the default permissions for new file system shares have changed. Windows XP and Windows Server 2003 grant the Everyone special identity only the Read permission and give the Administrators group the Full Control permission. This means that if you plan to rely on NTFS permissions for access control, you must remember to modify the permissions for your shares to grant full control to everyone.

Creating a File System Sharing Strategy

The most obvious file system sharing strategy is simply to share the root of each volume on every networked computer. There are two main reasons why this is a bad idea:

- **Confusion**   When users are faced with a dozen different shares representing the disk drives on a dozen different computers, it can be difficult for them to figure out where the files they need are located. They might have to search through the shares on several different systems before they locate their files. Even a single large drive shared from its root can present a large and complicated directory structure.

- **Security**   Sharing an entire drive, particularly a system drive, grants users access to many files and folders that they would be better off not seeing. Users typically do not need access to operating system and application files on other computers, and they can cause damage if they inadvertently delete a required file or directory.

The solution to this problem is to create shares from specific folders and not from entire volumes. In fact, the Shared Folders snap-in even displays a message box when you try to share an entire volume, warning you that root sharing is not recommended for security reasons. The files that users are most likely to access over the network are documents and data files. Therefore, you should organize the directory structure of your systems in such a way as to store documents and other shared files in logically named folders, and then create shares out of those folders.

Sharing Removable Drives

One exception to this practice should be when you are sharing files on removable drives, such as CD-ROM, DVD-ROM, or cartridge drives. While nothing prevents you from sharing a specific folder on these types of drives, keep in mind that the share will be usable only when the disk or cartridge containing that folder is in the drive. Sharing the root of the drive enables you to swap media as needed and still have the share remain available.

Nesting Shares

As mentioned earlier, you can share any folder on a volume, even one that is already included in another share higher in the directory. For example, you can share the root of drive D, calling the share D, and then create a separate share out of the D:\docs folder, calling it Docs. These two shares can even have different permissions. However, you must remain conscious of the fact that even though the shared folders are nested in Windows Explorer, to network users they are two separate and completely independent shares. What's more, the permissions for the two shares are separate as well. If, for example, you give users full control of the D share and then give them read-only access to the Docs share, their limited access to the D:\docs folder through the Docs share does not affect the full control they have when they access the exact same folder using the D share.

USING NTFS PERMISSIONS

Windows Server 2003 supports two main file systems: FAT and NTFS. The file allocation table (FAT) file system is a holdover from the MS-DOS operating system that provides basic functionality but few of the features required for network storage. The only advantage to using FAT drives is that you can start a computer with an MS-DOS boot disk and still access the drives. NTFS is a file system first introduced in Microsoft Windows NT 3.1 that includes a number of features beneficial to network administrators. Chief among these is the system of permissions that provides detailed access control for all of the individual files and folders on a drive.

> **NOTE**   **Exam Objectives**   *The objectives for exam 70-290 require students to be able to "configure file system permissions."*

Every file and folder on an NTFS drive has an ACL containing ACEs that list the security principals that have been granted permissions for that file or folder. When a user attempts to access a file or folder, the system compares the user's security access token, which contains the security identifiers (SIDs) of the user's account and those of the groups to which the user belongs, to the SIDs in the ACEs of the ACL. Once the system authorizes the user, access is granted to the file or folder.

Compared to the share permissions discussed earlier in this chapter, NTFS permissions have many distinct advantages, including the following:

- **Scope**   NTFS permissions apply to files and folders no matter how they are accessed. Users at the system console or connecting over the network by any means are subject to the same permissions.

- **Flexibility**   NTFS provides a long list of special permissions, which are combined into standard permissions, either of which you can apply to any file or folder on a drive, with complete control over permission inheritance.

- **Replication**   NTFS permissions are replicated by the FRS.

- **Resilience**   NTFS permissions are included in a backup or restore of a data volume.

- **Less fragile**   NTFS permissions are not lost if you move or rename the file or folder to which the permissions are applied (as long as the file or folder remains on an NTFS volume).

- **Auditing**   You can audit access to NTFS files or folders based on the security principals who have permission to access them.

Working with NTFS permissions is understandably more complex than using share permissions, but the additional protection provided is usually worth the trouble to network administrators.

Managing Standard Permissions

Most of the time, administrators work with NTFS standard permissions because they usually provide enough flexibility to control access to shared files and folders. In Windows Explorer, every file and folder on an NTFS volume has a Properties dialog box with a Security tab, as shown in Figure 9-14, which you use to assign standard permissions for that file or folder, as well as access the more advanced permission controls discussed later in this chapter.

Figure 9-14   The Security tab for an NTFS folder

> **NOTE** **Remote NTFS Administration**   Windows Explorer is capable of configuring NTFS permissions for any file or folder on the network, as long as the user has the appropriate privileges. This is in contrast to Windows Explorer's share permission capabilities, which are limited to the local system.

The process of assigning standard permissions to an NTFS file or folder is similar to that of assigning share permissions. You select a security principal in the Group Or User Names list box or click Add to specify a new security principal, and then, in the Permissions list box, you select the appropriate Allow or Deny check boxes for the permissions you want to apply. The standard permissions for the NTFS file

system and the tasks that can be performed with each permission are listed in
Table 9-1.

> **NOTE** **File and Folder Permissions** There are slight differences when a particular permission is applied to a file as opposed to a folder. One permission, List Folder Contents, is not applicable to files.

Table 9-1 **NTFS Standard Permissions**

Standard Permission	When Applied to a Folder, Enables a Security Principal to:	When Applied to a File, Enables a Security Principal to:
Read	■ See the files and subfolders contained in the folder ■ View the ownership, permissions, and attributes of the folder	■ Read the contents of the file ■ View the ownership, permissions, and attributes of the file
Read and Execute	■ Navigate through restricted folders to reach other files and folders ■ Perform all actions associated with the Read and List Folder Contents permissions	■ Perform all actions associated with the Read permission ■ Run applications
Write	■ Create new files and subfolders inside the folder ■ Modify the folder attributes ■ View the ownership and permissions of the folder	■ Overwrite the file ■ Modify the file attributes ■ View the ownership and permissions of the file
Modify	■ Delete the folder ■ Perform all actions associated with the Write and the Read & Execute permissions	■ Modify the file ■ Delete the file ■ Perform all actions associated with the Write and the Read & Execute permissions
List Folder Contents	■ View the names of the files and subfolders contained in the folder	■ Not applicable
Full Control	■ Modify the folder permissions ■ Take ownership of the folder ■ Delete subfolders and files contained in the folder ■ Perform all actions associated with all of the other NTFS folder permissions	■ Modify the file permissions ■ Take ownership of the file ■ Perform all actions associated with all of the other NTFS file permissions

Practice creating NTFS permissions by doing Exercise 9-3, "Configuring NTFS Permissions," now.

> **NOTE** **Inherited Permissions** When a check box in the Security tab is selected and shaded gray, this indicates that the permission has been inherited from a parent folder.

Using Advanced Security Settings

This basic interface in the Security tab enables administrators to perform common permissions assignment tasks quickly and easily, but it does not provide a great deal of information, nor does it provide full access to all of the features provided by the NTFS permissions system. Clicking the Advanced button displays the Advanced Security Settings dialog box, as shown in Figure 9-15, which is as close as you can get to viewing the file or folder's actual ACL in the Windows graphical user interface.

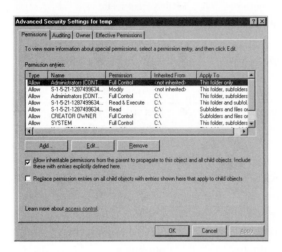

Figure 9-15   The Advanced Security Settings dialog box

The default Permissions tab of the Advanced Security Settings dialog box contains a Permission Entries list, which is essentially a list of the individual ACEs in the file or folder's ACL. Each entry in the list contains the following information:

- **Type**   Specifies whether the entry allows or denies the permission.
- **Name**   Specifies the name of the security principal receiving the permission.
- **Permission**   Specifies the standard permission being assigned to the security principal. If the ACE is used to assign special permissions, the word *Special* appears in this field.
- **Inherited From**   Specifies whether the permission is inherited and, if so, where it is inherited from.
- **Apply To**   Specifies whether the permission is inherited by subordinate objects and, if so, by which ones.

The Permission Entries list might contain multiple entries for a particular security principal, indicating that there are permissions originating from more than one source, such as one explicitly assigned permission and one inherited permission, or that the principal has both Allow and Deny permission types assigned to it. When this is the case, each entry in the list is managed separately.

To work with one of the entries in the list, you select it and click Edit to open a Permission Entry dialog box. Other than this, the only active controls in the Advanced Security Settings dialog box are the two following options:

■ **Allow Inheritable Permissions From The Parent To Propagate To This Object And All Child Objects**   Specifies whether the file or folder should inherit permissions from parent objects. This check box is selected by default. Clearing it causes a Security message box to appear, in which you can choose to remove all of the inherited ACEs from the list or copy the inherited permissions from the parents to the file or folder. If you choose the latter, the effective permissions stay the same but the file or folder is no longer dependent on the parents for permission inheritance. If you change the permissions on the parent objects, the file or folder remains unaffected.

■ **Replace Permission Entries On All Child Objects With Entries Shown Here That Apply To Child Objects**   Causes child objects to inherit permissions from this folder, to the exclusion of all permissions explicitly assigned to the child objects. This check box is available on folders only.

Managing Special Permissions

Editing one of the permission entries in the Advanced Security Settings dialog box or adding a new entry in that dialog box displays a Permission Entry dialog box, like the one shown in Figure 9-16. Here, for the first time, you have direct access to the special permissions that form the underlying fabric of the NTFS permissions system.

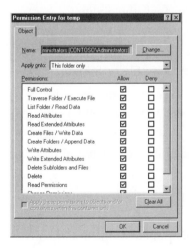

Figure 9-16   A Permission Entry dialog box

NTFS has 14 special permissions, the functions of which are as follows. In cases where the special permissions are presented in pairs, separated by a slash, the first permission applies to folders and the second to files.

■ **Traverse Folder/Execute File**   The Traverse Folder permission allows or denies security principals the ability to move through folders that they do not have permission to access, so they can reach files or folders that they do have permission to access. This permission applies to folders only. The Execute File permission allows or denies security principals the ability to run program files. This permission applies to files only.

■ **List Folder/Read Data** The List Folder permission allows or denies security principals the ability to view the file and subfolder names within a folder. This permission applies to folders only. The Read Data permission allows or denies security principals the ability to view the contents of a file. This permission applies to files only.

■ **Read Attributes** Allows or denies security principals the ability to view the NTFS attributes of a file or folder.

■ **Read Extended Attributes** Allows or denies security principals the ability to view the extended attributes of a file or folder.

■ **Create Files/Write Data** The Create Files permission allows or denies security principals the ability to create files within the folder. This permission applies to folders only. The Write Data permission allows or denies security principals the ability to modify the file and overwrite existing content. This permission applies to files only.

■ **Create Folders/Append Data** The Create Folders permission allows or denies security principals the ability to create subfolders within a folder. This permission applies to folders only. The Append Data permission allows or denies security principals the ability to add data to the end of the file but not to modify, delete, or overwrite existing data in the file. This permission applies to files only.

■ **Write Attributes** Allows or denies security principals the ability to modify the NTFS attributes of an existing file or folder.

■ **Write Extended Attributes** Allows or denies security principals the ability to modify the extended attributes of an existing file or folder.

■ **Delete Subfolders and Files** Allows or denies security principals the ability to delete subfolders and files, even if the Delete permission has not been granted on the subfolder or file.

■ **Delete** Allows or denies security principals the ability to delete the file or folder.

■ **Read Permissions** Allows or denies security principals the ability to read the permissions for the file or folder.

■ **Change Permissions** Allows or denies security principals the ability to modify the permissions for the file or folder.

■ **Take Ownership** Allows or denies security principals the ability to take ownership of the file or folder.

■ **Synchronize** Allows or denies different threads of multithreaded, multiprocessor programs the ability to wait on the handle for the file or folder and synchronize with another thread that might signal it.

The Permission Entry dialog box for an ACE displays the individual special permissions that are the functional equivalent of the standard permission specified in the Advanced Security Settings dialog box. The special permissions that make up the six standard permissions are listed in Table 9-2.

Table 9-2   **NTFS Standard Permissions and Their Special Permission Equivalents**

Standard Permission	Special Permissions
Read	■ List Folder/Read Data
	■ Read Attributes
	■ Read Extended Attributes
	■ Read Permissions
	■ Synchronize
Read and Execute	■ List Folder/Read Data
	■ Read Attributes
	■ Read Extended Attributes
	■ Read Permissions
	■ Synchronize
	■ Traverse Folder/Execute File
Modify	■ Create Files/Write Data
	■ Create Folders/Append Data
	■ Delete
	■ List Folder/Read Data
	■ Read Attributes
	■ Read Extended Attributes
	■ Read Permissions
	■ Synchronize
	■ Traverse Folder/Execute File
	■ Write Attributes
	■ Write Extended Attributes
Write	■ Create Files/Write Data
	■ Create Folders/Append Data
	■ Read Permissions
	■ Synchronize
	■ Write Attributes
	■ Write Extended Attributes
List Folder Contents	■ List Folder/Read Data
	■ Read Attributes
	■ Read Extended Attributes
	■ Read Permissions
	■ Synchronize
	■ Traverse Folder/Execute File

(continued)

Table 9-2   **NTFS Standard Permissions and Their Special Permission Equivalents**

Standard Permission	Special Permissions
Full Control	■ Change Permissions
	■ Create Files/Write Data
	■ Create Folders/Append Data
	■ Delete
	■ Delete Subfolders and Files
	■ List Folder/Read Data
	■ Read Attributes
	■ Read Extended Attributes
	■ Read Permissions
	■ Synchronize
	■ Take Ownership
	■ Traverse Folder/Execute File
	■ Write Attributes
	■ Write Extended Attributes

When you edit a permission entry, you can change any of the following parameters:

■ **Name**   Specifies the name of the security principal that receives the permission assignment. When you want to switch permissions from one principal to another, rather than create an entirely new ACE, you can use this interface to change the name of the assignee.

■ **Apply Onto**   Specifies which objects should receive the permission assignment, using the options shown in Figure 9-17. This selector provides the most complete control over the inheritance of the assigned permissions available; you can limit inheritance to any combination of files, folders, subfolders, and child files.

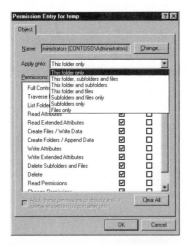

Figure 9-17   The Apply Onto options

■ **Permissions**   Specifies the special permissions to be assigned to the security principal. The Permissions list box includes all of the applicable special permissions listed earlier, plus the Full Control standard permission.

NOTE   Using the Apply Onto Option   When you use the Apply Onto selector to limit the targets for permission inheritance, all of the child folders and files still receive the ACE from the parent. Excluding certain child objects from inheritance just prevents those objects from enforcing the permissions in the ACE. In situations where the ACE is inherited by a large number of child objects, possibly causing network performance problems, using the Apply Onto option to limit the inheritance of the permissions is no help.

Viewing Effective Permissions

Considering the complexities of the NTFS permission system, it is fortunate that Windows Server 2003 includes a mechanism for viewing a security principal's effective permissions for a particular file or folder. To view effective permissions, you open the Advanced Security Settings dialog box for a file or folder and select the Effective Permissions tab, as shown in Figure 9-18. When you click Select and specify the name of a security principal in the Select User, Computer, Or Group dialog box, the check boxes in the Effective Permissions list change to reflect the cumulative permissions assigned to that principal.

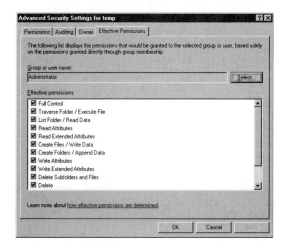

Figure 9-18   The Effective Permissions tab of an Advanced Security Settings dialog box

NOTE   Exam Objectives   The objectives for exam 70-290 require students to be able to "verify effective permissions when granting permissions."

While the Effective Permissions tab is useful for troubleshooting shared file access problems, it is not perfect. The effective permissions displayed in this interface are compiled by factoring together the following:

■ Permissions explicitly assigned to the security principal

■ Permissions the security principal inherits from parent objects

■ Permissions the security principal inherits from local and domain group memberships

However, the Effective Permissions list does not account for share permissions or for permissions inherited from special identities that depend on the security principal's logon status.

For example, the Effective Permissions tab might show that a particular group has the Full Control permission for a folder on a shared drive. However, if the default share permissions are still in place, granting the Everyone special identity only the Read permission, the group is actually limited to read-only access, despite what the Effective Permissions display says.

In the same way, the Effective Permissions cannot anticipate the logon status of a security principal at any given time. Windows Server 2003 makes it possible to assign permissions based on special identities, such as Anonymous Logon, Dialup, and Interactive. As you learned in Chapter 7, these identities are determined based on the way in which a user logs on to the system or the network. A user who accesses the network using a dial-up connection, for example, is a part of the Dialup special identity for the duration of that connection. Because security principals need not be logged on when you view their effective permissions, there is no way for the system to know which identities will have an effect on the principals when they do log on.

> **NOTE Effective Permissions Workaround** To account for the permissions assigned to special identities that might affect your users, you can use the Effective Permissions tab to display the effective permissions for a particular special identity, and then you can factor those results into your users' effective permissions.

Resource Ownership

Every file and folder in the NTFS file system (as well as every object in Active Directory) has an owner. By default, the owner is the user who created the file or folder. In the case of files and folders created by the operating system, the Administrators group is the owner. However, the ownership of any file or folder can be taken at any time by a member of the Administrators group, or by any user who possesses the Take Ownership special permission for the file or folder.

> **NOTE Exam Objectives** The objectives for exam 70-290 require students to be able to "change ownership of files and folders."

File or folder ownership has two main purposes:

- **Owners can modify ACLs.**   No matter what other permissions the owner of a file or folder has, the owner can still modify the file or folder's ACL. Ownership therefore functions as a fallback mechanism, in case someone locks all users out of a file or folder. If, for example, you create a new file and accidentally revoke all of your permissions to that file, your ownership enables you to modify the ACL for the file again and restore your permissions.

- **Disk quotas are determined by ownership.**   Disk quotas enable administrators to track and control how much server disk space each user is occupying. These quotas work by adding up the sizes of all the files owned by a particular user. You learn more about disk quotas in Chapter 12.

In addition to the Take Ownership permission, there are also two user rights that provide the ability to manage the ownership of NTFS files and folders:

- **Take Ownership Of Files Or Other Objects**   Users or groups possessing this user right can take ownership of any NTFS file or folder. By default, the Administrators group receives this user right from the Default Domain Controllers Policy GPO.

- **Restore Files And Directories**   Users or groups possessing this user right can take ownership of any NTFS file or folder or assign ownership to any other user or group. By default, the Default Domain Controllers Policy GPO grants this user right to the Administrators, Backup Operators, and Server Operators groups.

To view or take ownership of a file or folder, open its Advanced Security Settings dialog box and select the Owner tab, as shown in Figure 9-19. This tab lists the file or folder's current owner. If you have the Take Ownership special permission for the file or folder or the Take Ownership Of Files Or Other Objects user right, you can select your user account in the Change Owner To box and click Apply or OK to take ownership of the object. If you have the Restore Files And Directories user right, you can also click Other Users Or Groups to select another security principal and give it ownership of the object.

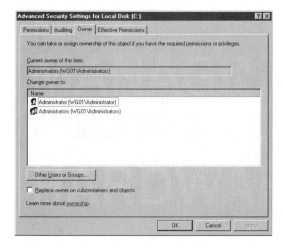

Figure 9-19   The Owner tab of the Advanced Security Settings dialog box

If you are the current owner of a file or folder and you want to pass ownership to another user, but you lack the Restore Files And Directories user right, you can still modify the ACL for the object and grant the other user the Take Ownership permission. The other user can then use the procedure described in the previous paragraph to take ownership of the file or folder.

ADMINISTERING INTERNET INFORMATION SERVICES

So far in this chapter, you have learned how to provide network users with access to the files on a computer running Windows Server 2003 by publishing shares with the Server service, which are accessible by clients running the Workstation service.

However, this is not the only way to share files using Windows Server 2003. You can also use Internet services, such as those provided by Microsoft Internet Information Services (IIS), even when your clients are on the local network.

> **NOTE**   **Exam Objectives**   *The objectives for exam 70-290 require students to be able to "manage Internet Information Services (IIS)."*

IIS is a Windows Server 2003 application that can publish files and applications using Internet standard protocols such as Hypertext Transfer Protocol (HTTP), which is the standard protocol for Web communications, and File Transfer Protocol (FTP). Compared to file system shares, IIS in its default configuration is a limited method of publishing files. For security reasons, IIS is installed in a secure, locked mode that enables the server to supply only static content to clients. Users can retrieve files from an IIS server to their local systems and work on them there, but they cannot open files directly from the server drives and save modified versions back to their original locations, as they can with a file system share. However, even in its locked-down state, IIS does provide a means of disseminating files easily and securely.

In the following sections, you learn how to install and configure IIS on a computer running Windows Server 2003 and manage the security of an IIS server.

Installing IIS

Unlike Windows 2000, Windows Server 2003 does not install IIS with the operating system by default. This is to prevent a potential security breach in the operating system. Earlier versions of Windows installed IIS by default, activated the World Wide Web Publishing Service, and created a default Web page. In cases where administrators did not use the service and neglected to shut it down, this provided a potential entry point for unauthorized users. In Windows Server 2003, you must install IIS manually, after the operating system installation is completed.

To install IIS, open Add Or Remove Programs in Control Panel and select Add/ Remove Windows Components to launch the Windows Components Wizard. In this wizard, you select Application Server, click Details, and then select Internet Information Services (IIS). You can click Details again to specify which IIS components to install. By default, the wizard installs the following components:

- **Common Files**   Installs required IIS program files.

- **Internet Information Services Manager**   Installs the Internet Information Services (IIS) Manager snap-in for MMC. You use this snap-in to manage the IIS services and configure site security.

- **World Wide Web Service**   Installs the service providing HTTP connectivity with TCP/IP clients on the network.

> **NOTE**   **Installing Additional Components**   *Although they are not needed for the functions described in this chapter, you can select additional IIS components to provide greater functionality to your server, but do not omit any of the default components listed here.*

When you complete the wizard, Windows Server 2003 installs the components you selected and activates the World Wide Web Publishing Service.

Managing an IIS Web Site

When IIS is installed, a default Web site is created, enabling you to implement a Web environment quickly and easily. Initially, the default site has no content (except for an Under Construction message). By adding your own files to the home directory for the default site, you can create a home page that provides clients with access to whatever files, folders, and other information you want to publish.

> **NOTE** **Exam Objectives** *The objectives for exam 70-290 require students to be able to "manage a Web server."*

To manage the Web sites on an IIS server, you use the Internet Information Services (IIS) Manager snap-in, as shown in Figure 9-20, which is accessible from the Start menu's Administrative Tools program group. This snap-in enables you to create and manage as many separate Web sites as your server hardware is capable of running.

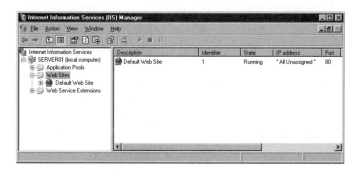

Figure 9-20 The Internet Information Services (IIS) Manager snap-in

Initially, there is only one Web site on the server, called Default Web Site. To view the sites on the server, expand the server node in the scope pane and then expand the Web Sites folder. By selecting one of the listed sites and, from the Action menu, selecting Properties, you open the Properties dialog box for that site. This dialog box contains a wealth of controls that enable you to configure this Web site's parameters. The following sections examine some of the most critical controls in this important dialog box.

Using the Web Site Tab

The Web Site tab of the Properties dialog box, shown in Figure 9-21, contains settings that specify how clients are able to access the Web site. IIS is able to host a virtually unlimited number of Web sites on a single computer, but for clients to access them, there must be a way to differentiate one site from another.

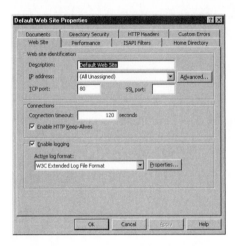

Figure 9-21   The Web Site tab of a Web site's Properties dialog box

Web servers typically use techniques such as the following to host multiple sites:

- **Different IP addresses**   By configuring the computer with multiple IP addresses and assigning a different IP address to each Web site, the Web server can direct incoming requests to the appropriate site, based on the IP address specified in the request.

- **Different port numbers**   By default, the HTTP protocol uses the well-known port number 80 for its TCP/IP communications. When you connect to a Web site, your browser assumes the use of port 80 unless you specify otherwise, using a Uniform Resource Locator (URL) like *http://www.contoso.com:81*. By assigning different port numbers to Web sites, a server can direct incoming requests to the appropriate site based on the port number specified in the request.

- **Host headers**   Despite the fact that clients typically use names to access Web sites, TCP/IP communications are based on IP addresses. Domain Name System (DNS) servers are responsible for converting the names supplied by users into the correct IP addresses. A **host header** is an optional field in an HTTP request message that contains the name of the Web server specified in the URL. Requests with different host header values can then be directed to a single Web server using one IP address and one port number. The server can then direct incoming requests to the appropriate site based on the host header value. For example, a company might run two Web sites, www.adatum.com and www.contoso.com, using one Web server. The company's DNS server resolves both names into the same IP address, so the request messages destined for each site all end up at the same server. The server then distinguishes between the two destinations by examining the contents of the host header fields.

With the controls in the Web Site tab, you can use any one of these three methods to differentiate this particular Web site from others running on the server. The Default Web Site is configured to use port 80 and all of the computer's IP addresses that are not assigned to other Web sites. If you create additional Web sites on the server, you might want to change these values by selecting a specific IP Address value, changing the TCP Port value, or clicking Advanced to specify a host header name for the site.

This tab also enables you to specify a time limit before inactive users are disconnected from the server, and also to control the server's logging behavior for this site, by selecting a log format, specifying what information is to be logged, and configuring a logging schedule.

Using the Home Directory Tab

A Web site's home directory is the default location for its content files. When you specify a URL in a Web browser that contains only a site name (such as *www.contoso.com*), the server automatically supplies the content files in the site's home directory. In the Home Directory tab, shown in Figure 9-22, you specify the location of the home directory for this particular Web site. By creating different home directories for the various sites running on a single server, you can maintain separate content for each site.

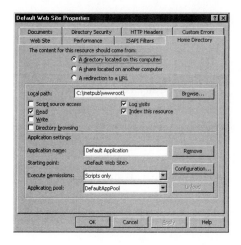

Figure 9-22   The Home Directory tab of a Web site's Properties dialog box

IIS enables you to specify a home directory by selecting any one of the following three options:

- **A Directory Located On This Computer**   Uses standard drive letter notation to specify a home directory on one of the computer's local drives

- **A Share Located On Another Computer**   Uses **Universal Naming Convention (UNC)** notation to specify a home directory on a share that's elsewhere on the network

- **A Redirection To A URL**   Uses URL notation to specify a home directory on another Web server

The default Web site uses a local home directory, which the IIS installation creates in the C:\Inetpub\wwwoot folder by default. Initially, this folder contains no actual content except for the files producing the Under Construction page, but by placing your own content files in this folder, you make them immediately available to clients.

In addition to allowing you to specify the actual location of the home directory, this tab also enables you to configure the types of access that clients have to this directory. The following options are available when you specify a home directory on a local drive or a network share:

- **Script Source Access**   Enables clients to access script files in the directory, assuming that the Read or Write permission is set.

- **Read**   Enables clients to read and download files in the directory.

- **Write**   Enables clients to upload files to the directory or change the content of write-enabled files.

- **Directory Browsing**   Assuming the absence of a default document, enables users to view a hypertext listing of the files and folders in the directory.

- **Log Visits**   Assuming that logging is enabled for the site, causes visits to this directory to be recorded in the log.

- **Index This Resource**   Causes a full-text index of the directory to be created in the Microsoft Indexing Service. (You must install the Indexing Service by clicking Add/Remove Windows Components in the Add Or Remove Programs utility.)

- **Application Settings**   Enables you to specify the types of Web applications clients are permitted to run.

Using the Documents Tab

In the Documents tab, shown in Figure 9-23, you can specify the name of the content file that IIS delivers to clients by default. When a client enters a URL that does not contain a file name in a browser, the Web server delivers the file with the default name specified in the Enable Default Content Page box. If the first file name listed does not exist in the directory, the server checks each of the listed names and delivers the file with the highest name in the list. If none of the listed files exist in the directory, the server either displays a hypertext listing of the directory's contents (if the Directory Browsing option is enabled in the Home Directory tab) or an error message (if Directory Browsing is disabled).

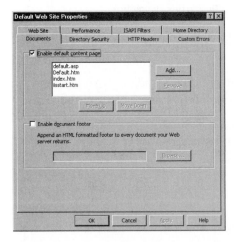

Figure 9-23   The Documents tab of a Web site's Properties dialog box

The Enable Document Footer box enables you to supply the name of a footer file to be appended to all documents published by the Web site.

Using the Performance Tab

In the Performance tab, shown in Figure 9-24, you can limit the amount of network bandwidth used by this site, and also the number of users that are able to connect simultaneously. This enables you to prevent one Web site from monopolizing all of the system's bandwidth.

Figure 9-24   The Performance tab of a Web site's Properties dialog box

Creating Virtual Directories

When you specify a home directory for an IIS Web site, all of the files in that directory and its subdirectories are published by the server and made available to clients. However, if you have existing files and folders you want to publish, it is not necessary to move them all to the home directory structure. Instead, you can create a virtual directory. A **virtual directory** is a pointer to a folder at another location, which appears to clients as part of the Web site's directory structure.

To create a virtual directory on an IIS Web site, you select the site in the Internet Information Services (IIS) Manager's scope pane and, on the Action menu, point to New and select Virtual Directory. This launches the Virtual Directory Creation Wizard, in which you supply the following information:

- **Virtual Directory Alias**   Specifies the name by which the virtual directory will be known to clients. The alias you enter here will appear as a subdirectory of the Web site in client URLs. The alias you choose need not (and often should not) conform to the actual name of the folder you are publishing.

- **Web Site Content Directory**   Specifies the path to the directory you intend to share with the virtual directory. The path you specify can use drive letter or UNC notation and be located on a local drive or a network share.

- **Virtual Directory Access Permissions**   Specifies the permissions granted to clients accessing the virtual directory (such as Read, Run Scripts, Execute, Write, and Browse).

Once you have created the virtual directory, the files in the content directory you specified appear on the Web site in a subdirectory identified by the alias you specified.

Configuring IIS Security

Most Web servers on the Internet provide clients with anonymous access. When you configure an IIS Web site to use anonymous access, all clients connect to the server using a special account dedicated to this purpose. The default name of the account in Windows Server 2003 is IUSR_*servername*, where *servername* is the name of the computer. Technically, the clients are authenticated, but there is no exchange of secure credentials and clients are not restricted in their access to the Web site.

> **NOTE   Exam Objectives**   *The objectives for exam 70-290 require students to be able to "manage security for IIS."*

However, if you want to restrict access to a Web site, you can increase the security level in several ways, including the following:

- **Authentication and Access Control**   Requires clients to supply a username and password for access to the site. IIS supports several types of encryption, with varying degrees of security.

- **IP Address and Domain Name Restrictions**   You can configure an IIS Web site to grant or deny specific clients access to the site, based on their IP addresses or domain names.

- **Secure Communications**   Requires clients to use a secured communications protocol or a digital certificate to gain access to the site.

You can configure all of these security mechanisms in the Directory Security tab of a Web site's Properties dialog box, as shown in Figure 9-25.

Figure 9-25   The Directory Security tab of a Web site's Properties dialog box

> **NOTE   IIS and NTFS Permissions**   *In addition to the security mechanisms just mentioned, you can also use NTFS permissions to secure Web sites. As explained earlier in this chapter, NTFS permissions apply no matter how a user accesses the NTFS file system. This means that a user who accesses a Web site with content stored on an NTFS drive must have the appropriate permissions to access the content files. See "Using NTFS Permissions," earlier in this chapter, for more information.*

Configuring IIS Authentication

To configure an IIS Web site to use any form of authentication other than the default anonymous access option, you click the Edit button in the Authentication And Access Control group box on the Directory Security tab to display the Authentication Methods dialog box (shown in Figure 9-26).

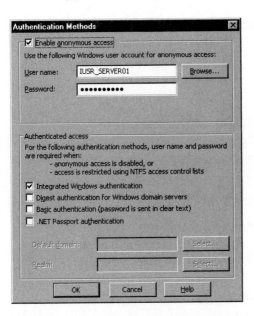

Figure 9-26   The Authentication Methods dialog box

To prevent unauthenticated access to the Web site, you must clear the Enable Anonymous Access check box; otherwise, the other authentication options have no effect. You must also apply NTFS permissions to the files and folders you want to protect. Then you must select an alternative form of authentication from the following options:

■ **Integrated Windows Authentication**   The server performs a cryptographic exchange with the client so that the username and password are transmitted in the form of a hash that prevents eavesdroppers from accessing the user's credentials. This form of authentication is not usable across proxy servers or firewalls.

■ **Digest Authentication For Windows Domain Servers**   For clients with Active Directory accounts only, the server collects user credentials and stores them on the domain controller as an MD5 (Message Digest 5) hash.

■ **Basic Authentication**   The client transmits the username and password to the server in clear text, creating a potential security breach. Use this option only when none of the more secure options is available.

■ **.NET Passport Authentication**   Clients connect to the server using their existing .NET Passport accounts, which are authenticated by a central .NET Passport server on the Internet.

Configuring IP Address and Domain Name Restrictions

When you click the Edit button in the IP Address And Domain Name Restrictions group box, you see the IP Address And Domain Name Restrictions dialog box, as shown in Figure 9-27. Here you can specify individual IP addresses, network addresses, and domain names, and then grant or deny them access to the site.

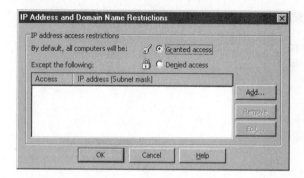

Figure 9-27   The IP Address And Domain Name Restrictions dialog box

In the IP Address And Domain Name Restrictions dialog box, you first specify whether you want the addresses or names you select to be granted or denied access to the site, and then you click Add to open a Granted Access or Denied Access dialog box, in which you enter the IP address of a specific computer, a network address and subnet mask, or a domain name.

This type of restriction is computer-based, rather than user-based. When you grant a specific IP address access to the site, anyone working on the computer with that address can access the site unless other security mechanisms are in place. Because these restrictions are separate from the Web site's authentication requirements, you can use them instead of or in combination with authentication. For example, you might want to grant a specific user access to the site, but make sure that the user connects only from a specific workstation. By enabling authentication and configuring an IP address restriction, you can do both of these things.

Configuring Secure Communications

When you click the Edit button in the Secure Communications group box, the Secure Communications dialog box (shown in Figure 9-28) appears, in which you can configure the following options:

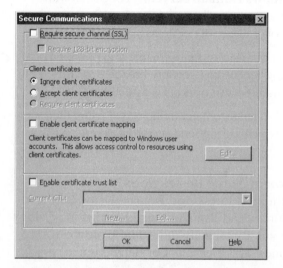

Figure 9-28   The Secure Communications dialog box

- **Require Secure Channel (SSL)**   Requires clients to use an encrypted communications protocol when connecting to the Web server, such as the Secure Sockets Layer (SSL) protocol. You can also require clients to use 128-bit encryption for greater security.

- **Client Certificates**   Specifies whether clients can, cannot, or must use digital certificates to access the Web site. To require certificates, you must select the Require Secure Channel (SSL) option.

- **Enable Client Certificate Mapping**   Configures the server to authenticate clients logging on with valid certificates. Click Edit to map certificates to specific user accounts.

- **Enable Certificate Trust List**   Configures the server to use a list of trusted certification authorities to validate user certificates. Users not possessing a certificate from one of the listed authorities are denied access.

SUMMARY

- Windows Server 2003 includes a number of independent permissions systems, including share permissions, NTFS permissions, Active Directory permissions, and registry permissions. Each of these systems enables you to control access to a specific type of system resource.

- Every object protected by permissions has an access control list (ACL), which is a list of access control entries (ACEs) that contain a security principal (such as a user, group, or computer) and the permissions assigned to that principal.

- File system shares enable network users to access files and folders on other computers. To create file system shares, you can use Windows Explorer, the Shared Folders snap-in, or the Net.exe command-line utility.

- Share permissions provide basic protection for file system shares, but they lack the granularity and flexibility of NTFS permissions. Share permissions also apply only to network access through the Server service. Files protected by share permissions are still accessible from the system console or through other network services, such as IIS and terminal servers.

- NTFS permissions can be allowed or denied, explicit or inherited. A Deny permission takes precedence over an Allow permission; and an explicit permission takes precedence over an inherited permission. The result is that an explicit Allow permission overrides an inherited Deny permission. The effective permissions for a file or folder are a composite of all the permissions assigned to the element, either explicitly or by inheritance.

- Access granted by NTFS permissions can be further restricted by share permissions and other factors, such as IIS permissions on Web sites. Whenever two permission types are assigned to a resource, such as share permissions and NTFS permissions, you must evaluate each set of permissions and then determine which of the two is more restrictive.

- Inheritance enables an administrator to control access to files and folders by applying permissions to a single parent folder and letting those permissions flow downward to the child objects beneath the parent.

- Every NTFS file and folder has an owner. The owner of a file or folder is always permitted to modify the file or folder's ACL, even without permissions.

- Any user with the Take Ownership permission or the Take Ownership Of Files Or Other Objects user right can take ownership of an object. A user with the Restore Files And Directories user right can assign ownership of any object to any user.

- IIS is a Windows Server 2003 application that makes it possible to share files and folders using Web and FTP server services. You can secure IIS sites by applying NTFS permissions and requiring user authentication, by restricting access to specific IP addresses or domain names, or by using encrypted communications protocols and digital certificates.

EXERCISES

Exercise 9-1: Creating a Share Using Windows Explorer

In this exercise, you share a folder on your computer using Windows Explorer.

1. Log on to Windows Server 2003 as Administrator.

2. Click Start and select Windows Explorer. The Windows Explorer window appears.

3. Expand the My Computer icon and Local Disk (C:).

4. Right-click the Documents And Settings folder and, from the context menu, select Sharing And Security. The Documents And Settings Properties dialog box appears, with the Sharing tab active.

5. Click Share This Folder and, in the Share Name text box, type **Test Share**. Click OK. The icon for the Documents And Settings folder is modified to indicate that it has been shared.

Exercise 9-2: Using the Shared Folders Snap-In

In this exercise, you use the Shared Folders snap-in to create a new share and configure permissions for it.

1. Log on to Windows Server 2003 as Administrator.

2. Click Start, point to Administrative Tools, and select Computer Management. The Computer Management console appears.

3. Expand the Shared Folders icon in the scope pane and select the Shares subfolder.

4. On the Action menu, select New Share. The Share A Folder Wizard launches.

5. Click Next to bypass the Welcome page. The Folder Path page appears.

6. In the Folder Path text box, type **C:\Windows**, and then click Next. The Name, Description, And Settings page appears.

7. In the Share Name text box, type **Test Share 2**, and then click Next. The Permissions page appears.

8. Select the Administrators Have Full Access; Other Users Have Read-Only Access option, and then click Finish. The Sharing Was Successful page appears.

9. Click Close.

Exercise 9-3: Configuring NTFS Permissions

In this exercise, you configure the NTFS permissions for a folder on your computer using Windows Explorer.

1. Log on to Windows Server 2003 as Administrator.

2. Click Start, and select Windows Explorer. The Windows Explorer window appears.

3. Expand the My Computer icon and Local Disk (C:).

4. Right-click the Documents And Settings folder and, on the context menu, select Sharing And Security. The Documents And Settings Properties dialog box appears, with the Sharing tab active.

5. Select the Security tab, and then click Add. The Select Users, Computers, Or Groups dialog box appears.

6. In the Enter The Object Names To Select text box, type **Guests**, and then click OK. The Guests group is added to the Group Or User Names list box in the Security tab.

7. Select the Guests security principal, and in the Permissions For Guests list box, select the Modify and Write check boxes in the Allow column.

8. Click OK to apply the permissions and close the Documents And Settings Properties dialog box.

REVIEW QUESTIONS

1. Which of the following tools enables you to create a share on a remote server? (Choose all correct answers.)

    a. A custom MMC console containing the Shared Folders snap-in

    b. Windows Explorer running on the local machine, connected to the remote computer's ADMIN$ share

    c. Net.exe

    d. The Computer Management console

2. A folder is shared on a FAT volume. The Project Managers group is given the Allow Full Control permission. The Project Engineers group is given the Allow Read permission. Julie initially belongs to the Project Engineers group. Later, she is promoted and is added to the Project Managers group. What are her effective permissions for the folder after the promotion?

3. A folder is shared on an NTFS volume, with the default share permissions. The Project Managers group is given the Allow Full Control NTFS permission. Julie, a member of the Project Managers group, calls to report problems creating files in the folder. Why can't Julie create files?

4. What are the minimum NTFS permissions required to allow users to open documents and run programs stored in a shared folder?

    a. Full Control

    b. Modify

    c. Write

    d. Read & Execute

    e. List Folder Contents

5. Bill complains that he is unable to access the spreadsheet document containing the departmental budget. You open the Security tab for the document, and you find that all permissions for the document are inherited from its parent folder. The Deny Read permission is assigned to a group called Acctg3, of which Bill is a member. Which of the following methods would enable Bill to access the plan? (Choose all correct answers.)

   a. Modify the permissions on the parent folder by adding the permission Bill:Allow Full Control.

   b. Modify the permissions on the parent folder by adding the permission Bill:Allow Read.

   c. Modify the permissions on the spreadsheet document by adding the permission Bill:Allow Read.

   d. Modify the permissions on the spreadsheet document by deselecting Allow Inheritable Permissions, selecting Copy, and removing the Deny permission.

   e. Modify the permissions on the spreadsheet document by deselecting Allow Inheritable Permissions, selecting Copy, and adding the permission Bill:Allow Full Control.

   f. Remove Bill from the group that is assigned the Deny permission.

6. You want to ensure the highest level of security for your corporate IIS intranet server without the added infrastructure of certificate services. The goal is to provide authentication that is transparent to users and to allow you to secure intranet resources with the group accounts existing in Active Directory. All users are within the corporate firewall. Which of the following authentication methods should you choose?

   a. Anonymous Access

   b. Basic Authentication

   c. .NET Passport Authentication

   d. Integrated Windows Authentication

7. You are configuring share permissions for a shared folder on a file server. You want all Authenticated Users to be able to save files to the folder, read all files in the folder, and modify or delete files that they own. What are the minimum permissions that you need to set on the shared folder to achieve your objective? (Choose all correct answers.)

   a. Authenticated Users: Full Control

   b. Authenticated Users: Read

   c. Creator Owner: Change

   d. Creator Owner: Read

CASE SCENARIOS

Scenario 9-1: Web Server Publishing

The content files for your corporate Web server are currently stored on drive D of a Windows Server 2003 computer with IIS installed. The server is called Web1 and its URL is *http://intranet.contoso.com*. You have been instructed to create an IIS solution that will enable the human resources department to publish documents containing company benefit and policy information from its own server. You have also been told that the URL to access the HR information should be *http://intranet.contoso.com/hr*. What must you do to fulfill the instructions?

a. Install IIS on the HR server.

b. Create a new Web site on Web1 called hr.

c. Install the FTP service on Web1.

d. Create a virtual directory on Web1 with the alias hr.

Scenario 9-2: Configuring Share Permissions

Acctg01 is a file server running Windows Server 2003 that is used by the accounting department to provide timesheet and expense report forms for employees. You are the network administrator responsible for configuring the share permissions on the file system shares, which must meet the following requirements:

- Employee-specific forms are stored in the Forms folder, which is shared using the name Forms. These forms must be accessible by all employees.

- Only Authenticated Users can access the forms.

- Employees can upload completed forms to a folder called Forms\Reports *username* that is shared as *username*.

- Users must be able to read their own forms, but not forms submitted by other users.

- Supervisor-specific forms are stored in the Forms\Supervisors folder, which is shared using the name Supervisors. These forms must be accessible only by members of the Supervisors global group.

To accomplish these goals, you have created the share permission assignments shown in the following table:

Shared Folder	Share Permissions
Forms	Everyone: Allow Read
Supervisors	Supervisors: Allow Read
Username	*username*: Allow Change

Assuming that the NTFS permissions for all of the folders are set to Authenticated Users – Modify, which of the following requirements have you met with your permission assignments? (Choose all correct answers.)

a. All employees can download their forms.

b. All employees can upload completed forms to their folders.

c. Employees can read only their own submitted forms.

d. Only Authenticated Users can download forms.

e. Only Supervisors can download Supervisor-specific forms.

CHAPTER 10
WORKING WITH PRINTERS

In addition to file sharing, the primary motivation for the development of local area networks (LANs) was the ability to share printers. Printers are often the bane of a network administrator's existence because they involve not just electronic components but also dirty things such as ink and toner and mechanical processes such as paper feeding. Microsoft Windows Server 2003 provides a powerful feature set to support enterprise print services, and understanding how to use these features can help you minimize the frustrations of dealing with network printing problems. In this chapter, you learn how to install, administer, and troubleshoot local, network, and Internet printers.

Upon completion of this chapter, you will be able to:

- Understand the model and terminology used for Windows printing

- Install a logical printer on a print server

- Prepare a print server to host clients

- Connect a printer client to a logical printer on a print server

- Manage print queues and printer properties

- Troubleshoot printer failures

UNDERSTANDING THE WINDOWS SERVER 2003 PRINTER MODEL

Windows Server 2003 provides print services that are powerful, secure, and flexible. By using a computer running Windows Server 2003 to manage printers, administrators can make them available to applications running locally on the Windows Server 2003 computer or to users on any client platform, including previous versions of Windows as well as Novell NetWare, UNIX, and Macintosh OS.

Windows Server 2003 and previous versions of Windows support two types of printers:

- **Locally attached printers** Printers that are connected to a physical port on a **print server**, typically a universal serial bus (USB) or parallel port.

- **Network-attached printers** Printers connected directly to the network instead of to a physical port on a computer. A network-attached printer contains (or is connected to) a network interface adapter and functions as a node on the network. Computers communicate with the printer using a standard networking protocol such as Transmission Control Protocol/ Internet Protocol (TCP/IP) or Data Link Control (DLC).

When you install a printer of either type on a computer that uses Microsoft Windows, the operating system creates a **logical printer**, which represents the physical printer device. The logical printer defines the characteristics and behavior of the printer; it contains the printer driver, printer settings, print setting defaults, and other properties that control the manner in which a print job is processed and sent to the physical printer. This virtualization of the printer by a logical printer enables administrators to exercise a great deal of creativity and flexibility in configuring enterprise print services.

Using Locally Attached Printers

When you install a **locally attached printer** in Windows Server 2003 (or any other version of Windows), the computer to which the printer is attached can, of course, use it to process print jobs. It is possible to share the printer with other computers on the network. When you create a printer share, the computer hosting the printer functions as a print server. A print server is a computer (or stand-alone device) that receives print jobs from network clients, stores the jobs in a **print queue**, and sends them one by one to the physical printer.

> **NOTE** **Printing Terminology** In the documentation for previous versions of Windows, the physical printer was referred to as a *print device* and the logical printer was referred to as a *printer*. Microsoft has altered this terminology in Windows Server 2003 in an attempt to eliminate the confusion this terminology causes. It now uses *printer* and *logical printer*.

Using Network-Attached Printers

When you are using a network-attached printer, there are two network printing models you can use, which are described in the following sections.

Create a Logical Printer on Every Client Computer

In this model, you install a logical printer on each client computer and connect those logical printers directly to the network-attached printer. There is no print server in this arrangement; each computer maintains its own print settings, processes its own print jobs, and stores the jobs in its own print queue. In a network environment, this model has distinct disadvantages, such as the following:

- When users examine the contents of the print queue, they see only their own jobs.

- Users have no way of knowing what jobs have been sent to the printer by other users.

- Administrators have no way of centrally managing the print queue.

- Administrators cannot implement advanced printing features such as printer pools.

- Error messages appear only on the computer that is printing the current job.

- All print job processing is performed locally on the client computer, rather than being offloaded to a print server.

This model might be practical for a small workgroup network, but for an enterprise, it provides virtually no centralized administrative capabilities. The only real advantage to this arrangement is that it is easy to set up, even by individual end users. Each client computer installs the printer in the normal manner and remains oblivious of the other clients (except when waiting for their print jobs to complete).

Create a Print Server

Because of the significant drawbacks just described, the most typical printing configuration for enterprise networks is the three-part model, which consists of the following components:

- The physical printer

- A print server containing a logical printer, which is connected to the physical printer

- Printer clients, which are connected to the server's logical printer

Printing with a print server provides the following advantages:

- The logical printer on the print server defines the printer settings and manages the printer drivers.

- The logical printer uses a single print queue that is visible to all client computers, so users and administrators can see a complete list of jobs waiting to be printed.

- Error messages, such as out-of-paper or printer-jam messages, are visible to all client computers, so users and administrators can be informed of printer problems.

- Most applications and most printer drivers can offload part of the print-job processing to the print server, which increases the responsiveness of the client computers. In other words, when a client prints a document, the job is sent quickly to the print server and control of the computer returns to the user, while the print server assumes the task of processing the job.

- Security, auditing, monitoring, and logging functions are centralized.

DEPLOYING A SHARED PRINTER

The process of deploying a shared printer using the print server model consists of the following three steps:

- Install the printer on the print server.

- Create a printer share on the print server.

- Connect the clients to the print server.

These steps are described in the following sections.

Installing a Windows Server 2003 Print Server

The first step in deploying a print server on a network is to install the printer on the computer that is to function as the print server. This process is no different from installing a printer for exclusive use by the local system. It is the act of sharing the printer that enables Windows Server 2003 to function as a print server.

In Windows Server 2003, you manage printers using the Printers And Faxes window, which is accessible from Control Panel or directly from the Start menu. Double-clicking the Add Printer icon launches the Add Printer Wizard. After clicking Next to bypass the Welcome page, you complete the wizard pages described in the following list.

> **NOTE   Using USB Printers**   Printers that connect to the computer using the universal serial bus (USB) do not require you to manually launch the Add Printer Wizard. Because USB devices are plug and play, the computer detects and installs them automatically. You might have to supply drivers for printers that are not supported by Windows, however.

- **Local Or Network Printer**   On this page, you specify whether you are installing a local printer or a **network printer**. In the context of this wizard, *local printer* refers to a physical printer that is either locally attached or network-attached but is not currently shared by another print server. *Network printer* refers to a printer shared by another computer on the network. Therefore, to install a print server, you always select Local Printer Attached To This Computer. If the printer is currently connected and ready, you can select the Automatically Detect And Install My Plug And Play Printer check box to attempt to install the printer automatically. However, it is also possible to install the logical printer without the physical printer actually being present.

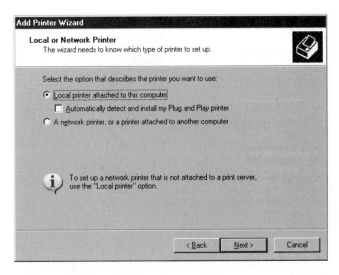

- **Select A Printer Port**   On this page, you specify how the computer communicates with the printer. If the printer is connected to a parallel (LPT) or serial (COM) port in the computer, you select the Use The Following Port option and select the correct port from the drop-down list. If the printer is connected by some other means, you select Create A New Port and select one of the port types from the drop-down list. Network-attached printers, for example, typically require a TCP/IP port. When you select the Standard TCP/IP Port option, the Add Standard TCP/IP Printer Port Wizard appears, in which you specify the IP address you assigned to the printer and, if necessary, the type of network interface adapter connecting the printer to the network.

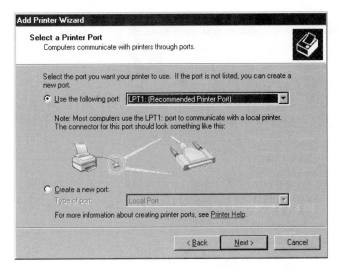

- **Install Printer Software**   If plug and play does not detect and install the correct printer driver, you can select your printer from a list of printer drivers included with Windows Server 2003, which is categorized by manufacturer and printer model. If your printer does not appear in the list, you can click Have Disk to install printer drivers supplied by the device manufacturer.

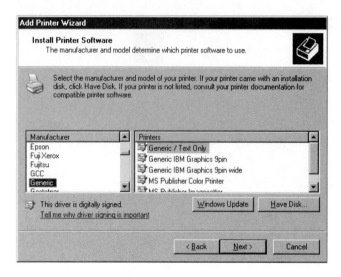

- **Name Your Printer** On this page, you specify the name by which the printer will be known to the applications running on the computer. By default, the wizard supplies the manufacturer and model name associated with the printer driver it is installing, but you can modify the Printer Name to any value you want. For full application compatibility, you should limit printer names to no more than 31 characters. When other printers are installed, this page also enables you to specify whether you want to designate this printer as the default printer for the computer, which means that applications will print to this printer unless you select a different one. This setting applies only to applications running on the local system, not to network clients.

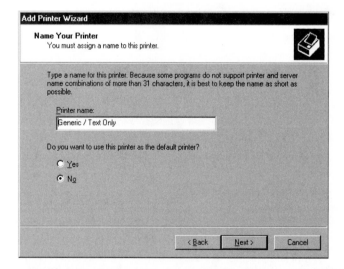

- **Printer Sharing** On this page, you specify whether you want to share the printer, thereby causing the computer to function as a print server. To create a printer share, you select the Share Name option and specify the name by which the printer will be known on the network. By default, the wizard supplies the first eight nonblank characters of the printer name you supplied in the previous page, but you can use any share name you want. For compatibility reasons, it is best to stick with 8.3 printer names that do not contain spaces.

NOTE **Sharing Printers**   The Printer Sharing page of the Add Printer Wizard provides only the most basic printer-sharing functionality. To configure other printer-sharing options, you must use the printer's Properties dialog box, as described in the next section.

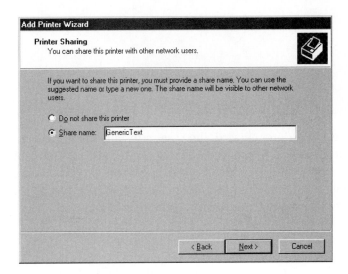

■ **Location And Comment**   This page contains fields in which you can supply information about the printer's location or capabilities. This information is visible to users browsing the network and might help them to locate the correct printer.

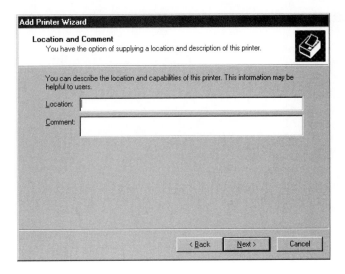

■ **Print Test Page**   This page enables you to print a test job to determine whether the computer can communicate with the printer.

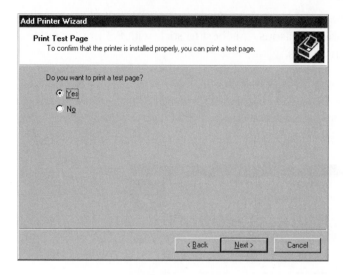

Practice
installing
a logical printer
by doing
Exercise 10-1,
"Creating a
Logical Printer,"
now.

When you complete the Add Printer Wizard, the system installs the appropriate printer driver and creates a logical printer icon for the printer in the Printers And Faxes window. You use this icon to access all of the configuration and maintenance tools for the printer. At this point, the printer is ready for use by the local system and, if you elected to share it, by clients on the network as well.

Sharing a Printer

It is possible to share a printer when you install it using the Add Printer Wizard, but you can get greater control over the share by using the Sharing tab of the printer's Properties dialog box (shown in Figure 10-1), which the wizard creates. To access this tab, select a printer icon in the Printers And Faxes window and, from the File menu, select Sharing.

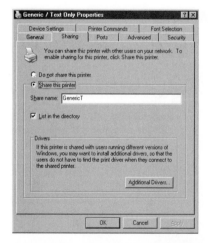

Figure 10-1   The Sharing tab of a printer's Properties dialog box

To share the printer (if it is not shared already), select the Share This Printer option and specify a name for the share in the Share Name text box. You can also select the List In The Directory check box to create a printer object for the printer in

Microsoft Active Directory. As with a shared folder object, a printer object is a pointer that enables users to locate a printer by searching Active Directory for its name or its capabilities. One benefit of specifying values for the Location field and similar properties is the ability to search for a printer based on these properties.

Click Additional Drivers to open the Additional Drivers dialog box, shown in Figure 10-2. When a client on the network accesses a shared printer, it can automatically download a printer driver from the Print$ share on the server, a capability that Windows calls Point And Print. This dialog box enables you to install printer drivers for other operating systems that your clients might be using. This is particularly beneficial if the printer uses drivers that are not included with Windows Server 2003. When you select other operating systems in this dialog box and click OK, the system installs the required drivers, prompting you to insert the manufacturer's driver disk, if needed.

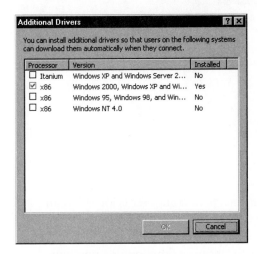

Figure 10-2   The Additional Drivers dialog box

> **NOTE   Updating Printer Drivers**   Client computers running Microsoft Windows NT, Microsoft Windows 2000, Microsoft Windows XP, and Windows Server 2003 download the printer driver from the print server when they first connect to the shared printer. They also verify that they have the current printer driver each time they print, and if they do not, they download an updated driver from the server. For these client computers, you need only keep the printer drivers updated on the print server. Client computers running Microsoft Windows 95, Microsoft Windows 98, and Microsoft Windows Me can automatically download and install printer drivers when they first connect with the share, but they do not check for updated printer drivers after the initial installation. If you obtain an updated driver, you must manually install it on these clients as well as on the server.

Connecting Clients to a Print Server

Once the printer is installed on the print server and shared, it is available for access by clients. Clients can access a shared printer in several ways, as described in the following sections.

Using the Add Printer Wizard

The procedure for installing a print client using the Add Printer Wizard is similar to that of installing a print server, except that on the Local Or Network Printer page, you select the A Network Printer, Or A Printer Attached To Another Computer option. This takes you to a Specify A Printer page, shown in Figure 10-3, in which you are presented with the following ways to indicate the printer you want to use:

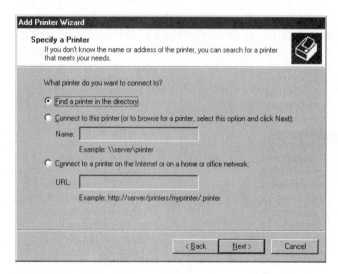

Figure 10-3   The Specify A Printer page of the Add Printer Wizard

- **Find A Printer In The Directory**   If the client computer is joined to an Active Directory domain, the Specify A Printer page displays this option, which causes the wizard to display a Find Printers dialog box that you can use to search for printers by name, location, or other criteria you have specified when creating the printer objects.

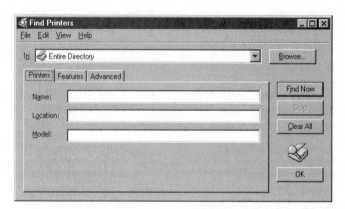

- **Browse For A Printer**   If the client computer is a member of a workgroup, the Specify A Printer page displays this option first. Selecting this option causes the wizard to display a Browse For Printer page, enabling you to browse in domains or workgroups for specific computers and select from the shared printers installed on each computer.

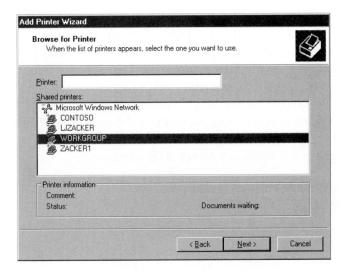

- **Connect To This Printer**   Selecting this option enables you to specify the name of a printer share on the network, using Universal Naming Convention (UNC) notation, such as *servername\printershare*. Clicking Next without specifying a name produces the same Browse For Printer page that the Browse For A Printer option produces.

- **Connect To A Printer On The Internet Or On A Home Or Office Network**   Selecting this option enables you to specify the name of a printer on the network or on the Internet using a Uniform Resource Locator (URL), such as *http://www.adatum.com/printers/printername*.

Once you identify the printer you want to install, the wizard installs the appropriate driver (presuming that one is available on the server or the client) and creates a logical printer in the Printers And Faxes window.

Browsing in Windows Explorer

You can also install a shared printer on a client simply by browsing in My Network Places using Windows Explorer. When you expand a computer icon in My Network Places, Windows Explorer displays a list of the shares on the computer. The printer shares are located in a container called Printers And Faxes, as shown in Figure 10-4. Select one of the shared printers and, from the File menu, select Connect to begin the process of installing the driver and logical printer.

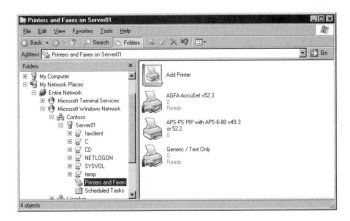

Figure 10-4   Browsing for printers in Windows Explorer

Searching in Active Directory

For clients in Active Directory domains, the Add Printer Wizard provides the ability to search the directory for printer objects. You can search the directory for printers in other ways as well, such as from the Start menu's main Search page. When you select the Other Search Options, this page enables you to specify various search criteria, including a Printers, Computers, Or People option, as shown in Figure 10-5. Choosing to search for a printer on the network displays the same Find Printers dialog box that the Add Printer Wizard displays. This dialog box is accessible in many other ways throughout the Windows Server 2003 interface.

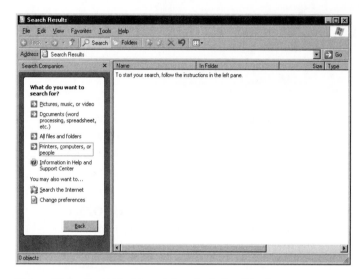

Figure 10-5   Searching for printers in Active Directory

CONFIGURING PRINTER PROPERTIES

After installing the logical printer on the print server, you can configure numerous properties by opening the printer's Properties dialog box, shown in Figure 10-6. Some of the controls in this dialog box are the same for all printers, but others that are provided by the printer driver can be specific to the printer. For example, a color printer might have color management controls that black-and-white printers don't need.

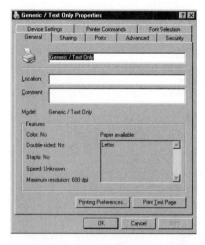

Figure 10-6   The General tab of a printer's Properties dialog box

The General tab enables you to configure the printer name, location, and comments, all of which were initially configured based on your responses to prompts in the Add Printer Wizard. The Sharing tab, as discussed earlier, enables you to specify whether the logical printer is shared and available to other clients on the network. Some of the other functions you can control in the Properties dialog box are discussed in the following sections.

Controlling Printer Security

Just as you can use permissions to secure file system shares, you can control printer usage and administration by assigning permissions through the Security tab of the printer's Properties dialog box, as shown in Figure 10-7.

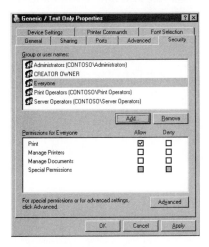

Figure 10-7   The Security tab of a printer's Properties dialog box

The standard permissions that you can set for a printer are as follows:

- **Print**   Enables security principals to connect to a printer and submit print jobs to it. By default, this permission is assigned to the Everyone special identity. To restrict access to a printer, you can revoke the permission from the Everyone identity and assign it to other security principals, or you can deny the permission to specific security principals.

- **Manage Printers**   Enables security principals to perform all tasks associated with the Print permission, and also provides complete administrative control of the printer. Holders of this permission can modify printer properties, pause and restart the printer, control the printer's share status, adjust spooler settings, and modify printer permissions. By default, this permission is assigned to the Administrators and Power Users groups, and on domain controllers, the Server Operators and Print Operators groups.

- **Manage Documents**   Enables security principals to manipulate the documents in the print queue by pausing, resuming, restarting, canceling, and reordering them. However, this permission does not provide the ability to send documents to the printer or control the printer's status. By default, this permission is assigned to the Creator Owner special identity. Because a permission assigned to Creator Owner is inherited by the user who creates an object, this permission enables users to manage print jobs that they have created. The Administrators, Print Operators, and Server Operators groups are also assigned the Manage Documents permission, which means they can manage any document in the print queue. On computers that are not domain controllers, the Power Users group has this permission.

In addition to providing standard permissions, the Security tab also provides access to an Advanced Security Settings dialog box, as shown in Figure 10-8, which you can use to manage individual ACL entries and work with special permissions, just as you can with the NTFS permission system. Unlike with NTFS, however, the special permissions for printers include only three additional capabilities, enabling security principals to read permissions, change permissions, and take ownership of a printer.

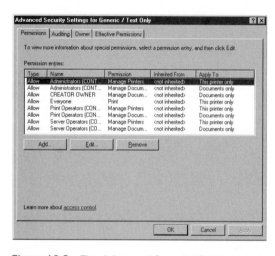

Practice working with printer permissions by doing Exercise 10-2, "Setting Printer Permissions," now.

Figure 10-8   The Advanced Security Settings dialog box

> **NOTE   For More Information**   *See Chapter 9 for more information on using standard and special permissions to control access to system resources.*

Assigning Forms to Paper Trays

If a print device has multiple trays that you use to hold different paper sizes, you can assign a form to a specific tray. A form defines a paper size. When users print a document of a particular paper size, Windows Server 2003 routes the print job to the paper tray that holds the correct form. Examples of forms include Legal, Letter, A4, Envelope, and Executive.

To assign a form to a paper tray, select the Device Settings tab of the printer's Properties dialog box, as shown in Figure 10-9. The number of trays shown in the Form To Tray Assignment section depends on the type of printer you have installed and the number of trays it supports. For each tray listed, you can select a different form. Further down the Device Settings tree are settings that specify the installation state of printer options, such as additional paper trays, paper handling units, fonts, and printer memory. These settings are all specific to the printer and depend on the capabilities of the printer and its driver.

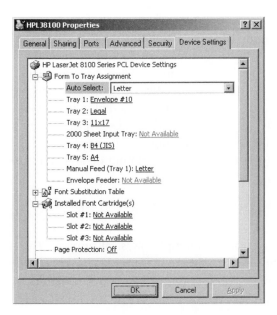

Figure 10-9   The Device Settings tab of a printer's Properties dialog box

Setting Print Job Defaults

The General tab of the printer's Properties dialog box includes a Printing Preferences button, and the Advanced tab includes a Printing Defaults button. Both of these buttons display a dialog box that lets you control the manner in which jobs are printed by the logical printer, including page orientation (portrait or landscape), duplex (double-sided) printing (if supported), paper source, resolution, and other document settings, as shown in Figure 10-10. These dialog boxes are identical to each other and are also identical to the dialog box displayed when you click Properties or Preferences in an application's Print dialog box.

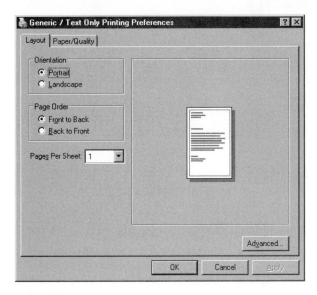

Figure 10-10   The Printing Preferences dialog box

The existence of three separate dialog boxes with identical controls is not an accident or simple redundancy. The Printing Defaults dialog box configures default settings for all users of the logical printer. If the printer is shared, these printing defaults become the default properties for all of the printer's clients as well. The Printing Preferences dialog box configures the user-specific, personal preferences for a printer. Any conflicting settings in the Printing Preferences dialog box override the printer's defaults. The Properties or Preferences dialog box provided by applications configures the properties for the specific print job the application is processing. These job-specific properties override both printing defaults and printing preferences.

Creating a Printer Pool

A printer pool is one logical printer that supports multiple physical printers. The physical printers can be attached to the server, to the network, or both. When you create a printer pool, the print server sends jobs submitted by clients to the first available printer. The logical printer representing the pool checks for an available port and forwards the job accordingly.

You configure printer pooling in the Ports tab of the printer's Properties dialog box. If you select the Enable Printer Pooling check box, you can specify multiple ports containing print devices that will be part of the pool. Figure 10-11 shows a printer pool connected to three network-attached printers.

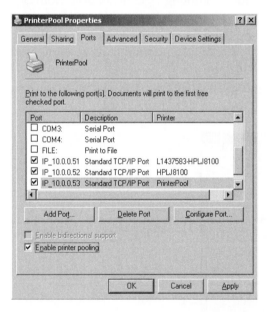

Figure 10-11   The Ports tab of a printer's Properties dialog box, showing a three-printer pool

> **NOTE   Printer Pooling Hardware Requirements**   Because a printer pool consists of multiple physical printers driven by a single logical printer, only one printer driver is installed. While the printers in the pool don't have to be completely identical, they must all be compatible with the driver installed in the logical printer.

Configuring Multiple Logical Printers for a Single Printer

While a printer pool is a single logical printer connected to multiple physical printers, the reverse structure—multiple logical printers connected to a single physical printer—is more common and more powerful. By creating more than one logical printer that directs jobs to the same physical printer, you can configure different properties, printing defaults, security settings, auditing, and monitoring for each logical printer.

For example, you might want to allow company executives to print jobs immediately, bypassing documents that are being printed by other users. To do so, you can create a second logical printer directed to the same physical printer as the other users, but with a higher priority.

To create this type of configuration, you simply use the Add Printer Wizard to create additional logical printers, using the same port as the first one. Each logical printer must have a unique name and share name. Then you configure the logical printers individually, with settings suitable for the clients that will have access to that logical printer.

To configure different priorities for the logical printers, you select the Advanced tab of the Properties dialog box, as shown in Figure 10-12, and specify a value for the Priority property in the range from 1 (lowest) to 99 (highest). If you assign the value 99 to the executives' logical printer and 1 to the logical printer used by all other users, documents sent to the executives' logical printer will print before documents queued in the users' logical printer. An executive's document will not interrupt a user's print job, but when the printer is free, it will accept jobs from the higher-priority logical printer before accepting jobs from the lower-priority logical printer. To prevent unauthorized users from printing to the executives' logical printer, you configure its ACL and remove the print permission assigned to the Everyone special identity, and instead allow only the executives the Print permission.

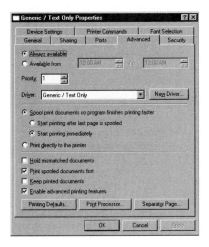

Figure 10-12   The Advanced tab of a printer's Properties dialog box

MONITORING PRINTERS

Once you have created, configured, and shared the logical printer on your print server, and once the network clients have been connected to those printers, you must begin to consider the administration tasks that inevitably result during the printing process. The following sections describe how you can use the various tools provided by Windows Server 2003 to monitor the network printing process and, when necessary, intervene.

> **NOTE Exam Objectives**   The objectives for exam 70-290 require students to be able to "monitor file and print servers. Tools might include Task Manager, Event Viewer, and System Monitor."

Monitoring Print Queues

Double-clicking a printer icon in the Printers And Faxes window opens another window, named for the printer, like the one shown in Figure 10-13. This is a print queue window, which lists all of the jobs currently waiting to be sent to the physical printer. Depending on the permissions they possess, users can manipulate the print queue and the individual jobs in it in various ways and to various degrees, using the menus in the window. Common tasks performed by users and administrators might include pausing, resuming, and canceling specific jobs in the queue, reordering jobs, and pausing and resuming the entire queue.

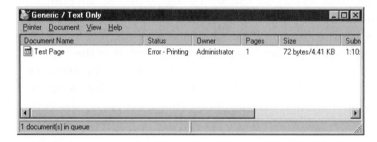

Practice working with queued print jobs by doing Exercise 10-3, "Canceling a Print Job," now.

Figure 10-13   A print queue window

> **NOTE Exam Objectives**   The objectives for exam 70-290 require students to be able to "monitor print queues."

Redirecting Print Jobs

If a printer is malfunctioning, you can send documents in the queue for that printer to another printer that is connected to a local port on the computer or is attached to the network. This is called *redirecting* print jobs. Redirection enables users to continue sending jobs to the same logical printer and prevents users with documents in the queue from having to resubmit the jobs.

To redirect a printer, you simply change the port to which the logical printer is sending the jobs. You do this by opening the printer's Properties dialog box, selecting the Ports tab, and selecting a different port or adding a new one. The check box of the port connecting the malfunctioning printer is immediately cleared—unless printer pooling is enabled, in which case you must manually clear the check box. Because the print jobs in the queue have already been prepared by the logical printer, the printer to which you redirect the jobs must be compatible with the driver used by the logical printer. All print jobs are redirected to the new port. (You cannot redirect individual documents, however, and any documents currently printing cannot be redirected.)

In most cases, print job redirection is most practical when you are using network-attached printers that are accessible through TCP/IP ports. When one printer malfunctions, you can change the port in its logical printer to the IP address of another physical printer on the network. This physical printer then services two logical printers until you fix the malfunctioning printer and change the port setting back again.

Using the Performance Console

The Performance console, accessible from the Administrative Tools program group in Windows Server 2003, contains two MMC snap-ins, System Monitor and Performance Logs And Alerts, that enable you to observe real-time performance of printers, log metrics for later analysis, or set alert levels and actions.

> **MORE INFO** For More Information   To review the capabilities of and procedures for using the Performance console, see Chapter 3.

To configure System Monitor or Performance Logs And Alerts to monitor network printing activities, you typically select the Print Queue performance object in the Add Counters dialog box, as shown in Figure 10-14. This performance object provides an instance for each of the printers installed on the computer and a number of performance counters that you can use to monitor the printing process, including the following:

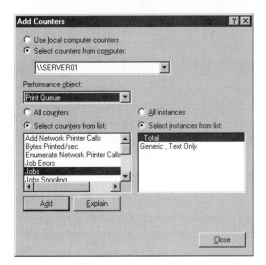

Figure 10-14   Selecting performance counters to monitor printer activity with the Performance console

- **Bytes Printed/Sec** Specifies the number of bytes of raw data per second that are sent to the printer. Low values for this counter can indicate that a printer is underutilized, either because there are no jobs, print queues are not evenly loaded, or the server is too busy. This value varies according to the type of printer. Consult the printer documentation for acceptable printer throughput values.

- **Job Errors** Specifies the number of job errors that have occurred since the spooler was last started. Job errors are typically caused by improper port configuration; check the port configuration for invalid settings. A printing job instance increments this counter only once, even if the error occurs multiple times.

- **Jobs** Specifies the current number of jobs in the print queue. A high or constantly increasing value might indicate the printer is overworked or that jobs are not being printed properly.

- **Not Ready Errors** Specifies the number of printer-not-ready errors that have occurred since the spooler was started.

- **Out Of Paper Errors** Specifies the number of out-of-paper errors that have occurred since the spooler was started.

- **Total Jobs Printed** Specifies the number of jobs sent to the printer since the spooler was started.

- **Total Pages Printed** Specifies the number of pages printed since the spooler was started. This counter provides a close approximation of printer volume, although it might not be perfect, depending on the type of jobs and the document properties for those jobs.

  NOTE **Using Performance Counters** Some of the print queue performance counters are better suited for performance logging, such as those tracking the amount of printer activity, and others are best suited for alerts, such as the error counters. Using alerts, you can configure the system to notify administrators when a specific type of error occurs.

Using Event Viewer

Using Event Viewer, you can examine the Windows Server 2003 System log as a source of information on printer and print spooler activity. By default, the spooler registers events concerning printer creation, deletion, and modification. The log also contains events with information about printer traffic, hard disk space, spooler errors, and other maintenance issues.

To control or modify spooler event logging, open the Printers And Faxes folder and select Server Properties from the File menu. Select the Advanced tab to access the properties shown in Figure 10-15. In this tab, you can control printer event log entries and print job notifications. This is also the tab that enables you to move the print spooler folder—an important task when you configure an active print server or when an existing print spooler folder's disk volume becomes full.

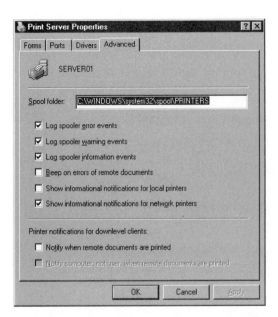

Figure 10-15   The Advanced tab of the Print Server Properties dialog box

Auditing Printer Access

Printer access, like file and folder access, can be audited. You can specify which groups or users and which actions to audit for a particular printer. After enabling the object access auditing policy, you can view the resulting audit entries in the Event Viewer console's Security log.

To configure auditing for a printer, open its Properties dialog box, select the Security tab, and then click Advanced. In the Advanced Security Settings dialog box, select the Auditing tab and add entries for specific groups or users. For each security principal you add to the audit entry list, you can configure auditing for successful or failed access based on the standard printer permissions, including Print, Manage Documents, and Manage Printers.

Next you must enable the Audit Object Access policy, which is located in the Group Policy Object Editor or Local Security Policy console under Computer Configuration\Windows Settings\Security Settings\Local Policies\Audit Policy. After the policy has taken effect, you can examine the Security event log to see and analyze entries made based on printer auditing.

> **TIP**   **When to Audit Printing**   Printer auditing creates dozens of log entries for a single print job, so it is useful only when you're troubleshooting specific problems. Do not use printer auditing to monitor printer use or to bill for printer usage. Instead, use performance counters such as Total Jobs Printed or Total Pages Printed.

TROUBLESHOOTING PRINTERS

Troubleshooting is an important part of printer management. This section can help you understand, identify, and address the types of incidents and problems that might occur in Windows Server 2003 printing.

NOTE Exam Objectives   *The objectives for exam 70-290 require students to be able to "troubleshoot print queues."*

Remember when troubleshooting that printing includes multiple components, including the following:

- The application that is attempting to print

- The logical printer on the computer on which the application is running

- The network connection between the print client and the shared logical printer on the server

- The logical printer on the server—its spooler, drivers, security settings, and other components

- The connection between the print server and the printer

- The printer itself—its hardware, configuration, and status

An efficient way to solve most problems associated with printing is to troubleshoot each component logically and methodically.

Identify the Scope of Failure

If a user cannot print a job from one application on the computer but can print from another application on the same computer, the error is most likely related to the failed job's application rather than the computer, the network, the print server, or the printer hardware. However, in some cases, using a different driver or data type can solve an application's print errors.

If the user cannot print to the printer from any application, identify whether the user can print to other printers on the same print server or on other print servers. If all possibilities fail, and if other users can print to the printers on the network, the error is likely local to the user's computer.

If the printer is networked, try creating a local printer on the problematic system that points directly to the printer's port. In other words, bypass the print server. If this process succeeds, there is a problem on the print server or with the communication between the user's system and the print server.

Verify That the Print Client Can Connect to the Print Server

You can confirm connectivity between the print client and the print server by opening the print queue window from the Printers And Faxes folder on the client computer. If the print queue window opens and shows any documents in the print queue, the client is successfully connecting to the print server. An error opening the print queue window would indicate a potential networking, authentication, or permissions problem. If this is the case, you can use the Ping utility to test the connection to the print server's IP address, or click Start, select Run, and type **\\\printserver**. If the ping test is successful or a window opens showing the Printers And Faxes folder and any shared folders, the client is connecting to the server. In that case, double-check security permissions on the logical printer.

Verify That the Printer Is Operational

Check the printer itself and ensure that it is in the ready state (ready to print). Check for depleted consumables, paper jams, and other obvious problems, and then print a test page from the printer console. Check the cable connecting the printer to the print server or the network. If the printer is network-attached, confirm that the network interface card light is on, indicating network connectivity.

Verify That the Printer Is Accessible from the Print Server

Some printers can display their IP address on the printer console or by printing out a configuration page. Confirm that the printer's IP address matches the IP address of the logical printer's port. The port's IP address can be seen in the printer's Properties dialog box, in the Ports tab. Ensure that it is possible to communicate with the printer over the network by pinging the printer's IP address.

Verify That the Print Server's Services Are Running

Using the Services console, check that the following print-related services are running properly:

- **Print Spooler**   Manages local and network print queues. If this service is not running, no printing will occur.

- **Remote Procedure Call (RPC)**   Required for standard network connections to shared printers.

You can also examine the volume on which the spool folder is stored to ensure that there is sufficient disk space for spooling. The spool folder location can be discovered and modified in the Server Properties dialog box, which you can access by selecting Server Properties from the File menu of the Printers And Faxes folder. By default, print jobs spool to the *Systemroot*\System32\Spool\Printers folder. For a high-volume print server, consider moving the spool folder to a partition other than the system or boot partition. If the partition where the spool folder resides fills to capacity with print jobs, printing will stop and, more importantly, the operating system might become unstable.

You should also look at the System log to see if the spooler has registered any error events, and, in the Printers And Faxes folder, make sure that the printer is not in Offline mode.

Attempt to print a job from an application on the print server. If you can print to the printer from the print server, the problem is not with the printer. If you cannot print to the printer from an application on the print server, create a new logical printer directed at the same port and attempt to print to the new printer. If that job succeeds, there is a problem with the configuration of the original logical printer. If that job is unsuccessful, there is a problem communicating with the printer, or with the hardware itself.

SUMMARY

- The printing architecture in Windows Server 2003 is modular, consisting of the physical printer itself, a print server with a shared, logical printer connected to the physical printer through a local or network port, and a logical printer on a client that connects to the shared, logical printer on the print server.

- A local printer is one that supports a printer directly attached to the computer or attached to the network. A network printer connects to a logical printer maintained by another computer, a print server.

- Shared printers are published to Active Directory by default, which enables users to easily search for printers based on location or other printer properties.

- To create a logical printer, you run the Add Printer Wizard and specify the printer driver and port to use.

- A single logical printer can direct jobs to more than one port, creating a printer pool.

- A single physical printer can be served by multiple logical printers, each of which can be configured with unique properties, drivers, settings, permissions, or monitoring characteristics.

- The print queue window, event logs, and performance counters enable you to monitor printers for potential signals of trouble and for utilization statistics.

- If a printer is to be taken offline or has already failed, you can redirect all its jobs not already in progress to another printer by adding or selecting the new printer's port in the properties of the original logical printer. The alternate port must represent a printer that is compatible with the driver in use by the original logical printer.

- Because the Windows Server 2003 printer model is modular, with the printer itself, the logical printer on a print server, and the logical printer on a client connected to the server's shared printer, you can methodically troubleshoot a printer failure by addressing each component and the links between those components.

EXERCISES

Exercise 10-1: Creating a Logical Printer

In this exercise, you install a logical printer on your computer.

1. Log on to Windows Server 2003 as Administrator.

2. Click Start, and select Printers And Faxes. The Printers And Faxes window appears.

3. Double-click the Add Printer icon. The Add Printer Wizard appears.

4. Click Next to bypass the Welcome page. The Local Or Network Printer page appears.

5. Select the Local Printer Attached To This Computer option. Be sure the Automatically Detect And Install My Plug And Play Printer check box is cleared, then click Next. The Select A Printer Port page appears.

6. In the Use The Following Port drop-down list, select LPT3: (Printer Port), and then click Next. The Install Printer Software page appears.

   Few, if any, computers have an LPT3 port. If your computer does, select a port that is unused by your computer, such as COM3 or COM4.

7. In the Manufacturer column, select Generic. In the Printers column, select Generic/Text Only, then click Next. The Name Your Printer page appears.

8. In the Printer Name text box, type **Test Printer**, and then click Next. The Printer Sharing page appears.

9. Click Next to accept the default sharing parameters. Click Next again to bypass the Location And Comment page. The Print Test page appears.

10. Select the No option, and then click Next. The Completing The Add Printer Wizard page appears.

11. Click Finish.

Exercise 10-2: Setting Printer Permissions

In this exercise, you configure permissions for your shared printer.

1. Log on to Windows Server 2003 as Administrator.

2. Install a logical printer, as described in Exercise 10-1.

3. Click Start, and select Printers And Faxes. The Printers And Faxes window appears.

4. Select the Test Printer icon for the logical printer you created and, from the File menu, select Properties. The Properties dialog box appears.

5. Select the Everyone security principal on the Security tab and then click Remove.

6. Click Add. The Select Users, Computers, Or Groups dialog box appears.

7. In the Enter The Object Names To Select text box, type **Users**, and then click OK. The Users group appears in the list of security principals.

8. Select the Allow check box for the Manage Documents permission, and then click OK.

Exercise 10-3: Cancelling a Print Job

In this exercise, you cancel a queued print job that has not completed.

1. Log on to Windows Server 2003 as Administrator.

2. Install a logical printer, as described in Exercise 10-1.

3. Click Start, and select Printers And Faxes. The Printers And Faxes window appears.

4. Right-click the Test Printer icon for the logical printer you created, and select Properties. The printer's Properties dialog box opens.

5. Click Print Test Page in the General tab to send a test page to the printer. A Test Printer message box opens. Click OK to close the message box, and click OK to close the printer's Properties dialog box.

6. Double-click the Test Printer icon for the logical printer you created. The Test Printer window appears.

7. Select the Test Page document in the list, and note its error status, which is due to no physical printer being connected to the selected port.

8. On the Document menu, select Cancel. A Printers message box appears, prompting you to confirm your decision to delete the print job.

9. Click Yes. The print job is deleted from the queue.

REVIEW QUESTIONS

1. You are installing a printer on a client computer. The printer will connect to a logical printer installed on a Windows Server 2003 print server. What type or types of information could you provide to set up the printer? (Choose all correct answers.)

    a. A TCP/IP printer port

    b. The physical printer's manufacturer and model

    c. The URL to the printer on the print server

    d. The UNC path to the printer share

    e. A printer driver

2. One of your networked printers is not working properly, and you want to prevent users from sending print jobs to the logical printer serving that device. What do you do?

    a. Stop sharing the printer

    b. Remove the printer from Active Directory

    c. Change the printer port

    d. Rename the share

3. You are administering a Windows Server 2003 computer configured as a print server. You want to perform maintenance on a physical printer connected to the print server. There are several documents in the print queue. You want to prevent the documents from being printed to the printer, but you don't want users to have to resubmit the documents to the printer. What is the best approach to take?

    a. Open the printer's Properties dialog box, select the Sharing tab, and select the Do Not Share This Printer option.

    b. Open the printer's Properties dialog box, and, in the Ports tab, select a port that is not associated with a print device.

    c. Open the print queue window, select the first document, and then select Pause from the Document window. Repeat the process for each document.

    d. Open the print queue window, and select Pause Printing from the Printer menu.

4. You are administering a Windows Server 2003 computer configured as a print server. Users in the Marketing group complain that they cannot print documents using a printer on the server. You view the permissions in the printer's Properties dialog box. The Marketing group is allowed Manage Documents permission. Why can't the users print to the printer?

    a. The Everyone group must be granted the Manage Documents permission.

    b. The Administrators group must be granted the Manage Printers permission.

    c. The Marketing group must be granted the Print permission.

    d. The Marketing group must be granted the Manage Printers permission.

5. You are setting up a printer pool on a Windows Server 2003 computer. The printer pool contains three print devices, all identical. You open the Properties dialog box for the printer and select the Enable Printer Pooling option in the Ports tab. What must you do next?

    a. Configure the LPT1 port to support three printers.

    b. Select or create the ports mapped to the three printers.

    c. In the Device Settings tab, configure the installable options to support two additional print devices.

    d. In the Advanced tab, configure the priority for each print device so that printing is distributed among the three print devices.

6. A Windows 2003 Server is configured as a print server. In the middle of the workday, the printer fuse fails and must be replaced. Users have already submitted jobs to the printer, which uses IP address 192.168.1.81. An identical printer uses address 192.168.1.217, and it is supported by other logical printers on the server. What actions do you take so that users' jobs can be printed without resubmission? (Choose all correct answers.)

    a. In the failed printer's Properties dialog box, select Enable Printer Pooling.

    b. In the failed printer's Properties dialog box, click Add Port.

    c. In the Printers And Faxes folder, right-click the failed printer and select Use Offline.

    d. In the failed printer's Properties dialog box, select the port 192.168.1.217.

7. Which of the following approaches gives you the clearest picture of printer utilization, allowing you to understand the consumption of printer toner and paper?

   a. Configure auditing for a logical printer, and audit for successful use of the Print permission by the Everyone system group.

   b. Export the System log to a comma-delimited text file, and use Microsoft Excel to analyze spooler events.

   c. Configure a performance log, and monitor the Total Pages Printed counter for each logical printer.

   d. Configure a performance log, and monitor the Jobs counter for each logical counter.

CASE SCENARIOS

Scenario 10-1: Updating Printer Drivers

The marketing department is complaining about print quality on its shared printer, which is called MarketingPrinter. When users print from their Windows XP desktops using Microsoft Office applications, documents print perfectly. But when they print from Adobe applications, the documents do not always reflect the desired results. The sales department, which has an identical shared printer called Sales-Printer and uses a mix of Windows 2000 and Windows XP workstations and Office, does not report any problems. As you consider the situation, it occurs to you that some applications produce different results depending on whether the printer is using PostScript or a non-PostScript driver. Where do you deploy the properly functioning printer driver so that the computers needing it are updated?

   a. The Server Properties dialog box of the print server

   b. The printer Properties dialog box of MarketingPrinter

   c. The printer Properties dialog box of SalesPrinter

   d. The printer Properties dialog box for the logical printers installed on the desktops of each marketing department user

Scenario 10-2: Enhancing Print Performance

You are the systems administrator for a law firm with a group of 20 legal assistants who provide administrative support to the attorneys. All of the assistants use a single, shared, high-speed laser printer installed on a Windows Server 2003 system. They must print large documents on a regular basis. Although the laser printer is fast, it is kept running almost constantly, printing documents. At times, the assistants have to wait 20 minutes or more after submitting a print job for their documents to reach the top of the queue. None of the assistants wants to scroll through a list of available printers to check which one has the fewest jobs before submitting a document. Which of the following options should you consider to minimize the amount of time that printers take to finish printing documents for all the assistants?

a. Install a second laser printer of the same make and model and create a printer pool.

b. Set different printer priorities for each legal assistant based on a list generated by the head of the group. The most important assistant should be set a priority of 1, and the least important a priority of 99.

c. Set different printer priorities for each legal assistant based on a list generated by the head of the group. The most important assistant should be set a priority of 99, and the least important a priority of 1.

d. Purchase three more identical laser printers, and install them with their own individual printer shares on the print server.

PART 4
MANAGING AND MAINTAINING HARDWARE

CHAPTER 11
MANAGING DEVICE DRIVERS

When you are working with a complex operating system such as Microsoft Windows Server 2003, which contains many elaborate pieces of software, it can be easy to forget about the small, invisible pieces that make everything else you do possible. For an operating system to make use of the hardware in the computer, it must have a software element called a *device driver* for each hardware component. Working with device drivers might not be an everyday task, but system administrators must be aware of them and know what to do when it comes time to update or troubleshoot them.

Upon completion of this chapter, you will be able to:

- Understand the relationship between hardware devices and drivers
- Install a device driver
- Use Device Manager to view and manage hardware devices and their device drivers
- Troubleshoot device driver problems

UNDERSTANDING DEVICE DRIVERS

A **device driver** is a set of software routines that implement device-specific functions for generic input/output (I/O) operations. For example, when an application running on a Windows Server 2003 computer writes a file to disk, it calls a generic operating system function called *WriteFile*. This function defines a basic action: the data at a specific memory location should be copied to a specific storage device installed in the computer. However, the WriteFile function knows nothing about the actual hardware involved; it only deals with the device-independent aspects of the procedure. To implement the device-specific functions required to complete the task, the operating system calls routines provided by the device driver for the storage hardware.

In all likelihood, the application will be storing the file on a hard disk drive, but it could also be storing it on a floppy disk or some other storage device. Different device drivers provide access to the storage devices the application might use. Device drivers also provide access routines for specific devices of a given type. The hard disk drive in the computer might use the IDE interface or SCSI. The drive might be made by any one of a dozen manufacturers. The device driver provides the access routines required for that particular model drive running on that specific operating system. The manufacturer of the drive probably also produces device drivers for other operating systems, and for the other drives it manufactures.

Device Driver Functions

Device drivers provide two basic functions:

- **They expose device-specific routines to device-independent functions in the operating system.**   This enables applications and other software components to communicate with the hardware installed in the computer. When an application calls the WriteFile function, the operating system calls the hard disk's device driver to execute the routine, enabling the drive to receive the data from the system and write it to the disk.

- **They manipulate the physical properties of hardware devices.**   When called on to do so by an application or operating system routine, a device driver can modify the physical configuration of a hardware device. For example, when you specify in an application that you want to print a document in landscape orientation rather than portrait, the device driver is responsible for modifying the physical configuration of the printer.

These two functions are actually two aspects of the same process, but in Windows Server 2003, they can conceivably be implemented by different device drivers. When this is the case, a low-level device driver is responsible for the actual communication with the hardware and a high-level driver interacts with the application or operating system routines. This duality is invisible from the Windows interface, however; you do not have to obtain and install two separate drivers.

> **NOTE**   **Drivers and Operating Systems**   In the days before Windows, device drivers were implemented by individual applications. When you installed a word processing product, for example, you had to select a device driver for your exact model of printer. If you then installed a spreadsheet application, you could not use that same driver. The spreadsheet application required its own printer driver. Windows revolutionized the device driver model by integrating drivers into the operating system rather than using separate drivers for each application. When you install a driver for a printer in any version of Windows, all of the applications running on the system can make use of that driver's routines.

Devices and Drivers

A computer, of course, consists of many different hardware devices that function as individual components, and all but the most benign (such as the computer's case) require a device driver. However, some devices are more standardized than others in the way that they function. The more standardized the device is, the more generic its driver is, and the more generic the driver, the fewer concerns the system administrator will have about updates and maintenance.

For example, virtually every computer has a keyboard, and every operating system requires a keyboard device driver. However, the functionality of the keyboard and the signals it exchanges with the computer are so standardized and consistent that it is rare for a system to require anything but a generic keyboard driver that is suitable for most any keyboard used with the computer. The only time a special keyboard device driver is necessary is when you are using an unusual piece of hardware with special capabilities, such as an input device intended for people with specific disabilities.

At the other end of the spectrum are devices such as video display adapters, which require a device driver that is designed to work with a specific hardware product. Highly specific device drivers such as these can be more problematic for system administrators in several ways, including the following:

- **They are less likely to be included with the operating system.**   Windows Server 2003 (like all of the Windows operating systems) includes a library of device drivers that provide compatibility with a long list of hardware devices of every type. The more generic devices, such as keyboards, are almost certain to be supported by the operating system drivers, but more esoteric components, and particularly new or off-brand devices, might not have device driver support in Windows or might not have the most recent version of a driver. In cases like these, you must furnish the operating system with drivers obtained from the hardware manufacturer.

  NOTE   Microsoft and Device Drivers   Although Windows Server 2003 and the other Windows operating systems include hundreds of device drivers for many different hardware products, few of these drivers are actually created by Microsoft. Microsoft receives the drivers from the hardware manufacturers and includes them with the operating system as a courtesy. For this reason, when you are having driver difficulties, you are far more likely to get the help you need from the hardware manufacturer than from Microsoft.

- **They might not be available from the hardware vendor.**   In some cases, hardware manufacturers develop Windows Server 2003 drivers for their products after they release Microsoft Windows XP drivers, because XP has a larger installed user base, or not at all, because they do not consider Windows Server 2003 to be part of the product's target market.

- **They are more likely to cause compatibility or functionality problems.**   Some types of device drivers are more prone to problematic behavior than others, often because the device is simply called upon to do more. For example, video display drivers tend to be the most problematic because of their many complex functions and because many applications push them to their limit. This becomes truer as you push the cutting edge of hardware technology. The latest video adapter designed for hardcore gaming is far more likely to experience driver problems than the simple integrated video adapter in a low-end system. When drivers are a problem, system administrators must deal directly with the hardware manufacturer to obtain replacements.

■ **They are likely to be updated more often than generic drivers.**   As a result of their complex or problematic nature, some drivers are more likely to be updated than others. Here again, the video adapter driver is a good example. Drivers for the latest video adapter products are often updated frequently by the manufacturer. Depending on when the hardware device was released and what version of Windows you are using, the driver included with the operating system might be several versions old. In most cases, the driver supplied with Windows is sufficient to get you through the operating system installation process, but you might have to install updated drivers for the device to achieve its full performance potential.

All hardware devices that have been approved for use with Windows Server 2003 are listed in the Windows Server Catalog, available at *www.microsoft.com/windows /catalog/server*. This catalog replaces the hardware compatibility lists used for earlier versions of Windows. When selecting hardware for Windows Server 2003 computers, you should always make sure that the devices you choose are listed in the catalog.

Device Drivers and Hardware Resources

A personal computer consists of a variety of hardware components connected (directly or indirectly) to a central motherboard. Processors, memory modules, hard disk drives, monitors, and other devices all have their unique functions, and the system must be able to communicate with each component individually. For this to occur, each device has to have some means by which the system can address it uniquely, so that when the computer generates output data that is intended to be displayed on the monitor, that data goes only to the video adapter and not to the keyboard or the hard disk drive.

To make this individualized component communication possible, PCs use various types of hardware resources (also called *system resources*). Each device driver is configured to use a unique combination of resources that enables it to communicate with the correct hardware device, and only that device. The types of hardware resources that devices can use are as follows:

■ **Interrupt request (IRQ) line**   An **interrupt request**, as the name implies, is a signal sent from one component to another (although typically from a peripheral device to the system processor) indicating that the sender requires the attention of the receiver and that it should stop what it is doing and do something else instead. For example, each time you press a key on a computer's keyboard, the keyboard sends an interrupt request to the system processor, notifying it that there is new input for it to process. A PC has 16 IRQ lines, which are designated for the use of various hardware devices (some of which can share an IRQ line).

- **I/O address** An **I/O address**, also called an I/O port, is a location in memory that is allocated for use by a particular hardware device, to exchange information with the system. Virtually every device in a computer has a unique I/O address assigned to it, enabling the system to communicate with individual devices.

- **Direct memory access (DMA) channel**   **DMA channels** are pathways that some hardware devices use to transfer data directly to and from system memory without involving the processor. Relatively few devices (such as floppy disk drives and audio adapters) use DMA channels, as compared to IRQ lines, mainly because there are fewer of them (only eight) in a PC.

- **Memory address**   A few devices, such as video display adapters and network interface adapters, require space in the upper memory area, usually to install a supplemental basic input/output system (BIOS). Another device that commonly requires this hardware resource is a SCSI (Small Computer System Interface) host adapter that provides its own BIOS, to enable the system to boot from a SCSI drive.

The Windows Server 2003 Device Manager makes it possible to view the hardware resources in your computer and the devices that are using them, as shown in Figure 11-1.

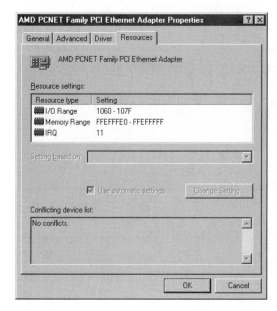

Practice displaying the hardware resources on your computer by doing Exercise 11-1, "Viewing Hardware Resources," now.

Figure 11-1   A device's hardware resources display in Device Manager

Configuring Hardware Resources

For communication between a hardware device and the computer to occur, the device and its driver must both be configured to use the correct hardware resource settings. For example, when you connect a printer to a computer's LPT1 parallel port, you must also configure the printer driver to use LPT1 to communicate with the printer. If the printer is connected to LPT1, and you configure the driver to use LPT2, no communication will occur and the computer will not be able to use the printer.

This relationship between hardware resource settings seems simple when you discuss printers, but for the computer's internal components, it becomes more complex. Installing a network interface adapter in a computer, for example, typically requires an IRQ line and an I/O port. For the computer and the adapter to communicate, the adapter hardware and the adapter driver must be configured to use the same IRQ line and I/O port. In addition, there must not be any conflicts from other devices trying to use the same IRQ line and I/O port.

At one time, it was necessary to configure both the hardware device and the device driver manually. To configure the network adapter, you either set jumpers on the card itself or ran a special configuration program supplied by the hardware manufacturer. Then you installed the driver and configured it to use the same hardware resource settings you configured on the adapter. Apart from the time and inconvenience involved, several things could go wrong with this process, such as the following:

- **Limited resource settings**   Some devices had a limited selection of hardware resource settings that they could use. For example, some older network interface adapters had a selection of only two or three IRQs they could use. If none of those IRQs was available on the computer, you either had to reconfigure another device or use a different adapter.

- **Resource depletion**   In the days when IRQ sharing was less common, well-equipped systems could easily have all of the IRQ lines occupied by other devices, preventing the installation of new components.

- **Device conflicts**   When two devices were configured to use the same hardware resource, usually neither of them functioned properly. When selecting the hardware resources for a new component, you had to be conscious of the resources already allocated to all of the other components in the computer.

Plug and Play

Fortunately, these problems were largely eliminated by the introduction of the Plug and Play standard in 1995. **Plug and Play** (PnP) is a standard that defines characteristics for computer components that enables them to automatically detect and configure the hardware in a computer. For PnP to function, all of the following components must support the standard:

- System hardware

- Peripheral hardware

- System BIOS

- Operating system

Most of the PC hardware devices manufactured since 1997, and virtually all of the PC hardware manufactured today, conform to the PnP standard, as do most system BIOS products and all of the Microsoft operating systems since Windows 95. This means that when you install a new device in a computer running Windows Server 2003, most of the time you do not have to be concerned with hardware resources or device configuration; the system takes care of everything (assuming a driver is available). When you install a new PnP device, the computer does the following:

- Detects the new hardware

- Installs the appropriate device driver
- Determines what hardware resources the device requires
- Scans the system for available hardware resources
- Selects appropriate resource settings for the device
- Configures both the device and the device driver to use the selected resources

If none of the resource settings the new device can use is available, PnP is capable of dynamically reconfiguring the other hardware in the computer to free up resources needed by the new device. If Windows Server 2003 does not have a driver for a device it detects, the operating system prompts you to supply a driver disk or search for an appropriate driver.

When you install a new hardware device that does not conform to the PnP standard, Windows Server 2003 might or might not be able to detect and identify it. Depending on the device in question, any of the following can occur:

- **The system fails to detect the new device.**   If the computer remains unaware of the new hardware, you must run the Add Hardware Wizard from Control Panel and manually identify, install, and configure the device and its driver.

- **The system detects the presence of the new device but cannot identify it.**   Sometimes the computer detects a new hardware presence but cannot even identify its type. Here again, you must manually select the device type, manufacturer, and model for the new component in the Add Hardware Wizard.

- **The system detects the new device and identifies its basic type but cannot identify the specific model.**   The computer might be able to identify the type of hardware installed, such as a network interface adapter, but not identify its manufacturer and model, so you must select them manually in the Add Hardware Wizard.

- **The system detects and identifies the new device and then installs and configures the device driver, but it cannot configure the hardware itself.**   If the computer successfully identifies the new hardware and installs the appropriate device driver, the system can usually configure the driver to use the device's current hardware resource settings. However, if the device's default settings conflict with other components in the computer, the system might not be able to reconfigure the hardware to use other settings. In this case, you have to configure the resource settings for the hardware device manually.

CREATING A DRIVER MAINTENANCE STRATEGY

In addition to installing the correct drivers initially, system administrators are also responsible for the ongoing maintenance of device drivers and their configurations. Driver updates are common because functional changes in operating systems and hardware devices dictate corresponding changes in drivers. In some cases, driver updates are incorporated into the regular service pack releases for the operating system, while other driver updates are available as hotfixes from the

Windows Update Web site. However, in many cases, it is left to the system administrator to check with the various hardware manufacturers for new driver releases and decide when and if to install them, as well as who should be responsible for performing the installation.

To Update or Not?

One of the first questions that a system administrator has to consider when faced with a new driver update release is whether to install it at all. Unfortunately, this problem can't be resolved with a hard-and-fast rule or a company policy. Hardware manufacturers generally release driver updates for three possible reasons:

- To enhance performance of existing features
- To implement new features
- To address problems with previous driver releases

In the first two cases, the installation of an update is certainly desirable, as long as the release does not introduce new problems. In the latter case, you might want to consider carefully whether your current configuration is suffering from the problem the update is designed to address. If not, it might be more prudent to hold off on installing the update.

Above all, the question of whether to install driver updates should depend on the hardware devices involved and the policies and reputation of the hardware manufacturer. Some manufacturers release driver updates frequently and haphazardly, often introducing new problems in the course of repairing old ones. This can be particularly true in the case of a hardware product that is new to the market, with driver code that has not been adequately tested. In cases like these, the latest driver might not be the greatest, and automatically installing every new driver release can lead to disastrous performance problems, especially if you have the same hardware device installed on dozens or hundreds of computers.

The best practice for a system administrator is to subject driver update releases to a rigorous testing regimen, just as you would use for any software update, before deploying them on production computers.

Users, Administrators, and Device Driver Installation

In most environments, it is preferable for end users to not have the ability to install or update device drivers. This is particularly true in a network environment, where administrators want to maintain a consistent system configuration throughout the network. This simplifies the process of maintaining and troubleshooting the network computers because technical support personnel do not have to examine each system to determine which updates have been installed.

However, device drivers are often more difficult to deploy on a large fleet of computers than other types of software updates. It is sometimes necessary to install a driver on each computer individually, and many administrators do not have the time or inclination to travel to every computer to configure devices and their drivers individually. Windows Server 2003 includes driver signing options and the ability to grant selective driver installation privileges to appropriate users, to create a flexible environment for device configuration and driver installation.

Controlling Device Driver Access

As with most installation tasks, members of the Administrators group have the unrestricted ability to install any hardware device and its associated drivers. This ability is provided by a user right called Load And Unload Device Drivers, which the Administrators group receives through local policies or through the Default Domain Controllers Policy group policy object (GPO). Members of the Users and Domain Users groups, however, are not granted this user right, so their hardware and driver installation abilities are limited. By default, users can install only PnP devices, as long as the following conditions are met:

- The device driver has a digital signature.
- No further action requiring Windows to display a user interface is needed to install the device.
- The device driver is already present on the computer.

What this generally means is that users can install printers and universal serial bus (USB) and IEEE 1394 (FireWire) devices. If any of the three conditions is not met, the user cannot install the device without being granted additional administrative privileges.

Driver Signing Options

All of the device drivers and operating system files included with Windows Server 2003 have a Microsoft digital signature, which indicates that the file has been tested by Microsoft and has not been altered since the manufacturer produced it. Digital signatures are intended to prevent device drivers and other software from being intercepted and altered by individuals trying to deploy unauthorized code, such as viruses and Trojan horses. They also indicate that the device has been tested for compatibility with the operating system. Device drivers supplied by third-party vendors might or might not be signed.

In Windows Server 2003, you can control how the computer responds to unsigned driver files during their installation. To do this, log on using the local Administrator account, double-click System in Control Panel and, in the System Properties dialog box, select the Hardware tab. Click Driver Signing to display the Driver Signing Options dialog box, shown in Figure 11-2.

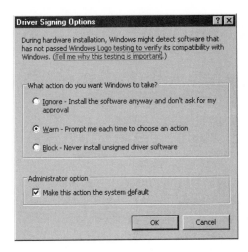

Figure 11-2   The Driver Signing Options dialog box

The available driver signing options are as follows:

- **Ignore**   Enables the installation of all device drivers on the computer, regardless of whether they have a digital signature. This option is available only if you are logged on as a member of the Administrators group.

- **Warn**   Causes the system to display a warning message whenever an installation program or Windows attempts to install a device driver that does not have a digital signature. The user can then choose whether to proceed with the device driver installation. This is the default option.

- **Block**   Prevents the system from installing device drivers that do not have a digital signature under any circumstances.

   NOTE   Exam Objectives   *The objectives for exam 70-290 require students to be able to "configure driver signing options."*

When you are logged on as a member of the Administrators group, this tab also includes a Make This Action The System Default check box. Selecting it causes the selected driver signing option to be the default setting for all users logging on to the system.

In addition to configuring the driver signing options manually for individual computers, you can also use group policies to enforce them for all or part of the network. In the Group Policy Object Editor console, browse to the User Configuration /Administrative Templates/System folder, where you will find a policy called Code Signing For Device Drivers. When you open the Code Signing For Device Drivers Properties dialog box, shown in Figure 11-3, you can specify the same options as in the Driver Signing Options dialog box.

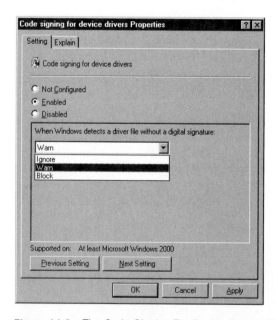

Practice configuring driver signing options in Windows Server 2003 by doing Exercise 11-2, "Configuring Driver Signing Options," now.

Figure 11-3   The Code Signing For Device Drivers Properties dialog box

USING THE ADD HARDWARE WIZARD

The Add Hardware Wizard is designed to walk you through the process of installing and configuring a new hardware device and its device driver. How the wizard is triggered and how much interaction is required from the user depends on the nature of the hardware device being installed. In most cases, the wizard is triggered when the system detects a new hardware device, either through PnP or its standard hardware detection routines.

> **NOTE Exam Objectives** *The objectives for exam 70-290 require students to be able to "install and configure server hardware devices."*

With PnP devices, the wizard often requires no interaction from the user. The system displays some progress indicators as it locates and identifies the new hardware, and then it installs and configures a device driver for it. If Windows Server 2003 does not include a driver for the device, the wizard prompts you to supply or search for one. If the system cannot identify the device, the wizard takes you through the process of specifying its type, manufacturer, and model.

If the system does not detect the presence of the new hardware device, you can start the wizard manually, in the following ways:

■ Select Add Hardware in Control Panel.

■ Open the System Properties dialog box, select the Hardware tab, and click Add Hardware Wizard.

When you click Next to bypass the wizard's Welcome page, the system performs a PnP hardware detection routine. If the system does not detect any new hardware, an Is The Hardware Connected? page appears, as shown in Figure 11-4, prompting you to specify whether you have installed the new hardware. This is a trick question: if you select the No, I Have Not Added The Hardware Yet option and click Next, the wizard terminates, instructing you to install the hardware and then run the wizard again. In fact, there are some types of hardware that you can install without the physical device actually being present. For example, you can install a local printer and its device driver before connecting the physical printer to the computer.

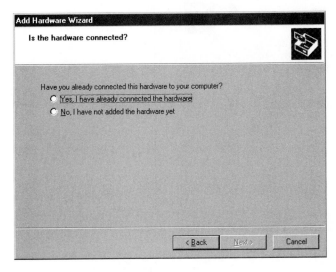

Figure 11-4 The Add Hardware Wizard's Is The Hardware Connected? page

If you select the Yes, I Have Already Connected The Hardware option and click Next, the wizard displays a page listing all of the hardware devices installed in the computer, as shown in Figure 11-5. To install a new device, scroll down to the bottom of the list, select Add A New Hardware Device, and click Next.

Figure 11-5   The Add Hardware Wizard's Installed Hardware list box

> **NOTE**   **Hardware Troubleshooting**   The list of installed devices provides the wizard's other primary function, that of troubleshooting the existing hardware in the system. For more information on hardware and device driver troubleshooting, see "Troubleshooting Devices and Drivers," later in this chapter.

On the next page, shown in Figure 11-6, you specify whether you want the wizard to search for new hardware or let you select the hardware from a list. This might seem odd because the wizard already ran through a hardware detection routine immediately after launching. However, that was the PnP hardware detection routine. Selecting the Search For And Install The Hardware Automatically option initiates a search for non-PnP hardware devices.

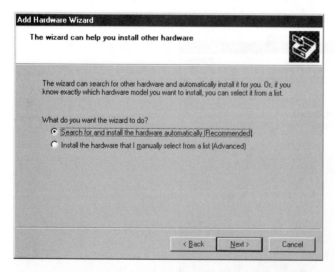

Figure 11-6   The Add Hardware Wizard's hardware detection options

If the wizard fails to locate your new hardware or if you select the Install The Hardware That I Manually Select From A List option and click Next, a page appears with a list of common hardware types from which you can choose, as shown in Figure 11-7. Select the type of hardware you want to install, and click Next.

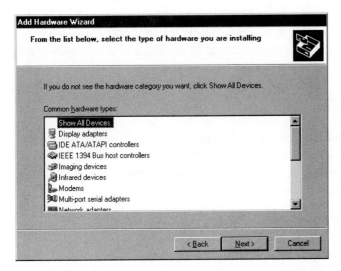

Figure 11-7   The Add Hardware Wizard's Common Hardware Types list box

Depending on the hardware type you select, you might see an additional hardware detection page, but the wizard will eventually display a page like that shown in Figure 11-8, in which you can select the manufacturer of the hardware device and a specific model produced by that manufacturer. All of the hardware devices listed have drivers included with the operating system. If your hardware device is not listed, you must click Have Disk and specify the location of a device driver you have obtained from the hardware manufacturer.

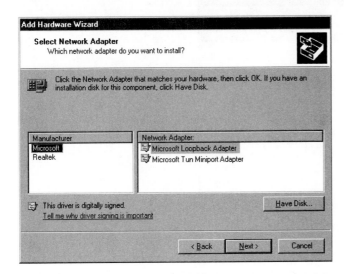

Figure 11-8   One of the Add Hardware Wizard's hardware selection lists

Once you have specified the exact hardware device you want to install, the wizard displays device-specific controls in which you specify how the system will access the hardware. For example, if you are installing a modem, the wizard prompts you for the COM port the modem is using. In some cases, if the wizard cannot locate the hardware you selected, it installs the device driver using default settings. You might then have to reconfigure the device driver manually before the system can communicate with the device.

Practice installing device drivers by doing Exercise 11-3, "Installing a Device Driver," now.

When the wizard is completed, the new device is added to the computer's hardware configuration, whether or not it is accessible. You can work with any of the hardware devices installed and the computer and their device drivers, using the Device Manager console, as described in the next section.

USING DEVICE MANAGER

Device Manager is the primary hardware and device driver management tool in Windows Server 2003. Although it is not immediately apparent from its default appearance (shown in Figure 11-9), Device Manager is an MMC snap-in that you can access in any of the following ways:

- Click Start, point to Control Panel, and select System. In the System Properties dialog box, select the Hardware tab, and then click Device Manager.

- Click Start, point to Administrative Tools, and select Computer Management. Then, in the Computer Management console's scope pane, select the Device Manager icon.

- Open the Run dialog box, type **mmc** in the Open text box, and click Enter to open an empty Microsoft Management Console window. Then select Add/Remove Snap-In on the File menu and add the Device Manager snap-in to the console.

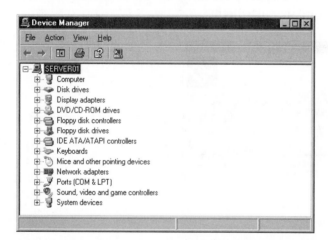

Figure 11-9   Windows Server 2003 Device Manager

The default Device Manager display consists of a hierarchy with the computer at the root and the various hardware device types beneath the root. Expanding one of the device types displays a list of all the components of that type installed on the computer. Components that are configured and functioning properly appear with an icon representing the component type. When there is a problem with a device, the icon is modified in one of the following ways, as shown in Figure 11-10.

- **Yellow exclamation point**   Indicates that the device cannot be started, is improperly configured, or does not have a device driver installed

- **Yellow question mark**   Indicates a device that cannot be identified

- **Red X**   Indicates a device that is disabled

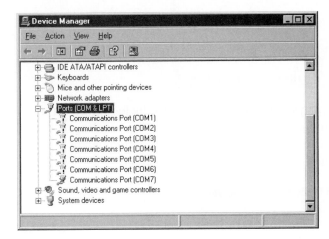

Figure 11-10   Device Manager icons

Device Manager is capable of displaying information in four modes:

- **Devices by type**   Displays a list of device types, which you can expand to show a list of devices of each type. This is the default Device Manager view.

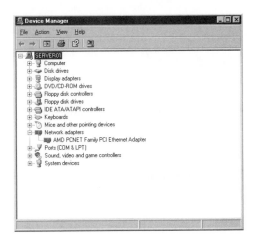

- **Devices by connection**   Displays a list of the connections used by hardware devices to communicate with the computer. Expanding a connection lists the devices using that connection. For example, the PCI Bus connection contains the icons for all of the expansion cards and other devices connected to the system's PCI bus.

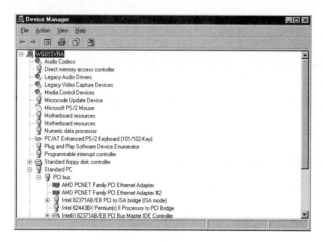

- **Resources by type**   Displays a list of resource types, including Direct Memory Access (DMA), Input/Output (I/O), Interrupt Request (IRQ), and Memory, which you can expand to show a list of the individual resources of each type and the devices that are using them.

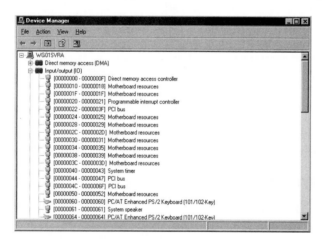

- **Resources by connection**   Displays a list of resource types, including Direct Memory Access (DMA), Input/Output (I/O), Interrupt Request (IRQ), and Memory, which you can expand to show the connection associated with each individual resource and the device using each connection.

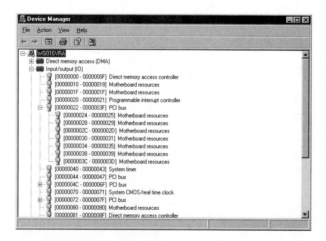

Whichever mode you use for the Device Manager display, you can select any one of the computer's devices and work with the hardware and its device driver, as described in the following sections.

> **NOTE Remote Device Management** Like many MMC snap-ins, Device Manager can work with the local system or with another system on the network. However, when Device Manager is connected to another computer, it operates in read-only mode exclusively. You can view information about the hardware on the remote computer and its drivers, but you cannot manipulate the devices or drivers. To manipulate them, you must run Device Manager from the remote computer's own console or within a Remote Desktop or Terminal Services session with the other computer.

> **NOTE Exam Objectives** The objectives for exam 70-290 require students to be able to "monitor server hardware. Tools might include Device Manager, the Hardware Troubleshooting Wizard, and appropriate Control Panel items."

Enabling and Disabling Devices

By selecting a device in Device Manager and choosing Disable from the Action menu, you can render that device inoperative until you manually enable it again. Disabled devices appear in Device Manager with a red X on their icons.

Disabling a device does not affect the hardware in any way; only the driver is disabled, preventing the system from accessing the device. Some devices, such as processors, cannot be disabled, and in some cases, you are instructed to restart the system to fully disable the device.

Once you have restarted the computer after disabling a device, the hardware resources it was using are released to the operating system and can be reassigned to other devices if necessary. When you reenable the device (by selecting Enable from the Action menu), it might not be assigned the same hardware resources that it used originally.

Uninstalling Device Drivers

By selecting a device and choosing Uninstall from the Action menu, you can remove a device driver from the system. The effect of uninstalling a driver depends on how the device was installed in the first place:

- **If the device was installed by Plug and Play** Uninstalling it removes the device driver and deletes the hardware device from Device Manager completely. However, if the hardware is still physically present in the computer, PnP will attempt to install it again the next time you restart the system, choose Scan For Hardware Changes from the Action menu, or run the Add Hardware Wizard.

- **If you installed the device manually using the Add Hardware Wizard** Uninstalling the device will remove the driver, but the device itself will remain in Device Manager. The device's icon will then appear with an exclamation point.

> **NOTE Another Way to Uninstall Drivers** You can also uninstall a device driver by clicking Uninstall on the Driver page of the device's Properties dialog box.

Managing Device Properties

When you select a device in Device Manager and, from the Action menu, select Properties, a Properties dialog box appears. This dialog box contains tabs with an assortment of controls that enable you to manage and configure the device and its driver. The contents of the Properties dialog box can vary, depending on the type of device and the capabilities of the driver, but most devices have at least the four tabs described in the following list.

> **NOTE** **Exam Objectives**   *The objectives for exam 70-290 require students to be able to "configure device properties and settings."*

- **General**   Displays information about the device, including its type, manufacturer, location, and current operational status. Also includes controls to enable, disable, and troubleshoot the device.

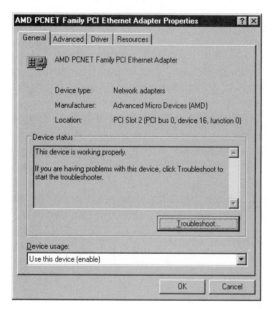

- **Advanced**   Contains device-specific controls that are implemented by the driver. This tab is not always present, and it is sometimes called Advanced Settings.

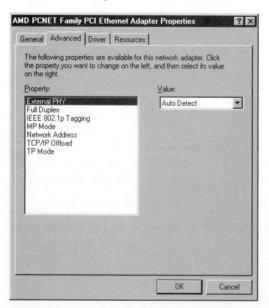

■ **Driver**   Displays information about the device driver, including its provider, date, version, signer, and filename, and also contains controls for
updating, rolling back, and uninstalling the driver.

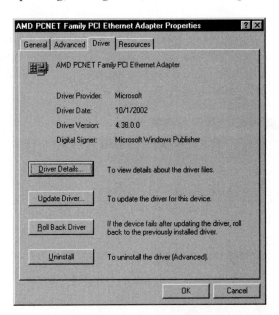

■ **Resources**   Displays the hardware resources currently being used by
the device and, under certain conditions, provides controls for modifying the
resource configuration. This tab is not always present.

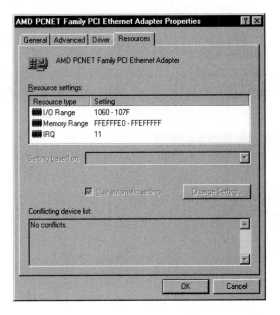

Updating Drivers

To update a device driver, you open the device's Properties dialog box in Device
Manager, select the Driver tab, and click Update Driver. This launches the Hardware Update Wizard, which enables you to specify the location of the updated
driver you want to install or search for one. To update a device driver, you must
have the same privileges needed to install it in the first place, such as membership
in the Administrators group or the Load And Unload Device Drivers user right.

NOTE   *Driver Updates for the Underprivileged*   *One exception to the privilege requirements for updating device drivers applies when you obtain the driver through the Windows Update Web site. In this case, any user can install an updated device driver.*

When you select the Install From A List Or Specific Location option on the wizard's welcome page, the wizard displays the page shown in Figure 11-11, on which you can specify the locations where the wizard should search for drivers or indicate that you want to select a driver from a list.

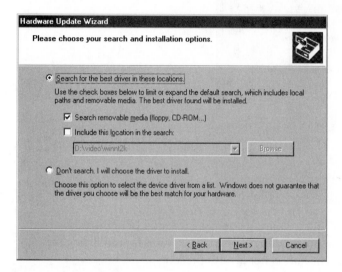

Figure 11-11   Driver update options

Instead of searching for a driver, you can also choose the Don't Search option, which displays a page like that shown in Figure 11-12. This page lists all of the drivers already on the system that are compatible with the selected hardware component. You can also click the Have Disk button to specify an alternative location for a driver.

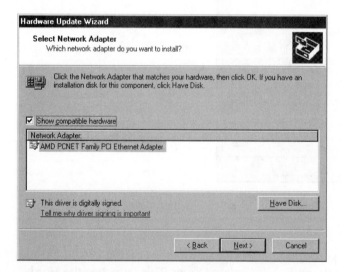

Figure 11-12   Selecting an updated driver

When the wizard completes the installation of the updated driver, you might be required to restart the computer, depending on the device involved.

Rolling Back Drivers

In some cases, you might discover that a device driver you recently updated is not functioning as expected, and you would like to go back to the version you were using originally. Fortunately, when you use Device Manager to update a device driver, Windows Server 2003 automatically saves a backup copy of the file being replaced. To revert to the previously installed version of the driver, you open the device's Properties dialog box and, in the Driver tab, select Roll Back Driver.

Managing Hardware Resources

Although it happens infrequently, you might need to manually configure the hardware resources used by a Windows Server 2003 device. This is usually necessary only when you are forced to install an older piece of hardware that does not support the PnP standard, such as an Industry Standard Architecture (ISA) expansion card. To work with hardware resources in Device Manager, you open a device's Properties dialog box and select the Resources tab, as shown in Figure 11-13.

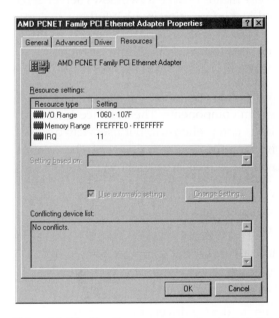

Figure 11-13   The Resources tab of a device's Properties dialog box

> **NOTE** **Exam Objectives**   *The objectives for exam 70-290 require students to be able to "configure resource settings for a device."*

In this tab, the Resource Settings box specifies the resources that the device is currently using, by type and by setting. For devices installed using PnP, the Resources tab is informational only; you cannot modify the resource configuration. For manually configured devices, however, you can change the resource settings that the driver is configured to use.

To modify a device's resource settings, you must clear the Use Automatic Settings check box to enable the other controls on the tab. Then you can use the Settings Based On drop-down list to select a preset hardware configuration, if any are available. You can also modify the setting for any of the resources listed in the Resource Settings box by selecting it, clicking Change Settings, and choosing a different value.

If the resource setting you specify is currently in use by another device on the system, the other device appears in the Conflicting Device list box. You must select resources that are not being used; otherwise, the conflicting devices are likely to prevent the system from functioning properly.

> **WARNING**   **Manual Resource Allocation**   *Once you manually configure hardware resources for a device driver, the resources you select are permanently allocated. PnP cannot use these settings when configuring other devices, even to free up specific resources for use by another device.*

USING CONTROL PANEL

Device Manager provides comprehensive access to a computer's hardware and device driver configuration, but not the only means of access. Windows Server 2003 actually stores the hardware and device driver information in the Windows registry, and tools such as Device Manager are just front ends that provide access to the registry data. The other Windows Server 2003 tool that provides user-friendly access to registry information is Control Panel.

A number of Control Panel applications provide access to hardware and device driver configuration data for various system components. The interface is not as consistent as that of Device Manager, or as comprehensive, but users can access some of the more important device drivers on the system in this way. The Control Panel applications providing access to device drivers are as follows:

- **Add Hardware**   Provides access to the Add Hardware Wizard, as described earlier in this chapter, enabling users to install new device drivers and troubleshoot existing ones

- **Display**   Provides access to device drivers for the computer's video display adapter and monitor, enabling users to modify display properties such as screen resolution and color depth

- **Game Controllers**   Provides access to device drivers for any game controllers installed on the computer

- **Keyboard**   Provides access to device drivers for the keyboard installed on the computer

- **Mouse**   Provides access to device drivers for the mouse or other pointer device installed on the computer

- **Network Connections**   Provides access to the device drivers for the network interface adapters installed on the computer

- **Phone and Modem Options**   Provides access to the device drivers for any modems installed on the computer

- **Printers and Faxes**   Provides access to the device drivers for the printers installed on the computer

- **Scanners and Cameras**   Provides access to the device drivers for scanners and cameras installed on the computer

- **Sounds and Audio Devices**   Provides access to the device drivers for the audio adapters and other sound-related components installed on the computer

- **System**   Provides access to the System Properties dialog box, which includes access to Device Manager, the Add Hardware Wizard, and the driver signing controls

In most cases, Control Panel provides access to the same Properties dialog boxes for specific hardware devices as Device Manager. These controls are also subject to the same access restrictions as Device Manager.

TROUBLESHOOTING DEVICES AND DRIVERS

At some point, you'll probably experience problems with hardware components and device drivers, particularly if you are working with non-PnP components. Windows Server 2003 provides a number of tools you can use to troubleshoot problems like these. Some of these tools are described in the following sections.

Device Manager Status Codes

When a device or its driver malfunctions, Device Manager is usually able to detect the failure and modify the device's icon to indicate an error condition. However, more information is available if you open the offending device's Properties dialog box. In the General tab, the Device Status box typically contains an explanation of the problem, and this explanation might include an error code. The most common error codes and suggested troubleshooting strategies are listed in Table 11-1.

Table 11-1   Device Manager Error Codes

Code	Explanation	Troubleshooting Strategy
1	This device is not configured correctly.	Use Update Driver to update the device driver. If no updated driver is available, try removing the device from Device Manager, restarting the system, and reinstalling the device.
3	The driver for this device might be corrupted, or your system might be running low on memory or other resources.	The driver might be corrupted. If you attempt to load a file that is corrupted, the system might think that it needs more memory. Use Task Manager to confirm that your system is not low on memory. If the memory is sufficient, use Update Driver to install another copy of the same driver from a different location.
10	The device cannot start.	Check that the hardware is properly installed in the computer. If it is, run the Hardware Update Wizard using the Update Driver button, but do not let Windows Server 2003 automatically detect devices. Instead, select Install From A List Or Specific Location (Advanced), and manually point the wizard to the appropriate driver.

(continued)

Table 11-1   **Device Manager Error Codes**

Code	Explanation	Troubleshooting Strategy
12	This device cannot find enough free resources that it can use. If you want to use this device, you will need to disable one of the other devices on this system.	Select the Resources tab of the Properties dialog box containing the error. Windows Server 2003 will most likely be able to identify the hardware component that is in conflict with the device in question. Either disable or remove the component that is in conflict. You can then re-add the device you removed and see if the system assigns different resources to it. If not, you might have to assign resources manually.
Most other codes	Various.	Most other codes involve an inappropriate driver or incorrect driver configuration. Try using a different driver or removing the device from Device Manager and reinstalling it.

Using Hardware Troubleshooters

Earlier in this chapter, you saw that the Add Hardware Wizard enables you to select a component that is already installed on the computer, using the interface shown in Figure 11-14. The Installed Hardware list box shown in the wizard always begins with the devices that are having problems. This is because you can use the wizard to troubleshoot a device that is malfunctioning. When you select an item in the Installed Hardware list box, the wizard displays its current status and enables you to start a troubleshooter that can sometimes help you find the cause of the problem.

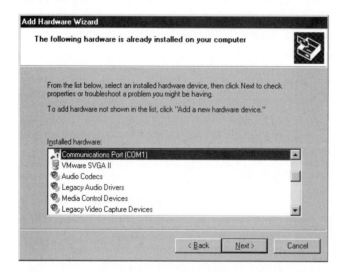

Figure 11-14   The Add Hardware Wizard's Installed Hardware list

The Windows Server 2003 hardware troubleshooters are implemented in the Help And Support Center, as shown in Figure 11-15. The screens that appear depend on the device experiencing a problem and the current status of the hardware. For example, a typical troubleshooter might ask you to confirm that the device is on the Windows Server 2003 hardware compatibility list (HCL) and then ask if you recently installed a new device driver. The troubleshooter can then provide instructions for possible remedies, such as rolling back the driver and reinstalling the device.

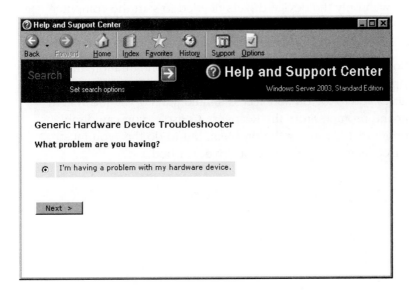

Figure 11-15   A Windows Server 2003 hardware troubleshooter screen

Recovering from Device Disaster

Sometimes, installing or upgrading a device driver can cause a serious problem with your computer. Depending on the importance of the device, the effect of the problem can range from annoying to catastrophic. This is particularly true for core system components such as video display drivers, because a faulty configuration can render the computer unusable. Rolling back the driver is difficult if you cannot see the screen.

Windows Server 2003 provides multiple methods for recovery from driver-related system failures. The tools are suited for specific purposes and have varying chances of success. Some of the tools that you can use to recover from a faulty driver installation, in escalating order of severity, are as follows:

- **Driver Rollback**   As you learned earlier, rolling back to an earlier driver version is an easy way to resolve a bad driver problem, as long as you have sufficient system access to run Device Manager and perform the rollback.

- **Last Known Good Configuration**   Used when a device driver update requires a restart and the computer will not boot to the point of allowing you to log on. When you change drivers that require a restart but the system fails to boot, pressing F8 as the system restarts and selecting the Last Known Good Configuration option restores the registry key HKLM\System\CurrentControlSet to its earlier value, which contains the old driver information. If the driver problem does not manifest itself until you have successfully logged on (as is often the case with video display driver updates), the Last Known Good Configuration option is of little use because the configuration is overwritten during each successful logon.

- **Safe mode**   When a device driver installation renders the computer completely unusable, pressing F8 as the system starts and selecting the Safe mode boot option causes Windows Server 2003 to start in a minimal configuration with only the device drivers needed to start the computer and log on. Once the system is running in Safe mode, you can use Device Manager to disable the offending device.

- **Recovery Console**   When the Last Known Good Configuration and Safe mode options fail to provide access to the computer, the Recovery Console enables you to log on and access limited parts of the file system from a command prompt. From the Recovery Console, you can disable the device driver that is causing the problem, but to do this, you must know the correct name of the device or driver (or both).

SUMMARY

- Device drivers are software components that enable applications and operating systems to communicate with specific hardware devices. Every hardware device you install in a computer must have a corresponding driver that is designed for use with the operating system the computer is running.

- Plug and Play is a standard that enables computers to detect and identify hardware devices, and then install and configure drivers for those devices. PnP dynamically assigns hardware resources to each device and can reconfigure other devices to accommodate each component's special needs.

- Windows Server 2003 includes a large library of drivers for many different hardware devices. If Windows does not include a driver for a device in your computer, you must obtain one from the hardware manufacturer.

- The drivers included with Windows Server 2003 are all digitally signed, to ensure that they have not been tampered with. You can configure the operating system's behavior when installation of an unsigned driver is attempted, by using the Driver Signing Options dialog box.

- To communicate with the computer, hardware devices use hardware resources, such as interrupt request (IRQ) lines, I/O addresses, DMA channels, and memory addresses.

- Device Manager is an MMC snap-in that lists all hardware devices in the computer and indicates problems with identification or driver configuration.

- Using Device Manager, you can enable and disable devices, update and roll back drivers, manage device and device driver properties, and resolve hardware resource conflicts.

- Users must have administrative privileges to install and manage hardware devices and their drivers. The one exception to this rule is that users without administrative privileges can install PnP devices, as long as no additional drivers or user intervention are required.

- Many hardware manufacturers periodically release driver updates, and it is up to system administrators to decide whether to install the updates, as well as who should install them and when.

- The Last Known Good Configuration option is useful for reverting to a previously used driver, but only if you have not logged on to the system after restarting.

- Starting the computer in Safe mode loads a minimal set of drivers, enabling you to access Device Manager and to disable, uninstall, or roll back a driver that is preventing the system from functioning properly.

EXERCISES

Exercise 11-1: Viewing Hardware Resources

In this exercise, you use Device Manager to view the hardware resources in your computer and the devices that are using them.

1. Log on to Windows Server 2003 using the local Administrator account.

2. Click Start, point to Control Panel, and select System.

   The System Properties dialog box appears.

3. Select the Hardware tab, and then click Device Manager.

   The Device Manager window appears.

4. On the View menu, select Resources By Type.

5. Expand the Interrupt Request (IRQ) heading and note the devices using the system's IRQ lines.

Exercise 11-2: Configuring Driver Signing Options

In this exercise, you configure the computer's driver signing options.

1. Log on to Windows Server 2003 using the local Administrator account.

2. Click Start, point to Control Panel, and select System.

   The System Properties dialog box appears.

3. Select the Hardware tab, and then click Driver Signing.

   The Driver Signing Options dialog box appears.

4. Select the Block option, and click OK.

   You have disallowed the installation of unsigned drivers.

Exercise 11-3: Installing a Device Driver

In this exercise, you install the device driver for a nonexistent network interface adapter on your computer.

1. Log on to Windows Server 2003 as Administrator.

2. Click Start, point to Control Panel, and select System.

   The System Properties dialog box appears.

3. Select the Hardware tab, and then click Add Hardware Wizard.

4. Click Next, and wait for the wizard to scan your computer for new devices. If you have not added any devices, the wizard asks whether the new device has been connected.

5. Select Yes, I Have Already Connected The Hardware, and then click Next.

6. Scroll to the bottom of the Installed Hardware list, select Add A New Hardware Device, and then click Next.

7. Select the Install The Hardware That I Manually Select From A List (Advanced) option, and then click Next.

8. In the Common Hardware Types list, select Network Adapters, and then click Next.

9. Select Microsoft as the Manufacturer, and Microsoft Loopback Adapter as the Network Adapter, and then click Next.

10. Click Next to install the adapter, and then click Finish to close the wizard.

Windows Server 2003 loads the driver and installs the device. A new network adapter named Microsoft Loopback Adapter appears in Device Manager under the Network Adapters category.

REVIEW QUESTIONS

1. A user with membership only in the Users group wants to install a USB printer connected to her computer. The drivers for the printer are included with Windows Server 2003. Can the user install the printer without help from an administrator? Why or why not?

2. A user with membership only in the Users group wants to install a USB printer connected to his computer. The driver for the printer is not included with Windows Server 2003, but the manufacturer has supplied a digitally signed driver for the printer on CD-ROM. Can the user install the printer without help from an administrator? Why or why not?

3. Under what circumstances do you have to modify the hardware resource settings for a device?

4. You need to remove a PnP device from a computer's hardware configuration temporarily, but you want to leave it physically connected to the computer. You also want to minimize the amount of work required to restore the device later. Which of the following is the best option to accomplish your goal?

    a. Use Device Manager to uninstall the device.

    b. Physically remove the hardware device from the computer.

    c. Use Device Manager to disable the device.

    d. Move the device driver file to another folder on the local drive.

5. The vendor for a wireless network card installed in your computer has released a new driver. You want to test the driver for proper functionality. Which Device Manager option should you use to test the new driver?

6. You want to view a list of devices connected to your Windows Server 2003 system listed numerically by IRQ. Which of the following methods do you use to do this? (Choose all correct answers.)

    a. Use Device Manager, and from the View menu, select Resources By Connection.

    b. Use Device Manager, and from the View menu, select Resources By Type.

    c. Use Device Manager, and from the View menu, select Devices By Connection.

    d. Use Device Manager, and from the View menu, select Devices By Type.

7. You have recently installed three legacy network cards on a Windows Server 2003 member server. Two of the network cards are working properly, but a third appears to be conflicting with another device on your system. How can you determine which other device on the system is conflicting with the third network card?

    a. Run Device Manager, and look for another device with a yellow and black exclamation mark beside it.

    b. View the application log, and look for an entry that describes the device that is conflicting with the network card.

    c. Run Device Manager, and select the network card that has the yellow and black exclamation mark beside it. On the Action menu, select Properties. In the Resources tab, a Conflicting Device list is displayed with the resources that conflict.

    d. Run the Hardware Troubleshooting Wizard, and select Resolve All Device Conflicts.

CASE SCENARIOS

Scenario 11-1: Troubleshooting Video Display Driver Problems

You have finished configuring a new driver for the computer's video display adapter and are prompted to restart the computer for the changes to take effect. Shortly after you log on, the computer screen goes blank. Which troubleshooting techniques or tools will enable you to recover from the problem with the display driver most easily?

    a. Last Known Good Configuration

    b. Driver Rollback

    c. Safe mode

    d. Recovery Console

Scenario 11-2: Modifying Hardware Resource Settings

You are the part-time systems administrator for a small desktop publishing business, which has a Windows Server 2003 standalone server. You have recently come into possession of a legacy fax board, a device that allows multiple faxes to be sent and received at the same time. You install the board on the Windows Server 2003 system, but it does not work. You open Device Manager and notice that a fax board's icon has a yellow warning with a black exclamation point. You suspect that there is an IRQ conflict with another device on this same system, a legacy RAID controller. Which of the following describes the correct method of altering the fax board's configuration so that there is no IRQ conflict between the legacy fax board and the legacy RAID controller?

a. Select the RAID controller in Device Manager. On the Action menu, select Properties. Select the Resources tab, and then clear the Use Automatic Settings check box. Select the IRQ, and click Change Settings. Scroll through the IRQs until you find one that does not conflict with any others. Click OK, and then restart the server.

b. Select the fax board in Device Manager. On the Action menu, select Properties. Select the Resources tab, and then clear the Use Automatic Settings check box. Select the IRQ, and click Change Settings. Scroll through the IRQs until you find one that does not conflict with any others. Click OK, and then restart the server.

c. Select the RAID controller in Device Manager. On the Action menu, select Properties. Select the Resources tab, and then clear the Use Automatic Settings check box. Select the I/O Range, and click Change Settings. Scroll through the I/O Range until you find one that does not conflict with any others. Click OK, and then restart the server.

d. Select the RAID controller in Device Manager. On the Action menu, select Properties. In the Device Usage drop-down list in the General tab, select Do Not Use This Device (Disable).

CHAPTER 12
MANAGING DISK STORAGE

If there is one truism about information technology, it's that no matter how much storage you have today, it will be full tomorrow. Only a decade ago, hard drives were nearly all measured in megabytes; a 1-GB drive was the size of a shoebox and cost thousands of dollars. Many organizations now measure their storage capacities in terabytes, and managing all that data can create an enormous strain on the storage subsystems in your servers.

Some large organizations are turning to storage area networks (SANs) made up of fiber-connected, fault-tolerant disk arrays, but it is still common to see servers with large amounts of storage, and it is important to configure the server storage to provide the optimum balance of storage capacity, performance, and fault tolerance. Microsoft Windows Server 2003 provides tools that enable you to extend the system's storage capacity, provide fault tolerance, and boost performance of the storage subsystem. System administrators should have a thorough understanding of these tools to keep their drives running smoothly and perhaps delay the inevitable exhaustion of their capacity.

Upon completion of this chapter, you will be able to:

- Understand disk storage concepts and terminology

- Distinguish between basic and dynamic storage

- Identify the types of storage volumes supported on Windows Server 2003 managed disks

- Identify the best RAID implementation given a particular storage requirement, in terms of capacity utilization, fault tolerance, and performance

- Add storage to a Windows Server 2003 computer

- Manage disks using Check Disk, Disk Defragmenter, and disk quotas

UNDERSTANDING WINDOWS SERVER 2003 DISK STORAGE

Before you can fully appreciate the disk storage capabilities of the Windows Server 2003 operating system, it is important to understand some basic underlying concepts. The following sections examine some of the nomenclature that Windows Server 2003 uses when referring to disk storage, and the basic structures that you use to create a data storage strategy.

Although the distinction might at first seem obvious, it is important, when you work with the storage subsystem in Windows Server 2003, to remain conscious of the distinction between physical storage devices and the logical divisions you can create on them. A *physical disk*, as the term implies, is a single, independent drive unit, usually a hard disk drive. Technically, the term *disk* refers to the magnetically coated platters inside the drive unit. A drive can have a single platter or a stack of platters, all of which are referred to collectively as the hard disk inside the drive.

To store data on a physical disk, you must first partition it. In the simplest possible configuration, a physical disk has a single partition that is represented in the operating system by a single drive letter. However, it is also possible to create multiple partitions on a single physical disk. A *partition* is an area of space on a disk that functions as a physically separate unit of storage. When a physical disk has more than one partition on it, each partition can be represented by a different drive letter in the operating system.

> **NOTE Drive Letters and Physical Disks**   Just because you see multiple drive letters in the operating system does not necessarily mean that there are multiple disk drives in the computer. Some applications recommend that certain data structures be stored on separate disks, to maximize the efficiency of the application's storage operations. For example, the Active Directory Installation Wizard recommends that the Active Directory database and log be stored on separate disks. However, specifying different drive letters for these data structures does not necessarily mean that they will be stored on different physical disks. You must be aware of the actual physical disk infrastructure to know which drive letters actually refer to different physical disks.

Unlike disks and partitions, which are rooted in the physical configuration of the storage subsystem, a *volume* (sometimes called a *logical drive*) is a logical unit of disk storage that you can create and manage using the Windows Server 2003 storage tools. A volume can consist of all or part of one or more physical disk partitions. Here again, the simplest possible configuration would be one in which a single volume encompasses an entire partition, which in turn encompasses an entire physical disk.

However, you can also create multiple volumes out of a single partition, or a single volume out of disk space from multiple partitions. There are valid reasons for both of these approaches to disk management. Creating multiple volumes out of a single partition enables you to logically separate various types of data. For example, you can use one volume to install applications and another to store data files. This simplifies the access control process for administrators and prevents the data types from being accidentally mixed. Combining partitions from multiple physical disks into a single volume enables you to consolidate all of your disk space into a single pool, which is represented by one drive letter. This technique also enables you to implement advanced disk storage technologies that provide added performance and fault tolerance, such as disk mirroring, disk striping, and redundant array of independent disks (RAID).

> **NOTE**   **Volumes and Drive Letters**   In most cases, a volume is represented by a single drive letter, even when the volume consists of multiple partitions on differ-ent physical disks. However, a volume does not have to have a drive letter at all. It is possible to mount a volume as a folder in another volume, effectively combining the two volumes into one logical drive letter.

The number and nature of the partitions and volumes you can create out of the space on physical disks depends on the Windows Server 2003 storage type you use: basic storage or dynamic storage, as discussed in the following sections.

> **NOTE**   **Confusing the Terminology**   If you have some difficulty recalling the distinctions between physical disks, partitions, and volumes, you are not alone. Many reference works, and even some Microsoft documents, misuse the terms. However, as you explore the capabilities of the basic and dynamic storage systems in Windows Server 2003, the differences between these storage concepts should become increasingly clear.

Using Basic Storage

Basic storage is the industry standard for hard disk management and the default storage mode for Windows Server 2003. All versions of Windows, and MS-DOS as well, support basic storage and can access basic disks. In Windows Server 2003, all disks are basic disks until you convert them to dynamic storage.

In basic storage, a physical disk is divided into partitions, and each partition functions as a physically separate unit of storage. The information about the loca-tion and size of each partition is stored in the partition table of the Master Boot Record (MBR) on the drive. To create multiple volumes on a single physical disk, you must create multiple partitions. Windows Server 2003 supports up to four partitions on a basic disk, and there are two partition types:

- **Primary**   A basic disk can have up to four primary partitions, with each primary partition functioning as a separate volume. One of the primary partitions can be designated as the **active partition**. The computer looks on the active partition for the boot files needed to load the operating system. After creating a primary partition, you must format it with a file system before you can store data on it.

- **Extended**   A basic disk can have one extended partition, utilizing the space left over after the creation of the primary partitions. Because a basic disk can have no more than four partitions, having an extended partition limits the number of primary partitions on the drive to three. To use the space on an extended partition, you must first create one or more *logical drives* out of the extended partition space, and then format each logical drive individually. You can create as many logical drives out of the extended partition space as you need.

NOTE **Using Extended Partitions** In earlier versions of Microsoft operating systems, including Windows 95, Windows 98, and MS-DOS, a physical disk could only have one primary partition. If you wanted to create multiple volumes on a single physical disk, you had to create an extended partition and divide it into one or more logical drives. Because Windows NT, Windows 2000, Windows XP, and Windows Server 2003 all support the use of multiple primary partitions, the only reason to create an extended partition is if you need more than four logical volumes on a single basic disk.

NOTE **Basic Disks and Removable Storage** Removable storage devices can contain only primary partitions. You cannot create extended partitions or logical drives on removable storage devices. You also can't have an active partition on a removable storage device. Note, however, that for these purposes, external hard drives that connect using USB 2.0 or IEEE 1394 (FireWire) are not considered to be removable drives.

Using Dynamic Storage

In addition to basic storage, Windows 2000, Windows XP, and the Windows Server 2003 family also support dynamic storage. In dynamic storage, partitions and logical drives are deemphasized in favor of volumes, which provide greater flexibility. All dynamic disks consist of only one partition, which encompasses its entire usable storage space. The individual storage units on the partition are called volumes.

As with basic disks, the single partition on a dynamic disk is defined by information stored in the drive's MBR. However, the volume information is stored not in the disk's partition table, but in a database controlled by the operating system's Logical Disk Manager (LDM) service. Because the volume database is not limited by the size and structure of the disk's MBR, you can create an unlimited number of volumes on a dynamic disk. Volumes are also more flexible than partitions in a variety of ways. The types of volumes supported by dynamic disks are as follows:

- **Simple volume** The functional equivalent of a primary partition on a basic disk. **Simple volumes** use space on a single physical disk and correspond to a single logical volume. When a computer has only one dynamic disk, all volumes must be simple volumes. After creating a simple volume of a given size, you can extend it by appending unallocated space from other regions of the same disk, without erasing the contents of the volume. Because simple volumes exist on only one physical disk, they are not fault tolerant.

- **Spanned volume** A **spanned volume** includes space on more than one physical disk. You can create a spanned volume using storage space from up to 32 physical disks, and the amount of space used on each disk can be different. When the system writes data to a spanned volume, it begins by filling up the space on one physical disk, and then it proceeds to each of the others in turn. As a result, spanned volumes provide no fault tolerance. You can extend a spanned volume without losing data by adding space from any of the system's physical disks. The main disadvantage of spanned volumes is that their potential for loss is multiplied by the number of physical disks contributing space to the volume. If one of the disks fails, the entire spanned volume is lost.

- **Striped volume**   A **striped volume** (also known as RAID Level 0, or RAID-0) combines areas of free space from up to 32 physical disks into one logical volume. Unlike a spanned volume, however, Windows Server 2003 writes data to all of the physical disks in the volume (called a stripe set) at the same rate. The system writes successive blocks to each physical disk in turn, and because multiple spindles are in use, read and write performance is increased as additional physical disks are added to the stripe set. However, as with spanned volumes, if one of the physical disks in a stripe set fails, the entire volume is lost.

  NOTE   Striping and Performance   You might not experience a performance improvement on a striped volume using IDE drives unless you use a separate IDE adapter channel for each physical disk. This is because two disks sharing a channel do not receive and execute commands simultaneously. Separate adapter channels improve performance by distributing I/O requests among controllers as well as among drives. For best performance, use SCSI drives for the volume. SCSI host adapters can send commands to all of the drives on the bus, and the drives can execute them at the same time.

- **Mirrored volume**   A **mirrored volume** (also known as RAID-1) consists of two identical copies of a simple volume, each on a separate physical disk. All data stored on the volume is written to both disks simultaneously. Mirrored volumes provide fault tolerance; if one physical disk fails, the other continues to function. The disadvantage of mirroring is that the volume's capacity is only half of the physical disk space.

- **RAID-5 volume**   RAID-5 is a fault-tolerant data storage technology that stripes data across three or more physical disks, which appear as a single unified volume. As with a striped volume, in a **RAID-5 volume** the system writes data to all of the physical disks at the same rate, but in RAID-5, the data is interlaced with checksum information, called *parity*. Although the parity is distributed among all of the disks in the array, the total amount of space used for parity is no greater than the size of one disk. If a single disk in the volume fails, the remaining disks can regenerate the missing data through calculations involving the parity. The calculation of parity during a write operation means that RAID-5 creates a substantial load on the system processor. RAID-5 provides improved read performance, however, because data is retrieved from multiple spindles simultaneously.

  NOTE   System Volume Limitations   Because of the importance of the system volume to the system's functionality, Windows Server 2003 imposes special limitations on the system volume. You cannot install the operating system on a spanned, striped, or RAID-5 volume, nor can you extend or span the system volume after the installation. However, you can mirror the system volume.

Basic vs. Dynamic Disks

The question of whether you should use basic or dynamic storage on your Windows Server 2003 computers requires careful consideration. As mentioned earlier, all Windows Server 2003 disks are basic disks initially, until you explicitly convert them to dynamic disks. The basic-to-dynamic conversion process is simple and quick and can be performed at any time with no loss of data. However, converting a dynamic disk back to a basic disk is more difficult because all data on the drive is lost and must be restored using a backup copy. Therefore, you should be sure that you want or need dynamic storage before performing the conversion.

Dynamic disks are easy to transfer between servers (except in the case of system disks), enabling you to move a disk from a failed server to a functioning server with little downtime. Each Windows 2000, Windows XP, and Windows Server 2003 computer can support one disk group, which itself can contain multiple dynamic disks. The LDM database is replicated among all disks in the disk group, which increases the resilience of disk configuration information for all the group's disks. However, unless you require more than four partitions on a single disk, dynamic storage does not offer any significant advantage on a computer with a single physical disk drive. It is only when you have two or more dynamic disks that you can take advantage of advanced volume types, such as spanned and striped disks.

Despite the advantages of dynamic storage, however, there are still reasons to use basic disks, such as the following:

- The behavior of the LDM database makes it difficult to transfer a dynamic disk used for starting the operating system to another computer when the original computer fails.

- Dynamic disks are not supported for removable or external media and are not supported on laptops.

- Basic storage is the industry standard, so basic drives are accessible from many operating systems, including MS-DOS, all versions of Windows, and most non-Microsoft operating systems. Therefore, you cannot access dynamic disks if you boot the system using any operating system other than Windows Server 2003, Windows XP, or Windows 2000.

> **NOTE** **Exam Objectives** *The objectives for the 70-290 exam state that students should be able to "manage basic disks and dynamic disks."*

USING DISK MANAGEMENT

The primary Windows Server 2003 tool for creating and managing basic and dynamic disks is an MMC snap-in called Disk Management. The Disk Management snap-in is part of the Computer Management console, which you can access from the Start menu's Administrative Tools program group, or you can add the snap-in to a custom console.

> **TIP** **Running the Disk Management Console** *Windows Server 2003 also includes a standalone Disk Management console, but there is no shortcut for it on the Start menu. To open the console, click Start, select Run, type **diskmgmt.msc** in the Open text box, and then click OK.*

The Disk Management interface is different from that of most MMC snap-ins. It has no scope pane functions; all of the controls are in the details pane. The details pane itself is split into top and bottom panes, as shown in Figure 12-1. The top pane, by default, contains a volume list that displays the volumes on all of the physical disks in the computer. This list actually displays volumes only for dynamic disks; on basic disks, the top pane contains a list of the primary partitions and logical drives.

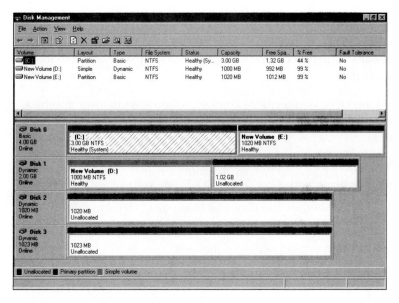

Figure 12-1   The Disk Management console

Each entry in the volume list contains the following information:

- **Volume**   Specifies the drive letter and/or volume name

- **Layout**   Specifies the volume type, such as simple, spanned, or striped for volumes on dynamic disks, or partition for volumes on basic disks

- **Type**   Specifies the type of disk on which the volume is located: basic or dynamic

- **File System**   Specifies the file system that was used to format the volume

- **Status**   Specifies the current status of the volume, using one of the following values:

  - ❑ **Failed**—Indicates that the volume could not be started

  - ❑ **Failed Redundancy**—Indicates that a mirrored or RAID-5 volume is no longer fault tolerant because of a disk failure

  - ❑ **Formatting**—Indicates that the volume is in the process of being formatted

  - ❑ **Healthy**—Indicates that the volume is operating normally

  - ❑ **Regenerating**—Indicates that a RAID-5 volume is in the process of re-creating data on a newly restored disk

  - ❑ **Resynching**—Indicates that a mirrored volume is in the process of re-creating data on a newly restored disk

  - ❑ **Unknown**—Indicates that the boot sector for the volume has been corrupted

- **Capacity**   Specifies the total capacity of the volume, in megabytes or gigabytes

■ **Free Space** Specifies the total amount of free space on the volume, in megabytes or gigabytes

■ **% Free** Specifies the percentage of the volume's capacity that is free

■ **Fault Tolerance** Specifies whether the volume type provides fault tolerance

■ **Overhead** Specifies the percentage of the volume's capacity devoted to storing redundant data

The bottom pane of the Disk Management console window contains a graphical view of the physical disks in the computer. For each disk, the view specifies the following information:

■ **Disk identifier** Specifies the number assigned to the disk by the system. Hard disk identifiers begin with Disk 0 and CD-ROMs with CD-ROM 0.

■ **Disk type** Specifies whether the disk is a basic disk, dynamic disk, CD-ROM, or DVD-ROM

■ **Disk size** Specifies the total capacity of the disk

■ **Disk status** Specifies the current status of the disk, using one of the following values:

❑ **Audio CD**—Indicates that a CD-ROM or DVD-ROM drive contains an audio CD.

❑ **Foreign**—Indicates a dynamic disk that has been moved from another computer but has not yet been imported into the current system's configuration. Run the Import Foreign Disks command to access the disk.

❑ **Initializing**—Indicates that the disk is in the process of being converted from a basic disk to a dynamic disk.

❑ **Missing**—Indicates that a dynamic disk has been removed from the computer, disconnected, or corrupted. Use the Reactivate Disk command to access a previously disconnected disk.

❑ **No Media**—Indicates that a CD-ROM, DVD-ROM, or removable disk drive is currently empty.

❑ **Not Initialized**—Indicates that the disk does not contain a valid signature. Use Initialize Disk to activate the disk.

❑ **Online**—Indicates that the disk is accessible and functioning normally.

❑ **Online (Errors)**—Indicates that I/O errors have been detected on a region of a dynamic disk.

❑ **Offline**—Indicates that a dynamic disk is not accessible.

❑ **Unreadable**—Indicates that the disk is not accessible, due to hardware failure, I/O errors, or corruption of the LDM database.

The horizontal bar representing each disk is divided into segments representing the various volumes or partitions on that disk. Each volume or partition segment is color coded to indicate whether it is a basic volume, a dynamic volume of a particular type, or unallocated space. The segments also contain some of the same information found in the volume list, such as the volume name, capacity, file system, and current status.

The Disk Management snap-in enables you to specify what should appear in the top and bottom panes by using the commands on the View menu. You can reverse the volume list and the graphical view, or you can replace either one with a disk list, as shown in Figure 12-2. The disk list contains much of the same information for each disk as the graphical view, plus a Device Type, such as IDE or SCSI, and a Partition Style, such as MBR or GPT (GUID partition table, used by Itanium-based computers).

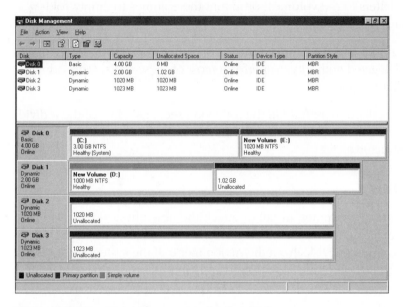

Figure 12-2   The Disk Management disk list display

Disk Management can manage disk storage on local or remote systems. The snap-in does not manipulate the disk configuration directly; rather, it works in concert with the Logical Disk Manager Administrative Service that it starts on the computer you are managing when you launch the Disk Management snap-in.

When you select one of the elements in the Disk Management interface, you can access a variety of functions from the Action menu and from the element's context menu. The specific functions are determined by whether you have selected a disk, a partition on a basic disk, or a volume on a dynamic disk. You can also open a Properties dialog box for each element, which provides access to additional functions. Some of the functions you can perform are described in the following sections.

> **NOTE   Using Diskpart.exe**   Virtually all of the tasks you can perform using the Disk Management snap-in can also be performed from the command prompt using the Diskpart.exe utility. Diskpart.exe is a program that you can use interactively or in scripts to automate disk management tasks. For more information on using Diskpart.exe, see the online help in Windows Server 2003.

▶ Adding Storage

The process of adding more storage capacity to a Windows Server 2003 computer consists of the following steps:

1. Physically install the disk(s).

2. Initialize the disk.

3. On a basic disk, create partitions and (if an extended partition) logical drives, or, on a dynamic disk, create volumes.

4. Format the volumes.

5. Assign drive letters to the volumes, or mount the volumes to empty folders on existing NTFS volumes.

You must be a member of the Administrators or Backup Operators group, or have been otherwise delegated authority, to perform most of these tasks. Only administrators can format a volume.

These steps are described more fully in the following sections. Most of the individual steps are also functions that you can perform on existing disks or volumes, as well as on new structures.

Installing a Disk

To add a new disk to a computer, install or attach the new physical disk. Then, open the Disk Management snap-in and, if the system has not detected the drive automatically, select Rescan Disks from the Action menu. If the system must restart to complete the installation of the new disk, do so, and then open Disk Management again.

Initializing the Disk

When you add a disk to a Windows Server 2003 computer, you must initialize the disk before you can begin to allocate its space to partitions, logical drives, and volumes. Initializing a disk enables the operating system to write a disk signature, the end of sector marker (also called a signature word), and an MBR or GPT to the disk.

If you start the Disk Management snap-in after installing a new disk, the Initialize And Convert Disk Wizard usually appears automatically. The wizard enables you to create a signature on the new disk and convert the default basic disk to a dynamic disk. To initialize a disk manually using Disk Management, right-click the disk's status box on the graphical view and, from the Action menu, point to All Tasks and select Initialize Disk.

> **NOTE   Converting New Disks**   The Initialize And Convert Disk Wizard does not convert new disks by default; you must select the disk for conversion manually.

Creating Basic Disk Partitions

After you have initialized the disk, you can begin to implement a storage structure of partitions, logical drives, or volumes. As mentioned earlier, all newly initialized disks in Windows Server 2003 are basic disks by default. If you want to maintain the disk as a basic disk, you can create partitions by selecting the unallocated space in the graphical view and, on the Action menu, pointing to All Tasks and selecting New Partition. This launches the New Partition Wizard, in which you specify whether you want to create a primary partition or an extended partition (as shown in Figure 12-3) and what size the partition should be.

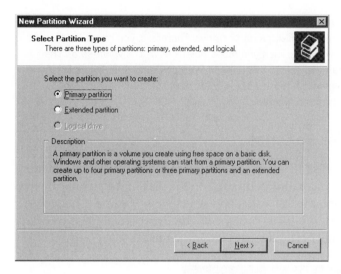

Figure 12-3   The New Partition Wizard

If you create a primary partition, the wizard takes you through the process of assigning a drive letter to the partition and formatting it, or you can choose to perform these tasks later. If you create an extended partition, you must select the Free Space area you just created and run the New Partition Wizard again, this time opting to create a logical drive. You can create any number of logical drives you want, until you have used all of the space in the extended partition. Here again, the wizard enables you to format the logical drives as you create them, or you can choose to format them later.

> **MORE INFO**   For more information on assigning driver letters to partitions and formatting them, see "Assigning Drive Letters" and "Formatting Volumes," later in this chapter.

Converting a Basic Disk to a Dynamic Disk

If you want to use dynamic storage, you must convert a basic disk to a dynamic disk before you can create new volumes. To do this, select the disk's status box in the graphical view and, on the Action menu, point to All Tasks and select Convert To Dynamic Disk. After the conversion is complete, the disk's status box shows it as being dynamic, and you can proceed to create volumes.

> **NOTE**   **Converting the System Disk**   In most cases, you can begin to use the dynamic disk immediately after you complete the conversion from basic storage. However, when you convert the system disk to dynamic storage, you must restart the system before you can perform any further actions on the disk.

You can convert a basic disk to a dynamic disk at any time, even when you have data stored on the disk. The structure of data on the disk is not modified, so the existing data is not lost. However, the best practice when performing any major disk manipulation is to back up your data first.

When you convert a basic disk that already contains partitions and logical drives to a dynamic disk, those elements are converted to the equivalent dynamic disk elements. In most cases, basic partitions and logical drives are converted to simple volumes. Windows NT volume sets and stripe sets are converted to spanned volumes and striped volumes, respectively.

> **NOTE   Converting a Dynamic Disk to a Basic Disk**   Converting a dynamic disk back to basic storage wipes out all data on the drive. Therefore, you must first back up all of the data on the disk. Then you must delete all of the volumes on the dynamic disk. Only then can you select the disk and select Convert To Basic Disk from the Action/All Tasks menu. After creating basic partitions and logical drives, you can restore the data back to the disk.

Creating Dynamic Disk Volumes

Once you have converted a disk to dynamic storage, you can proceed to create volumes on it. Select an area of unallocated space on the disk in the graphical view and, on the Action menu, point to All Tasks and select New Volume. The New Volume Wizard appears. In this wizard, you specify the type of volume you want to create in the Select Volume Type page, shown in Figure 12-4.

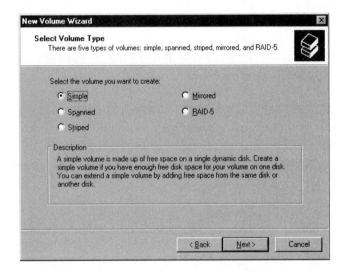

Figure 12-4   The Select Volume Type page of the New Volume Wizard

The volume types that are available for selection depend on the number of dynamic disks in the computer with unallocated space available.

Creating Simple Volumes

If you have only one disk in the computer, you can create only simple volumes. All you have to do to create a simple volume is specify its size. Then the New Volume Wizard takes you through the process of assigning a drive letter to the volume and formatting it, as described later in this chapter.

Creating Other Volume Types

To create spanned, striped, or mirrored volumes, you must have at least two dynamic disks with unallocated space available. To create a RAID-5 volume, you must have at least three dynamic disks. When you select any one of these volume types, the New

Volume Wizard displays the Select Disks page (shown in Figure 12-5), in which you select the disks you want to use to create the volume.

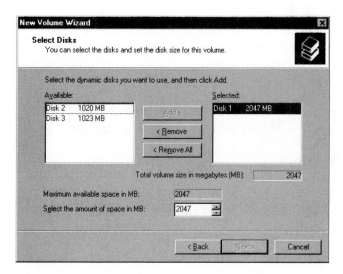

Figure 12-5   The Select Disks page of the New Volume Wizard

By default, the disk you chose when creating the volume appears in the Selected list. All of the other dynamic disks in the computer appear in the Available list. To add a disk to the volume, you make a selection in the Available list and click Add. You can add up to 32 disks to a spanned, striped, or RAID-5 volume; mirrored volumes use only two disks.

Once you have selected the disks you want to use to create the volume, you must specify the volume's size. The process varies slightly, depending on the type of volume you are creating:

- Spanned volumes can use any amount of space from each of the drives. For each of the disks in the Selected list, you specify the amount of space (in megabytes) that you want to add to the spanned volume. The Total Volume Size In Megabytes (MB) field displays the combined space from all the selected drives.

- Striped, mirrored, and RAID-5 volumes must use the same amount of space on each of the selected disks. After you select the disks you want to use for the volume, the Select The Amount Of Space In MB control specifies the maximum amount of space that each disk can contribute, which is determined by the disk with the least amount of space free. When you change the amount of space for one disk, the wizard changes the amount of space contributed by the other disks.

The total size of the volume is also calculated differently for the various volume types:

- For a spanned volume, the total size of the volume is the number of megabytes you specified for the selected disks combined.

- For a striped volume, the total size of the volume is the number of megabytes you specified, multiplied by the number of disks you selected.

- For a mirrored volume, the total size of the volume is the number of megabytes you specified. This is because each of the disks contains an identical copy of the data on the other disks.

- For a RAID-5 volume, the total size of the volume is the number of megabytes you specified, multiplied by the number of disks you selected minus one. This is because the RAID-5 volume uses one disk's worth of space to store the parity for the rest of the disk array.

After you configure these parameters, the wizard enables you to assign a drive letter to the volume and format it, as described in the following sections.

Working with Mirrored Volumes

A mirrored volume provides good performance along with excellent fault tolerance. Two disks participate in a mirrored volume, and all data is written to both volumes simultaneously. For the best possible fault tolerance, you should use disks connected to separate host adapters. This creates a configuration called **duplexing**, which provides better performance and enables the volume to survive an adapter failure as well as a disk failure.

Converting a Simple Volume to a Mirrored Volume   In addition to creating a new mirrored volume, you can also convert a simple volume into a mirrored volume by selecting the simple volume and, on the Action menu, pointing to All Tasks and selecting Add Mirror. You must have another dynamic disk in the computer with sufficient unallocated space to hold a copy of the simple volume you selected. Once you have created the mirror volume, the system begins copying data, sector by sector, to the newly added disk. During that time, the volume status is reported as Resynching.

Recovering from Mirrored Disk Failures   The recovery process for a failed disk within a mirrored volume depends on the type of failure. If a disk has experienced transient I/O errors, the volume on both disks will show a status of Failed Redundancy. The disk with the errors will report a status of Offline or Missing, as shown in Figure 12-6.

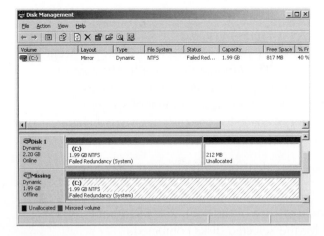

Figure 12-6   A mirrored volume showing a Failed Redundancy status

After you correct the cause of the I/O error—perhaps a bad cable connection or power supply—select the volume on the problematic disk and, on the Action menu, point to All Tasks and select Reactivate Volume. Or you can select the disk and choose Reactivate Disk. Reactivating brings the disk or volume back online. The system then resynchronizes the disks.

If you want to stop mirroring, you have three choices, depending on what you want the outcome to be:

- **Delete the volume**   If you delete the volume, the volume and all the information it contains is removed. The resulting unallocated space is then available for new volumes.

- **Remove the mirror**   If you remove the mirror, the mirror is broken and the space on one of the disks becomes unallocated. The other disk maintains a copy of the data that had been mirrored, but that data is of course no longer fault tolerant.

- **Break the mirror**   If you break the mirror, the mirror is broken but both disks maintain copies of the data. The portion of the mirror that you select when you select Break Mirror maintains the original mirrored volume's drive letter, shared folders, paging file, and reparse points. The secondary drive is given the next available drive letter.

If you have a mirrored volume in which one physical disk has failed completely and must be replaced, you can't simply remirror the mirrored volume, even though one of the disks in the mirror set no longer exists. You must first remove the failed disk from the mirror set to break the mirror. Select the volume and, on the Action menu, point to All Tasks and select Remove Mirror. In the Remove Mirror dialog box, it is important to select the disk that is missing. The disk you select is deleted when you click Remove Mirror, and the remaining disk becomes a simple volume. Once the operation is complete, you can select the simple volume and use the Add Mirror command to use the replacement disk to create a new mirror volume.

> **EXAM TIP**   *Fault Tolerance for System and Boot Volumes*   Because you can create a mirror volume from an existing simple volume, mirroring is the only native Windows Server 2003 technique you can use to provide fault tolerance for a computer's system and boot volumes. You cannot use the RAID-5 capabilities of Windows Server 2003 for system or boot volumes because you must convert the disks to dynamic storage and create the volume before any data is written to it. Obviously, you cannot do this before the operating system is installed. However, hardware RAID implementations do make it possible to install the operating system on a RAID-5 volume.

Working with RAID

As mentioned earlier in this chapter, RAID is a series of fault tolerance technologies that enable a computer or operating system to respond to a catastrophic event, such as a hardware failure, so that no data is lost and work in progress is not corrupted or interrupted. You can implement RAID fault tolerance as either a hardware or a software solution.

In a hardware solution, a RAID adapter handles the creation and regeneration of redundant information. Some vendors implement RAID data protection directly in their hardware, as with disk array adapter cards. Because these methods are vendor specific and bypass the operating system's fault tolerance software drivers, they offer performance improvements over software implementations of RAID, like that included in Windows Server 2003.

Consider the following points when you decide whether to use a software or hardware RAID implementation:

- Hardware RAID implementations are more expensive than software RAID and might limit equipment options to a single vendor.

- Hardware RAID implementations generally provide faster disk I/O than software RAID.

- Hardware RAID implementations might include features such as hot swapping of hard disks, to allow for replacement of a failed hard disk without shutting down the computer, and hot sparing, so that a failed disk is automatically replaced by an online spare.

Windows Server 2003 supports three levels of RAID:

- **RAID-0**   Striped volumes do not provide fault tolerance, but they are considered a RAID implementation.

- **RAID-1**   Mirrored volumes are the most basic type of fault-tolerant RAID, but they suffer from relatively low efficiency. Fully 50 percent of the disk space devoted to the array is used to store redundant data.

- **RAID-5**   Striped volumes with parity provide fault tolerance with enhanced performance and a better level of efficiency than RAID-1. At maximum, only 33 percent of the disk space devoted to the array is used to store redundant parity information.

With Windows Server 2003 implementations of RAID-1 and RAID-5, the fault tolerance applies only to a single drive failure. If a second failure occurs before the data lost from the first failure is regenerated, data is lost that can be recovered only by restoring it from a backup.

> **NOTE   RAID and Backups**   RAID technologies are not designed to replace regular system backups. No matter how fault tolerant your storage solution, you should still back up your data at regular intervals.

Because RAID-5 volumes are created as native dynamic volumes from unallocated space, you cannot convert any other type of volume into a RAID-5 volume without backing up that volume's data and restoring into a newly created RAID-5 volume.

If a single disk fails in a RAID-5 volume, the entire data store on the volume remains accessible. During read operations, any missing data is regenerated on the fly through a calculation involving remaining data and parity. Performance is degraded during this time, and if a second drive fails, data is lost irretrievably.

Once the failed drive is returned to service, you might need to use the Rescan Disks command in Disk Management and then reactivate the volume on the newly restored disk. The system then rebuilds missing data from the parity information and repopulates the disk, leaving the volume fully functional and fault tolerant again.

Choosing a RAID Technology

Mirrored volumes (RAID-1) and RAID-5 volumes provide different levels of fault tolerance and performance. Your choice will depend on the level of protection you require and your hardware budget. The major differences between mirrored volumes and RAID-5 volumes are summarized in Table 12-1.

Table 12-1   Comparison of RAID-1 and RAID-5

Mirrored Volumes (RAID-1)	Striped Volumes with Parity (RAID-5)
Can protect system or boot partition	Cannot protect system or boot partition
Requires two hard disks	Requires a minimum of three hard disks and allows a maximum of 32 hard disks
Has a higher cost per MB	Has a lower cost per MB
50 percent redundancy	33 percent maximum redundancy
Good read and write performance	Excellent read and moderate write performance
Uses less system memory	Requires more system memory

> **NOTE   Exam Objectives**   The objectives for the 70-290 exam state that students should be able to "implement a RAID solution."

Assigning Drive Letters

When you create a partition on a basic disk or a volume on a dynamic disk, the New Partition Wizard or New Volume Wizard gives you the opportunity to assign a drive letter to the partition or volume, using the interface on the Assign Drive Letter Or Path page, shown in Figure 12-7. By default, the wizard assigns the next available drive letter (excluding A and B) to the new partition or volume. You can also select any other available drive letter.

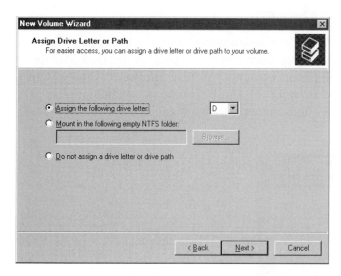

Figure 12-7   The Assign Drive Letter Or Path page of the New Volume Wizard

Instead of assigning a drive letter to a volume, you can also mount the volume in an empty folder on an NTFS drive. Mounting a volume in this way makes the entire contents of the volume appear as a folder on another drive. This capability makes it possible to extend a Windows Server 2003 storage subsystem beyond the limitations of the 24 available drive letters and to expand the available drive space on an existing volume.

When you select the Mount In The Following Empty NTFS Folder option, you must enter or browse to an empty folder on any other NTFS drive in the system. The NTFS drive can be on a basic or a dynamic disk, and there are no limitations on the types of volumes you can mount. You can, for example, mount a striped volume in an empty folder of a mirrored volume, or you can mount a basic partition in a folder on a RAID-5 volume. Each volume retains its own performance and fault tolerance characteristics. There are also no limitations on the file system of the volumes you mount. The mounted volume can use FAT or NTFS; only the disk containing the folder to which you mount the volume must use NTFS.

Figure 12-8 shows a computer in which a folder on a drive is a mount point to another volume. Note that the folder appears in the Explorer hierarchy exactly where it should, but it displays a drive volume icon. When users navigate to that folder, they are transparently redirected to the mounted volume.

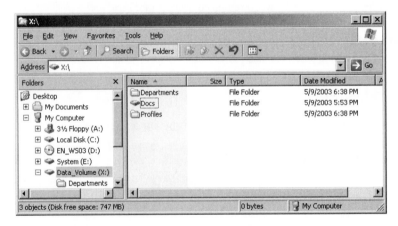

Figure 12-8   A volume mounted to a folder path

It is also possible to modify drive letter assignments and mount volumes after you have created them. To do this, select a drive in either pane of the Disk Management snap-in and, on the Action menu, point to All Tasks and select Change Drive Letter And Paths. The Change Drive Letter And Paths dialog box that appears displays the current drive letter and mounted path assignments for the drive, as shown in Figure 12-9.

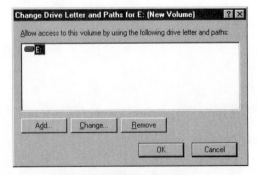

Figure 12-9   A Change Drive Letter And Paths dialog box

By clicking the Change button, you can modify the existing drive letter assignment or mounting path, and by clicking Add, you can create a new one. You can even do both, giving a volume or partition a drive letter and mounting it to an NTFS folder at the same time.

> **NOTE** **Modifying Drive Letters** *You cannot change the drive letter of the volume that is a system partition or boot partition. If the volume you are trying to modify is currently in use, such as if an application has files on the volume locked open, the system can create a new drive letter assignment for the volume, but it will also leave the existing drive letter assignment in place until the next time you restart the computer.*

Formatting Volumes

The final step in the New Partition Wizard and the New Volume Wizard gives you the opportunity to format the new partition or volume you created, using the interface shown in Figure 12-10.

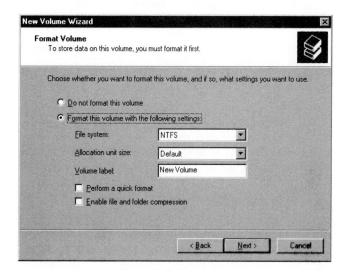

Figure 12-10   The Format Volume page of the New Volume Wizard

The controls on this page are as follows:

- **File System**   Windows Server 2003 supports three file systems: FAT, FAT32, and NTFS. FAT and FAT32 are included in the operating system only for backward compatibility reasons. FAT is the original MS-DOS file system, and FAT32 is an improved version of FAT first implemented in Windows 95. Both of these file systems offer no advantages other than compatibility with older operating systems. If you were to start a Windows Server 2003 computer with an MS-DOS disk, for example, only the drives formatted with FAT or FAT32 would be accessible. NTFS, on the other hand, includes many advanced features, including access control, compression, and disk quotas. In short, unless you have a specific reason for using FAT or FAT32, you should format your partitions and volumes using the NTFS file system.

> **NOTE** **Formatting Dynamic Disk Volumes** *When you format a volume on a dynamic disk using this interface, only the NTFS option is available. It is possible to format dynamic disks using FAT or FAT32, but to do so, you must use the Format.exe utility from the command line.*

■ **Allocation Unit Size**   Specifies the size of the clusters that the file system will use to allocate disk space. Larger cluster sizes enable the disk to access files with fewer reads and writes, but it also wastes more disk space when blocks are only partially filled. Smaller cluster sizes waste less space but require more disk reads and writes. In most cases, selecting the Default value (which is 4 KB for drives larger than 2 GB) is sufficient. If you intend to use the volume to store only large files, you might want to use a larger cluster size; for small files, a smaller cluster size might be preferable.

■ **Volume Label**   Specifies a name for the volume of up to 32 characters.

■ **Perform a Quick Format**   Selecting this option causes the wizard to format the volume without scanning it for bad sectors. If the disk has been formatted before and you are convinced that it is not damaged, selecting this option greatly decreases the time required for the formatting.

■ **Enable File and Folder Compression**   Causes all data to be stored on the volume in compressed form. To use compression, the volume must be formatted using the NTFS file system with an allocation unit size of 4 KB or smaller.

It is also possible to format a drive at any time by selecting it and, on the Action menu, pointing to All Tasks and selecting Format.

Extending Dynamic Volumes

Unlike partitions on basic disks, which are permanently locked at the size you specify when you create them, it is possible to extend a volume on a dynamic disk as long as unallocated space is available on the disk. This enables you to enlarge a volume when it nears its capacity, without taking the volume offline and interrupting user access.

You can extend simple or spanned volumes on a dynamic disk, as long as the volume is formatted using NTFS, and as long as the volume is not the system or boot volume. To extend a volume, select it in Disk Management and, on the Action menu, point to All Tasks and select Extend Volume. This launches the Extend Volume Wizard, in which you can specify the new size for the volume as well as add space from other disks, creating a spanned volume.

MANAGING DISK STORAGE

Windows Server 2003 disk volumes are efficient and stable if formatted with NTFS, but somewhat less so when formatted with FAT or FAT32. The NTFS file system logs all file transactions, replaces bad clusters automatically, and stores copies of key information for all files on the NTFS volume. With these mechanisms, NTFS actively protects the integrity of the volume structure and the file system metadata (the data related to the file system itself). However, user data can occasionally be corrupted and can certainly become fragmented. Users also have the annoying habit of storing enormous amounts of data on the volumes to which they have access. The following sections explain how to maintain the integrity of disk volumes, optimize volumes through defragmentation, and set storage limits using disk quotas.

> **NOTE   Exam Objectives**   The objectives for the 70-290 exam state that students should be able to "optimize server disk performance."

Using Check Disk

Check Disk, or Chkdsk.exe, is a Windows Server 2003 tool that enables you to scan a disk volume for file system errors and, optionally, test for and attempt to recover bad sectors on the hard disk.

There are several ways to run Check Disk:

- Open Windows Explorer, select a local drive in My Computer, and, from the File menu, select Properties. In the Properties dialog box for the drive, select the Tools tab and then click Check Now.

- Open the Disk Management snap-in, select a volume, and, on the Action menu, point to All Tasks and select Properties. In the Properties dialog box for the drive, select the Tools tab and then click Check Now.

- Open a Command Prompt window and, on the commend line, type **chkdsk** **x: /f /r**, where *x:* is the drive letter of a local drive. Then press Enter.

- When a partition is mounted on another drive and doesn't have a drive letter, open the Properties dialog box for the mount point in Windows Explorer, select the General tab, and click Properties to open a Properties dialog box for the actual partition. Then select the Tools tab and click Check Now.

When you run Check Disk from a drive's Properties dialog box, you see the Check Disk dialog box shown in Figure 12-11, in which you can select the tasks you want to perform.

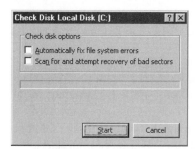

Figure 12-11   The Check Disk dialog box

When you select Automatically Fix File System Errors (or add the /f switch to the Chkdsk.exe command line), Check Disk attempts to fix inconsistencies in the file system catalog, such as files that appear in the catalog but don't appear in a directory on the volume. Check Disk makes three passes over the drive to examine the metadata, which is the data describing how files are organized on the disk. The passes attempt to ensure that all files on the volume are consistent with the master file table (MFT), that the directory structure is correct, and that the security descriptors are consistent.

If you select Scan For And Attempt Recovery Of Bad Sectors (or add the /r switch to the Chkdsk.exe command line), Check Disk makes a fourth pass, which tests the sectors in the volume reserved for user data (as opposed to file system metadata, which is always checked). If the program finds a bad sector, it recovers the data and moves it to a good sector if the volume is fault tolerant; if the volume is not fault tolerant, data cannot be recovered using Check Disk and must be restored from a backup. The bad sector is then removed from active use.

All files with open handles must be closed before Check Disk can run. If all handles cannot be released (which is the case if you run Check Disk on the system volume), you are prompted to schedule Check Disk to run the next time the system restarts. When Check Disk is running, the volume is inaccessible to other processes. Depending on the size of the volume, the options you have selected, and the other processes running on the computer, Check Disk can take a significant amount of time to complete, and it is quite processor-intensive and disk-intensive while it runs.

Practice using Check Disk by doing Exercise 12-1, "Using Check Disk," now.

Using Disk Defragmenter

Files are stored on a volume in units called *clusters*. As you learned earlier, you configure the cluster size when formatting a drive. Many NTFS volumes use the default cluster size of 4 KB. Each cluster can contain only one file, even if that file is smaller than the cluster size. If a file is larger than the cluster size, the file is saved to multiple clusters, with each cluster containing a pointer to the next segment of the file. When a drive is new, all clusters are free, and as files are written to the drive they tend to occupy physically adjacent clusters. But as files are deleted or expanded and contracted in size, free clusters are no longer completely contiguous, so a file might be saved to clusters that are not physically close to each other on the disk drive. This **fragmentation** of files results in slower read and write performance because the drive heads must move to many different locations on the disk.

Windows Server 2003 provides a disk defragmentation utility that you can use to analyze your volumes and reorganize the clusters so that files are stored on contiguous areas of disk space. The defragmentation utility is significantly improved over the Windows 2000 version; it can now defragment volumes with cluster sizes greater than 4 KB and can defragment the master file table. You can use the tool to defragment any local disk volume.

To use the built-in Disk Defragmenter, as shown in Figure 12-12, open the Properties dialog box for a disk volume using either Windows Explorer or the Disk Management snap-in and, in the Tools tab, click Defragment Now. You can also open the Disk Defragmenter snap-in in the Computer Management console or in a custom MMC console, select a volume, and click Analyze. The tool displays a recommendation based on the amount of fragmentation it detects. The tool might also advise you to run Check Disk on the volume before defragmenting (which is always a good idea).

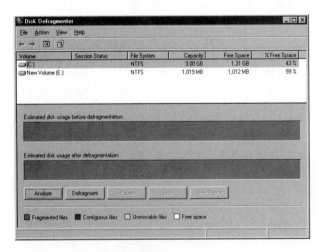

Figure 12-12   The Disk Defragmenter

If the recommendation is to defragment, click Defragment. You can defragment any type of volume: FAT32 or NTFS, basic or dynamic. The volume can have files open during the defragmentation process, but the open files might not be efficiently defragmented and might slow down the whole process, so closing all open files before defragmenting is recommended. Disk Defragmenter moves files around the drive in an attempt to collect all of the clusters for each file into a contiguous area of disk space. The result also consolidates free space, making it less likely that new files will be fragmented.

To completely defragment a volume, the volume must have at least 15 percent free space. The tool uses this space to stage files as it defragments them. If the volume contains numerous fragmented large files, the amount of free space required for effective defragmentation will be larger. If the volume contains less then 15 percent free space, then the volume will be only partially defragmented.

Practice using Disk Defragmenter by doing Exercise 12-2, "Defragmenting a Disk," now.

> **NOTE** **Exam Objectives** *The objectives for the 70-290 exam state that students should be able to "defragment volumes and partitions."*

Implementing Disk Quotas

One of the most persistent challenges in storage management is keeping track of how much server disk space each user is occupying. Until Windows 2000, there was no way to track drive usage on a per-user basis in Windows. Windows 2000 introduced NTFS-based quota management as a built-in feature, enabling administrators to set limits on the storage space allotted to each user, and Windows Server 2003 provides the same functionality. When disk quotas are enabled, the quota manager tracks the files on a volume that are owned by particular users. The manager then compares the total disk usage for each user to limits configured by an administrator. When users reach their limits, the manager notifies them or prevents them from writing to the disk, or both.

The Windows Server 2003 quota manager reports the amount of free space on a volume based on each user's quota, so if a user has a 50-MB quota on a 500-GB RAID volume, the user initially sees the amount of free space reported as 50 MB. When the user approaches the quota limit, the messages that appear are similar to those indicating that a volume is filling up or is full; the system warns that space is low and suggests deleting unneeded files. In actuality, there might be plenty of free space on the volume, but none of it is available to the user.

The process of configuring quotas consists of the following steps:

1. Enable quotas on a volume.

2. Configure default quota settings.

3. Create quota entries for specific users.

Enabling Quotas

Disk quotas are disabled by default in Windows Server 2003; you must enable them on a volume-by-volume basis. To enable quotas, open the Properties dialog box for a volume using Windows Explorer or the Disk Management snap-in, and select the Quota tab, as shown in Figure 12-13. Then select the Enable Quota Management check box.

TIP   *Opening a Volume's Properties Dialog Box*   *Most documentation suggests opening the properties of the volume from Windows Explorer, by right-clicking a drive and selecting Properties. Unfortunately, that process limits you to configuring quotas for volumes with drive letters only; Windows Explorer cannot display the Quota tab for a volume mounted to a folder path. Therefore, it is recommended that you configure quotas using the Disk Management snap-in. Disk Management enables you to open the Properties dialog box for any volume and access its Quota tab.*

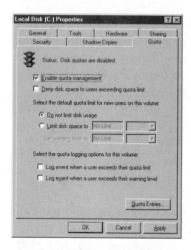

Figure 12-13   The Quota tab of a volume's Properties dialog box

If you select the Deny Disk Space To Users Exceeding Quota Limit check box, users who reach their storage limits are denied additional space on the volume. Any attempts to write additional data to the volume will fail. If this check box is not selected, users are warned when they reach their limits but are not prevented from writing additional data to the volume.

Configuring Quota Defaults

You can manage disk quotas in two ways: by setting a default storage limit that applies to all users, and by creating quota entries that define limits for specific users. To configure the default storage limit, you select the Limit Disk Space To option in the Quota tab and specify the maximum amount of storage allotted to each user. You can also specify that users receive a warning that they are nearing their limits.

Finally, you can specify logging options that cause the quota manager to register events in the computer's System log, identifying users by name and specifying that they have exceeded their warning or quota limits. Administrators can view these entries in the Event viewer console.

Creating Quota Entries

Quota entries are essentially exceptions to the rule you defined in the quota defaults. When you create a quota entry for a specific user, the default quota settings do not apply to that user. The entry settings apply instead, whether they set a higher or lower storage limit for that user. To create quota entries, click the Quota Entries button to open the Quota Entries window, as shown in Figure 12-14.

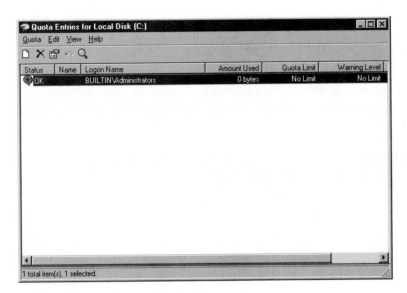

Figure 12-14   The Quota Entries window

> **NOTE   Quota Entries**   By default, one quota entry appears in the window,
> granting the Administrators group No Limit to their storage capacity. This
> enables administrators to install the operating system, services, applications,
> and data without exceeding a quota. Note that this is the only group quota entry
> assignment permitted. When creating your own quota entries, you can only select
> users; you can create new quota entries for groups.

Click the New Quota Entry button on the toolbar or select New Quota Entry from
the Quota menu, and you can select one or more users for which to create a quota
entry. Once you select users, an Add New Quota Entry dialog box appears, as
shown in Figure 12-15, in which you specify the storage limits and warning threshold for the selected users. When you create an entry for multiple users, each user
receives the specified limit individually.

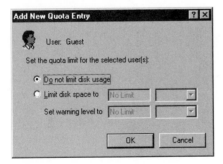

Figure 12-15   The Add New Quota Entry dialog box

Exporting Quota Entries

If you want to apply the same quota entries to another NTFS volume, you can
export the entries and import them to the other volume. Select one or more quota
entries and, on the Quota menu, click Export and specify a filename. On the other
volume, select Import and select the file containing the entries you want to import.

Monitoring Quotas and Storage

The Quota Entries dialog box displays the current disk storage utilization per user and whether that storage is at or above warning levels or limits. You can sort by column to identify users who have exceeded their quota levels or limits. There is no mechanism to generate alerts warning administrators about users approaching their quota limits, so you must monitor the Quota Entries dialog box or the System log in Event Viewer.

> **NOTE   Exam Objectives**   The objectives for the 70-290 exam state that students should be able to "monitor disk quotas."

Practice configuring disk quotas by doing Exercise 12-3, "Configuring Default Disk Quotas," now.

SUMMARY

- Windows Server 2003 supports two types of storage, basic and dynamic, and three file systems, FAT, FAT32, and NTFS. Most of the advanced storage management features are available only on dynamic disk volumes formatted using NTFS.

- Basic disks and the FAT file system provide backward compatibility with older Windows operating systems but are limited in their capabilities. A basic disk can have up to four partitions of two types, primary and extended. There can be only one extended partition on a disk, but you can create as many logical drives in the extended partition as you need.

- Dynamic disks provide flexible and powerful options in configurations with more than one disk. A dynamic disk has only one partition, but you can create any number of volumes on that partition.

- Basic disks can be converted to dynamic disks with no data loss, but all data and volumes must be deleted to convert a dynamic disk to a basic disk.

- Dynamic disks support simple, spanned, striped, mirrored, and RAID-5 volumes, to provide storage according to capacity, performance, and fault tolerance requirements.

- Fault tolerance is provided by mirrored (RAID-1) volumes, which maintain a full copy of the volume's data on each of two disks, and striped-with-parity volumes (RAID-5), which stripe the data across multiple disks and use parity and remaining data to calculate data missing from any one failed disk.

- Simple volumes, spanned volumes, striped volumes (RAID-0), and all basic disk logical drives are not fault tolerant. All data is lost if any disk supporting such volumes fails. The larger those volumes, or the more physical disks supporting those volumes, the greater the likelihood of failure.

- To create and manage basic and dynamic disks, you use the Disk Management snap-in. Common disk management tasks include creating and deleting partitions and volumes and assigning drive letters and mount points.

- Disk volumes can become corrupted or fragmented and often fill to capacity. The Check Disk, Disk Defragmenter, and Quota Manager tools help you manage existing volumes.

- Disk quotas allow you to set and monitor storage limits and to deny write access to users exceeding those limits. Quotas are configured on a per-user, per-volume basis.

EXERCISES

Exercise 12-1: Using Check Disk

In this exercise, you use the Check Disk utility to examine the condition of your computer's C drive.

1. Log on to Windows Server 2003 using the local Administrator account.

2. Click Start, and then click Windows Explorer.

3. Select the C drive in Windows Explorer and, from the File menu, select Properties. The Local Disk (C:) Properties dialog box appears.

4. Select the Tools tab, and then click Check Now. The Check Disk Local Disk (C:) dialog box appears.

5. Select the Automatically Fix File System Errors and Scan For And Attempt Recovery Of Bad Sectors check boxes, and click Start. A Checking Disk Local Disk (C:) message box appears, stating that Check Disk requires exclusive access to the drive.

6. Click Yes to schedule the disk check to occur the next time you restart the computer.

7. Restart the computer, and watch as the disk check occurs.

Exercise 12-2: Defragmenting a Disk

In this exercise, you use the Disk Defragmenter utility to defragment your computer's C drive.

1. Log on to Windows Server 2003 as Administrator.

2. Click Start, and then click Windows Explorer.

3. Select the C drive in Windows Explorer and, from the File menu, select Properties. The Local Disk (C:) Properties dialog box appears.

4. Select the Tools tab, and then click Defragment Now. The Disk Defragmenter console appears.

5. Click Analyze. After the analysis, a Disk Defragmenter message box appears, specifying whether you should defragment the drive.

6. Regardless of the program's recommendation, click Defragment to begin defragmenting the drive. When the defragmentation process is complete, another message box appears, enabling you to view a report on the procedure.

Exercise 12-3: Configuring Default Disk Quotas

In this exercise, you configure the default disk quotas for your computer's C drive.

1. Log on to Windows Server 2003 as Administrator.

2. Click Start, and then click Windows Explorer.

3. Select the C drive in Windows Explorer and, from the File menu, select Properties. The Local Disk (C:) Properties dialog box appears.

4. Select the Quota tab, and then select the Enable Quota Management check box.

5. Select the Limit Disk Space To option, and specify a maximum capacity of 500 MB.

6. In the Set Warning Level To controls, specify a warning level of 450 MB.

7. Select both of the quota logging option check boxes, and click OK. A Disk Quota message box opens.

8. Click OK to dismiss the message box and enable the quota system.

REVIEW QUESTIONS

1. Which of the following provides the ability to recover from the failure of a single hard drive?

    a. Logical drive

    b. Simple volume

    c. Mirrored volume

    d. Striped volume

    e. Extended partition

    f. Spanned volume

    g. RAID-5 volume

    h. Primary partition

2. You are dual-booting a system in your test lab. The computer has Windows NT 4 installed on the first primary partition and Windows Server 2003 installed on the second primary partition. The computer is running low on disk space, so you add a new disk drive. You boot to Windows Server 2003 and configure the drive as a dynamic disk. When you later restart to Windows NT 4, you are unable to see the disk. Why?

3. To provide fault tolerance, maximum performance, and the ability to hot-swap a failed drive, you purchase a seven-disk hardware RAID. After installing the array, you see only one new disk on Windows Server 2003. Why?

4. In which of the following disk regions can you create logical drives?

    a. Primary partitions

    b. Simple volumes

    c. Spanned volumes

    d. Extended partitions

    e. Unallocated space

5. You recently added a disk to a computer. The disk had previously been used in a Windows 2000 server. The disk appears in Device Manager but is not appearing correctly in Disk Management. What menu item must you select?

    a. Import Foreign Disk

    b. Format

    c. Rescan Disks

    d. Change Drive Letter And Paths

    e. Convert To Dynamic Disk

6. You attempt to convert an external FireWire disk from basic to dynamic storage, but the Convert option is not available. What is the most likely reason for this?

7. You're the administrator of a Windows Server 2003 computer. You want to fix any file system errors and recover any bad sectors on your computer's hard disk. Which tool should you use?

    a. Check Disk

    b. Disk Defragmenter

    c. Diskpart.exe

    d. Disk quotas

8. What is the required amount of free disk space on a volume to perform a complete defragmentation?

    a. 5 percent

    b. 10 percent

    c. 15 percent

    d. 25 percent

    e. 50 percent

9. You're implementing software RAID on your Windows Server 2003 computer. You want to provide fault tolerance to the system and boot partitions. Which version of RAID should you use?

    a. RAID-0.

    b. RAID-1.

    c. RAID-5.

    d. You cannot use software RAID to protect a boot partition.

10. You're setting up a Windows Server 2003 computer, and you want to protect the data on the hard disk. You want to implement a solution that provides the fastest disk I/O possible and supports the hot swapping of hard disks. Which RAID solution should you use?

    a. RAID-0

    b. RAID-1

    c. RAID-5

    d. Hardware RAID

11. You're setting up RAID-5 on your Windows Server 2003 computer. You plan to use five hard disks, which are each 20 GB in size. What percentage of redundancy can you anticipate with this configuration?

    a. 20

    b. 25

    c. 33

    d. 50

12. You're setting up software RAID on your Windows Server 2003 computer to provide fault tolerance to the data stored on that system. The computer is used as a database server. The server performs many read operations but relatively few write operations. As a result, you want a fault-tolerant solution that provides excellent read performance. Which RAID solution should you use?

    a. RAID-0

    b. RAID-1

    c. RAID-5

13. A computer on which you want to implement RAID-5 contains three disks, each with 2 GB of unallocated space. Using the Disk Management snap-in, you start the New Volume Wizard by right-clicking one of the regions of unallocated space. When you reach the Select Volume Type screen, the RAID-5 option is not available. What is the most likely reason for this behavior?

    a. RAID-5 is already implemented in hardware.

    b. One or two of the disks are configured with the basic storage type.

    c. All three disks are configured with the dynamic storage type.

    d. All three disks are configured with the basic storage type.

    e. RAID-5 is already implemented in software.

CASE SCENARIOS

Scenario 12-1: Using RAID

Lee has two 100-GB SCSI hard disk drives connected to a Windows Server 2003 server that he is responsible for administering. The server also has a single hardware RAID controller that supports RAID-0, RAID-1, and RAID-5. Currently 70 GB on the first drive is used and the second drive is empty. Lee is concerned that the first hard disk drive might fail, causing him to lose all the data on that drive. Lee has considered regular backups but does not have the equipment with which to back up 70 GB on a regular basis. He would like to configure a solution that provides fault tolerance for the first drive. Which of the following should he consider, given the current configuration of his Windows Server 2003 server?

    a. He should configure volume shadow copy services on the first hard disk drive by using disk properties.

    b. He should configure the disks in a RAID-5 configuration using the hardware RAID controller's configuration utility.

    c. He should configure the disks in a RAID-0 configuration using the hardware RAID controller's configuration utility.

    d. He should configure the disks in a RAID-1 configuration using the hardware RAID controller's configuration utility.

Scenario 12-2: Adding Storage

Mark is the system administrator of a Windows Server 2003 file server. The server currently has two disk drives. The first disk drive, which is 30 GB in size, hosts all the operating system files. The second disk drive, which is 80 GB in size, hosts user data on five separate shares. Each share corresponds to a specific department in the organization and is divided into three separate folders. The first folder is a departmental documents folder, the second is a collaboration folder, and the third is an individual user data folder.

All users have read access to the departmental documents folder and have read and write access to the collaboration folder. In addition, each individual user has full control over her unique data folder. Only the individual user can access her data folder; other users cannot read or write to that folder. The five-share system works well, and all employees in the organization understand where to store and find documents.

A problem has developed in that the user data sections of each of the five departmental shares are expanding so quickly that the disk hosting the user data is almost filled to capacity. It is up to Mark to conceive and implement a solution to this problem. Mark's primary goal is to add more space to each share so that the disk hosting the shared folders does not become full.

Mark is also assigned these secondary goals by his manager:

■ Retain only five shares, and keep the user data directory as a folder off each departmental share.

■ Provide fault tolerance for the file share.

■ Retain the security scheme currently in use so that individual users have full control over their own directories and other users cannot access them.

To achieve these goals, Mark performs the following actions. During a scheduled period after midnight, when no users are connected to the server, Mark shuts down the server and installs five new 100-GB hard disk drives on the server. He then formats each drive as a single volume using the NTFS file system, and he creates a new folder called Temp under each of the folders hosting each department's share. One by one, he mounts the five disks to each of the Temp folders so that each Temp folder points to its own individual mounted hard disk. He then copies the entire contents of the user data folder into the Temp folder under each share, and then he deletes the original user data folder. Finally, he renames the Temp folder with the name of the user data folder.

How many of his goals has Mark achieved?

a. He has not achieved any primary goals but has achieved all his secondary goals.

b. He has achieved the primary goal and one secondary goal.

c. He has achieved the primary goal and two secondary goals.

d. He has achieved all primary and secondary goals.

e. He has achieved none of his goals.

GLOSSARY

access control entry (ACE) An entry in an access control list (ACL) that defines the permissions granted to a particular security principal.

access control list (ACL) A collection of access control entries (ACEs) associated with a file, folder, Active Directory object, or other resource that defines the permissions that security principals, such as users, groups, and computers, have for accessing the resource.

ACE *See* access control entry (ACE).

ACL *See* access control list (ACL).

active partition The partition on which the system's boot files are stored.

archive bit A 1-bit flag included with every file on a drive that backup software programs use to determine which files to back up. Newly created files have their archive bits activated, and performing a full backup clears them. Whenever a file is modified, its archive bit is reactivated so that an incremental or differential backup can back up only the files that have changed.

attribute A component element of an Active Directory object that contains information about that object. For example, a user object might consist of attributes such as the user's first name, last name, and e-mail address.

autochanger A data storage hardware device that consists of one or more tape drives, a media array, and a robotic mechanism that inserts selected tapes into the drives. Autochangers make it possible for administrators to implement extended, unattended backup strategies.

baseline A set of performance levels taken under normal conditions that is used for comparison with levels taken later, when problems occur.

bottleneck A component that is not providing the same level of performance as the other components, causing a systemwide slowdown.

CAL *See* Client Access License (CAL).

Client Access License (CAL) A license that allows a user or device to connect to a server product for functionality that uses server components, including file and print service or authentication. Unauthenticated access through the Internet does not require a CAL.

commit memory The amount of memory allocated to user programs and the operating system.

computer object An Active Directory object representing a specific computer in a domain. The object includes a computer account that enables the system to establish a secure channel with a domain controller, as well as informational properties about the computer.

container object Any Active Directory object that can act as a parent to other objects.

details pane The right pane in a Microsoft Management Console (MMC) window, which displays information about whatever element is selected in the left (or scope) pane.

device driver A set of software routines that implement device-specific functions for generic input/output (I/O) operations.

differential backup A type of backup job that uses a filter so only the files that have changed since the last full backup job are backed up. The filter evaluates the state of each file's archive bit, which a full backup job clears. Creating or modifying a file sets its archive bit, and the differential job backs up only the files that have their archive bit set. The differential job does not modify the state of the bit, so the next differential job also backs up only the files that have changed since the last full backup. Differential jobs use more tape or other media than incremental jobs because they repeatedly back up the same files, but they're easier to restore in the event of a disaster. You have to restore only the last full backup and the most recent differential backup to completely restore a drive. *See also* incremental backup.

direct memory access (DMA) channel A pathway used by a hardware device to transfer data directly to and from system memory.

directory service   A database containing information about network entities and resources, which is used as a guide to the network and as an authentication resource by multiple users. Early network operating systems included basic flat-file directory services, such as Windows NT domains and the Novell NetWare bindery. Today's directory services, such as Microsoft's Active Directory and Novell's eDirectory, tend to be hierarchical and are designed to support large enterprise networks.

distribution group   An Active Directory group type that cannot function as a security principal and is used primarily to create e-mail distribution lists.

DMA channel   *See* direct memory access (DMA) channel.

domain   A group of users, computers, and other resources for which information is stored in a directory service on a server called a domain controller.

domain controller   A computer running Windows Server 2003, Windows 2000, or Windows NT that has been designated to store and process directory service information. Windows NT domains and the Windows Active Directory service store their directory service databases on domain controllers, which also authenticate users who want to access network resources.

domain functional level   A setting that indicates which Active Directory features are available in the domain. The Active Directory implementations in the various versions of Windows have slightly different feature sets, and the domain functional level controls what group nesting and conversion tasks are possible.

domain local group   An Active Directory group scope that is used primarily to provide access to resources in a single domain.

duplexing   A disk-mirroring installation in which each physical disk is connected to a different host adapter. Duplexing provides increased performance and enables the volume to survive the failure of an adapter as well as a disk drive.

effective permissions   A combination of allowed, denied, inherited, and explicitly assigned permissions that provides a composite view of a security principal's functional access to a resource.

forest   A group of Active Directory trees that use different namespaces.

forest functional level   A setting that indicates what Active Directory features are available in the forest. Raising the forest

functional level has no effect on Active Directory group activities.

fragmentation   The tendency of a disk to contain files stored on clusters that are scattered all over the drive. Because the drive heads have to access clusters all over the disk to read a single file, overall performance decreases.

global group   An Active Directory group scope that is most commonly used to manage permissions for directory objects that require frequent maintenance, such as user and computer accounts.

GPO   *See* group policy object (GPO).

group policy object (GPO)   A collection of group policy settings that can be applied to a domain, site, or organizational unit (OU) object.

host header   A method of differentiating multiple Web sites running on a single server when the server uses only one IP address and port number. By specifying a Web server name in HTTP request messages, the Web server is able to forward each request to the appropriate site.

hotfix   A patch or update for a Microsoft product that addresses a single issue that is explained in an accompanying Microsoft Knowledge Base article. Hotfixes might be recommended for installation only on computers that are performing certain tasks or are experiencing a specific problem.

incremental backup   A type of backup job that uses a filter so only the files that have changed since the last backup job are backed up. The filter evaluates the state of each file's archive bit and backs up only the files with an archive bit that is set. Performing an incremental backup resets the archive bits (unlike a differential job, which does not reset the bits). Incremental jobs use the least amount of tape (or other medium), but they are more difficult to restore in the event of a disaster. To fully restore a drive, you must restore the last full backup job and all the incremental jobs performed since that last full backup, in chronological order.

interrupt request (IRQ)   A signal sent from one component to another (typically from a peripheral device to the system processor) indicating that the sender requires the attention of the receiver.

I/O address   A location in memory that is allocated for use by a particular hardware device, to exchange information with the system.

IRQ   *See* interrupt request (IRQ)

leaf object An Active Directory object that cannot act as a parent to other objects.

license group Because the License Logging service allocates licenses based on username and not device name, Windows Device Client Access Licenses (CALs) are given to a license group. A license group has one or more users and is allocated licenses equivalent to the number of devices used by that group to connect to server products.

local group A group account on a Windows Server 2003 standalone or member server. Local groups can have local users and domain global groups as members, but they provide access only to resources on the local system.

locally attached printer A physical printer that is directly attached to a computer, typically using a parallel or USB port.

local user profile A collection of folders and files that make up the desktop environment for a specific user, stored on a local drive.

logical printer Represents a physical printer on a computer by sending print jobs out through a specific port. The logical printer includes the print queue, the printer driver, settings, permissions, and printing defaults that manage the creation of print jobs for the printer.

mandatory user profile A read-only user profile that does not maintain modifications between sessions. Users can modify mandatory profiles, but their changes are not saved when they log off.

memory leak The result of a program allocating memory for use but not freeing up that memory when it is finished using it.

mirrored volume Two disks that contain identical copies of data. The only software RAID supported on the system volume. Good read and write performance; excellent fault tolerance; but costly in terms of disk utilization because 50 percent of the volume's potential capacity is used for data redundancy.

network-attached printer A physical printer that is connected directly to the network rather than to a computer. Computers typically communicate with network-attached printers using IP addresses.

network printer In the context of Windows, a logical printer that is a client of a shared logical printer on another computer. Not to be confused with a network-attached printer.

object The fundamental building block of the Active Directory directory service.

Objects are elements that represent a network resource, such as a user, computer, domain, or group. Objects are composed of individual attributes, which contain information about the object. For example, the attributes of a user object might include the user's first name, last name, and e-mail address.

organizational unit (OU) A type of Active Directory container object used within domains. OUs are logical containers in which you can place users, groups, computers, and other OUs. An OU can contain objects only from its parent domain. An OU is the smallest scope to which you can apply a group policy or delegate authority.

OU *See* organizational unit (OU).

Per Device or Per User licensing mode A licensing requirement that allows a single CAL to authorize a user (who might use more than one device) or a device (which might be used by more than one user) to connect to any number of servers.

performance counter A data-reporting item associated with a performance object.

performance instance An individual occurrence of a performance counter. If there are four processors in a server, there are four instances for each performance counter in the Processor object, numbered 0 through 3.

performance object A logical collection of data-reporting items or counters connected with a resource, service, or application that can be monitored.

Per Server licensing mode A licensing requirement that is allocated when a user or device connects to the server or product. When the user disconnects, the license is returned to the available license pool. This mode requires sufficient licenses to support the maximum number of concurrent connections on each individual server.

Plug and Play (PnP) A standard that defines characteristics for computer components that enables the components to automatically detect and configure the hardware in a computer.

PnP *See* Plug and Play (PnP).

print queue A list of print jobs waiting to be submitted to a physical printer.

print server A computer that is configured to share a printer with clients on a network. The print server queues the print jobs submitted by the clients and submits them to the physical printer.

RAID-5 volume   A volume on which data is written to multiple (from 3 to 32) physical disks at the same rate and that is interlaced with parity to provide fault tolerance for a single-disk failure. Has good read performance and good utilization of disk capacity, but is expensive in terms of processor utilization and write performance because parity must be calculated during write operations.

roaming user profile   A server-based user profile that is stored on a shared network drive, where the user can access it from any computer.

scope pane   The left pane in a Microsoft Management Console (MMC) window, which displays the snap-ins installed in the console.

security group   An Active Directory group type that is used as a security principal in access control lists (ACLs).

security identifier (SID)   A unique value assigned to every Active Directory object when it is created.

service pack   A collection of patches and updates for a Microsoft product that have been tested together and recommended for installation on all computers running the product.

SID   *See* security identifier (SID).

simple volume   The equivalent of a basic disk partition. Simple volumes exist on only one physical disk, so they are not fault tolerant.

slipstreaming   The process of integrating service packs and/or hotfixes into a Windows operating system installation.

snap-in   A special-purpose application module that runs within the Microsoft Management Console (MMC) shell. There are two types of snap-ins: standalone snap-ins, which you can add directly to an MMC console, and extension snap-ins, which must be associated with a specific standalone snap-in.

spanned volume   A volume that includes space on more than one physical disk.

Because their size tends to be greater and because multiple physical disks are involved, spanned volumes have a higher risk of failure and are not fault tolerant.

special permission   An element providing a security principal with a highly specific degree of access to a resource.

standard permission   A combination of special permissions used to provide a security principal with a frequently used level of access to a resource.

striped volume   A volume on which data is written to multiple (from 2 to 32) physical disks at the same rate. It offers maximum performance and capacity but no fault tolerance.

tree   A group of Active Directory domains sharing a contiguous namespace.

UNC   *See* Universal Naming Convention (UNC).

Uniform Resource Locator (URL)   A standard notation for identifying a resource on the Internet. For example, *http://www. adatum.com*. The most common way to use a URL is to enter it in a Web browser.

universal group   An Active Directory group scope that is typically used to grant access to related resources across multiple domains.

Universal Naming Convention (UNC)   A standard notation used to identify resources on a network. UNC uses the following format: \\Server\Share.

URL   *See* Uniform Resource Locator (URL).

virtual directory   An Internet Information Services (IIS) object that enables a folder on any local or remote volume to appear as a subfolder of a Web site.

volume shadow copy   A feature in Windows Server 2003 and Windows XP that maintains a library containing multiple versions of selected files. Users can select a version of a file to restore as needed, and the Backup program uses the shadow copies to back up open files.

INDEX

Number

64-bit server support, 8

A

access control lists. *See* ACLs (access control lists)
Account Operators group, 226, 228
accounts, computer. *See* computer accounts; computer objects
accounts, user. *See* user accounts
accounts, vulnerability of, checking for, 133
ACEs (access control entries)
  NTFS permissions with, 295
  permissions in, 277
  purpose of, 276
  special permissions, table of, 301–302
ACLs (access control lists)
  ACEs. *See* ACEs (access control entries)
  defined, 210
  displaying, 210
  editing, 277
  FAT file system with, 277
  groups in, 210
  NTFS permissions with, 295
  ownership of folders, 304
  purpose of, 276
  security principals, 210, 244, 276, 302
  special identities, 229–230
  storage of, 277
Action menu, MMC, 39
activating Windows Server, 18, 34
Active Directory
  attributes, 30
  authoritative restores, 121
  backups, 114, 120–121
  client OS compatibility, 201
  computer objects in. *See* computer objects
  container objects, 31, 34
  creating user objects, 205–206
  CSV for importing objects, 191–192
  directory services overview, 27–28
  domain controller server role, 20–21
  domain model, 28
  domain objects, 30
  Dsadd.exe, 193–194, 207
  features for legacy clients, 201–202
  forests, 29
  functional levels, 212–214
  global catalogs, 30
  group objects, 30
  group policy objects, 32
  groups. *See* Active Directory groups
  leaf objects, 31
  legacy OS issues, 202
  MMC consoles for, 38
  modifying objects with Dsmod.exe, 195
  moving user objects, 206
  multiple-master replication, 28
  Ndsutil.exe, 121
  nonauthoritative restores, 120
  objects, 30
  organizational unit objects, 30–31
  OU hierarchy, 170
  permissions, 31, 276
  printer objects, 30
  publishing shares, 291
  purpose of, 27–28
  replication, 28
  restoring, 120–121, 124
  schemas, 31
  shared folder objects, 30
  Standard Edition with, 6
  Sysvol, 28
  templates for user objects, 190–191
  trees, 29
  user accounts, hierarchy for, 170
  user objects, 30, 205–206
  viewing objects, 34
  Web Edition with, 5
Active Directory Domains and Trusts console, 213
Active Directory groups
  Account Operators, 226, 228
  adding members, 235–236, 243, 244
  Administrators, 226, 228
  automating management of, 239–241
  Backup Operators, 227–228
  Builtin container, 226
  built-in domain local groups, 226–229
  CertPublishers, 224
  changing types, 237
  consoles for managing. *See* Active Directory Users and Computers console
  converting, 220
  creating, 234–235, 239–240, 242, 245
  defined, 215
  deleting, 238, 244
  distribution groups, 216
  Domain Admins, 224, 226
  Domain Computers group, 224
  Domain Controllers group, 225
  Domain Guests, 225
  domain local groups, 217, 220, 221, 244
  Domain Users, 225
  Dsadd.exe, 239–240, 245
  Dsget.exe, 240–241
  Dsmod.exe, 240
  Enterprise Admins, 225, 226
  finding with Dsget.exe, 240–241
  global groups, 217–218, 220
  Group Policy Creator Owners, 225
  Guests, 227
  management of, 235–236, 239–241
  nesting, 219, 237, 243
  Network Configuration Operators, 227
  Performance Log Users, 227
  Performance Monitor Users, 227

SYSTEM REQUIREMENTS

To complete the exercises in this textbook, you need to meet the following minimum system requirements:

- Microsoft Windows Server 2003, Enterprise Edition (A 180-day evaluation edition of Windows Server 2003, Enterprise Edition is included on the CD-ROM.)

- Microsoft Windows Server 2003, Standard Edition (Evaluation edition is not included, but all textbook exercises will run on the Standard Edition.)

- Microsoft PowerPoint or Microsoft PowerPoint Viewer (PowerPoint Viewer is included on the Supplemental Student CD-ROM.)

- Microsoft Word or Microsoft Word Viewer (Word Viewer is included on the Supplemental Student CD-ROM.)

- Microsoft Internet Explorer 5.01 or later

- Minimum CPU: 133 MHz for x86-based computers and 733 MHz for Itanium-based computers (733 MHz is recommended.)

- Minimum RAM: 128 MB (256 MB is recommended.)

- Disk space for setup: 1.5 GB for x86-based computers and 2.0 GB for Itanium-based computers.

- Display monitor capable of 800 x 600 resolution or higher

- CD-ROM drive

- Microsoft mouse or compatible pointing device

Uninstall Instructions

The time-limited release of Microsoft Windows Server 2003, Enterprise Edition, will expire 180 days after installation. If you decide to discontinue the use of this software, you will need to reinstall your original operating system. You might need to reformat your drive.